Rethinking U.S. Labor History

RETHINKING U.S. LABOR HISTORY

Essays on the Working-Class Experience, 1756–2009

Edited by

Donna T. Haverty-Stacke
and
Daniel J. Walkowitz

continuum

NEW YORK • LONDON

2010

The Continuum International Publishing Group
80 Maiden Lane, New York, NY 10038
The Tower Building, 11 York Road, London SE1 7NX

www.continuumbooks.com

Library of Congress Cataloging-in-Publication Data
Rethinking U.S. labor history : essays on the working-class experience, 1756-2009 / edited
by Donna Haverty-Stacke and Daniel J. Walkowitz.
    p. cm.
Includes bibliographical references and index.
ISBN-13: 978-0-8264-0198-4 (hbk. : alk. paper)
ISBN-10: 0-8264-0198-8 (hbk. : alk. paper)
ISBN-13: 978-1-4411-4575-8 (pbk. : alk. paper)
ISBN-10: 1-4411-4575-3 (pbk. : alk. paper)
    1. Working class–United States–History. 2. Labor–United States–History.
3. Labor movement–United States–History. I. Haverty-Stacke, Donna T.
II. Walkowitz, Daniel J. III. Title.
HD8072.5.R48 2010
331.0973–dc22
                                                              2010003377

ISBN: 978-0-8264-0198-4 (Hardback)
       978-1-4411-4575-8 (Paperback)

Columbia FLI Partnership
HB8072.5 .R48 2010

Typeset by Newgen Imaging Systems Pvt Ltd, Chennai, India
Printed in the United States of America by Sheridan Books, Inc

Contents

Contributors

Eric Arnesen is Professor of History at The George Washington University and a historian of race, labor, politics, and civil rights. He is the author or editor of seven books, including *Brotherhoods of Color: Black Railroad Workers and the Struggle for Equality* and *Waterfront Workers of New Orleans: Race, Class, and Politics, 1863–1923*. He is a frequent contributor to the *Chicago Tribune* and his review essays have also appeared in the *New Republic*, the *Nation*, the *Boston Globe*, *Historically Speaking*, and the *Christian Century*.

Daniel E. Bender is the Canada Research Chair in Cultural Analysis and an Associate Professor of History and Comparative Literature at the University of Toronto. He is the author of *Sweated Work, Weak Bodies: Anti-Sweatshop Campaigns and Languages of Labor* (2004) and *American Abyss: Savagery and Civilization in the Age of Industry* (2009). His current research explores American zoos and the working-class confrontation with empire.

Eileen Boris is Hull Professor and Chair, Department of Feminist Studies, University of California, Santa Barbara, where she holds affiliate appointments in History and Black Studies and directs the Center for Research on Women and Social Justice. Among her recent books are *Intimate Labors: Cultures, Technologies, and Politics of Care*, co-edited with Rhacel Parreñas, and *Workers Across the Americas: The Transnational Turn in Labor History*, for which she serves as an Associate Editor. With Jennifer Klein, she is the coauthor of *Caring for America: Home Health Workers Under the Shadow of the Welfare State*.

Theresa Ann Case is an Associate Professor of History at the University of Houston-Downtown, where she teaches US women's history and courses on US social and cultural history. She is the author of *The Great Southwest Railroad Strike and Free Labor* (2010).

Elizabeth Faue is Professor of History at Wayne State University. She is the author of *Writing the Wrongs: Eva Valesh and the Rise of Labor Journalism* and *Community of Suffering and Struggle: Women, Men and the Labor Movement in Minneapolis,*

1915–1945, and essays on labor, gender, and politics. She is currently working on a project entitled, "Remembering Justice: Labor, the State, and Working Class Memory."

Elizabeth Fones-Wolf is a professor of history at West Virginia University. She is the author of *Selling Free Enterprise: The Business Assault on Labor and Liberalism, 1945–60* (1994) and *Waves of Opposition: Labor and the Struggle for Democratic Radio* (2006).

Ken Fones-Wolf is the Stuart and Joyce Robbins Distinguished Chair in History at West Virginia University, where he teaches courses on Appalachia and American working-class history. He is the author or editor of six books and numerous articles.

Donna T. Haverty-Stacke is an associate professor of history at Hunter College, CUNY, where she teaches courses in U.S. working-class, urban, and cultural history. She is the author of *America's Forgotten Holiday: May Day and Nationalism, 1867–1960* (2009). Her current research focuses on the history of the 1941 Smith Act trial of members of the Minneapolis Teamsters and Socialist Workers Party and explores issues of trade union democracy and political dissent in wartime.

Jennifer Klein is Professor of History at Yale University. She is the author of *For All These Rights: Business, Labor, and the Shaping of America's Public-Private Welfare State*. She has co-authored with Eileen Boris *Caring For America: Home Health Care Workers in the Shadow of the Welfare State*.

Joseph A. McCartin is Associate Professor of History and Executive Director of the Kalmanovitz Initiative for Labor and the Working Poor at Georgetown University. He is the author of *Labor's Great War: The Struggle for Industrial Democracy and the Origins of Modern American Labor Relations*. He is completing a book on the 1981 air traffic controllers' strike.

Steve Rosswurm, who teaches history at Lake Forest College, is the editor of *The CIO's Left-Led Unions* (1992) and the author of *Arms, Country, and Class* (1987) and *The FBI and the Catholic Church* (2009). The CIO and the Catholic Church is the subject of his next book.

Zachary Schwartz-Weinstein is a Ph.D. candidate in the American Studies Program, department of Social and Cultural Analysis, New York University and an organizer with GSOC-UAW Local 2110. His dissertation looks at the history of service workers at U.S. universities and university hospitals between 1945 and the present.

Shelton Stromquist is Professor of History at the University of Iowa and the author of *Reinventing "the People": The Progressive Movement, the Class Problem, and the*

Origins of Modern Liberalism and numerous other works. His is currently working on a transnational and comparative history municipal labor and socialist politics, 1890–1920.

Daniel J. Walkowitz is Professor of Social and Cultural Analysis and Professor of History at New York University. Co-author (with Michael B. Frisch) of *Working-Class America*, his most recent books include *Working with Class: Social Workers and the Politics Of Middle-Class Identity in 20th Century America* and *City Folk: English Country Dance and the Politics of the Folk in Modern America.*

Peter Way, Professor of History and Head of the Department at the University of Windsor in Canada, is a social historian, whose research and teaching interests lie in the history of working people in North America and within the Atlantic world. His first book, *Common Labor: Workers and the Digging of North American Canals, 1780–1860* (1993), won the 1994 Frederick Jackson Turner Prize awarded by the Organization of American Historians. He is currently writing a monograph titled "Artisans of War: Common Soldiers and the Making of Britain's American Empire in the Seven Years' War," which examines soldiering and warfare from the perspective of labor history and cultural studies, seeking to place the war in the context of merchant capital and the imperial state.

Introduction

Donna T. Haverty-Stacke and Daniel J. Walkowitz

This volume, *Rethinking U.S. Labor History,* appears at an auspicious moment in labor history. Approximately 25 years ago a path-breaking edited collection, *Working-Class America, Essays on Labor, Community and American Society* (co-edited by Michael B. Frisch and Daniel J. Walkowitz), introduced 11 young scholars who would help to define the "New" labor history and announce its coming of age.[1] Much good and important work has appeared since, but that 1983 collection still stands as a marker of an important transitional moment in labor history worth examining with a look backward and forward from that juncture.

The present moment is equally auspicious, however, for organized labor and for the working class, which is found both in and outside of union ranks. For the American labor movement stands at a precipice. As the first decade of the New Millennium comes to close, fewer than one in ten workers belong to unions; one in three did so only half a century ago. The reasons for this change are complex and merit asking hard questions, as much about attitudes of workers as about the hostile antilabor climate they have faced in the past quarter century. The 1980s marked the growing hegemony of neoliberalism—state-sponsored privatization of services, industry, and the economy that constituted a frontal attack on labor. President Ronald Reagan's crushing of the air traffic controllers' strike in 1981 with the use of nonunion workers announced a new antilabor state regime in the United States. Paralleled by similar policy laid out by Prime Minister Margaret Thatcher in Britain, Reagan-Thatcherism would dictate a transatlantic state policy and labor-management relations that labor would have to grapple with on a global scale for the next three decades. With the partial exception of the Clinton-era interlude, American workers struggled in the post-1980 era with the consequences of a hostile national political environment that was sustained by conservative courts, a Congress enamored of "free market" open trade, and a conservative, antiunion National Labor Relations Board. The social consequences of this new order would be what the *New York Times* has called a "new Gilded Age" —an era with a widening gap between the "have" and the "have nots." Corporate salaries and "golden parachutes" rose astronomically in these years, while an expanding service sector that was disproportionately black, Hispanic, Asian, and female cleaned the offices of those corporate magnates, bused their food at restaurants, tended to their children, and otherwise made the "good life" of the rich possible. Only recently, with the election of a pro-labor president, Barack Obama, has there been any glimmer of change in federal policy, but as we write in the summer of 2009, the change remains more a promise than a new reality.

The labor movement has not been idle in the face of these changes. In the wake of its decline, the union movement has reorganized, striving to rethink strategies that could meet the global restructuring of business, work, and state policies. In the fall of 2008, the fragility of the "gilded" veneer showed cracks and gave new openings to the U.S. labor movement, offering new hope to unions that had recently reorganized. In 2005, powerful new unions like the SEIU and UNITE HERE had formed the "Change to Win Coalition" to confront the challenges wrought by the antiunion climate of the past decades. The new coalition, moving now with a renewed sense of purpose, broke with the craft and industrial unions in the AFL-CIO, which had represented labor for most of its first century, and gave voice to the more socially diverse workforce of the modern era. And workers responded dramatically to the call to action. Coincident with the 2008 election drive, union membership witnessed its largest growth in over 25 years. Unfortunately, division within the labor movement and in-fighting among leaders of rival factions presented new challenges, and the impact of the hemorrhaging of the economy in 2009 on labor is a story yet to be written. While the deepest "recession" since the Great Depression of the 1930s has seen the evisceration of the American auto industry and threatens the future of one of the nation's leading unions, the United Auto Workers, unions can take hope from some prior experiences: hard times have traditionally fueled worker discontent and labor organizing. This is, then, an uncertain and auspicious moment to reflect on the state of labor and labor history in America.

A century of vital writing by labor historians frames this present historiographical moment. John R. Commons, working with colleagues he had himself trained at the University of Wisconsin, began to publish his seminal four-volume *History of Labor in the United States* in 1918. A pioneering historian of the organized labor movement during the era of the American Federation of Labor, Commons led a distinguished first generation of what were more properly labor economists than historians. In the next decades, Commons et al.'s *History of Labor* (1918–1935) and its ten-volume companion documentary collection established the field of labor history as institutional political history that privileged (and celebrated) the economistic policy and leading role of organized labor in the AFL.[2] This first generation of labor economists actually spanned three careers. Commons' student at Wisconsin, Selig Perlman, would write the authoritative volume on labor theory, *A Theory of the Labor Movement* (1928), that would track his own rejection of Marxist economics for the more economistic functional approach of the AFL, and in turn, Perlman's student, Philip Taft, would pen what would remain for decades the definitive history of the AFL, *The A.F.L. in the Time of Gompers* (1957). It is comment as much on the hegemonic role the Wisconsin School played as on the patriarchal nature of the profession that it took the resurgence of feminism in the 1970s to give the extraordinary work of a trio of important women labor economists and historians during this same period its due. The three—Caroline F. Ware, Vera Shlakman, and Hannah Josephson—each penned histories of New England textile workers in the first half of the nineteenth century, an industry dominated, as they note, by women workers. The genealogy of labor history takes a very different tack with their inclusion, as their focus on workers outside the union movement and on women more nearly aligns with the work of the next generation than that of Commons et al.[3] Ware's, Shlakman's, and Josephson's attention to textile mills where women labored provided a broader social history than that which had been offered by their male counterparts at Wisconsin, but their contributions remained outside the historiographic canon until the 1970s.

The New Social History of the 1960s represented a conscious break with the "old" Commons historiographic tradition. Reflecting the new population of white ethnics who entered higher education in the 1960s and the social ferment of the decade, a new second generation of labor historians reinvented labor history as the history of labor and the working class. Historian giants in England such as Edward P. Thompson and Eric Hobsbawm, and their American counterparts—most notably the triad of David Brody, Herbert G. Gutman, and David Montgomery—reshaped the historical terrain. In particular, in his magisterial account of the early industrial revolution in Britain, *The Making of the English Working Class,* Thompson gave new meaning to the notion that class, while "largely determined by the productive relations into which men are born—or enter involuntarily," was not a structure but a relationship. In Thompson's widely cited Preface, he noted,

> class happens when some men, as a result of common experiences (inherited or shared), feel and articulate the identity of their interests as between themselves, and as against other men whose interests are different from (and usually opposed to) theirs. . . . Class-consciousness is the way in which these experiences are handled in cultural terms: embodied in traditions, value-systems, ideas, and institutional forms.[4]

In the United States, Gutman and Montgomery took much the same tack in developing the New Social History. Focusing on the workplace and community, they sought to re-explore the past "from the bottom up" by empowering the voices "from below," and labor historians strained to hear the voices of the rank and file, not just those of labor leaders. The new work valorized the study of union and nonunion workers, in the community, on the shopfloor, and in the family in order to tell a fuller story of their struggles. In doing so, these historians of the working class heralded the efflorescence of the New Social History as a remaking of how historians understood the past. Working people, in and outside of unions, in the workplace and in the community, and acting as a class and as ethnic and racial fractions, became vital subjects of and agents in histories of their own making. The social history of black labor—free and unfree—also flourished as historians uncovered the lives and labor of workers in textile, garment, and shoe industries and in the mines and mills of industrial America.

Brody, Montgomery, and Gutman advanced the new history of labor and the working class as much by writing their own groundbreaking works as by training a generation of new, young scholars who stood on their broad shoulders. Published in 1983, *Working-Class America* was as much a testament to the legacy of this extraordinarily influential transatlantic group of historians as it was to an announcement of future work. Indeed, in retrospect, the volume marked the heyday of this earlier era of labor history. Frisch and Walkowtiz offer in their Introduction an impressive review of the state of labor history up until then and gather in their volume a series of cutting-edge essays that showcase the original research of leading scholars in the field at that time. A chief concern of many scholars then was the fragmentation of historical inquiry in general since the 1960's social history turn, with its favoring of local studies of discrete social structures. In their Introduction, Frisch and Walkowitz argue that the contributors to their collection sought to reintegrate the field of *labor* history specifically by "integrat[ing] multiple dimensions of the working-class experience within a framework that reveals their interconnections." These include essays that explore interclass relations, changing forms of working-class culture, a "more precise history of capitalism," and subjects that expose the lived experience of unity between political and social history. The volume, whose ten essays ranged from early textile mill workers before the "golden age" of the Lowell mills to postwar rank-and-file reactions of auto workers to the anticommunist assault on the CIO, demonstrated new approaches in the field. It gave voice to radical workers in the Knights of Labor and communist transit workers; it highlighted the role of ideology, religion, and ritual in working-class organization; and it placed women, the family labor economy, and consumption as equally at the center of labor history as industrial production. In sum, the volume trumpeted the extraordinarily rich potential and breadth of what these then young historians had helped reconceptualize as working-class history.

Historians have enough trouble figuring out the past, much less imagining the future, and so it was difficult for the editors of *Working-Class America* to imagine that labor history in the mid-1980s might be at a crossroads rather than a take-off. Labor history suffered a decline in the academy in the 1980s that paralleled the rise of Reagan-Thatcherism. The reasons are complicated, but in part reflected how members of the 1980s' "me generation" turned away from social activism at a time when new postmodern academic fashions and identity politics championed ethnic, gender, and race identities over those of class and the worker. Both Reagan-Thatcherism and, in turn, the dissolution of the Soviet socialist states coincided with and may have even encouraged this new focus on cultural history and a decentering of class as a central category of scholarly inquisition.

Significant new work in labor history continued to appear in the next decade in both monographs and articles, but these contributions worked largely in the framework established by the New Labor History in the 1970s. A summer 1974 edition of the *Journal of Social History* published the essays presented at the foundational Anglo-American Labor History Conference held at Rutgers University two years earlier. That landmark event, which brought leading British and American labor historians such as Hobsbawm, Thompson, Gutman, and Montgomery together in the United States for the first time, advanced the transatlantic theoretical tradition that nourished the new work.[5] A subsequent 1986 conference at Northern Illinois University reflected on the legacy of the New Social History fifteen years later. Like the previous work, the focus remained on industrial workers in the nineteenth and early twentieth centuries, but engaging recent concerns Gutman had raised about the tendency of community studies to balkanize labor history, many of the essays addressed "synthesis." The papers from the conference subsequently appeared in a book, *Perspectives on American Labor History* (Northern Illinois University Press, 1989), coauthored by J. Carroll Moody and one of the participants at the earlier Rutgers conference, Alice Kessler-Harris. Notably, in addition to review essays by the coauthors and Brody, two of the other five authors, Sean Wilentz and Leon Fink, had published in *Working-Class America*, and the others were young scholars who had recently authored highly influential monographs on gender and politics and economics of work and worker consciousness in the New Labor History—Alan Dawley, Mari-Jo Buhle, and Michael Reich.[6]

Twelve years after the publication of the Illinois conference collection and 15 years after the publication of *Working-Class America*, three students of David Montgomery, Eric Arnesen, Julie Greene, and Bruce Laurie, edited a volume "to celebrate and reflect upon the influence of . . . Montgomery" on the field. In *Labor Histories: Class, Politics, and the Working-Class Experience*, the editors remarked (in retrospect, perhaps wistfully) on the "renewed ferment" then characterizing both the labor movement and the field of labor history and outlined three main concerns of historians such as Montgomery who considered labor's past through the lens of contemporary issues. In exploring the themes of "politics and the state" and "class and culture," the scholars contributing to this volume reflected increased attention to the state that had increasingly characterized labor history and was a sign of the new centrality of feminist and postcolonial study to labor history. Indeed, even as cultural history began to undercut the social moorings that anchored the new working-class history, one could see in this volume how labor historians were stimulated by new work on the state[7] and the social construction of race. Thus, examining the extent of racism and misogyny that complicated the history of the working class, these histories took care to uncover as well the "materialist moorings" for these attitudes.

It was a third area, however, gender history, that most dramatically transformed the writing of labor history at the end of the century—and challenged (and threatened may not be too strong a word) male labor historians in particular. Women workers in cotton mills, textile workshops, and as domestic servants had long been the subject of study, but few scholars interrogated how gender "mattered"; how the place of women and their subjectivities shaped the historical experience. Fewer still engaged similar questions of men: how masculinity, patriarchy, or male culture, for instance, shaped their experiences. In time women's history morphed into gendered history, as it would expand to include men and women, queer and straight. Feminist scholarship, most notably Ava Baron's 1991 collection *Work Engendered*, led the way down this new path, but equally important was the conceptual work done by European historians of gender and labor, including Joan Scott and Judith Walkowitz.[8] Yet with the emergence of this gendered history during the late 1980s and early 1990s, came the opposition of many male labor historians. Worried that the linguistic turn and post-structuralism undercut the materialist paradigms of class analysis, they rejected the engendered approaches such methods had spawned. Bryan Palmer's *Descent into Discourse* was one of the more full-throated outcries against the cultural turn and its impact on labor history. Arguing that post-structuralism, which had profoundly galvanized feminist labor historians, reified discourse, Palmer believed the central focus on language had obscured structures of oppression and forms of resistance. His opening salvo threw down the gauntlet: "Critical theory is no substitute for historical materialism; language is not life."[9]

Almost two decades later, it is hard to imagine all the furor over the linguistic turn, gendered history, and the hyperbolic caricatures critics drew of one another. Even Palmer, in a monumental 2000 exploration of transgressions and resistance, *Cultures of Darkness*, acknowledges postmodern appreciation of difference (though he warns still of its limits to understanding capitalist particularities).[10] Whether the theoretical battle was won or the opposition simply wilted before seemingly larger threats to a withering organized labor movement is not clear, but the divisive tone of 1990s-era labor panels has given way to a unified new movement of labor and labor historians in the new millennium.

Labor historians' new esprit has had its institutional base in a new organization for the advancement of labor and working-class history, the Labor and Working Class History Association (LAWCHA). In annual meetings and in their writing and organizing on behalf of pro-labor legislation, labor historians have mobilized new explorations of the history of labor in the United States. They have asked new questions about the character and meaning of transformations of work and capital and the impact of those transformations on a potentially revitalized U. S. labor movement. These scholars are eager not only to reconstruct a more sophisticated picture of the past, but also to come to understand better how workers and the labor movement have gotten to where they are today. Transformations of workplaces and labor in United States and Western European countries trouble the older focus on industrial or blue-collar work. Working people, as C. Wright Mills famously observed more than a half century ago, imagine themselves as "middle class" and as an increasingly smaller part of the workforce. Labor historians, building on these new workplace realities, are charting new approaches to and exploring new territory in the history of labor and the working class.[11]

* * *

Much new work in labor history has begun to appear in specialized journals and merits a wider audience. This volume, *Rethinking U.S. Labor History*, seeks to chronicle this rejuvenation and change by showcasing the current research of leading scholars alongside three thought-provoking essays on the future directions of the field. Although one of the coeditors of this volume and the coauthor of one of its essays contributed to *Working-Class America*, this collection blends the work of some senior labor historians who have penned major monographs in the field with young scholars working at the frontiers of what we think will be the field's future. All express a continued interest in questions surrounding the relationship of class and culture, especially the association between the changing experience of class and the broader context of American political culture. Their work also reflects a revived interest in the links between workers' experience and the changing political economy, especially as American workers confront the continued flight of manufacturing jobs and the transformation of the nation's retail sector. As the face of unions has changed to reflect the nation's female and minority working-class populations, historians in this collection continue to grapple with the role that gender and race have played in America's labor history. They are concerned not just with tracing those categories as lived experiences in the past, however, but also with exploring their meanings as cultural, social, legal, and political constructs that had ramifications for the shape and direction of the labor movement. And several of the labor historians in this collection have embraced the transnational turn, some engaging in comparative national studies, others working to break down the epistemological barriers of the nation-state to chart the broader patterns of labor migrations and workers' communities that flowed over such borders throughout history. Finally, some essays also reflect the new concerns of labor history since the 1990s with the state, as some scholars examine how the political apparatuses of local and federal policy shape workers lives and the fate of unions. In this spirit, while not denying the importance of workers' agency, in the essays that follow we see how some historians have called for a fresh look at just how much the political atmosphere structures agency, something that they (and many workers) became acutely aware of under the hostility of the Bush administration and, now, with the opportunities promised by that of Obama.

The above themes animate the work of the authors whose scholarship is showcased in this volume. The essays that make up the section on "current research" demonstrate the broad chronological, thematic, and methodological range of historians' current work, reflecting the richness of the field's recent renaissance. These chapters are organized, for the most part, chronologically so the reader can appreciate the change over time in terms of the content explored by each author. But there are some interesting thematic links among many of the pieces that also serve to organize this main section of the volume. Such themes include explorations of alternative working-class identities, the experiences of laborers who have not traditionally been considered workers, the significance of the state to the definition of certain work experiences as well as to the fate of unions, and the insights that can be gained by going beyond the limits of the nation-state to appreciate the lives, expectations, and struggles of workers.

Alternative working-class identities emerge in this volume in a variety of guises. How workers understand themselves as workers—their identity or consciousness—has been something labor historians have attempted to uncover since many of them took the cultural turn. Most of their works have traditionally focused on revealing and reconstructing the experiences of the most militant of laborers and the most politically radical of workers. But what about those folks who were workers but who chose not to strike, who decided to vote against the union, or who vehemently opposed the communist organizers among them? Four chapters in this volume grapple with these kinds of questions.

In her richly detailed narrative of the 1886 Southwest railroad strike, Theresa Case explores both the social and ideological "middle ground" that existed between the strikers and the strikebreakers during the great upheaval along the rails. Moving beyond the tendency of many scholars to denounce strikebreakers, Case seeks to understand them better as laborers of a different stripe by uncovering a community in which traditional divisions of ethnicity, race, and sex did not play a part, but which found itself under stress during the strike nonetheless. Outlining the materialist moorings of her subjects, Case explores the ways in which the personal connections in the community and on the job between skilled and unskilled workers constituted one fault line along which workers took sides as the strike widened and spread. Drawing on the contributions and methods of cultural history, she also explicates how shared ideas and a shared language constituted the other fault line. Specifically, Case finds that the idea of free labor—and the concept of "manhood" that was at the center of the expression of that idea—was employed in different ways and for different ends during the strike. Locating railroad workers along a spectrum of more communal or more individual interpretations of free labor, Case demonstrates how both strikers and strikebreakers created alternative *working-class* identities for themselves even as they stood on opposite sides of the fight.

Like strikebreakers, religiously devoted workers have not always been fully understood or appreciated by those who have written their history. Ken and Liz Fones-Wolf acknowledge the hesitancy of labor historians to consider the role of religion in working-class life, specifically the hesitancy to consider it as something other than a conservative, red- and race-baiting force that has prevented the growth of unions. While not denying this reactionary facet of many faith communities, the Fones-Wolfs delve more deeply into the history of various Protestant sects in the South during the 1930s and 1940s, uncovering the dynamic changes that such popular Christian denominations underwent in the face of the social and economic changes brought about by the depression and war. In so doing they reveal how "social and religious upheaval also created spaces where dissident voices clamored for change." As the CIO attempted to work within those spaces for change by recognizing the significance of religion to the lives of Southern white workers, its mainstream organizers in the Southern Organizing Committee (SOC) failed to grasp fully the diversity, locally based nature, and highly valued autonomy of those workers' primitive, rural faith traditions. In a region where there was "no common creed" the work of radical organizers, like Claude Williams, Ward Rodgers, and Don West, who grasped the significance of prophetic gospel teachings, bore greater fruit. In their insightful chapter the Fones-Wolfs demonstrate just how significant religion was to the white working class of the South in these decades and how there was no simple formula for translating that system of beliefs into either a commitment to or rejection of unions. Such a reality, the Fones-Wolfs remind us, was difficult to understand fully, not only for the mainstream organizers of the SOC (like Lucy Mason, John Ramsay, Franz Daniel, and Charles Webber), but also for historians who may continue to try to pigeonhole those workers into one camp or the other too hastily.

In his study of the struggle within Mine-Mill in Connecticut during World War II, Steve Rosswurm also seeks to move away from easy dichotomous categorizations. In this case, Rosswurm rejects the tendency to cast communist organizers as heroes and anticommunist working-class Catholics as villains in the story of the CIO's organizing campaigns in the brass valley. And he also seeks to appreciate the significance of religion in the lives of the workers in that valley in a way that moves beyond the familiar story of faith as merely a force for conservative union opposition and red-baiting. Just as the Fones-Wolfs show the difficulty CIO SOC leaders had in appreciating the meaning of Southern white workers' primitive rural Christianity, so does Rosswurm uncover the failure of the Communist Party to engage or take seriously the culture of workers, which in this case was a deeply conservative, traditional Catholicism. Rosswurm does not ignore the anti-Semitic, racist, and sexist strains of those workers' religiously informed opposition to outsiders and communists, but he also demonstrates how the Catholic workers who, alongside the efforts of Father Donnelly, opposed the communist presence in their union did so, they believed, not to destroy Mine-Mill but to save it.

While the brass workers that Rosswurm investigates fought to build a union free of those they deemed a threat to their white, Catholic working-class world of the 1940s, the blue, pink, and white collared ranks of the post-1968 period that Joseph McCartin studies have found unions not to be worth any effort at all. Although the thrust of McCartin's chapter is an argument for the role that structural factors have played in the decline of unions since the late 1960s, he acknowledges that some of the "solvents of solidarity" were cultural as well. The American worker's embrace of an antiunion position stemmed, in part, from his/her attitudes, beliefs, and values about work and his/her perception of him/herself as a worker. This has been especially true for white-collar workers, whose numbers increase over the time frame McCartin explores. These laborers tended not to see themselves as workers and have not embraced unions, contributing to the other factors McCartin cites as explanation for the decline of organized labor in the latter half of the twentieth century. Although many historians have not focused closely on these workers, their antiunion attitudes—even, antiunion identities, as some historians like Lawrence Richards have argued[12]—form a legitimate subject for study. They too need to be located within the broader history of labor and the working class, just as much as the stories of strikebreakers, religiously conservative workers, and anticommunist union men. The chapters offered by Case, the Fones-Wolfs, Rosswurm, and McCartin begin this work.

In addition to exploring alternative working-class identities, this volume offers chapters that consider the lives and experiences of those who traditionally have not been appreciated—either by their contemporaries or by historians—as workers. Peter Way's study of soldiering as the work that built the world of imperial capitalism during the eighteenth century breaks new ground in both military and labor history. In making his case, Way narrates the story of James Miller, a British soldier, from the time he first enlisted in 1756 through his many exploits in the Caribbean and Canada, most notably Miller's participation in the bloody battle on the Plains of Abraham during the Seven Years' War. In this narrative Way shows the soldier as worker in making war and empire—not just through Miller's fighting but also in the grunt work that he and his fellow fighter-laborers do, including digging ditches and building forts. Noting how the reality of the soldier as worker has been (and continues to be) "masked" by calls to duty and adventure, Way explores the existence of what he terms a "plebian opposition culture" in the actions of soldiers who slow down their labor in protest against low pay and difficult working conditions. He demonstrates how these "hidden class transcripts" of anger over pay and conditions unfold over time to climax in a mutiny, which he reads as a labor conflict. Way's innovative study informs military history by reminding us that nationalist "gains were paid for through the exploitation of a class of military laborers." And it also contributes to labor history not only by reclaiming the work experiences and class politics of soldiers, but also by locating them "among that transnational proletariat that transited much of the globe" in the eighteenth century, including Boston's Stamp Act protestors, Irish "whiteboys" guerillas, and rebellious Jamaican slaves.

Although there is a rich and growing literature on the history of domestic workers as laborers, scholars have just recently begun to turn their attention to exploring the experiences of home health care workers through the lens of labor history. Eileen Boris and Jennifer Klein offer an engaging study of the nature of home care work as it has evolved during the twentieth century, considering the effects of this development both on the nature of the work itself and on the lives of those who carry out that work. Such home care workers have been predominately female and immigrant and traditionally have "appear[ed] in public narratives as marginalized workers, hidden in the home, a space that remains unrecognized as a workplace." Boris and Klein bring these women out of the shadows and show in their chapter how the homes in which they care for others are workplaces, sites of labor situated within a formal market that has been shaped, in large part, by the state. As the intimate labor of care—in terms of both personal care and household chores—became a social service, Boris and Klein argue that it became part of a labor market influenced by government policies beginning in the 1930s with the New Deal and continuing through the 1960s with the reforms of the Great Society.

In addition to seeing these mostly immigrant women workers as laborers who toiled within a formal (if largely hidden) labor market, Boris and Klein also bring the state back into the narrative of labor history in their study. They argue that home care work was located at the center of an ideal vision within modern government reform policy. Reformers geared such policy to achieve "dual rehabilitation": the provision of home care work itself for seniors and the disabled on the one hand, and the employment of mostly poor and minority women who might otherwise end up on the state's welfare rolls on the other. Yet such a hope for fostering independence for both home care clients and providers—both would be "rehabilitated" in the pro- cess—has resulted in reality in something much different: reinforced racial, gender, and class inequities. As Boris and Klein argue, "low wages and lack of benefits [have] kept workers poor despite state promotion of such jobs as an alternative to welfare dependency." And those low wages and lack of benefits have resulted from the dif- ficulty home care workers have faced as they have tried to organize as workers to protest such conditions. Such organization has been challenged (and remains chal- lenging) because the public and the state have refused to recognize such workers as workers in a distinct labor market, seeing them instead as independently contracted social workers employed largely by the state through the Medicare and Medicaid systems. Since the 1980s and 1990s homecare workers around the country, especially in California and New York, have developed new organizing strategies to overcome these challenges. They have woven together the tactics of "political unionism, because they had to influence the state; social movement unionism, because they depended on mobilizing clients and communities; and service sector unionism, because they helped create this new epicenter of organized labor" into what Boris and Klein have terms "careworker unionism"—"a solidaristic attempt to move the labor of care away from its marginalized status to recognize its centrality to the contemporary political economy." While many home care workers have gained recognition of their unions, they still struggle with low pay, living at or just above the poverty level.

Like Eileen Boris and Jennifer Klein, Joseph McCartin considers the role of the state in the history of labor organizing during the late twentieth and early twenty- first centuries. He too brings the state back into the narrative in a way that goes beyond a consideration of labor law. In his exploration of organized labor's decline from 1968 through 2005 (when union density fell to 12%), McCartin considers the role of the state within a broader discussion of the political economy. In particular he weighs the state's role in the deregulation of the economy as he traces out the many structural factors that have constituted what he terms the "solvents of solidarity" eroding the union movement during the past 40 years. While he acknowledges the significance of the weakness of U.S. labor law since the passage of the Taft-Hartley Act in 1947 in opening the door to employers' resistance to unions (including many abusive tactics, like illegal firings of those who participate in organizing drives), McCartin argues that the ultimate reason for union decline has been a "crisis of collective action" among workers. He believes that this crisis can be charted most clearly by the rapid and unexpected drop-off in the number of strikes (from an average of 350 per year during the 1950s to just about 25 in the first five years of the new century). And, McCartin argues, this phenomenon—of workers so rapidly and dramatically turning away from using their most powerful weapon—has been a result of a confluence of changes in the nation's political economy that happened roughly from 1978 until about 1983. Those changes included:

> [T]he economic turmoil of the late 1970s; the growing phenomenon of deregulation which undermined the stability of workers in many highly unionized industries; the first effects of a new stage in the process of globalization made possible by the shipping container, the satellite, and the computer; a wave of plant closings that foretold the accelerating phenomenon of de-industrialization; the resurgence of conservatism in the face of economic crisis; and the spreading use of striker replacements from the public to the private sector."

McCartin explores each of these changes in depth, arguing that they help to explain why the "crisis of organized labor that emerged in the last third of the 20th century was not only measured by the erosion of workers' rights to organize or the failure of unions to devote greater resources to organizing, but also by the erosion of workers' capacity to act collectively even when organized." He thus challenges his readers to bring the state back into the narrative of union decline while at the same time pushing them to see beyond it to the many interrelated structural changes of the past decades that have proven to be such potent antidotes to worker solidarity.

Shelton Stromquist also challenges his readers both to consider the role of the state and to look beyond it in quite specific ways in his study of working-class politics at the turn of the twentieth century. He calls for an appreciation of the transnational context for local—specifically municipal—proletarian political action. Yet he also argues that the nation-state should not be dismissed altogether in the study of transnational working-class politics. Rather, Stromquist argues, the nation must be understood as a historical construction that proletarian political activists both shaped and were shaped by. This constituted and constitutive role of the state vis-à-vis radical working-class politics was especially potent during the late nineteenth- and early twentieth centuries when such movements functioned within the context of heightened national consciousness.

In his chapter Stromquist thus calls for a new way of doing the history of labor politics and a new way of imagining transnational history. He acknowledges that there have been many ways historians have sought to capture the meaning of working-class life and politics beyond national boundaries, going back to the most basic comparative studies of the Commons era, through the multicountry studies of workers in a given industry, like coal mining or the maritime trades, to the more recent subaltern studies that have focused attention on "informal sector workers" as part of a global working class. Stromquist also recognizes those who have advanced the idea of the transnational by exploring workers' migrations and the international networks of socialism and communism. But while each of these alternative approaches considers different kinds of transnational ties, Stromquist argues that many of them fully appreciate neither the continued pull of the nation-state nor the significance of the local community as a space for working-class transnational action. A narrative that explores such complicated interconnections among the transnational, national, and local spheres is what Stromquist offers in his study of labor and socialist municipal political activity in Wellington, New Zealand, Brisbane, Australia, and Milwaukee, Wisconsin. In his exploration of these three case studies, Stromquist locates the pull of "national parliamentary affairs and national party competition" but discovers that the labor and socialist parties in each city also drew from "a different set of internationalist loyalties." They deployed those loyalties on the local level to challenge "the nationalist framework of their respective movements" in a phenomenon Stromquist has termed "localist internationalism." In so doing those labor and socialist party activists were able to "reshape Council debate and action around a set of issues to which labor was deeply committed" and to redefine "how council business was conducted." Looking at Brisbane, Wellington, and Milwaukee side by side allows Stromquist to locate the American example within a broader context of global municipal labor politics and thus to challenge the old Sombartan chestnut of American exceptionalism. And his three-city "localist internationalist" approach shows not only the development of that social democratic politics worldwide, but also the vital contribution played by municipal grassroots mobilization and the contestation between local-internationalists and parliamentary leaders for the soul of this political movement.

While Stromquist explores the contours of socialist labor politics, Eric Arnesen turns his attention to communism. Specifically, he calls on historians to reassess their understanding of the Communist Party (CP) and its relationship with labor and the civil rights movement during World War II. His chapter, along with Steve Rosswurm's, constitute a fifth thematic grouping in our volume: post-revisionist approaches to the nature of the CP and its place within the labor movement that have been taken up since the opening of the Soviet archives and the Venona cables during the early 1990s.

In his exploration of A. Philip Randolph's critique of the Communist Party as a grave danger to the civil rights movement (most famously articulated during the 1940 National Negro Convention), Arnesen makes the case for why historians need to appreciate the significance of such contemporary criticism. While he recognizes the important contributions of revisionist scholars who have studied the CP (noting their insights into the grass-roots activism of the party, for example) he is clear about his concerns with the limits of their work. Arnesen argues that most revisionists have essentially left out the politics in their explorations of the party's activities in the past, which has allowed them to overlook the communism that was at the heart of the Communist Party; the new social history brought many significant insights into the work of party activists on unemployed councils, in neighborhood tenement groups and with civil rights organizations, but it has failed to grapple with the core political realities of the party to which such activists belonged, including its shifting policy positions and ties to Moscow.

Arnesen takes issue with this oversight in terms of the Communist Party's relationship to black civil rights and black labor. In his discussion of Randolph's opposition to communism during and after World War II (and in his exploration of the fate of Randolph in labor-left history) he demonstrates that when revisionist scholars reject the criticisms of their traditionalist cohorts (like John Earl Haynes and Harvey Klehr) they lose sight not only of the implications of those criticisms but also of contemporary anticommunists like Randolph. In turn, Arnesen argues that there has been an oversimplification of anticommunists and anticommunism (a point also made by Rosswurm in his chapter on Mine/Mill) and a overlooking of the lived, historical experience of the CP among many blacks and workers. Arnesen insists (quite controversially) that if one takes this view of the history it can be argued that the Communist Party was as much complicit in the creation of anticommunist sentiment as was the right wing: opposition to communism on the part of African Americans, like Randolph, was not reactionary but rather a legitimate defense of democracy against the Soviet commitments and Stalinist discipline of the party.

Arnesen, along with the other contributing authors to this volume, thus expands the boundaries of the field. Thirty years ago the New Labor History broadened its purview to include the working class rather than to focus on institutional labor and mobilized social history for a different story "from the bottom up." It focused on the social history of the industrial working class and the era before the mid-twentieth century. The essays in this volume broaden the focus further, re-emphasizing the political history of labor (as in the essays by Stromquist, Arnesen, McCartin, and Boris/Klein) and the cultural institutions of working-class life (notably in terms of religion in the chapters by the Fones-Wolfs and Rosswurm). The essays also broaden the geographical and temporal reach of working-class history. From Peter Way's finely etched transatlantic study of the eighteenth-century soldier and the idea of what we might call the "military worker" to Shelton Stromquist's comparative and transnational context for understanding American socialism and exceptionalism at the beginning of the twentieth century, and to Joseph McCartin's structuralist study of union decline since the 1970s, the chapters span three centuries. And finally, these essays (like McCartin's and Boris/Klein's) heed the call of our three "new directions" essays (described below) in redefining the parameters of labor and work to reflect the reorganization of work in service and consumption more recently.

That said, the essays also reflect what some may find to be a disquieting revalorization of those formerly often discredited or marginalized in labor history—Case's strikebreakers or Rosswurm's and Arnesen's conservative working-class anticommunists, for example. Yet, the reasons for this reappraisal are worth considering, even if the answers are only partial and tentative. And some may feel these accounts, too, will demand rebalancing. In part, these latest revisions may reflect the dismemberment of the Soviet Union and failure of state socialism societies, that is, of communism. But at a time when labor seeks to rebuild itself and labor historians in LAWCHA strategize to assist that effort, the "humanizing" of nonunion workers and those who led efforts to discredit many communist organizers who built the labor movement in the last century, seems counterintuitive. For some, the new view seems offered as a corrective to what these historians have seen as an unproductive free pass. Any movement must be willing to learn from its mistakes if it is to grow.

With an eye to that growth this volume also offers three impressive chapters that posit new directions for the field and are presented in addition to the eight chapters representing the current research interests of both younger and leading scholars of labor history. The first of these "new directions" essays suggests how engaging with a history of the senses can enrich labor historians' understanding of both workers' past experiences and class as an historically constructed category. The second recommends exploring questions of gender in labor history beyond the shop floor to reach a deeper understanding of working-class identities and politics. The third grapples with the consequences of the appreciation of certain activities as labor that have not traditionally been considered work for historians' understanding of the past and for the future of the field. While a few of the authors whose works are showcased in the current research section of this volume have begun to explore some of these new approaches, the three studies in this "new directions" section delve more deeply into the significance and possibilities of such methods. They offer both veteran and aspiring researchers inspiration for the future of labor and working-class history.

In the first of these "new directions" chapters Daniel Bender makes a provocative suggestion for scholars to integrate the history of the senses into their explorations of and understanding of working-class history. He acknowledges that heretofore there generally has been hostility, if not an outright clash, between cultural and social historians, with the former interested in questions of representation and the latter in questions of agency. Most cultural historians have focused their attention on the middle class and elites in society and have thus not engaged significantly with working-class history. At the same time, most labor historians have been social historians and have thus rejected what they perceive to be the weak materialist moorings of cultural history. Because of that we do not know much about "how working people have been described, studied, and represented, for example, by elites." Bender believes that a history of the senses could help overcome this divide between labor and cultural history and "provide new ways of understanding class that include but also transcend definitions of class as a set of shared experiences." By drawing on insights from cultural history, labor historians could appreciate class "as a set of cultural representations, cultural differences, and physical perceptions that are experienced in multisensory ways" and cultural historians could then expand their focus to include questions of class.

Bender acknowledges that some scholars have already begun this type of synthesis, most notably scholars of gender and labor like Elizabeth Faue, Ava Baron, and Eileen Boris who have considered how workers have been "subjects of study and analysis" as well as "'objects of law and social policy.'"[13] He argues that Faue's, Baron's, and Boris' work "suggests that the same documents that labor historians have relied on to reconstruct the social history of the working class can be revisited for what they reveal about the representations of class and class difference" and serve as examples for the new approach he advocates. To bolster his argument, Bender demonstrates in his chapter how works like *The Jungle* and the Pittsburgh Survey have the potential to be used in this way. Through his multisensory reading of these works he shows just how important senses (other than the visual) were in representations of workers: they were described as noisy, smelly, and coarse. And he probes questions about the act of perceiving inherent in the works he explores asking how and why such things were or were not recorded and what that can tell us about class understood in this mutlisensory, representational way.

Some of what these explorations tell us, Bender argues, is that there was an ideology embedded in these sensory perceptions and representations that hinged on questions of power and control. Attitudes about sensory perceptions were and are also tied to class markers that relate to this kind of politics and denote the difference between "stink" and "smell." And especially during the late nineteenth- and early twentieth centuries when progressive reformers (like settlement house workers) who were engaged in the "liberal project" promoted reform of homes and workplaces they "sought to regulate proletarian sensory alterity. That is, they promoted middle-class norms of smell, sound, and taste." Bender argues that in response to such attempts at control there was "working-class resistance—including hidden transcripts—[that] can be read as a search for what we might term 'sensory autonomy.'" Such struggles for control and for freedom persist in the present—the blasting sound of a tricked out car stereo or the strong odors from a neighborhood block party, for example—and can serve as fruitful sources of inquiry for those interested in understanding the experience and representation of class and class difference.

More fully understanding the experience of class is something that many women's labor historians and feminist scholars have attempted to do since the 1970s through their explorations of women's roles in the workplace and in the home. Liz Faue considers the importance of these scholars' works in re-imaging labor through the lens of gender in her chapter on new directions in the field. Faue notes how the first wave of women's labor historians focused on reconstructing the experience of working women: what their lives were like in the factory or behind the counter and how they were discriminated against in the workplace or excluded from unions. At the same time, Faue reminds us how the early scholarship that grappled with questions of masculine self-definition—like David Montgomery's study of steel workers—did not critically probe the "manly" craftsman identities it described. It would take "the resurgence of feminist activism, adoption of gender analysis in the social sciences and the humanities, and the continued growth in and impact of women's labor force participation" to bring about more critical studies of the political meanings of such working-class masculinities (and to explore similar working-class femininities).

Faue celebrates these advances in the scholarship for the ways they have brought us closer to recognizing the complexities of working-class experiences in the past. Most notably she heralds Kathleen Barry's *Feminism in Flight* and Stephen Norwood's *Strikebreaking and Intimidation*. Faue argues that Barry's work moves beyond the old divide in feminist scholarship over "difference and equality in the pursuit of women's political agenda" by showing how women flight attendants could both organize within unions and yet also find their own ways, as women, to express their fight for justice in the workplace. She holds up Norwood's study as an example of how scholars can critique the construction of working-class masculinities and the violence that was so often attendant to the process of that construction.

Ultimately Faue argues that the questions a gendered approach to labor history raises—about how "gender both empower[s] as well as limit[s] class activism . . . how . . . such gender ideals, which have underwritten much of labor history, [have] changed in a deindustrializing economy . . . [and] how . . . racial and ethnic differences among men and women workers [have] altered how they think about their own gendered and class roles as working-class Americans"—must be considered "beyond the shop floor if they are at all to make sense of how class identity is ultimately gendered and ethnically and racially defined." For while we know a great deal about the interactions among these identities in the workplace we have yet to explore the "emotional histories" and "subjective understandings" of workers, which, Faue argues, "require not just gender analysis but feminist understandings of what gender difference and equality have meant and might mean." This new direction for labor historians could take them into working-class and labor biographies and studies of working-class childhood and adolescence, where such understandings and identities are first formed, and dramatically expand the boundaries of the field.

Zach Schwartz-Weinstein also poses a challenge to the field of labor history as a whole when he suggests in his "new directions" chapter that scholars must take up a critical investigation of the limits of work. Arguing that those limits have largely been placed by labor historians who have followed a definition of productive work tied to the wage relationship—a definition itself rooted in Marxist categories—Schwartz-Weinstein calls for "a continuing critical engagement with the history of the discipline" itself as a first step in pushing beyond such boundaries. By "troubling the limits of productive labor" he argues that historians can better recognize and document the work and working experiences of those who have largely remained invisible from labor history's narrative. At the same time they can both gain insights into why this may have been so—the prioritizing of a narrow definition of waged labor—and begin to construct new paradigms for future scholarship. Without such fresh historical approaches, Schwartz-Weinstein warns, "labor history risks a dangerous and parochial inability to understand living labor's broader dimensions."

Schwartz-Weinstein acknowledges that the process of criticizing what has been defined as the limits of work is not, in itself, new. The New Labor historians of the 1960s and 1970s were critical of the institutional focus of the Commons school that came before them. And the feminist scholars and cultural historians of the 1970s and 1980s critiqued the unquestioned male dominance and structural focus of the New Labor historians who came before them. Schwartz-Weinstein now calls for a third phase in this critique of the limits of labor that includes a continuation of the kind of inquiries posed by feminist and cultural historians but which also contains a focus on work that is "situated in relation to contemporary and historical capitalisms and articulations of race, gender and nation." In particular, he emphasizes the need to continue scholarly exploration of "racialized and gendered service work" and affective labor. Essentially Schwartz-Weinstein asks labor historians to take a broader view of what constitutes work and the workplace at the same time that they take a close view of the daily interactions in these often overlooked sites where not just race and gender are constructed but also work and labor itself.

Such a new approach is significant, and much needed, Schwartz-Weinstein argues, not only because it would expand the discipline's gaze and understanding of the past—the historical construction of capitalism and work—but also because over the last 25 years there have been many more workers doing such service work and affective labor. And, yet, those laborers have not been considered, by some historians and by society at large, to be workers. In terms of societal denial of the status of these laborers as workers Schwartz-Weinstein cites the NLRB cases *Brown University v. UAW* and *Oakwood Healthcare, Inc.* in which the Board decided that graduate students and nurses were not workers, but rather that the graduate teaching assistants were only students and the nurses, because of some training responsibilities, were supervisors. Such cases remind us of the human and political costs of such limited definitions of work. These students and nurses were not allowed to form or join unions and, largely as a consequence, were unable to demand effectively higher wages, better benefits, or job security.

Those in the service sector and those who carry out such affective labor pose a challenge to our comprehension (in both contemporary and historical contexts) of work because their labor is often masked. They are hidden in the home or behind informal or ambiguous work relationships (like the graduate student teaching assistant, the nurse who also trains other nurses, or the housekeeper and child minder who do what has long been deemed unproductive work). Understanding and unmasking that process of denial—and often of self-denial on the part of the worker—is a worthwhile task for labor historians, Schwartz-Weinstein argues. It allows us to ask questions of the "instability of labor as a category" and to see the complex and historically contingent relationship between such work and the construction of race, gender, and sexuality. Schwartz-Weinstein cites the important work by historians like Tera Hunter and Kathleen M. Barry in this vein.

Ultimately Schwartz-Weinstein calls on labor historians to engage in a new "archival practice" that sees *labor* as socially constructed and as found in unusual places. The workplace would then be defined broadly and though it historians could probe the interrelated constructions of race and gender and sexuality "in the most quotidian interaction with employer and coworkers." Such close-grained inquiries could take place across a vast expanse of contexts, thus expanding the topical reach of the discipline, while following a thematic synthesis that would narrow the focus back in along the lines of "troubling labor."

* * *

In addition to these three cutting edge "new directions" essays, this volume provides readers with additional resources that should be of particular use for students and those new to the field. First, we have included a chronology of labor and working-class history. It is intended to provide students and researchers new to the field with a quick overview of some of the more significant moments in the history of organized labor and in the experiences of the working class. But it can also serve as a reminder for everyone interested in the field, young and veteran alike, of the changes that have taken place in it over the past few decades. There are more things noted in our chronology than just the formation of union federations or the undertaking of nationwide strikes. We have also tried to include entries that reflect the more recent concerns of scholars for the role of women and minority workers, for those who may not traditionally be considered workers, and for social and cultural experiences that are hard to chart. In doing so we want our readers to recognize that such tools as chronologies are inherently limited, however, because of the choices we must make about what to include and what to leave out. We do not pretend to offer a chronology that has captured *every* important event. And we draw our readers' attention to our sensitivity in defining just what constitutes an "important" moment, what should be considered part of the labor movement, and who constituted the working class. While we strive to reflect the broader cultural changes and social phenomena of daily life that have been so central to working-class history in this timeline, such things are difficult to quantify. The mechanism of the chronology itself also favors a history that is institutional, legal, and political while showcasing the extraordinary moments of the past. We have attempted to make ours as inclusive as we can but draw attention to this challenge to provoke reflection and discussion about the relationship between method and subject in the field.

In addition to the chronology we also offer our readers a list of resources relevant to the field of labor and working-class history. These include information on important archives, professional organizations, union and library websites, and the like. Many of these tools that were not widely available 25 years ago —especially the websites, LISTSERVs, and chatrooms—have become important sources for research and teaching, as well as for the resurgence of the labor history community. They can be useful for those interested in finding source material for their own research or for the classroom. And they can also be a wonderful mechanism through which to create professional partnerships for conferences and publications. This virtual community of scholars and resources is transforming the field in ways yet to be appreciated fully. We hope that this section will prove to be of practical and meaningful use to our readers.

Finally, we have also provided a section that gives suggestions "for further reading" on each of the topics addressed in the volume. Our authors have each provided a list of 12 books that they believe are the most significant to their subject. These lists serve as a useful resource for researchers and young scholars who want to continue their exploration of the many themes raised in this book.

This volume then means to serve as both a practical and substantive contribution to the field of labor history and a comment on its current state and future prospects. The essays demonstrate that the state of labor history today is strong and its possibilities for the future bright. The works of scholars, young and senior, that are showcased here illustrate how the boundaries of labor and working-class history have expanded well beyond the first wave of growth that took place during the 1960s and 1970s with the social turn and even beyond that of the second wave of the 1980s cultural turn. Indeed, these essays suggest that we may now be facing a third wave of expansion, in terms of both subject matter and methodological approaches in the field. Such new terrain, explored in our essays here, include: those who are workers but who do not identify with the labor movement or who have not been and are still not recognized by it because of the nature of their work or their gender, race, religion, region, and/or politics; the place of the political economy and the state in shaping the parameters within which organized labor can and cannot function, particularly since the late twentieth century; the "localist internationalism" of transnational labor politics; the gendered assumptions behind definitions and experiences of class and class difference; and multisensory approaches to appreciating class as it was lived and represented in the past. Each of these essays, and the approaches and subjects they offer for contemplation, herald the rich and broad future of U.S. labor and working-class history.

Notes

1. Michael H. Frisch and Daniel J. Walkowitz, eds. *Working-Class America: Essays on Labor, Community and American Society* (Urbana: University of Illinois Press, 1983).
2. John R. Commons, *History of Labor in the United States* 4 volumes (New York: Macmillan, 1918).
3. Caroline F. Ware, *The Early New England Cotton Manufacture: A Study in Industrial Beginnings* (1929); Vera Shlakman, *Economic History of a Factory Town* (1935); Josephson, Hannah, *The Golden Threads: New England's Mill Girls and Magnates* (1949). For an insightful appraisal of these women, see Ardis Cameron, *Radicals of the Worst Sort: Laboring Women in Lawrence, Massachusetts, 1860–1912* (Urbana: University of Illinois Press, 1993).
4. E. P. Thompson, *The Making of the English Working Class* (London: Victor Gollanz, 1963).
5. The Conference, organized by Peter N. Stearns and Daniel J. Walkowitz, also included many younger historians who would go on to become leaders in the field: Alice Kessler Harris, James Green, Melvyn Dubofsky, Gareth Stedman Jones, and Pat Thane, among others.
6. Alan Dawley's brilliant study of the shoemakers of Lynn, Massachusetts, *Class and Community* (Cambridge: Harvard University Press, 1976), won the Bancroft Prize. Dawley's memorable phrase that the ballot had been the nail in the coffin of working class consciousness would influence the debate on nineteenth century working-class consciousness and questions of American exceptionalism. Mari Jo Buhle's book *Women and American Socialism, 1870–1920* (Urbana: University of

Illinois Press, 1983) integrated women's history with the history of politics, radicalism, and labor. The labor economist Michael Reich had published with David Gordon and Richard Edwards a widely influential synthetic account of labor economics and the organization of work, *Segmented Work, Divided Workers: The Historical Transformation of Work in the United States* (Cambridge, UK and New York: Cambridge University Press, 1982).

7. Theda Skocpol, *States and Social Revolutions: A Comparative Analysis of France, Russia and China* (New York: Cambridge University Press, 1979); Stephen Skowronek, *Building a New American State: The Expansion of National Administrative Capacities, 1877–1920* (New York: Cambridge University Press, 1982). This spawned increased focus on the history of the state and liberalism in America by labor historians. See, for example, Steve Fraser and Gary Gerstle, *The Rise and Fall of the New Deal Order, 1930–1980* (Princeton: Princeton University Press, 1989).

8. Joan W. Scott, *Gender and the Politics of History* (New York: Columbia University Press, 1988); Judith R. Walkowitz, *Prostitution and Victorian Society: Women, Class and the State* (New York: Cambridge University Press, 1980) and *City of Dreadful Delight: Narratives of Sexual Danger in late-Victorian London* (Chicago: University of Chicago Press, 1992).

9. Bryan D. Palmer, *Descent into Discourse: The Reification of Language and the Writing of Social History* (Philadelphia: Temple University Press, 1990).

10. Bryan D. Palmer, *Cultures of Darkness: Night Travels in the Histories of Transgression* (New York: Monthly Review Press, 2000).

11. C. Wright Mills, *White Collar: The American Middle Classes* (New York: Oxford University Press, 1951).

12. Lawrence Richards, *Union-Free America: Workers and Antiunion Culture* (Urbana: University of Illinois, 2008).

13. Ava Baron and Eileen Boris, "The Body as a Useful Category for Working-Class History" *Labor* 4 (Summer, 2007): 23–43; Joel Dinerstein, *Swinging the Machine: Modernity, Technology, and African American Culture between the World Wars* (Amherst: University of Massachusetts Press, 2003).

PART I

CURRENT RESEARCH

CHAPTER ONE

Memoirs of an Invalid: James Miller and the Making of the British-American Empire in the Seven Years' War

Peter Way

In Benjamin West's iconic painting "The Death of Wolfe" General James Wolfe lies dying on the Plains of Abraham, a pallid figured recumbent in the arms of others.[1] Officers in martial red, naval blue, and colonial green, the colors of the Empire, encircle him. A lone private soldier clasps his hands in prayer, while a lone Indian etched with tattoos looks on contemplatively, and a herald runs with news of impending victory, a Union Jack held high. In the background, men in work clothes toil at hauling heavy loads up a steep incline from ships moored in the St. Lawrence River, while red-coated common soldiers strive toward an enemy obscured by the smoke of battle, a front line discharging weapons signals the point of engagement. Their collectivity rendered figuratively, workers and soldiers congeal into an indistinguishable mass the further they retreat from the cynosure of our gaze, noble Wolfe. This painting, both in its imaginative drafting of the event and in the perspective it adopts, inadvertently captures the essence of much military history. The stated causes of war are largely taken at face value, the focus centers on commanding officers, death is portrayed as heroic, and common soldiers recede into the background, vulgar strokes of the brush. The militarist discourse captured on canvas and on printed page mystifies the labor involved in making war. Armies stood at the heart of fiscal-military states that arose in the early modern era and developed structures of taxation and borrowing to fund the armed conflict central to their fundamental goals: internal order, national defense, the acquisition and protection of dependent territories, and the security of colonial trade. Soldiers in these professional armies, whether conscripted or enlisted, received wages to work in the war industry and their labor combined powered European state formation and imperial expansion. They occupied a familiar world of masters and servants, the exchange of labor for pay, work discipline, and conflict over the meaning of the labor contract. Patriotic rhetoric, chain of command, army uniforms, and military justice obscured the commonality of martial labor with that in civil society to contemporary observers and later historians, but now the accumulated layers of obfuscation can be stripped away. Soldiers' central role in the making of the modern world requires attention, while the work they performed needs to be re-claimed as part of international labor history.

This essay thus adopts a different perspective, a deep focus intended to recapture the whole tableau of the Seven Years' War by bringing the background to the fore. Christ-like Wolfe blurs as once-faceless rank and file materializes. If rendered true to life, in viewing the "Death of Wolfe," we could perhaps espy one James Miller, a common soldier of the 15th regiment present on the Plains of Abraham, whose martial efforts involved no less heroism than Wolfe's. Whereas Benjamin West and countless others chronicled Wolfe's actions,[2] no one has rendered Miller's story. But, unlike his comrades by the thousand, Miller sought to speak for himself. He has left a memoir of service in the British army spanning the Seven Years' War that allows the historian to engage more closely the front rank experience of warfare. Miller sent his memoirs in 1792, to Sir Jeffery Amherst, his former commander. At that time, he served as acting fort major for his garrison of Chelsea Hospital Invalids[3] stationed on the Island of Jersey in the English Channel, and wrote requesting a promotion to a lieutenancy in the Invalids with the higher pension that would have gone with that rank.[4] Miller naturally adopted the language of a petitioner. "It is very possible that some may think it impertinent, others presumptious, for so humble an individual presuming to give a Narrative, which contains nothing of novelty, or in any degree equal to many in the army."[5] His narrative may not be novel in the experiences recounted, as many soldiers shared similar careers. However, unlike the provincial troops raised by the colonies,[6] few regular soldiers left written narratives of their military service in the Seven Years' War largely due to their low level of literacy. Moreover, Miller's record of service is remarkable in that he participated in many of the key battles of the Seven Years' War, and thus provides a much more complete rank and file narrative of the conflict. Finally, despite the fact that his memoirs constituted a petition to Amherst, they provide both candid and critical evaluations of his military service and his commanding officers. In this, it is exceptional, being a rare narrative of a common soldier's engagement with warmaking that was not meant to be published and thus not sanitized so as to appeal to subscribers or a wider reading public.[7] The chain of command may have operated to deny Miller an understanding of all that transpired in the battles in which he participated, just as the political economy worked to deny a voice to the subaltern. Nonetheless, Miller refused to remain mute.

Miller's memoir's unusual candor and historical sweep allow us to interrogate the elitist biases of military history and perform a critical reading of British military enterprise in a war that constituted a turning point in imperial history, revealing soldiers' fundamental role in the making of the British American Empire. Traditional military historians rely on the official papers generated by officers and government officials and, by default, have written in a similar vein about the command concerns with mobilization, provision and supply, strategy, and chain-of-command order. The so-called new military historians in the past 30 years have given more attention to common soldiers and their experience of warfare, building on the work of John Keegan,[8] but these studies tend to concentrate on how soldiers *experienced* war rather than on how they *made* war, how they served as victims to the misfortunes of war as opposed to agents acting to effect the historical changes flowing from war. The same official records also document numerous actions performed by common soldiers from the mundane to the mortal, which when read against the grain, can shed much light on their role in history. This usually involves an exercise in pastiche, sorting through numerous records, pulling out the evidentiary fragments addressing their lives, and assembling a mosaic that purports to capture the complex whole. Miller's is the document that provides a coherent and comprehensive account of life in the lower ranks. Juxtaposed to and joined with the fragmented view it helps provide a resolution comparable to the military master narrative.

Miller's memoirs allow the historian to do more than attach a name to the face of battle. His more critical observations of military life enable a reading of the class dynamic within the army and the labor history of warfare. Given the propensity of old soldiers to tell their war stories somewhat romantically, one could expect a stirring narrative of battles won. And the fact that Miller was requesting advancement in the Chelsea Invalids from his former commander would foster self-censoring in the re-telling of events. Yet Miller is quite forthright in complaining of the treatment of soldiers, the willingness of officers to sacrifice men with seemingly little remorse, and the unfair distribution of the spoils of war. He also spends as much time recounting the hard work that went into making war as he does recounting the great set-piece battles in which he participated. Miller's is as much an account of a life of labor as it is a trading in war stories. Realistically, this should not surprise the modern reader. Warfare is one of the central enterprises of human beings, something we have engaged in since we pulled together into collectivities. And it is at root an economic enterprise as much as a purely military endeavor, wars being waged over boundaries and the resources these boundaries sought to enclose. The term making war connotes the fact that warfare in its many manifestations has to be produced and reproduced, yet militarist rhetoric nationalizes the process as an inevitable element of statecraft, and patriotic calls to arms rationalize military service as sacrifice for the nation rather than as the paid labor of members of the working class. While one can excuse military historians for not casting soldiers as workers, labor historians cannot so easily be let off the hook. Yet virtually no work has been done on the subject of military labor. Colonial historians have given great attention to craftsmen, indentured servants, apprentices, slaves, unpaid domestic workers—and with just cause—but none to soldiers.[9] Yet warfare comprised the most heavily capitalized human enterprise at the time. Moreover, the Seven Years' War proved of crucial importance to Britain and its colonies. The war was fought over who would control North America east of the Mississippi, and the defeat and removal of the French from this region led to a huge land grab that changed the face of the British Empire and paved the way for the formation of both the United States of America and Canada.

Soldiers performed the work that made the war that gave rise to these modern states. Their contributions need to be recognized as labor and their stories be told as part of the international history of labor.

"not intended, for the public eye"

Miller opened his memoir with a disclaimer: "As this Journal, is not intended, for the public eye, he trusted that the few friends, who has the patience, to read it, will have the good nature, to pardon any imperfections."[10] All documents exhibit weaknesses; the trick lies in accounting for them. Miller apologized for failings in writing style but also of his recall. It is not clear when Miller committed his account to paper. He noted that several "ordinary books" recording the movements of the 15th Regiment in the Seven Years' War had been taken from his possession in 1781 when he had been captured by the *Black Princess*, a French Privateer.[11] Presumably he wrote from memory between that event and his sending the manuscript to Amherst in 1792. Miller's motive to secure promotion in the Invalids meant that the memoir naturally concentrates on recounting his military record. Enlisting with the 15th Regiment in 1756 while a youth, Miller embarked on a storied military career, taking part in: the 1757 expedition against Rochefort; the capture of Louisbourg in 1758; the fall of Quebec in 1759; the successful defense of Quebec and the surrender of Montreal in 1760; the capture of Martinique in 1761; and the taking of Havana from Spain in 1762. After a winter in Cuba, his regiment returned to Quebec, where it remained when a general mutiny broke out late that summer. After its suppression, he remained in Canada until his regiment returned in 1768 to Britain, where Miller continued to serve in the army. It is not clear but Miller apparently left the army in 1775 after hostilities with the American colonies erupted, and made his way to North Carolina where a relative had left him a property near Wilmington. A loyalist provincial company offered a lieutenancy to Miller, and in that capacity he served alongside the regular army against the rebels throughout the colonies and in the West Indies before being granted invalid status and dispatched to England. Taken by a French privateer en route and shipped to France, he ultimately returned to England as part of a prisoner exchange. He received orders to serve as a member of the Invalid Guards in Jersey, where he heard the sad news of the British surrender to the Americans. There he remained until sending his memoirs to Amherst in 1792.

Miller forthrightly offered his opinion on military and political matters, but he proved much more stingy with personal information. We know not his birth date but he tells us he enlisted in 1756 when still a youth, meaning he was likely born in the late 1730s. He places his birthplace "on the wrong side of the Tweed," that is, in Scotland in the Border region, but he does not tell us exactly where. As to his domestic situation, he makes but two fleeting references. In 1781, he noted that when he and other invalided members of the British army were sent home from Charleston, South Carolina, he "sailed with my family." And in 1792, he expressed his thanks for the patronage of officers who helped his son secure an appointment to the

26th Regiment, presumably as an officer.[12] That constitutes the sum of our knowledge. Equally cryptic is Miller's status. He is literate and writes with a fairly polished style, at times in Latin and others in French, and reveals a depth of knowledge, quoting Rousseau at one point, perhaps an artifact of his schooling. "A confin'd education was my lot, being sent to school at the distance of two miles, as soon as I could walk so far. The school master had been at college, and had therefore a smattering of latin, which he taught!"[13] But there is no indication of his parents' class status.

Miller's rank in the military proves equally evasive. In the letter to Amherst attached to his memoirs, he indicated that he was currently acting Fort Major of the garrison of Invalids on the Island of Jersey in the English Channel, but signs as James Miller, Ensign, the most junior of officer ranks. In the conclusion he refers to having held the rank of lieutenant, but in a colonial regiment within which holding the status of gentlemen was not a prerequisite to a commission. Miller never divulges his status in the 15th Regiment of the regular army, but he gives every indication that he served as a private soldier. A "crimp" (private individuals paid by regiments to perform recruiting in the stead of a formal military recruiting party) enlisted him to the army, certainly not the way officers entered the army, instead purchasing their commissions. And Miller writes of his service in the Seven Years' War as if he toiled in the front ranks: receiving wounds in combat, being frost bit while on guard duty.[14] Thus, it appears that Miller served as a common soldier in this war, perhaps being promoted to a noncommissioned officer (corporal and sergeant), then continued serving in its aftermath up to the Revolution when he secured a commission in a provincial regiment. While climbing out of the enlisted ranks into the officer class proved difficult in the regular army,[15] an experienced and connected individual like Miller could make the leap more easily in the colonial forces, especially if one had significant experience of warfare and local connections. Miller's reticence to divulge too much of himself leaves voids in his story, necessitating such informed supposition. And we do not have other sources to fill in these silences. This problem bedevils biographies of common people: when the records do exist, they often are all we have on the subject, as in this case. Luckily, Miller provides rich material with which to limn the contours of life as a common soldier engaged in the hard work of making war at what proved to be an epochal moment in British American history.

"To have the happiness, of being born a Briton"

James Miller proclaimed his "happiness, of being born a Briton."[16] He entered the world coincidental to Britain's entrance on the international scene as an important player. Britain had undergone a protracted process of state formation involving dynastic wars, union with Wales and Scotland, Civil War and Revolution that conspired to focus energies at home through the end of the seventeenth century. With the issues of internal state order largely resolved, however, Britain could contend for international rank with European powers. Military capability constituted the key ingredient.

Early Modern Europe underwent a "military revolution" involving: tactical and technological change; marked expansion in the size of armies; growing complexity of strategic thinking so as to marshal these larger forces; the resultant need for greater training and discipline of soldiers ultimately leading to professional standing armies; and state development geared to making war.[17] Many historians believed that England escaped this militarization, but John Brewer has argued that from 1688 to 1714, Britain in fact expanded its military commitments by sharply increasing taxation (customs and excise), engaging in "public deficit finance (a national debt)" in an unprecedented fashion, and creating an administrative structure for the military and fiscal needs.[18] Britain transformed into what Brewer termed a fiscal-military state with war constituting its "main business."[19]

Britain's newfound warmaking capabilities gave rise to a bellicose national culture that vaunted all things British.[20] At least from the Act of Union with Scotland of 1707, Protestantism, anti-Catholicism, and anti-Gallicism informed this culture. At its heart rested the concept of the Briton, a national identity cast in opposition to the "other." The Briton, unlike the French or Spanish, was Protestant, possessed liberties, lived at relative economic ease, exhibited manly traits, and pursued commerce with a vengeance. The Briton made for a particularly pugnacious identity, one that became entangled with imperialist endeavors, in particular the Seven Years' War.[21]

The war also constituted a change in the way that Britain fought war. Since the mid-seventeenth century, Britain had followed a "blue water" policy that prioritized defense of the British Isles and treated colonies as sources of wealth for that defense, leaving colonists largely to defend themselves.[22] As a result of the rising importance of commerce and its colonial sources, empire came to be conceived of in territorial terms, as landed wealth in need of protection. As the conflict over the Ohio Valley percolated in the aftermath of King George's War (ending in 1748), it appeared that the American colonies were at risk, and ultimately a decision was made to defend them at great cost. For the first time, Britain committed regular troops numbering in the tens of thousand to a colonial theater with the express purpose of removing the French threat. From its inception in 1754 to its denouement in 1763, the war witnessed armed conflict on a scale never seen before in the New World. In the end, Britain's defeat of France brought it North America east of the Mississippi, making the Seven Years' War "the most dramatically successful war the British ever fought," according to Linda Colley.[23]

The Seven Years' War comprised human endeavor on a vast scale, although the labor involved often goes missing in imperial and military history. Yet war is hard work. The actual fighting often seen as the sole occupation of soldiers becomes entangled in nationalist rhetoric in a way that mystifies the labor involved. Marching, bearing and firing arms, jabbing bayonets, slashing swords are drenched in glory by much historical prose but they also all are parts of a labor process with battlefield victory and its more material rewards the payoff. Equally important are all the supporting duties of a soldier: digging trenches, picket duty, cutting wood, and building roads and forts. Less prone to mythologizing, such hewing of wood and drawing of water comprises the proletarian labor of warmaking crucial to military enterprise; without it the infrastructure of empire remains unbuilt. For performing such work, British soldiers received six pence per day, the exchange of labor for wages no different than that of a miner or coalheaver, but arguably more central to the entire imperial project of merchant capital.[24]

"hearing a drumbeat, set the heart on fire!"

Recruitment, either voluntary or coerced, comprised a soldier's entry point to military labor just as labor recruitment of one form or another brought apprentices, servants, and laborers into civilian occupations. Yet patriotism and popular culture rendered soldiering as duty and adventure, masking the fact that military enlistment equated to a mundane agreement to a labor contract. Once listed, the recruit was introduced to the art of war, peculiar to the military but sharing with other forms of labor the performance of set tasks subject to work discipline that privileged the interests of employer and managers (the army and officers) over those of the laborer (the soldier).

Looking back near 40 years, Miller drenched the remembrance of his youthful enthusiasm for soldiering in golden hues. "From the earliest recollection, the hearing a drumbeat, set the heart on fire! A soldier, in my idea, must be the first of mortals, being the guardian of his country. Often did I throw myself in their way, wishing to be taken notice of." Such youthful patriotism drew Miller to the army like a moth to a flame, but when recounting his actual enlistment a note of the remorse of an old man creeps in: "at last in the year 1756 at a very tender age, had the happiness, as I then thought! Of being singled out, by one of those worthies called crimps, who deal in human flesh, he enter'd into conversation, praised the life, of a soldier, profer'd Gold and every good which was soon accepted of, and now behold me, in the high road to honor." Pride soon yielded to the true import of what he had done, as joining the army meant leaving his family and life as he had known it behind, though the adventure of travel would blunt these feelings. "The first night passed in delirium! But on the morning, being hurried away, without having permission to bid farewell to our dear relatives, for there were several boys of us, what grief, what sorrowing many a long and lingering look we cast behind during the first days march, but the grief went off, as the distance increas'd."[25]

Miller did not march alone on this road. In times of war, the fiscal-military state's appetite for soldiers proved voracious, and for the first time in the Seven Years' War the American colonies constituted the maw down which these men disappeared. From about 3,000 troops in the American colonies prior to the outbreak of hostilities to upwards of 30,000 active troops at the peak of the conflict (not counting all the troops needed to replace casualties and deserters and about the same number of provincial troops raised in the colonies), the labor needs of the military mushroomed in the mid-1750s. To help meet this demand officials resorted to coercion in the form of impressment. The state passed the first Press Act in 1704. It gave local justices of the peace the power to force into military service "such able-bodied men, as have not any lawful employment or calling, or visible means for their maintenance and livelihood." Here the logic of vagrant laws fused with needs of military revolution. Parliament again passed a Press Act in 1756 but abandoned it in 1758 due to popular opposition, but not before 500 men were pressed in London alone in 1756.[26] On the whole, however, the British army relied upon volunteers like Miller. Recruiting parties scoured the countryside, drums beating, colors flying, hoping to entice youths to answer the call. Some regiments recruited year round, establishing depots and having recruiters on permanent duty. Others hired "crimps" to do the job.[27]

While the army did exert a romantic attraction as Miller could attest, it also was a dangerous job as the crippled beggars in the street gave witness. Prospective recruits evaluated these prospects but did so also in light of prevailing social and economic forces, which could conspire to direct men into the military. Unemployment and high prices characterized the mid-1750s in England, marked by strikes in the west country textile industry. In Scotland, the combination of political proscription and agricultural "improvement" imposed on the country in the aftermath of the failed Jacobite uprising of 1745–46 pushed many off the land, while famine stalked parts of the Highlands in 1756–57.[28] That broader historic forces were at work is reflected in the demography of the army. Rather than "the scum of every county, the refuse of mankind," as Lieutenant Colonel Campbell Dalrymple described them, soldiers came from all the ranks of the laboring classes and from across the British Isles.[29] An analysis of data from the Chelsea Hospital for troops from Miller's 15th Regiment provides a glimpse. Those from a laboring background (laborers, husbandmen, servants, and soldiers' sons) accounted for 66 percent (138 of 208) of those pensioned from the regiment, those with some skill 34 percent (70 of 208).[30] The army proved indiscriminate, skimming the cream as much as the scum from Britain's plebeians. Likewise, recruiting parties ventured wherever bodies could be found within the realm: 48 percent had been born in England, 39 percent in Scotland, 9 percent in Ireland, and 3 percent in Wales. For those displaced by economic or political convulsions, or others merely seeking adventure, the army offered the prospect of a steady wage, clothing, and food. In hard economic times, such as in the late 1750s when army recruiting peaked, it could be seen as the lesser of evils. Military service constituted an option in the proletariat's subsistence strategies.[31]

"the glorious expectation of soon seeing a battle! . . . it was then, my folly, stared me full in the face"

James Miller's reinforced regimented soon received orders to repair to Portsmouth, where true wonders awaited. Arriving at the great naval port, "every Object that presented itself, ravished the astonished senses!" Here he first confronted the imperial war machine in which he constituted but a small cog. He marveled at the "Dock Yard, the blacksmiths shop, in particular, where they were forming anchors of prodigious magnitude," likening the craftsmen to Vulcan who forged thunder bolts for Jove; "as for the workmen, my fancy, painted them real Cyclops . . . and concluded at last that they must be, more than mortal, who could undertake, such arduous operations." He would soon be able to say the same of himself.[32] His youthful wonderment at the scale of martial enterprise naturally blinded Miller to the logical outcome of all this activity—bloody warfare that would exact its toll on many thousands. When the order came for his corps to set sail on a secret expedition, he could exclaim: "what cheerfulness in every countenance, with the glorious expectation of soon seeing a battle!"[33] Yet, as with many recruits, the banality, discomfort, and powerlessness of a soldier's life quickly punctured Miller's delusions of the grandeur of the military profession.

The Austrian victory over Frederick of Prussia outside Prague in June 1757 and the French defeat in July of the British Army of Observation at Hastenbeck in Germany prompted the British to attempt to divert the French from Germany with an expedition against Rochefort on the Bay of Biscay. The force of 30 warships and over 8,000 soldiers and marines sailed from the Isle of Wight in September for points unknown to Miller, who had more mundane concerns on his mind.[34]

> The accommodation of soldiers, on board ship, are not very conducive to ease or health, all between decks being separated by boards into births, of six foot by six, three feet, six inches high, one tier, over the other, four or five men are allotted to each birth, and they creep into their holes, in the best manner they can, one third of which, are generally kept on deck while at anchor. I seldom went below for there proceeds, such a Disagreeable Stench, of putrid breaths when you are going down the hatch way, that no being, accustomed to fresh air, can bear.[35]

When a strong gale hit the fleet, severe seasickness roiled his guts. "[I]t was then, my folly, stared me full in the face, and repentance came too late, for having embraced, a life, of so much misery."[36] Miller experienced first hand the commonplace for soldiers, whether at sea or on land: cramped, uncomfortable, obnoxious, and unhealthy living conditions.

Miller's remorse deepened as a result of his first campaign. The fleet, under command of Commodore Howe, sailed along the French coast into the Bay of Biscay, where it captured Aix, a small island guarding the approach to Rochefort. Next preparations were made for the attack on the port. At one point, the troops were ordered into the transports in preparation for a landing, but after hours waiting, "thumping" alongside the men of war, the commanders decided that the surf was too rough and the approach too shallow to insure success. The men returned on board and the ships sailed for England. This turn of events mortified Miller, opening the door to his first criticism of his superiors: "we certainly cut but a poor figure, on our return, and were frequently insulted, in our quarters, as if soldiers, were answerable, for the conduct of their superiors. I was now, pretty well cured, of all the romantic notions, imbibed in youth."[37] His bubble burst by the dullness and discomfort of soldiering and his commanders' lack of execution, Miller soured on military life before he had fired a shot. Lack of action soon would prove the least of his worries.

"with much perseverance, loss and fatigue"

Prime Minister William Pitt then irrevocably altered Britain's war goals and the essence of its foreign policy. Subsidized German forces and the allied Prussians would wage the war against France and Austria in Europe, but the real object now comprised eliminating France as an imperial power by striking her weak colonies in the Americas.[38] Miller would be swept along by this sea change. British military initiatives in the colonies thus far in the war had produced a litany of defeats: Braddock at Monongahela in 1755; the loss of Oswego the next year; and the fall of Fort William Henry and the failure to launch the expedition on Louisbourg in 1757. Pitt's unprecedented commitment of resources to North America upped the stakes. The force targeted on Louisbourg alone comprised the largest ever mounted in North America. In total, the planned campaign for 1758 involved upward of 50,000 British troops: over 14,000 regulars and 600 rangers would attack Louisbourg; near 8,000 regulars and 20,000 provincials would attack Fort Ticonderoga then invade Canada; and 1,880 regulars and 5,000 provincials would assault Fort Duquesne at present-day Pittsburgh.[39]

Early in 1758, Miller sailed for North America in a fleet under the command of Admiral Boscawen and the military generalship of Jeffery Amherst. "After a tolerable passage," Miller wrote, they "landed at Hallifax, in Nova Scotia, where the army was exercised, in the woods, bush fighting, after the Indian manner, making fascines, raising redoubts, attacking, defending them."[40] This is the first time that Miller mentions training. No doubt, he and his comrades had been regularly drilled in marching, maneuvers, the firing of weapons, and use of the bayonet before this time. The battlefield strategies of the professional armies that arose as a result of the military revolution required highly disciplined and coordinated movement in the face of enemy musket volleys that necessitated routine training.[41] As well as an introduction to the art of war, this instruction must be seen as workplace training familiarizing soldiers with the duties and expected performance of military labor. Miller mentions it at this point because the training expanded beyond that prescribed for the European battlefield to include the *guerilla* tactics that also were practiced in the Americas, and likely intensified as the battle approached. Louisbourg would be Miller's first taste of combat.

For soldiers the first "blooding" marked their true entrance into the warrior fraternity. The enormity of the risk involved, one's very life, prevented the men from seeing it as a job. Either exhorted by patriotism or cowed by discipline they had to fight, or face execution for cowardice if they fled. No other occupation put the labor dictum so starkly as did the army in warfare: work or die (and possibly die working). Though he did not express it, Miller must have felt trepidation when the combined expedition sailed in May for Cape Breton, where the French citadel of Louisbourg, the most substantial of European fortresses in North America, guarded the entrance to the St. Lawrence, the gateway to New France. The fortress overlooked Gabarus Bay, within which French ships anchored and acted as floating artillery installations, while an island in its middle provided another site for ordnance. The two points of land at the mouth of the harbor likewise had cannon emplacements. The defenses, setting up a number of points of crossfire, posed many dangers for the British forces. On June 8, Amherst ordered an amphibious assault to root out the cannons. Miller was about to experience the work of war for the first time. Troops loaded into flat boats set out, despite what Miller called "a great swell."

> Every precaution, had been taken by the enemy, to oppose our landing, the whole shore was one continuous battery, and the french troops, were concealed, from our sight by branches of trees, cut down. They reserved their fire until our boats got near the shore, when such a tremenduous one commenced, from their great guns, and small arms, as I have never since, beheld! Several boats, were sunk, others overset, by the swell, a boat carrying our grenadier company, was sunk by which, one Officer, two Serjeants, and thirty fine fellows were lost.[42]

In the midst of this chaos, it became clear that it was too late for the boats to retreat. James Wolfe, who commanded the assault, identified a part of the shoreline, where the army landed, and over the course of the next few days cannon were brought ashore and trained on the French artillery emplacement and ships in the harbor. Over the course of six weeks, the British dug siege trenches, gradually advanced the artillery, and bombarded the fortifications. Miller "expected every moment, orders to storm them," but avoided that dangerous tactic by a French surrender on July 26.[43] Miller noted: "Thus with much perseverance, loss and fatigue, we had taken the strongest Garrison in N[th]. America, and opened the road to Canada."[44]

A crown jewel of French holdings in the New World had been secured. British feats of arms also won them Fort Duquesne (and Fort Frontenac at the head of the St. Lawrence), but the army suffered a stinging defeat in early July, its assault of Ticonderoga repulsed with significant losses.[45] Even for Miller, the cost in human lives tempered pride in the victory at Louisbourg. If Rochefort opened his eyes to the hard life of the soldier and the human frailty of officers, Louisbourg made clear the price of British victories and those expected to pay it. To the deaths and casualties of the siege he also added those who perished later as a result of the hard labor. His corps removed to Halifax, "where we spent a severe winter, and lost, a number of men, from the fatigue of the late campaign."[46] Here he made the connection all too often lost on historians, that military work spanned combat and daily duties, and both taxed the soldier as the taking of Quebec would reaffirm.

"the most happy, the most glorious death, that a soldier could wish"

Pitt envisaged a three-pronged attack for the 1759 campaign. Wolfe would lead a force in excess of 8,000 men against Quebec; Amherst would again strike up the Lake Champlain corridor with 11,000 regulars and provincials; and another expedition of 3,000 regulars, provincials, and Indian allies would assault Fort Niagara.[47] Miller's regiment left Halifax in the spring to join a fleet from New York. The expedition sailed into the Gulf of St. Lawrence and arrived at Quebec in late June. In his narrative Miller compresses a campaign that lasted several months, detailing taking up camp across from the city, the failed French attempt to set the British fleet ablaze with fireships, the defeat of their attack on the north shore near the falls of the Montmorency River in late July, and skimming over General Wolfe's increasingly desperate efforts to find a way of getting his army safely across the river and in a position to attack the city. Instead he concentrates on the ultimate battle, not surprising in that strategizing is the domain of generals and fighting falls to soldiers.[48] Finally, Wolfe identified a cove upstream from Quebec, where he believed the cliffs could be scaled, and early in the morning of September 13, launched the attack. The troops rowed past Quebec at night in flat boats with oars muffled, landed at the cove and ascended the heights, securing position on the Plains of Abraham, where the enemy marched out to join them in battle.

> The french army, collected from their different posts, were formed in two lines, with Indians and Canadians in front, they attacked us with great spirit, however our men reserved their fire, until the enemy, was within forty paces, when every shot told [?], and the french were repulsed almost immediately and drove from the field. [49]

Miller sketches the soldiers' story of the fall of Quebec but reserves more color for the victory's emotional centerpiece: "the great loss to our army which check'd our joy was the Commander in Chief, Wolfe, who fell, after receiving three wounds. However he met with the most happy, the most glorious death, that a soldier could wish."[50] Could the same be said for the dead among the common soldiers? The campaign had exacted its toll. The failed assault at the Montmorency River on July 31 alone led to the death of 210 men and wounding of another 233. While only some 60 perished on the Plains of Abraham, 600 received wounds.[51] Among the wounded from Miller's 15th Regiment were: William McDuff, a laborer from Renfrew in Lowland Scotland; Jonathan Miles, a miller from Wiltshire; Arthur Cairns, a weaver from Monaghan in Ireland; Corporal James Smith, a cabinetmaker from Inverness in the Scottish Highlands; Sergeant William Babbige, a weaver from Manchester; and Michael Poole, a cordwainer from Gloucestershire, who lost his left leg. All paid the price at Quebec and received a pension in recompense when they returned to England the next year.[52]

With General Montcalm dead, the French army retreated from Quebec, believing the city now defenseless. Four days later, the commander surrendered to the British.

The second great piece of French dominion in North America had tumbled to British might of arms. Niagara had already fallen to the British that summer, while the French in the face of Amherst's advancing army had destroyed and abandoned first Ticonderoga then Crown Point, where the cautious British general decided to winter.[53] The remnants of New France lay exposed for a final campaign.

"The duty became extremely hard"

The British fleet provisioned the regiments left to garrison Quebec, Miller's among them, and sailed down the St. Lawrence before the river froze. Interestingly, his account of the hardships endured that winter achieves greater depth than did his rendition of the battle for Quebec.

> A severe winter, now commenced, while we were totally unprepared, for such a climate, neither fewel [fuel], forage, or indeed anything, to make life tolerable. The troops, were crouded into vacant houses, as well as possible, numbers fell sick, and the scurvy made a dreadful havock among us. The duty became extremely hard, for after being up all night, on guard, the men were obliged to go near six miles, through the snow, to cut wood, and then to drag it home on Sledges. From the severe frost, the wood was as hard as marble, and Europeans, who had never been accustomed to cut wood, made but small progress, a constant, and daily supply, was however necessary, and required the greatest perserverance. In short, the fatigues of the winter was so great, that the living, almost envied the dead.

Suffering such conditions, soldiers turned to an old friend. While liquor was scarce, "when the men, could procure them, they generally drank to excess, it was no uncommon thing in the morning, to find several men frozen to death, from the above cause." More often, troops suffered the effects of the cold as a result of doing their duty, as the army made several fruitless excursions up the frozen river looking for forage. "Many men, lost the use of their hands, and feet, during the winter. I was also frost bit, in the right foot, while on guard . . . however by taking it in time, lost no bones."[54] The garrison as a whole suffered, with a thousand men dying from poor conditions and 2,000 rendered unfit for service from an original garrison of 7,000.[55]

These casualties that occurred during the course of regular garrison duty must be understood in terms of workplace injuries and deaths within the war industry as much as battlefield wounds and mortality. A soldier's labor included chopping wood for fuel, finding forage for the work animals, and standing guard, while doing so in the harsh winter climate led to frostbite. Moreover, the army had the responsibility to provide adequate accommodation, food, and clothing, yet supplies proved insufficient to the point men died of malnutrition and scurvy. The fact that soldiers sought solace in drink does not excuse the army for failing to live up to the labor contract. Such harmful conditions could breed a feeling of grievance among war workers that some sought to act out. Disgruntled soldiers accommodated themselves to such situations by avoiding duty and performing assigned tasks in a slipshod fashion, or sought to moderate their condition temporarily by consuming alcohol. Others resisted their subordination at the hands of officers by insubordination, desertion, and in extreme cases, mutiny. While such acts tended to be individualistic in nature and did not develop out of any coherent class consciousness, they certainly were a product of class struggle and informed by an enduring plebeian oppositional culture that clearly perceived the difference of interests between masters and servants such as soldiers and the officer class within the military labor relationship.[56] In this context desertion approximated the flight of an indentured servant or slave from a master, and mutiny equated to such coordinated activities as bread riots and mob actions. Custom and communal expectations of just social and economic practice mediated class relations. Soldiers, as well as receiving their pay, expected to be clothed, provided for, and cared for by the military, and when these expectations were not met felt a certain right to take corrective action.

We catch a glimpse of such class struggle in Quebec that winter. While Miller characterized the garrison commander and military governor, James Murray, as "indefatigable being always present, at guards mounting, visiting the different posts daily, taking notice of, and rewarding those, whom he found attentive, and alert,"[57] other evidence suggests that soldiers felt discontented with the difficult situation. Charles Maclean of the 28th Regiment was brought before a general court martial on November 16 charged with being absent from duty, talking of desertion, and speaking disrespectfully of Governor Murray. A witness testified he heard him say of the great number of desertions lately, "if they were not used better, more would Desert." He also complained of not being paid:

> [I]f the Governor had not pay, he would desire none, but that if he had, he would insist upon his, that he would starve for no King &c. rather than that, He would Blow out the Best Gentlemans Brains in the Town & that it would be a pretty thing if there was a Note about that left under the Governor's Door some night or other.

He received 1,000 lashes from a whip in punishment.[58] Others apparently broke military law from hunger. In mid December, William Davis of the 58th Regiment and Nicholas Duggan and Daniel Coleman of the 43rd were tried by a general court martial for robbing the King's Stores of a bag of bread. Duggan was sentenced to 1,000 lashes, later reduced to 300. Davis and Coleman, on duty as sentries at the time, received the death penalty. The court later determined that Davis and Coleman "shall cast Lots and do reprive him whose fortune Shall Favour."[59] These cases not only reflect the dire conditions at Quebec that winter but also hint at the ways in which soldiers, just like other workers of the time, took action when the conditions of their employ did not meet expectations. They also demonstrate the might of the military, which could gamble away the lives of its workers.

"Thus after a series of hardships . . . an immense country was added to the British Empire"

The thaw of spring brought with it a French army numbering more than 7,000 that attacked Quebec in April, bent on its recapture. The smaller British army on the 28th marched out to give battle again on the Plains of Abraham, "but the french line, when hid by the bushes, kept up a fire, and with such effect, as threw us into confusion." Miller's regiment took refuge in a hollow that shielded it from French musketry. It advanced again, which gave the French

> an opportunity of cutting us up, they being drawn up under cover, and taking aim at leisure . . .. In short, in half an hour, ten Officers, from Twenty, were dropped, twelve Serjeants, from twenty four, and near two hundred, rank and file, from less than four hundred in the field! The corps was broken, and retreated to their former ground, happy would it have been, had they never left it.

The remainder of the British army fared no better and retreated "confusedly" to Quebec in defeat. The British lost some 259 men killed and 829 wounded in the battle. The French began entrenchments for a siege and the loss of the city seemed imminent, but the arrival of British warships on May 12 caused the French to decamp, sparing the defenders.[60] Thus, Miller's first experience of military defeat turned into a victory of sorts, yet his painful recording of the "butcher's bill" of casualties suggests a further souring of his view of military life.

Miller enjoyed but a brief respite, as his corps joined the expedition departing against Montreal under General Murray's command. Amherst had planned a three-pronged attack on the city. As well as the fleet advancing from Quebec, he himself led an army approaching 11,000 from Lake Ontario down the St. Lawrence and another numbering 3,500 commanded by William Haviland advanced up Lake Champlain and down the Richelieu River. The three armies converged at Montreal in early September, and the French, surrounded on all fronts, yielded to the British on the 9th. "A Capitulation took place," Miller reported, "and all Canada was given up, a Country of more extent than Britain, and Ireland, inhabited by at least, one hundred thousand inhabitants . . .. Thus after a series of hardships, in a climate, unknown to british constitutions, an immense country was added to the British Empire, a country producing every necessary for man. We flatter'd ourselves, with the hopes of enjoying repose, after such fatigues."[61] They would be disappointed.

Miller's corps was ordered to Crown Point on Lake Champlain, where "they were employed in raising a fort, but for what purpose, it is unknown, except, to enrich some individuals, for by the conquest of Canada, there was no enemy to dread, in that Quarter."[62] Here, we can see Miller's cynicism about the military and its priorities increasing, a cynicism born of experience with the class politics of the army. He joined the army to fight and, having won New France for the king, he balked at performing construction work to the possible profit of a war contractor. Yet, his experience as a soldier had taught him that he had to follow orders, however unjust he deemed them. The work discipline of the army may have secured his labor but it did not coerce his mental capitulation to military enterprise. Miller's disgruntlement thus must also be read as a hidden class transcript subverting the presumption of absolute military authority and the innate justice of the political economy for which it constituted the armed wing. This contrarian theme becomes more dominant in his memoirs from this point as, after a month of such construction work, the 15th regiment was ordered to New York, from whence they would depart on an expedition for the West Indies.[63]

"the blood of britons"

The conquest of New France had left French power in the Caribbean intact and the war unconcluded, thus for 1761, Pitt planned a campaign against Dominica, St. Lucia, and Martinique. In June, 2,000 men sailed to Guadeloupe for the assault on Dominica, which fell to the British by the end of the month. Martinique constituted the main objective, however, and Pitt instructed Amherst to mobilize a force totaling almost 14,000 troops including the 15th to be commanded by Major General Robert Monckton. The expedition sailed from New York in November after the hurricane season.[64] Although Miller does not mention it in his memoirs, he likely felt trepidation at being posted to the West Indies, military service there being notorious for its high mortality due to tropical diseases.[65]

On Christmas Eve, 1761, Monckton arrived at Barbados with 10 different regiments and some companies of American Rangers. The fleet left in January for Martinique and its main port, Fort Royal. The British forces made a landing four miles from the fortress. At one in the morning, the army marched through deep ravines against several elevated enemy redoubts. Arriving at daybreak, they immediately began pushing up the steep hill, and "the men were quickly out of breath." When they reached the summit, the French retreated, the main body to a battery, others hiding in the fields of sugar cane, both keeping up a withering fire. The British advanced on the battery under heavy enemy fire, but entered the embrasures, and drove the French out with bayonets.[66] Miller paid the penultimate price of war in the action.

> As we were entering the works . . . a musket ball grazed my neck, which in a few moments swelled to such a degree, that I thought I should have choaked and attempted to swallow water, but could not, I contin'd with the company in that Situation, the afternoon, and part of the next day when the Surgeon fearing, a mortification, sent me on board an hospital ship, where I remain'd in the same deplorable state three days, at last when all hopes of life was over, a violent perspiration came on, the swelling subsided, and I was soon able to join the corps.[67]

During his illness, the army had encircled the fort and the garrison surrendered on February 4. The island did so shortly afterward, followed soon thereafter by St. Lucia, Grenada, and St. Vincent.[68] "Thus a conquest was made, of the capital of the french Islands in those seas, it was striking at the root of their strength, in that quarter, and almost totally annihilated, their West India trade."[69] War with France had effectively ended, but the victory came at the near cost of James Miller's life.

War having been declared on Spain in January 1762, the government's next objective became Havana. The Earl of Albemarle, given command of the invasion force, brought 4,000 men from England to combine with Monckton's troops, making for an army of 14,000. Another 4,000 provincials and 2,000 regulars followed from America.[70] Yet sickness had already sapped Monckton's victors of Martinique, being "very sickly, many dead, and the sick list increasingly daily." On May 23, there were 9,857 rank and file returned fit for duty and 1,241 reported sick of the expeditionary force, with those regiments that had served under Monckton returning the vast majority of the sick.[71]

The army made a landing on Cuba in early June, and began its slow advance on the fortifications guarding Havana, under repeated assaults by enemy troops. Miller wrote that "the fatigues of this Siege pass description, the foundation, being a solid rock, an no earth to cover us, part of the army, were employed in bringing sand bags, two miles distance, amidst showers of grape shot. The soldiers named this road bloody lane!" Unfortunately, the battery they built, "the labour of several weeks," caught fire and was reduced to ruins, and they "had the whole work, to begin again, in this burning climate, when the men were less able, to perform that duty, being already exhausted, by the excessive fatigues." Here, quite literally, can be seen how war is "made," dirt dug by hand and hauled to erect a barrier from which to assail the enemy. Even more so than the hardest of manual labor it exacted a toll on those who performed it. As well as enemy fire the soldiers had to contend with harsh conditions: "the bad water brought on disorders, which were mortal, you would see the mens tongues hanging out parch'd like a mad dogs, a dollar was frequently given for a quart of water."[72] The siege against El Morro, the main fortress of Havana, carried on through July until the British breached its walls and took the fort on the 30th. A second fort fell on August 11, leading the Spaniards to surrender.[73] Miller recounted:

a capitulation took place, when the city, with all the riches, contained therein . . . fell into our hands. The wealth found in the custom house, was immense, the whole suppos'd to amount to near four millions sterling! Little however came to the share of Non commission'd Officers, and private men, owing to the two commanders in chief sharing one third of the whole between them! How far this was consistent with equity must be submitted to posterity, and whether after the most extraordinary fatigues, in such a climate, the blood of britons should be lavish'd to agrandize individuals. By the above conquest the key to all the riches, in america were in our hands.[74]

Almost £400,000 in booty fell to the army, with Lord Albemarle receiving £122,697. Soldiers earned much less: "when a distribution of Prize money, took place, a Serj.[t] received only 22 Dollars, and a private man, eleven, certain it is, that it cost each man more for water during the siege, exclusive of blood and fatigue."[75]

Miller's comments here only partially concern the unequal distribution of wealth. It more fundamentally addresses the justness of war making. Common soldiers formed the class expected to fight and die for their country. They expend the "blood of britons" but the officer class and the nation state profit from their sacrifice. Miller was clearly conscious of the class division that bifurcated the military and mirrored the common/gentry divide in British society, and cognizant that it operated in the interest of officers in the army and merchants and aristocrats at home. That consciousness did not translate into a complete rejection of the political economy that nurtured the unequal distribution of resources, Miller did continue to serve in the military for 20 more years after all, but it did provide him and other soldiers a platform from which to critique their employers and, ultimately as we shall see, reject their authority if only for a short period.

This stupendous victory of Havana cost dearly. Approximately 1,800 British troops had died during the siege, but the dying had just begun. With no real hospital, the British had to use tents and a large storehouse for the many sick, and lacking fresh food, the sick ate salt provisions. Two months after the taking of Havana, an accounting of casualties took place: 273 men had been killed during the conflict; 246 had perished afterward from wounds received in battle; and sickness had claimed the lives of 4,380 others, most likely to a combination of yellow fever and malaria. In the end, the taking of Havana led to death for 40 percent of the 14,000 soldiers involved.[76]

Miller remembered:

The army, in general became sickly, after marching into town . . . indeed the Reg.[ts] last from home, were the most sickly, and we were under the necessity, of giving, a party, to assist in doing duty, and bury the dead, of the 9.th and 72.[d] Reg.[ts], for N. America and Martinico had seasoned our men to hardships.[77]

Hardened to duty mayhap, but nonetheless aggrieved.

The army withdrew regiments from Havana but Miller's 15th remained behind to garrison the city, further exposed to tropical diseases but also to avaricious provisioning merchants. British officials established a board of customs, which imposed a 5 percent customs duty on imported goods "for the enriching of some favourite individuals," so soldiers could not afford the available produce, and "by these impositions, we soon got rid of our Prize money, and pay."[78] This arrangement exacerbated the grievance felt from the inequitable distribution of booty. The manner of the garrison's withdrawal from Havana cemented this cleavage.

Britain, France, and Spain concluded the Treaty of Paris peace in February 1763. When they heard the news, Miller and his mates "flatter'd ourselves, with the hopes, of soon being relieved from this unhealthy climate, an event that did not take place for more than six months after." Only in June, did they receive word that Cuba was to be returned to Spain and the garrison withdrawn.

> We now enjoyed in Idea, the happiness of being blessed once more, with a sight of all that is dear to man, his country, parents &ca &ca. But alas! there is nothing certain under the sun for before we cleared the gulph of Florida, a packet from England fell in with the fleet, she brought orders, for a distribution of the troops, our Corps, was order'd back to Canada . . . It is astonishing, what effect this disappointment had on some of the men, several of whom absolutely fell sick and died! Others never held up their heads untill we arrived at N. York, which was near three weeks after.[79]

The great Caribbean campaign ended thus, with the rank and file emotionally lost at sea, and the high command awash in emoluments drained from the Spanish Empire. The labor of soldiers had secured these riches, as they had the colonial wealth of France beforehand. Through campaign after campaign the rank and file had put their lives on the line for their country and brought new lands under the dominion of the king. They also constructed the infrastructure of empire, entrenchments, forts, and roads that opened and secured these lands to settlers and trade, which would increase the wealth and power of merchants and members of the upper class but contribute little to their own pockets. The experience of making war—doing the work, following officers' orders, suffering punishments, facing the enemy—bred camaraderie among the soldiers. This worked in the army's interest, making for a coherent fighting force, but it also bred class unity among the war workers that could be turned on the officers. The accumulating grievances of the troops combined with the mounting death toll led some such as Miller to question equity of the system. Many came to feel the labor contract had been severed, and, as is common with disgruntled workers, took action to secure justice. The hewers of men and drawers of fire engaged a new enemy, officers, the army, and their king, in a mass action that revealed a proletarian identity at work.

"Better to die on a gibbet! Than perish by inches!"

"I have always been an advocate for rigid discipline, knowing the absolute necessity of it," recalled Miller. "But here it was carried to a degree of excess, never before known in the Corps." After three weeks at sea they next faced an arduous 600 mile journey from New York to Quebec, by sloop to Albany, marching through Saratoga to Lake George and on to Crown Point, across Lake Champlain in Batteau, then on to the Saint Lawrence, across to Montreal, and on to Quebec.

> On the Corps, arriving at the Governors farm, near Quebec, he was pleas'd to look at them, they were reduced to few in number, notwithstanding they had been filled up twice, since leaving Quebec in less than three years. He order'd each man

a pint of wine, and expressed himself to one of the Grenadiers, of whom he used to take notice . . . I did not know you, you look so black! the soldier replied, we have been on black service, and have got very little white money for it![80]

The words of this unknown soldier capture the disgruntlement felt by many. The volatile situation erupted in a general mutiny that can best be understood in terms of labor conflict. A number of work-related issues fuelled the uprising. The hard service and unfair treatment experienced in the Caribbean constituted one cause for the mutiny. Soldiers also took umbrage at not being disbanded and returned to England at war's end. While they nominally had enlisted for life, custom held that service lasted only for the duration of the war. The catalyst for mutiny, however, came with alterations to the pay and provisioning of soldiers. With the official cessation of hostilities in 1763, the War Office sought to economize by ordering that stoppages (i.e. withholdings) to soldiers' wages of 4d. per diem for rations be implemented, as far as it could be done "without causing a disturbance among the Soldiers."[81] This hope proved forlorn as provisions for troops had been provided without deduction throughout the war in recognition that the American colonies constituted a "hardship" posting. Miller recognized that the stoppages constituted an assault on the pay relationship and jeopardized a soldier's subsistence. He believed it impossible for the men to pay the four pence stoppage, "and keeping themselves, in the necessarys suitable to the duty, of the severe climate," and this "ought to have been obvious to every one, that knew the service." Winter duty in Canada required soldiers to purchase every year "a duffle great coat, flannel mittens, a fur cap, long cloth leggings." Having performed such soldier's duty and suffering frostbite as a result, Miller understood why the stoppages led martial workers to combine and refuse to work unless under the old terms of employment.

Governor Murray communicated word of the stoppages on September 18, then

> one morning after guard mounting, a drum was heard, beating to arms, the different Corps, turned out, without Officers, and marched up to the grand parade, some Officers, who wanted to Stop their men, were on the point of being shot, for it is said, the bad men intended to murder every one, who did not join with them, they began firing in the Street.

Murray sent an officer inquiring as to "the meaning of their assembling in an unsoldier like manner," and it was decided that the mutineers would return to their barracks, and Murray would speak to them on the grand parade the following day.

> Next morning the Gen.[l], with all the Officers in the Garrison, come on the parade, where the soldiers were already drawn up, He then inquired what was their complaints, or cause of such mutinous conduct? One of the 60th Reg.[t] who was their commander and spokesman, replied, they . . . consider'd it as the heighth [sic] of injustice, after having at the risk of their lives, conquer'd countries, in every climate, that now on a general peace, the reward is want and misery, which

unavoidably must be the case, should four pence P^r day be stopped from their pay, for provisions, What is left? To provide cloathing, proper for this severe climate? Better to die on a gibbet! Than perish by inches!

The general assured them that no money would be stopped until further word came from England. On his orders, the soldiers marched under their regimental colors the next morning, and had the Articles of War read to them before they returned to quarters, symbolizing their readmission into good faith status within the army. Shortly afterward, Murray discharged the ringleaders. Though not an abolition of the stoppages, the reduction of the stoppages from four pence to two and a half pence placated most men.[82]

It is not clear exactly what role Miller played in the mutiny at Quebec. He wrote of the mutineers as if not one of them, and further isolated the "bad men" who wished to do violence to the officers. Miller also tended to play down the insurrectionary potential of the soldiers' actions, whereas other reports portrayed it as more threatening. Murray deemed it a "most horrid Mutiny." "It was so general, so violent, and so sudden, their [sic] was no resisting at the time."[83] And private Charles McDonell of the 60th Regiment called it a "Revolution."[84] Clearly, it was not in the best interests of Miller's petition to Amherst for promotion to side with a mutiny that occurred under his general command. Nonetheless, he certainly expressed his sympathy for the cause of the uprising and refused to deny the merit of their demand, a return to the preexisting pay relations. In this way, Miller from thirty years' distance (and while the French Revolution unfolded around him to his general approbation) acted as a spokesperson for the rights of soldier workers, who performed dangerous service for small recompense and should not have been further ground down by the army and the government.

Quebec was not alone in experiencing a mutiny: from Newfoundland to Florida the troops rose up. This wave of rebelliousness would force Amherst to reduce the wage deductions, placating many of the troops. And Quebec's mutiny fizzled much more quickly than elsewhere. Soldiers of the 40th Regiment in Halifax and the 45th at Louisbourg, un-persuaded by the reduction, refused to work unless freely supplied late into the spring of 1764. The mutineers finally yielded, but not before extracting further concessions from the King, who promised to rotate all regiments so that none would remain in North America endlessly. But all those who remained mutinous, the monarch warned, would be sent to the Caribbean islands, where they would continue until "the Advisers and first Movers in these unmilitary, disobedient Disturbances" were given up for punishment.[85] Many soldiers, Miller among them, knew all too well the dire nature of this threat.

"Is the population of Britain and Ireland adequate to such waste of men?"

The mutiny and promised rotation did not draw James Miller's war to a close. His regiment marched to Montreal in 1765. He served there and in the back forts for two years then returned to Quebec in the winter of 1767, before the regiment's repatriation in 1768. In the spring of that year, Miller recorded that "the Corps . . . sailed for England, a hundred and fifty, Officers included, had been filled up, four times during the course of ten years, a consumption of near twenty to one. Is the population of Britain and Ireland adequate to such waste of men?"[86] Sadly, time would answer this question in the affirmative as Britain soon embarked on another half century of international conflict with America and France for political economic ends.

James Miller's life offers an object lesson of what soldiers' stories can contribute to labor history. First, on the level of political economy, it nicely encapsulates the essential role the military played in imperial expansion and the triumph of merchant capital. Warfare constituted a crucial element in the process of primitive accumulation, freeing labor from the soil and crafts at home to fight in the military, and abroad removing lands from people to be converted to commercial production, the wealth generated as a result filling national coffers and the pockets of masters and merchants. Viewing the military on this macro scale places soldiers' labor at the center of profound historical change, and fixes class as a concept at the heart of national and international historical narratives. Simply, warfare rested upon the class relationship between soldier and the state (represented by the army and its officers) signified by the payment of a daily wage for service rendered, and this unequal exchange purchased the stuff of national dreams. These warrior workers built a new world order, with Britain the emergent superpower. We should not allow nationalist or militarist discourses to obscure the basic fact that these gains were paid for through the exploitation of a class of military laborers. The blood of Britons comprised the necessary ingredient to this empire won on the battlefield; it stained the ground, washed into the river systems, and flowed into the Anglo Atlantic.

Second, James Miller's memoirs allow labor historians to reclaim soldiers' work experience. Much more than the imagined glory of the battlefield, as Miller discovered, soldiering involved any number of tasks that needed to be performed under the watchful gaze of their employers. It can be approached in the same ways that labor historians address other forms of work: for example, in terms of the nature of the labor contract, the social origins of the workforce, the relations of production, labor discipline, and class cohesiveness. I have emphasized in this essay one main strand, how the experience of work led Miller to question the workings of military labor and moved others to outright resistance. More than just a cog in the war machine mindlessly acting out orders, Miller questioned the class hierarchy that dominated the army and broader British-American world. In the civil sphere this hierarchy rested upon dominance of the means of production through the ownership of land and its resources, and the control of labor, capital, and political office; in the military, holding an officer's commission, having access to political patronage, and controlling soldiers. In either instance labor constituted the crucial requirement, for from it flowed the products that generated wealth. Soldiers profited by but six pence per day and the occasional modest distribution of booty, while being asked to pay with their limbs and their lives. Some felt the injustice of this arrangement but were unable to articulate their grievance other than by slacking at their duties, drinking, and making do; others contested authority by being insubordinate or running away. In the extreme, soldiers mutinied and mounted a dangerous insurrection against the military and the political economy it protected, a harbinger of subaltern revolts to come. In this latter action we glimpse the class politics of soldiers, even have their words of rebellion recorded, as was the case of the mutineer at Quebec who avowed he would rather hang than perish slowly through the army's docking of his pay. While coined in the currency of custom and tradition, being an appeal to established practice and just social relations, such rhetoric concerned issues common to all free laborers, such as fair payment for work performed, and revealed an oppositional mentality that challenged the existing class relationship within the military. James Miller's memoirs prove so valuable because, rather than fragments of such radical thinking, they contain a sustained critique of the operation of the hierarchical social structure of the army and the state. Miller questioned his commanders' orders when he felt them to be unjust, attacked the distribution of the spoils of war on the basis of class status, and, above all else, resented the state's remorseless expenditure of human life in the pursuit of military victory.

Third, and finally, once we understand the role of the military in the conjoined projects of imperialism and merchant capital, and have recaptured soldier's labor from the army's camp, we need to situate the war worker in the swirling class forces of the eighteenth century, to array him alongside the ranks of other proletarians of the period. Though overlooked by historians of the Atlantic World, focused as they have been on the currents of the ocean and the shores upon which they broke, soldiers must be classed among that transnational proletariat that transited much of the globe. Moreover, as imperialism penetrated inland from the mid-eighteenth century seeking to establish territorial dominance, soldiers became ever more crucial to the enterprise, as the Seven Years' War demonstrated. Crossing the ocean four times in his life and having participated in world-changing events, no wonder Miller's thought reflected that stream of proletarian radicalism that flowed around the Atlantic and periodically erupted to challenge authority in all its forms. Such oppositional thought infused the actions of bread rioters, Jack Tars who rioted against impressment as occurred in Boston in 1747 and against the Stamp Act in 1765, slaves who rose against their masters as in the case of Tacky's Revolt in Jamaica in 1760, the Irish peasants who as "Whiteboys" used clandestine violence in an attempt to secure better terms from their landlords in early 1760s Ireland, or workers who fought changes to workplace conditions like the Spitalsfield silk weavers rioters of London in 1765, or the coalheavers and sailors who struck the London docks in 1768–69, and later, the British naval mutineers at the Nore and Spithead in 1797.[87] To this partial list can now be added the general mutineers in the British army of 1763–64, which included Miller's 15th regiment: workers of the Atlantic world all.

In conclusion, James Miller was no revolutionary. Despite his critical commentary, he soldiered on, fighting rebels in the American Revolution, who he thought were in the minority and responsible for taking the rights, property, and lives of fellow Britons. But his experience as a soldier, from training through drilling, building, fighting, getting wounded, right up to mutinying, did breed a critical perspective on society and governance that placed him closer to Thomas Paine than Edmund Burke. The British defeat by the Americans he attributed not to his fellow soldiers but to the British ruling class. "Some of our great men, had certainly mistaken, their talents. In a country where frivolous distinctions are allowed to birth, without merit, and whose children are taught to believe, that they were born to command, indifferent Ministers, ignorant Magistrates and poor Generals, may be expected."[88] Miller also wrote admiringly of the French Revolution in its early stages. While being escorted through France after his capture by the privateers in 1781, he noted "but two ranks of people, Viz. either very great, or very humble" and remarked: "The poor appear to be very oppressed." Later after the Revolution had occurred, Miller affirmed

> surely, no revolution was ever effected with less cruelties, and a government, has been settled, on the principles of equity, and liberty to all men . . . A Government fixed on this Basis, does honour to human nature, and must soon rise, superior to all others.

Lest his readers should think he wrote only of the particular situation of France, Miller scripted a warning to his own country. "Let England beware and amend your constitution, by a more equal representation, and a reduction of taxes, and totally abolish what remains of the feudal system, the good of the people ought always to be the end of Government."[89] Miller wrote in the early 1790s, before both the terror soon unleashed in France and the British government backlash against laboring radicalism. Still, such cutting observations may have came too close to the bone. No record survives that James Miller received his promotion from Jeffery Amherst.

Notes

1. C. P. Stacey, "Benjamin West and 'The Death of Wolfe,'" National Gallery of Canada *Bulletin* 7 (IV, 1), 1966; Fred Anderson, *Crucible of War: The Seven Years' War and the Fate of Empire in British North America, 1754–1766* (New York: Random House, 2000), 367. This painting has figured prominently in the recent literature on the Seven Years' War, being a centerpiece to Simon Schama's *Dead Certainties (Unwarranted Speculations)* (New York: Knopf, 1991), and gracing the covers of Anderson's *Crucible of War* and Matthew C. Ward's *The Battle for Quebec 1759* (Stroud, Gloucestershire: Tempus, 2005).
2. Most recently, Stephen Brumwell in *Paths of Glory: The Life and Death of James Wolfe* (Montreal and Kingston: McGill-Queen's University Press, 2006).
3. Established in 1681, the Chelsea Hospital cared for and/or paid pensions to soldiers made invalid by injury or 20 years of service. They could perform limited duties while on pension. See: G. Hutt, *Papers Illustrative of the Origin and Early History of the Royal Hospital at Chelsea. Compiled in the Secretary's Office at that Institution* (London: Eyre & Spottiswood, 1872); C. G. T. Dean, *The Royal Hospital Chelsea* (London: Hutchinson, 1950).

4. James Miller, Memoirs of an Invalid, Amherst Papers, U1350 Z9A, Centre for Kentish Studies, Maidstone, England; James Miller to Lord Amherst, 16 Jan. 1792, Amherst Papers, U1350 Z9, Centre for Kentish Studies. I would like to thank the Centre for Kentish Studies, Kent Archives and Local History Service, Kent County Council for permission to quote from the Miller materials at length in this essay.

5. Ibid., 1.

6. Fred Anderson mined the journals of provincial troops in *A People's Army: Massachusetts Soldiers and Society in the Seven Years' War* (Chapel Hill: University of North Carolina Press, 1984).

7. Examples of published accounts are: The Serjeant-Major of Gen. Hopson's Grenadiers, *A Journal of the Expedition up the River St. Lawrence . . .* (Boston: Fowle and Draper, 1759); Donald Macleod, *Memoirs of the Life and Gallant Exploits of the Old Highlander Serjeant Donald Macleod (1688–1791)* (London, 1791; rpt. edn, London: Blackie & Son, 1933); *Through So Many Dangers: The Memoirs and Adventures of Robert Kirk, Late of the Royal Highland Regiment*, ed. Ian McCulloch and Timothy Todish (orig. edn 1775; New York: Purple Mountain Press, 2004).

8. Keegan, *The Face of Battle: A Study of Agincourt, Waterloo, and the Somme* (New York: Viking Press, 1976). See also: Sylvia R. Frey, *The British Soldier in America: A Social History of Military Life in the Revolutionary Period* (Austin: University of Texas Press, 1981); Glenn A. Steppler, "The Common Soldier in the Reign of George III, 1760–1793," D.Phil. thesis, Oxford University, 1984; Stephen Brumwell, *Redcoats: The British Soldier and War in the Americas, 1755–1763* (New York: Cambridge University Press, 2002).

9. For some representative colonial labor histories, see: Richard B. Morris, *Government and Labor in Early America* (New York: Columbia University Press, 1946); Sharon V. Salinger, *"To Serve Well and Faithfully": Labor and Indentured Servants in Pennsylvania, 1682–1800* (Cambridge: Cambridge University Press, 1987); Robert J. Steinfeld, *The Invention of Free Labor: The Employment Relation in English and American Law and Culture, 1350–1870* (Chapel Hill: University of North Carolina Press, 1991); Allan Kulikoff, *From British Peasants to Colonial American Farmers* (Chapel Hill: University of North Carolina Press, 2000); Billy G. Smith, ed., *Down and Out in Early America* (University Park, PA: Penn State University Press, 2004).

10. Memoirs of an Invalid, 1–2.

11. Ibid., Preface.

12. Ibid., 3–4, 177, 217.

13. Ibid., 5–7, 207.

14. Ibid., 33, 56–57.

15. Brumwell, *Redcoats*, 91–97.

16. Memoirs of an Invalid, 3.

17. M. Roberts, *The Military Revolution, 1560–1660* (Belfast: Queen's University Press, 1956); Geoffrey Parker, *The Military Revolution: Military Innovation and the Rise of the West, 1500–1800* (Cambridge: Cambridge University Press, 1988; 2nd edn 1996); Michael Duffy, ed., *The Military Revolution and the State 1500–1800* (Exeter: Exeter Studies in History, No. 1, 1980); M. S. Anderson, *War and Society in the Old Regime 1618–1789* (Leicester: Leicester University Press, 1988); David Eltis, *The Military Revolution in Sixteenth-Century Europe* (London: I.B. Tauris, 1995); Jeremy Black, *A Military Revolution? Military Change and European Society 1550–1800* (London: Macmillan, 1991).

18. John Brewer, *The Sinews of Power: War, Money and the English State, 1688–1783* (London: Routledge, 1989), xi, xv, 65.

19. Ibid., xi, xv, xvii.

20. Linda Colley, *Britons: Forging the Nation, 1707–1737* (London: Vintage, 1996), 3–4, 9.

21. Kathleen Wilson, "Empire of Virtue: The Imperial Project and Hanoverian Culture c.1720–1785," in Lawrence Stone, ed., *An Imperial State at War: Britain from 1689 to 1815* (London: Routledge, 1994), 128–64; P. J. Marshall, "Introduction" to *The Oxford History of the British Empire*, Vol. II, *The Eighteenth Century* (Oxford: Oxford University Press, 1998), 1.

22. Daniel A. Baugh, "Great Britain's 'Blue-Water' Policy, 1689–1815," *The International History Review* 10 (1) (February 1988): 33–58, and "Maritime Strength and Atlantic Commerce: The uses of 'a grand marine empire'," in Stone, ed., *An Imperial State at War*, 185–223.

23. Colley, *Britons*, 73–76, 106, 108.

24. For a fuller treatment of the soldier as worker, see Way, "Class and the Common Soldier in the Seven Years' War," *Labor History* 44 (4) (December 2003): 455–81.

25. Ibid., 8–9.

26. Arthur N. Gilbert, "Army Impressment during the War of the Spanish Succession," *The Historian* 35 (August 1976): 689–790; Gilbert, "Charles Jenkinson and the Last Army Press, 1779," *Military Affairs* 42 (1978): 7; Gilbert, "An Analysis of Some Eighteenth Century Army Recruiting Records," *Journal of the Society of Army Historical Register* 54 (217) (Spring, 1976): 39; Loudoun to Daniel Webb, March 27, 1756, London, LO 974, box 21, Loudoun Papers, North America, Huntington Library, San Marino, CA [hereafter in form LO 974/21].

27. Steppler, "Common Soldier in the Reign of George III," 1–18; Frey, *British Soldier in America*, 3–4.

28. John Rule, *The Vital Century: England's Developing Economy, 1714–1815* (London: Longman, 1992), 148–49, 183–84; John Rule, *The Labouring Classes in Early Industrial England, 1750–1850* (London: Longman, 1986), 256–59; Robert W. Malcolmson, *Life and Labour in England 1700–1780* (London: Hutchinson, 1981), 113, 125; Andrew Mackillop, "More Fruitful than the Soil": *Army, Empire and the Scottish Highlands, 1715–1815* (East Linton, Lothian, Scotland: Tuckwell Press, 2000), passim [famine, 84–88].

29. Dalrymple, *A Military Essay*, quoted in Steppler, "Common Soldier in the Reign of George III," 39.

30. Admission Books, Out-Pension Records, Royal Hospital, Chelsea, Series 116, War Office Papers, Public Records Office, Kew, London [hereafter WO 116]; Royal Hospital Chelsea Regimental Registers, Series 120, War Office Papers, PRO, Microfilm reproductions held at Library and Archives Canada, Ottawa [hereafter WO120].

31. For a fuller presentation of this argument, see: Way, "Rebellion of the Regulars: Working Soldiers and the Mutiny of 1763–1764," *William and Mary Quarterly*, 3rd Ser., 57 (4) (October 2000): 761–92; Way, "Class and the Common Soldier."

32. Memoirs of an Invalid, 9–11.

33. Ibid., 12.

34. Lawrence Henry Gipson, *The British Empire before the American Revolution*, Vol. VII, *The Great War for the Empire: The Victorious Years 1758–1760* (New York: Alfred A. Knopf, 1949), 118–23.

35. Memoirs of an Invalid, 12–13.

36. Ibid., 14.

37. Ibid., 15–17.

38. Anderson, *Crucible of War*, 212–13.

39. [William Pitt] Disposition of His Majesty's Forces in North America [December 30, 1757], Abercromby Papers, AB 851, Huntington Library; Gipson, *The Victorious Years*, 177; Anderson, *Crucible of War*, 235–36.

40. Memoirs of an Invalid, 18.

41. J. A. Houlding, *Fit for Service: the Training of the British Army, 1715–95* (orig. edn 1981; Oxford: Oxford University Press, 1999).

42. Ibid., 20–21.

43. Ibid., 21–24. For accounts of the fall of Louisbourg, see: Gipson, *The Victorious Years*, 191–207; Anderson, *Crucible of War*, 250–56.

44. Memoirs of an Invalid, 24.

45. Gipson, *The Victorious Years*, 208–86; Anderson, *Crucible of War*, 240–49, 257–85.

46. Ibid., 24.

47. Brumwell, "British Soldier," 34–35, 37–39.

48. Gipson, *The Victorious Years*, 371–427; Anderson, *Crucible of War*, 344–68. Matthew Ward's *The Battle for Quebec 1759* offers a comprehensive recent study.

49. Memoirs of an Invalid, 28–30.

50. Ibid., 28–30.

51. Gipson, *The Victorious Years*, 397–400; Anderson, *Crucible of War*, 344.

52. McDuff: WO116/5/56, 23 Dec. 1760; WO120, 23 Dec. 1760. Miles: WO120, 20 Feb 1761. Cairns: WO116/5/56, 23 Dec. 1760; WO120, 23 Dec. 1760. Smith: WO116/5/56, 23 Dec. 1760; WO120, 23 Dec. 1760. Babbige: WO116/5/54, 8 Dec. 1760; WO120, Dec. 1760. Poole: WO120, 20 Feb 1761.

53. Anderson, *Crucible of War*, 330–43.

54. Memoirs of an Invalid, 31–33.

55. Anderson, *Crucible of War*, 392–93.

56. E. P. Thompson pointed out the fallacy of expecting plebeian laborers of the eighteenth century to act out of a completely formed class consciousness. Consciousness and class formation flowed historically from class struggle, and in eighteenth-century Britain that struggle was ongoing and modern classes not yet fully formed. Thompson, "Eighteenth-century English society: class struggle without class?" *Social History* 3 (2) (May 1978): 133–65.

57. Memoirs of an Invalid, 33.

58. Records of General Courts Martial, volume 46, pp. 2–3, November 16, 1759, War Office Papers, series 71, British National Archives, Kew, London [hereafter in form WO71/46/2–3].

59. WO71/46/8–10, 13–14.

60. Memoirs of an Invalid, 35–41; Anderson, *Crucible of War*, 391–96.

61. Memoirs of an Invalid, 42–44. Gipson, *The Victorious Years*, 397–400; Anderson, *Crucible of War*, 400–09.

62. Memoirs of an Invalid, 45.

63. Ibid., 45–46.

64. Lawrence Henry Gipson, *The British Empire before the American Revolution*, vol. 8, *The Great War for Empire: the Culmination, 1760–1763* (New York: Knopf, 1953), 187–90; J. W. Fortescue, *A History of the British Army*, vol. 2 (London: Macmillan, 1899), 537–41.

65. John R. McNeill, "The Ecological Basis of Warfare in the Caribbean, 1700–1804," in Maarten Ultee, ed. *Adapting to Conditions: War and Society in the Eighteenth Century* (Alabama: University of Alabama Press, 1986), 34–36, 38.

66. Memoirs of an Invalid, 52–54.

67. Ibid., 56–57.

68. Gipson, *The Culmination*, 190–96.

69. Memoirs of an Invalid, 58.

70. Julian S. Corbett, *England in the Seven Years' War: A Study in Combined Strategy*, vol. 2 (London: Longmans, Green, & Co., 1907), 249–50, 253; Gipson, *The Culmination*, 262; David Syrett, "American Provincials and the Havana Campaign of 1762," *New York History* 44 (October 1968): 376–79.

71. Albemarle to Amherst [4 May 1762], *Publications of the Navy Records Society*, vol. 114: *The Siege and Capture of Havana 1762*, ed. David Syrett (London: Spottiswoode, Ballantyne, & Co., 1970), 103; Abstract of the general return of His majesty's forces [May 23, 1762], Ibid., 126.

72. Memoirs of an Invalid, 64–65.

73. Gipson, *The Culmination*, 264–68; Syrett, *Siege and Capture of Havana*, 200, 210; Corbett, *Seven Years' War*, vol. 2, 270 ff.

74. Memoirs of an Invalid, 68–69.

75. Alan J. Guy, *Oeconomy and Discipline: Officership and Administration in the British Army 1714–1765* (Manchester: Manchester University Press, 1985), 107; Corbett, *Seven Years' War*, vol. 2, 283. Miller reported that another dividend was

paid four years later at Montreal, when privates received a further four dollars and sergeants eight, "but these may be consider'd as nothing compared with the gettings, of great men." Memoirs of an Invalid, 69–70.

76. General return . . . from the 7 June to 18 October, October 18, 1762, in Syrett, *Siege and Capture of Havana 1762*, 305; Corbett, *England in the Seven Years' War*, vol. 2, 282; Amherst to Murray, October 28, 1762, WO34/3/177–78; McNeill, "Ecological Basis of Warfare," 36.

77. Memoirs of an Invalid, 71–72. Miller partially blamed the British army's love of alcohol for the pervasive illness. "It was very usual to meet Officers, and soldiers, drunk every hour of the day!"

78. Ibid., 73–74.

79. Ibid., 74–76.

80. Ibid., 76–78.

81. W. Ellis to Amherst, May 20, 1763, Jeffrey Amherst Papers, vol. 1, schedule 1, William L. Clements Library, University of Michigan, Ann Arbor. Other fiscal flashpoints factored in. Soldiers worried about the support of their families, wished to continue receiving pay for extraordinary labor, wanted the clothing that the army owed them, and disliked being drafted into new regiments once war was over, especially those destined to remain in America. For a fuller treatment of the mutiny, see Way, "Rebellion of the Regulars."

82. Memoirs of an Invalid, 79–84.

83. Murray [to Amherst], September 21, 1763, WO34/2/225; Murray to Gage and Gov. Barton, September 21, 1763, WO34/2/227. See also: Orders to the Garrison of Quebec, September 18, 1763, WO34/2/231; Ja. Pitcher to Amherst, September 23, 1763, WO34/4/120.

84. Petition to Brig. General James Murray, n.d., WO34/2/239. An anonymous officer's report likewise painted a more mobbish picture of events with armed men confronting officers with swords drawn. *The Annual Register, or a View of the History, Politicks, and Literature, For the Year 1763* (Second edition; London, 1765), 159–60.

85. Ellis to Gage, January 21, 1764, Thomas Gage Papers, English Series, Clements Library; Gage to Ellis, December 9, 1763, April 13, May 12, 1764, ibid.

86. Memoirs of an Invalid, 86.

87. Jesse Lemisch, "Jack Tar in the Streets: Merchant Seamen in the Politics of Revolutionary America," *William and Mary Quarterly*, 3rd Ser., 25 (1968): 371–407; Jesse Lemisch, *Jack Tar vs. John Bull: The Role of New York's Seamen in Precipitating the Revolution* (New York: Garland, 1997); Peter Linebaugh and Marcus Rediker, *The Many-Headed Hydra: Sailors, Slaves, Commoners, and the Hidden History of the Revolutionary Atlantic* (London: Verso, 2000), 214–27, 277; Anderson, *Crucible of War*, 653, 677–87.

88. Memoirs of an Invalid, 192–93.

89. Ibid., 181–82, 199–200.

CHAPTER TWO

Losing the Middle Ground: Strikebreakers and Labor Protest on the Southwestern Railroads

Theresa Ann Case

In 1966, historian William M. Tuttle Jr published a short, remarkable, almost wholly forgotten piece on the 1904 Chicago meat-packing strike entitled "Some Strikebreakers' Observations of Industrial Warfare." Tuttle's point was that, although "strikebreakers have dashed the hopes of countless strikes by enabling factories to continue production," historians understand little about strikebreakers' motivations, backgrounds, and experiences. The two extended interviews with ex-strikebreakers that the union conducted, and which Tuttle's essay introduces, "give us a picture," he noted, "of experiences and impressions that are extraordinary . . . because they strip away some of the anonymity surrounding the participants," allowing them to "emerge as individuals."[1]

It is not that historians have disregarded strikebreakers. While some assumption lurks in the literature that a lack of moral fiber explains their actions, most scholars have been careful to place strikebreakers in a larger material context, understanding them as often part of a reserve army of labor—a "pool of unemployed workers" whose deprivation, anxiety, and lack of alternatives, especially in the context of state repression of labor protest, made them highly vulnerable to employer exploitation.[2] Stephen Norwood begins his book on professional strikebreaking with a discussion of chronic joblessness, noting that the street corners of early twentieth-century American cities teemed with the homeless and unemployed, a number of whom were recruited by strikebreaking entrepreneurs to serve in employers' private armies as armed guards or as replacement workers.[3] In addition to (and related to) rooting strikebreaking in economic need and insecurity, historians have explored the incidence of strikebreaking as both a manifestation of and a source of the division and animosity among workers along lines of race, ethnicity, sex, skill, and status. Some sources emphasize generational differences between earlier and later waves of various immigrant groups, for example. Others maintain that employers encouraged, and "labor aristocrats" identified with, an elaborate hierarchy in compensation and social rank, while feminist historians have explored how conceptions of masculinity and femininity have stratified working people.[4] A good deal of debate has focused on strikebreaking on the part of people whom unions traditionally excluded, particularly African Americans.[5] Finally, scholars have turned their attention to the mobilization of strikebreakers, ideologically, geographically, and logistically—specifically, the boom in the professional strikebreaking business in the early twentieth century, the views of army officers on the military's strikebreaking role, and the growth of market institutions to organize and match the needs of employers and job seekers.[6]

Still, Tuttle's point largely stands. With the possible exception of African-American strikebreakers, the ordinary men and women who took the places of striking workers during the late nineteenth century remain remote, shadowy, faceless figures, and their relationships to strikers mostly appear in the literature as desperate, bitter, violent exchanges—despite the elemental and often dramatic part that strikebreakers played in Industrial Era labor protest, the degree to which strikebreaking contributed to an especially violent strike history in the United States, and the leaps and bounds by which the field of social and cultural history has grown since Tuttle's piece was published.[7] Probably this is due to the challenge of sources. Typically, the stories of individual strikebreakers received scant mention in contemporary newspaper coverage, employer and union documents, and government investigations. Probably it is also a consequence of labor historians' tendency to cast industrialists, the state, and protesting workers and their leaders and sympathizers as the narrative linchpins, with strikebreakers making their chief appearance in the story when lines hardened and events escalated.

Several works nod in a new direction. Ardis Cameron traced the prevalence of English-speakers among strikebreakers in the 1912 strike by female mill-workers in Lawrence, Massachusetts, in part to cultural differences. Irish and English workers, in contrast to southern and eastern European immigrants, she discovered, were distant and even hostile to the very traditions that helped to sustain strikers as they faced "payless paydays" during the walkout—a willingness to call for public aid and an attachment to "a network of reciprocity" among extended family and neighbors. English-speakers were therefore much more likely to fill the positions of protesting workers. Using oral histories, newspapers, and union and company records, Timothy J. Minchin has investigated the use of "permanent replacements" in a number of late twentieth-century labor conflicts. His essays expose the colliding perceptions of workers on both sides of the strike divide, the efforts of some to bridge the gulf, and the agonizing, destructive consequences of employers' use of replacement workers on local workers in defeat, their communities, and the wider modern labor movement. Finally, James Sidbury's treatment of the slave informers who betrayed Gabriel's Conspiracy in early eighteenth-century Virginia demonstrates the value of scholarly skepticism regarding analyses that rely on "moral categorization." Such an approach "creates comfort" by "neatly classifying those who lived in Gabriel's world according to modern observers' sympathies," Sidbury notes, but overlooks the common, if contradictory, values that both informers and rebel slaves shared and, hence, the difficult moral questions that various enslaved actors—informers, potential conspirators, and Gabriel's cohorts confronted (or elided) as the insurrection date approached and as rebels' plans unraveled. Together, these scholars encourage historians to situate more fully those who undermined oppositional movements within the specific cultural circumstances that they inhabited. Strikers' and strikebreakers' choices were controversial in their own time and continue to be. An examination of the attempts of each to wrestle with the radical circumstances presented by the Industrial Era renders those decisions more comprehensible.[8]

In the course of my own work on the 1886 Southwest railway strikes, I discovered a possible springboard for such an examination: a long list of names of, and collection of interviews with, strikers and strikebreakers, that I gathered from newspaper sources and a transcript of the congressional investigation of the "labor troubles" at the root of conflict. Connected with data from the 1880 federal census, the list of names yields information on the backgrounds of a small but significant number of participants. The transcript is an especially rich source in that it includes the testimony of a wide variety of actors and observers only weeks after the strike's effective defeat. While most of the available evidence relates to strikers, a close reading allows a tentative reconstruction of the social and cultural history of strikebreakers and their multi-faceted interactions with strikers at various moments in one highly contentious Gilded Age labor protest. What emerges is a story involving men (and in a much more fragmentary way, women) from both sides of the strike divide who were not as dissimilar as one might think. This was not a "race" strike or one in which workers separated along ethnic or generational lines. Even the schism between many brotherhood and non-brotherhood men that had traditionally haunted railway labor protest was overcome during the strike's initial phase. To be sure, as grave obstacles mounted to the walkout, enmity and violence characterized the relationships between strikers and strikebreakers, some of whom were friends and neighbors. Yet, in this case, the similar backgrounds of a number of strikers and strikebreakers, the various positions that they took on violence, and the shifting allegiances of each, suggest that many strikebreakers shared with strikers a commitment to antebellum notions of "free labor" and an identity as railroaders. In myriad ways, strike participants sought to stand on some secure cultural ground between violent, industrial unionism and a purely individualist path to "dealing with, and sometimes overcoming dependence and inequality."[9] In the interest of understanding their dilemma, historians should further explore the larger web of values and traditions within working-class communities that shaped their debates over labor violence and strikebreaking.

The 1886 Great Southwest Strike

Historians have long considered the 1886 "Great Southwest Strike" a seminal episode. In the midst of a national upsurge in labor protest in 1886 called the Great Upheaval, it pitted railroad workers who belonged to the Knights of Labor, the nation's first mass industrial union, against the infamous financier-entrepreneur and "railway king"

Jay Gould, whose sprawling "Southwest" system of roads linked much of Texas and the Midwest to markets in the East and on the Pacific coast. At the heart of the conflict was a fight for union recognition, which sparked the largest sympathy strike that the nation had ever seen and a cross-racial alliance between black and white railway workers in an era of Jim Crow.

The significance of the massive discontent among railroad workers in March and April 1886 cannot be appreciated unless one begins with the labor contests of the previous year. In March 1885, railway officials on Gould's "Southwest" system enacted yet another across-the-board wage cut after a series of earlier pay reductions, galvanizing the vast majority of men in the yards and shops to walk out. "Starvation" wages threatened railroaders with dependence, undermined their ability to sustain the fraternal organizations and traditions that made their work more respectable and endurable, and intensified the already severe pressures of other cost-cutting policies such as the speed-up. The scale and suddenness of the walkout stunned officials; local communities' enthusiastic embrace of the largely peaceful, relatively short effort in the name of antimonopoly, and the cooperation of engineers and firemen in the shutdown of freight traffic, brought railway officials to the table to negotiate. The March 15 compact, combined with a September 1885 bargain secured between Gould and the national Knights of Labor on behalf of employees on his system, unlocked powerful, pent-up frustrations among working people nationally. Railroad workers, and workers of all kinds, adopted the inclusive Knights in astonishing numbers, so that 700,000 belonged to the order by 1886, a seven-fold increase over the year before.[10]

In March 1886, Gould system managers' routine violations of the 1885 agreements triggered another massive walkout in Texas, Missouri, Kansas, Arkansas, and Illinois, beginning on the Texas & Pacific and spreading to the Missouri Pacific. District Assembly 101 of the Knights of Labor, representing workers on the "Southwest" system, this time called for collective bargaining. Despite the large-scale participation of railroaders from an array of occupations in crowd actions that shut down freight traffic for more than three weeks, in the end, strikers met with a series of humiliating blows. A number of railroaders returned to work or resisted the order to strike, union violence escalated in response, and law-and-order leagues organized to aid railroad officials and local authorities in suppressing the walkout. Bloody clashes followed between pro-strike crowds and company-hired deputies in Fort Worth, Little Rock, and East St. Louis. Trains moved freely by mid-April 1886, leaving the Knights in defeat, the bulk of strikers out of work and many beset by legal troubles and targeted by a blacklist, and railway communities as well as railroaders deeply and bitterly divided.[11]

The Brotherhood Men and Moral Suasion

When workmen along the lines of the Texas & Pacific laid down their tools at the sound of the whistle on the afternoon of March 1, and when their compatriots did the same on the Missouri Pacific on March 6, few shared any immediate grievances with the skilled trainmen who operated and fueled the engines of freight and passenger trains.[12] The "Southwest" strikers represented a whole host of occupations—boilermakers, carpenters, machinists, apprentices, shop laborers, baggage-men, car repairers, track and section men, brakemen, switchmen, hostlers, and engine wipers.[13] Engineers and firemen generally did not leave their posts and join the Knights as they moved "together in one large body . . . out of the yards and up to the Knights of Labor hall" to hold a meeting. Most belonged to powerful, conservative, exclusive craft unions, the Brotherhood of Locomotive Engineers (BLE) and the Brotherhood of Locomotive Firemen (BLF), which feared the motley occupational, racial, and ethnic composition of the Knights and studiously avoided conflict with railway companies.[14]

With the 1885 strike, the brotherhoods' leadership and rank-and-file had departed from this cautious tradition. Engineers and firemen on the Gould system cooperated spontaneously and almost universally with strikers, and the BLE's Grand Chief Peter M. Arthur issued no directive to forbid it. The walkout ended quickly and was popular with the wider public and so did not imperil the BLE's reputation. This surely influenced Arthur. Also, engineers suffered a number of exploitative practices, and railway officials had failed to honor an agreement with the BLE made two years prior. The shutdown of freight traffic during the strike apparently reminded officials of the benefits of arbitration with the BLE. It thus afforded Arthur the opportunity to secure a separate agreement with Southwest system representatives that protected them from pay deductions for the loss or breakage of tools or damage of freight, the requirement that engineers perform work traditionally done by (unskilled) hostlers, and arbitrary discharges or suspensions. System representatives also promised to assign regular engines or runs "by seniority and capacity in regular road service" and to avoid employing part-timers. These stipulations appealed to engineers, who experienced, like other railroaders, heightened job competition and deteriorating conditions on western roads during the 1880s.[15]

That railroad officials had generally honored the agreement over the previous year encouraged brotherhood men to act cautiously in 1886. An open, formal alliance with the Knights would have jeopardized the measure of control that they had won over their work-life and prospects. Another powerful obstacle to aid was Arthur, who had a positive experience with management as an engineer and who had, since a series of disastrous BLE strikes in 1876–77, embarked as grand chief on a "go-it-alone" strategy that relied on the engineers' skill and respectable image. The head of the BLF, Frank Sargent, tended to acquiesce to the older and more experienced Arthur.[16]

In contrast to engineers, many strikers, particularly the semi-skilled and unskilled, were in a state of crisis that managers refused to acknowledge. Their grievances involved violations of the March 1885 compact, which company officials falsely claimed pertained only to shopmen. Strikers later testified at length that their pre-strike wages were never restored, as agreed upon, and managers discriminated against Knights or blacklisted them entirely and concocted various strategies for robbing workers of their pay, including stepping up the pace of their already physically taxing, life- and limb-threatening work. For example, brakemen received their pay for every full hour worked, so that "if you were on the road one hour and fifty minutes, you only got one hour extra time." Roundhouse and shop laborers in Kansas City and elsewhere testified that they regularly received pay for only ten hours a day when they had put in thirteen. Trackmen's hours were cut to only a few days per week, despite the safety risks associated with understaffed maintenance crews.[17] Besides enforcement of the March 1885 terms, strikers demanded $1.50 a day for their "downtrodden brethren," unskilled laborers, and, probably as a means of appealing broadly to the deep-seated racial and economic anxieties of less skilled white and black workers, sought the eviction of convict labor and Chinese workers from employment on the "Southwest" system roads.[18]

Not all strikers claimed grievances. Shopmen, especially, related that they had no particular complaints, even in hotbeds of Knights activity such as Parsons and Atchison, Kansas, and Pacific, Cypress, St. Louis, and Sedalia, Missouri.[19] Nonetheless, while some apparently contented or quiescent railroaders clearly resented and resisted the strike order, and others conveyed mixed feelings, most Knights energetically embraced the walkout as a matter of principle. To these men, the termination of a local leader of the order on the Texas & Pacific, which had precipitated the walkout on that road and the sympathy strike on the Missouri Pacific, dramatized the larger issue of anti-unionist discrimination and portended a system-wide plan on the part of railroad officials to break the power of the order. E. F. Pagett, a De Soto strike leader and chair of DA 101's grievance committee, told the congressional committee that investigated the walkout, "We made earnest and repeated efforts to get our grievances . . . before the officials of this road, and that we failed." He continued, "The longer it went the worse it was, and we saw very plainly that inside of another six months they would have the employés of the system back exactly where they were at the time that agreement was entered into," when the railroad introduced "the most notorious starvation cuts that ever wages the West received."[20] Texas Knights leader William E. Farmer sounded a similar theme at a mass meeting numbering 2,500 people in Fort Worth on March 9: "The time has come when [Reverend Henry Ward] Beecher declares that a dollar a day is sufficient to purchase bread and water, and that a man who can't live on bread and water, with his family, isn't worth living. This is the feast, my friends, to which you are invited." These strong sentiments resonated with rank-and-file railroaders. "The accepted impression" among the Knights, one Marshall, Texas, newspaper editor related, was that the walkout represented "a test case," the outcome of which "must determine the relative positions that labor and capital are to occupy in this country."[21]

Trainmen's decision to aid the strike, or not, was key, because a withdrawal of the labor of trackmen, bridgemen, and shopmen affected train and track repair, not, at least for some time, train operation. As long as engines, cars, switches, bridges, equipment, and roads were in fair condition, these workers held much less leverage, as freight could continue to move. Certainly, the popularity of the walkout among switchmen and brakemen helped the Knights a good deal. Switchmen controlled the switches in the railway yard in order to avoid having an engine or car thrown off track. They also brought cars onto the same track and helped the brakeman to couple and uncouple them in order to make up trains. Brakemen mainly ran along the top of the train cars to set and release the hand brakes upon the engineers' signals. Then again, braking and switching were semi-skilled tasks, even entry-level jobs under labor-scarce circumstances, that lacked the backing of the powerful railway brotherhoods.[22]

What is startling is that, despite the engineers' contract and despite the brotherhoods' general wariness of strikes and disdain for the less skilled, a significant number of engineers and firemen initially cooperated with the Knights, especially in Atchison, St. Louis, and Pacific. The scenes that dominated the news during the walkout's first week, when the Missouri Pacific attempted to send out its first freight trains, resembled almost exactly the ritual that had played out almost everywhere along the Gould lines between trainmen and strikers during the walkout the previous year. In St. Louis, when requested to by the crowd that gathered around him, fireman Harry Boggs "alighted from his engine and refused to go out," followed by the engineer W. S. Haley. One DA 101 official reported, "We have the best of reasons for saying that the engineers and firemen of the system will assist us whenever they are asked to do so." General Superintendent William Kerrigan acted as switchman the next day, with Engineer Marvin at the helm, but a young man known only as Williams approached both trainmen. The train started and again stopped, after which Kerrigan abandoned the endeavor, to the "approving shake" of strikers and a tearful Williams. Similar exchanges between strikers and trainmen, and the Knights' expressions of hope, were repeated for the next several days. "Get down Madden" called the member of a large assembly in Atchison that surrounded an outgoing locomotive. Fireman George Madden "stepped at once from the cab, and was applauded by the men around." Engineer Charles Benedict and fireman John Cain did the same. The strikers' "argumentary opposition," one newspaper predicted, may prove "more forcible than blows" and "bring victory to the banners of the Knights." An almost celebratory mood took hold in St. Louis, where one striker enlightened a reporter as to why he and his compatriots intervened with one attempt to take out an engine (successfully) but not another. "There is no use in doing it all here. We gain time by letting them go down [the track to the next pro-strike gathering] and come back, and so distribute the excitement. That is our policy."[23]

An abiding bitterness against Gould and the "spirit of 1885" apparently moved these sympathetic engineers and firemen to action. The rumor that the heads of both brotherhoods would endorse the strike likely emboldened them. In addition, the Missouri Pacific's use of nonunion men and company police to take out engines pushed these trainmen toward the Knights. Engineers' refusal to deal with strikebreaking elements extended to brakemen, one newspaper recounted. Brakemen across the system had declined to "touch a car or to aid the railroad company in any way to resume operations," one paper reported, so that "if the [braking] work is done by outsiders it is ranked as 'scab' work and the engineer and fireman will not consent to touch it." Firemen, who were less skilled than engineers, identified more with the Knights' industrial unionism and apparently urged engineers to aid the strikers.[24]

The clear evidence of skilled trainmen's sympathy lends some credence to reports that two strategies permitted engineers, in St. Louis at least, to have their cake and eat it, too, for a time. After a series of meetings, trainmen agreed to "run the engines if asked to do so," meaning that "if the engines were out from the round house ready for service they would take charge, and would obey orders in the matter of coupling, switching, and running cars, but would do no more than actually required by a strict construction of their duties." These stipulations, one engineer pointed out, did not require them to "submit or expose" themselves "to violence." One strike sympathizer divulged that there "seems to have been a hidden significance both for the strikers and the engineers" in that statement. "Although no violence will be attempted," he explained, "the notice to leave from the K of L will be regarded [publicly] as intimidation and the men will not go out. This course will be keeping a technical faith with the company and an honest one with the strikers."[25] Engineers also invoked the cause of public and trainmen's safety in refusing to run trains. The prospect of navigating an engine through the crowds that sought to block its way was "useless," commented one "prominent Brotherhood man," who opposed "risking any life for the company's sake." While the safety claim did not necessarily imply sympathy for the strike, many reportedly saw it as an "excuse": "The real cause of their leaving" is that "they were beckoned to by the Knights of Labor."[26]

The "spirit of 1885" was not universal. In some locales engineers and Knights squared off against one another early on, sometimes violently, a subject to which I will turn later.[27] One local brotherhood leader in Atchison argued that at least some of Knights' outwardly friendly requests for trainmen to leave their posts cloaked more coercive methods.[28] However, the aid rendered by many skilled trainmen to the strike, even in the face of strong incentives to refuse aid, points to a kind of cultural pact between these workers that centered in large part on the principle of moral suasion. The willingness of brotherhood men to extend their support partly depended on the fact that they were asked to do so, persuaded to, by other workers, on the basis of a call for justice. Their actions were in line with what David Brody calls the "rough compromise" between individual rights and the right to association conceived by Massachusetts judge Lemuel Shaw in *Commonwealth v. Hunt* (1842). Shaw held that workers could act collectively to place pressure on their employers as long as their collective efforts were lawful and voluntary. In recognizing the legality of trade unions, Shaw's ruling reflected popular antebellum notions about "free labor" that considered labor a form of property and a necessary condition for self-ownership but also linked freedom to equality before the law, citizenship, and the dignity of labor. Freedom required respect for both community standards and individual liberty.[29] Like a series of legal cases during the late nineteenth century that narrowed the meaning of freedom to freedom-of-contract, the injunctions issued against the 1886 Southwest strike undermined *Commonwealth v. Hunt* and thus the middle ground that railway workers had secured on the basis of moral suasion, leaving strikers and strikebreakers increasingly at odds but also ambivalent and divided about how to restore the balance between individualism and communalism.

The Mass Entry of Strikebreakers

Some of the early news regarding strikebreakers must have unsettled a number of Knights, particularly the unskilled. The *Dallas Morning News* reported that "green men" had replaced striking baggage handlers on the T&P, new crews of men ran the yards and warehouses at Fort Worth, and, in Marshall, a "foreman and a few raw hands," mostly black workers, were able to move the trains. By March 5, the T&P receivers considered those who had walked out as former employees and any new men as a permanent, not a temporary, labor force. A few days later General Superintendent William Kerrigan of the Missouri Pacific made a similar announcement.[30]

Yet prior to mid-March, strikebreakers did not seriously threaten the walkout. Reports that mention black strikebreakers specifically were rare, although railroad managers would have benefited from the exploitation of racial divisions between black and white Knights. In fact, blacks and whites populated the ranks of both strikebreakers and strikers, and race did not emerge as an overt tool of any one group until late in the conflict.[31] Also, skilled shopmen remained scarce in Marshall and Fort Worth, despite the brave face that railroad mangers put on before the press. In St. Louis, officials boasted that 20 craftsmen were at work, and strikers worried when they heard the shop bell ring. In reality, as the Knights discovered, only four workers were employed and the master mechanic himself had sounded the bell. In contrast, the ranks of the Knights were "gaining force every hour," especially among "now exasperated" men idled by the standstill in freight traffic, and 300 brakemen, switchmen, and firemen joined a St. Louis assembly in the strike's first week.[32]

The mood of Knights remained, for the time, "confident," and the newspapers frequently described strikers as "orderly," "quiet," "peaceable," and "well behaved." Sedalia Knights regarded officials' decision to lay off idled workers as a "game of bluff which does not frighten them in the least." St. Louis Knights leader J. J. McGarry declared, "We can win this time much easier than last year. Then we were scarcely organized and won, and now we have 1500 men in our district, all of whom we may call upon."[33]

While strikebreakers faced some physical risks—one was jostled out of the way and another received "two black eyes" and "a few lumps,"—in the main strikers relied, with a good deal of success, on moral suasion and the public disgrace that strikebreaking hazarded to carry the day. On March 12, the *Atchison Daily Globe* reported that the Knights had the full allegiance of brakemen and had convinced most new men to turn away from the roundhouses and shops "without violence or exhibition of ill temper."[34] Before a March 9 mass meeting in Fort Worth, William Farmer responded unequivocally to an audience member's request that he explain the term "scab": "It was a man who would take sides with his enemy to slay his brother." "Still," Farmer instructed, "I don't want you to hurt any of these fellows, and you ain't going to do it." Instead, he "wanted the workingmen to think."[35]

The new conditions that the walkout faced by the month's end would have confounded any thinking striker. First, the courts enjoined hundreds of striking employees from interfering, even peaceably, with traffic on the Missouri Pacific. Strikers had expected state intervention on the T&P, as that road was in receivership, meaning that it was a bankrupt road under federal reorganization. In fact, Knights had earlier expressed the belief that the T&P "was placed in the hands of receivers in order that the road might have the protection of the United States courts" in its fight against labor. The Missouri Pacific was solvent; the Knights had thought it a relatively safe road on which to make their fight against Gould. The massive scale and scope of the injunctions issued to protect it were unprecedented, as the chief lawyer for the Missouri Pacific acknowledged, and one federal judge went so far as to rule that a strike against the T&P was illegal.[36] Second, the brotherhood chiefs moved to distance their organizations from the trouble. BLE chief Arthur formally ordered engineers to do their duty and move trains, and Sargent, the head of the BLF, encouraged firemen to do the same. BLF Secretary-Treasurer Eugene Debs expressed some sympathy with strikers but seconded Sargent's message, as he saw the Knights' credo, "an injury to one is the concern of all," as unduly antagonistic and Gould system officials as friendly and reasonable.[37] Third, the governors of Kansas and Missouri publicly rejected strikers' claim that railroad officials had violated the 1885 compact. This seemed to hearten the Missouri Pacific's vice-president, who announced that the loss of revenue due to stalled traffic necessitated a reduction in the company's overall workforce.[38] Finally, strikers were confused and humiliated when the national Knights leadership, under the impression that Gould had agreed to arbitrate, first ordered them back to work and then, days later, after Gould denied the story, renounced the order. Strikers returned to retake their positions only to be told that their jobs were occupied, no work was available, or that their alleged participation in destruction of railroad property eliminated them from consideration for employment.[39]

It took time for strikers to see the enormity of the problem before them. A Dallas paper recounted how the injunctions "produced no other effect among employees than to raise a hearty and a general laugh." When J. J. McGarry received his writ, it fell [to] the ground as the deputy gave it to him; a crowd gathered and covered it with tobacco juice.[40] The injunctions eventually did their work, however, greatly restricting strikers' ability to win, or even protest their losses. By April 7, traffic moved freely on the Missouri Pacific at Fort Worth under the watch of U.S. marshals, about 30 state rangers, and company guards. A mass meeting in Galveston of 1,500 people demonstrated against U.S. marshals' arrest of strikers for "only standing on the side of the streets, guiltless of any crime, as an outrage on civil liberty" and denounced the practice of trying arrestees outside cities. A Marshall Knights leader was charged with contempt of court and placed under $1,500 bond for writing a letter simply requesting a strikebreaker to quit work, with no threat of violence intimated.[41] Many strikers seemed in a state of shock. When trains began to move under the direction of company detectives and police in St. Louis, and with the aid of deputized citizens in Palestine, Texas, the mood of those congregated was one of quiet observation.[42]

Once strikebreaking was fully protected and the strikes' prospects dimmed, labor was plentiful. In Marshall, strikers were "discouraged" as workmen filled the shops. By early April, the Fort Worth Typographical Union was moved to express its "deep sympathy with the strikers" in "their great struggle with tyrannical bigots and detestable scabs."[43] Among those who resumed work en masse were engineers and firemen. Martin Irons, the head of DA 101, grieved over "how new men were deserting at various points, how new men were being brought in as strikebreakers every day, how the members of the railroad brotherhoods had not lived up to their promises not to operate trains with strikebreakers."[44]

With moral suasion effectively criminalized and the BLE order in force, a host of new strike tactics emerged. Some Knights turned to physical force or the threat of it, so that accounts of clashes between skilled trainmen and strikers increasingly replaced descriptions of cooperation in local newspapers. In St. Louis, a crowd of strikers and their sympathizers surrounded an outgoing train and dragged down the engineer and fireman and disabled the engine. New men and returning strikers arrived with "bruised heads and faces." A number slept and ate inside the shops rather than stay at boarding houses, because, as one superintendent testified, "They dare not go out . . . or . . . they would most assuredly get beaten . . . and badly used beyond question, which a number of them was." Men who tried to go home to their families in the southern part of St. Louis were "waylaid." Strikebreakers and strike opponents received written and verbal warnings that threatened expulsion from town or death.[45] Knights also threw their energy into the prevention of track, yard, and engine maintenance by the seizure or sabotage of equipment and the forced occupation of shops and roundhouses. Crowds frustrated every attempt to switch by disabling or "killing" engines and taking engine parts. "Twenty-five draw-heads had been removed, over four hundred pins gone, wherever they could take slack on a car," a Palestine yard-master reported.[46] In Atchison, 30 to 40 masked strikers took over the roundhouse, held 13 guards at pistol point, and put the engines out of action. Outside of town, 2,000 men swarmed on top of a freight train, set the brakes, uncoupled its cars, "threw the links and pins into the river, and killed the engines." And, although strikers' culpability is uncertain, in only one week in late March, trainmen allegedly found a fire set on both ends of an Alvarado, Texas, bridge, a rail across the track outside of Little Rock, a missing spike that caused a train to derail near Marshall, and sabotaged tracks at Irondale, Mineral Point, Jacksonville, Sedalia, and Parsons.[47]

In the wake of these events, one of course finds unshakeable hostility between striker and strikebreaker, but the rift is not entirely captured by H. M. Hoxie, Vice-President of the Missouri Pacific, who early in the walkout appealed to "every independent, free thinking co-laborer" to abandon the "arbitrary, useless, and uncalled for" strike. The Knights, he held, had carelessly heeded the command of their leaders and betrayed their own interests and identities: "A few men whom you have voluntarily given the power, are depriving many thousands of their collaborators of their accustomed wages, divesting this company of the capacity to pay its employés for their services, shutting up the avenues of traffic in four States, and preventing some 4,000,000 of people from obtaining their customary supplies and the necessities of life." Hoxie's formulation of the issue drew upon the narrow, economic understanding of "free labor" that had emerged in the aftermath of emancipation. As Senator Henry Teller famously put it: "The difference between a slave and a freeman consists mainly in the fact that the freeman may freely dispose of his labor . . . on terms fixed by himself."[48]

Like Hoxie, some strikebreakers condemned what they saw as unthinking allegiance to the order at the expense of individual rights and ambition. One instance consists of a single retort to an indignant Knight, "I supposed there was somebody before you," the implicit assumption being that no job is the property of anyone else; a person has no legitimate claim on the position that they quit, in protest or otherwise.[49] Strikebreaker Joseph Cramer cast the Knights as a dictatorial force bent on the pursuit of power. Cramer was a painter in the Iron Mountain shop in De Soto. He went out on strike on March 6, but later objected to the tactic of blockading trains, which landed him in trouble with the Knights assembly. Allegedly, Master Workman Charles Laughlin instructed him, "If you don't want to do it you need not, but just go to swell the party," to which Cramer replied that he "would not violate the company's laws" and "it was not any of my business."[50] The same theme emerges in another former Knight's charge that the strikers "were not doing right . . . A man, because he has five or six hundred men at the back of him, wants to get another man out of his situation, and I don't believe in such business."[51] However, the focus of many strikebreakers' testimonies was not freedom-of-contract's unconditional assertion of the individual right to hire on and quit at will but pragmatic issues, ambivalence about the strike itself, and strikers' use of coercion in ways that violated community standards and workplace ties. These concerns were not only voiced by many strikebreakers but also by a significant section of Knights.

The Struggle for a Middle Ground

Before turning to the cultural basis on which some strikers and strikebreakers stood, an explanation of their common social ground is in order. The analysis here is tentative, because the data is quite limited. Altogether the names of 393 strikers and 99 strikebreakers were culled from the congressional investigation testimony and four newspapers. Only 30 strikebreakers and 64 strikers surfaced in the 1880 federal census (I excluded the two "scab" clerks and five police and marshals). I also considered information (age, years of service to the railway company) on an additional 16 strikebreakers and an additional 24 strikers available in the transcribed testimony. The data is skewed almost wholly toward white men. Just two black strikers were found in the census, and only a few black and female participants testified before the congressional committee, and briefly at that. Engineers are probably over-represented in the data on strikebreakers (eight of the thirty found in the census). Nonetheless, although the bulk of names are associated with events in just a few towns—Denison, De Soto, Sedalia, and Marshall—the sample otherwise provides a solid cross-section of people of various skills, occupations, and locales.[52]

Very little stands out in the quantitative material in terms of major social cleavages between strikers and strikebreakers. Strikebreakers were more likely to be married, native-born, and established in their own home. Seventy percent of strikebreakers were married in contrast to half (53%) of strikers, and only one-quarter of strikebreakers boarded or lived with one or both parents in 1880, compared to nearly twice as many strikers (47%). About one-third of strikebreakers were born outside of the United States or of immigrant parents. This was true for nearly half (47%) of strikers. These are appreciable differences, but, given the preponderance of engineers in the sample on strikebreakers, not entirely surprising. In other ways, these actors were very similar, as the numbers suggest. The median age of striker and strikebreaker was 35 and 37, respectively (40% of strikers and 44% of strikebreakers were in their thirties at the time of the walkout). Those of immigrant stock came almost exclusively from Ireland, England, and Germany, with no one group heavily dominating. About one-third of strikers and strikebreakers had children in 1880, and almost universally, the wives of strikers and strikebreakers were "keeping house," although, the census may not indicate what historian Paul Michel Tailon tells us, which is that many female relations of railroaders took in boarders, and washed or sewed clothes or sold small items to help the household get by. The reference to railroaders is important because 53 percent of strikebreakers and 39 percent of those strikers found in the census had worked for a sustained period as a railroader (they were railroad men in 1880 and 1886). Examining the biographical information that some participants gave the committee, we find that nine of fourteen of the strikebreakers for whom we have specific information had worked on the railroads for two years or more. For strikers, thirteen of twenty-two had done so.[53]

If a considerable number of participants were railroaders, probably it was the case that a significant number of strikers and strikebreakers were not strangers to one another, because 40 percent (of each group) had remained in the same town for at least six years, since at least 1880. Strikebreaker McGee was an established resident of Palestine, Texas, a major strike town. By 1886 he had labored nine years for the railroad. In a small place like Palestine, and as a one-time member of the order, he inevitably would have known striker F. M. Jones, who was a local Knights executive board member and, in 1880, a labor gang boss, or Charles Eika, a leader of Palestine's black local, New Hope Assembly. Strikers Ben Metz, Charles Williams, Thomas Robinson, and Thomas Dugan were neighbors in De Soto in 1880, and may well have known John Duffy, an engineer and a strikebreaker in 1886. Moreover, because railroading was an occupation that brought workers, especially trainmen, from different towns into frequent contact with one another, and because this was the "boomer" era in which railroaders worked for one road and then another, it makes sense to broaden our scope to consider men who may well have interacted in various places along the system. In addition to the 40 percent from each group who persisted in the same town between 1880 and 1886, an additional quarter of strikebreakers and quarter of strikers in 1880 lived in 1886 in a different small town located along the lines of Gould's Southwest system. Strikebreaker John Doyle was a Denison railroad employee in 1880 but a De Soto foreman by the time of the strike. Joseph Gettler was a Denison striker who worked in Marshall as a machinist in 1880. It is noteworthy that he also lived among railroaders of various skills, as did blacksmith Benjamin Holden, a Sedalia striker in 1886 and a laborer in Moberly, Missouri, six years prior. According to the data collected, which is in line with the general picture of living patterns in railroad towns, it was not at all uncommon to find men boarding with other railroaders, boarding railroaders in their homes, or living in neighborhoods that mixed boarders and more established residents.[54]

This comparison of participants' backgrounds indicates that the most significant fissure between strikers and strikebreakers was not social background. The qualitative evidence bears this statement out. Like race, ethnicity was not a subject of comment in the newspapers during the conflict or in the transcript. Nor did the conflict seem to revolve around insiders and outsiders or older, invested conservatives and youthful militants. If two newspapers were correct in their reports that about half of strikebreakers were "strangers"—probably unemployed men from out of town—then about half were not. They were returning skilled trainmen, men idled by the walkout, and ex-strikers. Strikebreakers and strikers often knew one another. Engineer Nathan Karl recognized many of the shopmen who raided the round-house that he guarded. Knights in Kansas City urged J. W. Shea to leave town when someone recognized him as a "Company Man" from Little Rock. While at least one Knight warned engineers that strikebreaking trainmen would endure the same treatment in the future—"Men no longer have to be gray-headed to run engines or steamboats"—other evidence points to the stability and recognition that a number of Knights enjoyed in their communities.[55] In numerous locales, early on, Knights "appointed a large number of guards, who took possession of the yards and shops."[56] The Knights often claimed that they sought to protect railroad property from damage by renegade strikers or vandals. Local authorities had enough confidence in them to appoint Knights as deputies for a time to safeguard yards, shops, and round-houses. Finally, while ultimately most brotherhood men opted to run the trains, this was not a conflict between the skilled and unskilled. Skilled shopmen played a prominent role in the Knights and no one skill or occupation dominates in the list of arrestees.[57]

The available evidence suggests that the chief fissure was instead cultural, or more precisely, philosophic. In the wake of various assaults on the Knights' legal right to conduct a peaceful strike, workers divided over the meaning of "free labor." Strikebreakers who identified with Hoxie's formulation, which held up an individual's choice on the labor market as sacrosanct and portrayed unionism as despotic and anarchic, stood at one pole of this debate. Knights who threatened the imperilment of strikebreakers' and railway officials' lives in order to secure collective power for workers occupied the other pole. In the middle, strikers and strikebreakers expressed an array of positions that sought some "rough compromise" between individual prerogatives and collective ones. The culture of railroading appears to have influenced some of the positions that they took.

On one part of this middle ground were strikebreakers who did not out-of-hand reject unions or strikes. Some had merely grown desperate. Knights urged Charles Redding of Atchison against going to work several times, but he started switching in the yard in early April. "I didn't feel, under the circumstances that I was in, that I could afford [not to]." A number regarded the strike as merely unwarranted. A former Knight stated simply to the committee, "I did not think that the cause was a just one." Peter McGee was also a one-time Knight who claimed that many Knights wanted to go back to work. When a committee visited him in the night to persuade him to stay out, he answered, "I had been out long enough, and I could not see any just reason for remaining out any longer." Others argued not with the justice of the strike but its wisdom, such as a local Knights assembly in Downs, Kansas, which resolved "to allow all of the striking employés . . . belonging to this local assembly to resume work."[58] In St. Louis, engineers were purportedly "to a man . . . ardently in sympathy with the strikers," but the BLE's order that its members run the trains convinced most to buckle. One revealed, "I am sorry we have got to do this, because some of the best friends I have got in this world work in that shop. But the Knights should remember we have got some obligations we are bound to respect."[59] None of these actors invoked an individualist ideology or intimated a rejection of the right to strike per se, or even the tactics of the Knights. Did the Knights have cause to walk out, the ability to maintain a lengthy, flagging effort, or the power to protect trainmen from their brotherhoods? These were the salient issues for these men. Their utilitarian outlook led them in the end to place self-preservation above what seemed an increasingly out-of-reach goal after mid-March—union recognition for Gould system Knights.

Some vacillated between their commitments to communalism and individualism. Machinist Daniel Millory was a strike leader who served on a local grievance committee and co-authored a major DA 101 document entitled "The Spark Which Kindled the Conflagration," but returned to work on April 1 "on account of Mr. Powderly's order," refused to quit again, and became "disconnected with the order." He had held a "dislike of the strike" from its inception, because, he maintained, DA 101 had failed to exhaust every possible alternative to the walkout. Although Millory told the congressional committee that he had "retired" from the Knights, when pushed to testify as to the identity of his co-author, he repeatedly refused. "I certainly do not want to injure my obligation," he insisted, relenting only when a prominent Knights representative reassured him.[60] A. N. Christy went back and forth across strike lines. Christy was a foreman painter who was laid off on the second day of the walkout and later discharged and so did not consider himself a striker. At some point he took up the Knights' cause because he "went back to work when we were ordered back [by DA 101]." However, although Christy disobeyed the subsequent order to go out again, the ordeal of laboring under the supervision of "a lot of deputy sheriffs" troubled his ideals about liberty enough that he quit. "I would just as soon go to work in the street with a ball and chain. I am no convict," he testified.[61] Both men revealed mixed feelings about the walkout. Millory was torn between his own personal stance and his ties and responsibilities to the Knights. Christy alternated between his allegiance to the Knights' emphasis on mutual protection and mutual sacrifice, and his willingness to remain at work as a strikebreaker, although, in the end, he found the latter more oppressive than the former. Ambivalence probably also plagued a number of engineers; the BLE's directive to refuse aid to the Knights reportedly caused a "wrangle" among them. In Sedalia, BLE members took a stand against the strike but only after meeting for two days.[62] One lamented, "If we stand with the strikers, 'scab' runners will take our places, and if we desert the strikers, they themselves will drive us from the road . . . It is plain that we hold the key to the situation and if we were free to act with these men the strike would be settled in twenty-four hours."[63]

Other strikebreakers were firmly anti-strike in part because they held a strong level of discomfort with those strike tactics that went far beyond moral suasion and the protection of railroad property. Outside of town, quite early in the strike, De Soto engineer and BLE representative M. Roberts saw a man throw a switch in front of his running engine, which was pulling a boycotted T&P car. "The result," he testified, "was it ditched my engine and nine cars right in the face of a passenger train on the south bound track." A wreck was averted, and nothing concrete pointed to the culpability of the union, but he considered the ditching of his engine a "cowardly low trick." A few days later, after a meeting with the Knights in which Roberts spoke against the walkout, a committee visited his home and sickened his wife with the news that he would be "roughly treated" if he continued to run trains. He also found that strikers had raided the roundhouse, disabled his engine as well as the others, and "carried away" the parts, which were never returned. At the meeting he had argued, "The company had lived up strictly to their contract and that we, as men, proposed to do the same thing." The strike would "only injure the prospect of those men in De Soto that had little homes there and living comfortably." He appealed to them to refrain from violence, which they promised to do. Roberts later related to the committee, "They [the Knights] were all friends of mine. I told them I had nothing but my duty, and that while I sympathized with them personally, I couldn't uphold the work they were doing."[64]

Roberts' narrative relates several reasons for his decision to refuse aid to the Knights. He hopes to protect the engineers' contract and established railroaders' pecuniary interest in their communities. Roberts is also hurt personally that he is a target of intimidation and possible assassination by people who had been friends of his. As a conservative brotherhood man, he extended the boundaries of solidarity to only engineers, and seemed to conceive of the contract as the embodiment of the harmony that was possible when capital and "responsible" labor respected the interests and integrity of the other. Perhaps even more than this, Roberts reacts to these events as a railroad man. Engine ditching endangered the crew and public safety, which engineers, as commanders of their locomotives and "heroes of the rail," were supposed to take to heart. Popular tales, published in the BLE journal and the mainstream press, had long celebrated those qualities that aided engineers in controlling massive, moving, complicated equipment under all sorts of dangerous conditions— technical know-how, "coolness and nerve" in a crisis, resourcefulness, and physical endurance and adroitness. While the public showered much of its attention on skilled trainmen, and white, native-born men claimed that only they possessed these qualities, in fact many kinds of railroaders, from unskilled trackmen to semi-skilled brakemen and skilled shopmen, required all or most of these attributes to perform their work well—to keep themselves in one piece and to preserve the lives and limbs of passengers and fellow railroaders.[65]

The sense of dignity and responsibility that railroaders identified with was linked closely to nineteenth-century notions of manliness; the traits of a good railroad man were understood to be naturally masculine and a measure of manliness. Beyond a workplace culture that "marked worth" between men and apart from women, railroading also reinforced the larger culture's association between manhood and a breadwinner role. Railroad companies' cost-cutting policies, as well as a prolonged strike in which Knights had little legal room to contest those policies, put railroaders' manhood in question. Thus, participants attacked one another as unmanly. "The same toughness workers displayed on the job" suggested to some that they should endure policies such as the speed-up and fight to provide for their families by returning to work. Strikebreakers characterized Knights as poor providers for jeopardizing their livelihoods and as cowards for hiding their identities in written warnings.[66] Strikers returned the insult. One impugned the character of those who would abandon fraternal ties: "We have not the railway company to fight, but the men in our own ranks who like you weaken and fall by the wayside . . .. Remember the obligation you have taken at the alter." The participation of women and boys in crowd actions seemed to strengthen the Knights' claim that Gould system policies threatened railroaders' provider role. More militant Knights likened the struggle against Gould to a battle, a true test of manhood: "Cowards to the rear, scabs to the enemy, and men to the front . . .. Let us die when victory is assured to the generations behind us."[67]

Strike tactics that deliberately placed the public and railroaders at great risk on the job violated a gendered workplace culture that Roberts and other railroaders, striker and strikebreaker alike, shared, as the case of Eugene Perry illustrates. Perry was a shopman and a Knights leader in Sedalia, who had led crowds in stopping and disabling engines. He returned to work, however, shortly after four strikebreakers suffered injuries in a train wreck allegedly caused by track tampering.[68] Indeed, Knights leaders distanced the organization from this form of violence. They charged that the increased incidence of fire, wrecks, and near-wrecks was a consequence of the railroads' negligence in maintaining the roads or conditions unrelated to the strike.[69] In this argument they had some support from even strike opponents, like the editor of the *Dallas Morning News*, who doubted that a train wreck outside of Fort Worth was necessarily the order's work. He ventured that perhaps it was due to a "bad place in the track," as the paper had only days before reported on the poor condition of T&P road given that few men would labor for the low wages offered. Regardless of the Knights' claims, the public blamed the incident, in which the engineer and firemen suffered gruesome deaths, on the walkout. A similar assumption reigned among Atchison's skilled trainmen, despite the Knights' protestations, after an alleged train-ditching badly injured the engineer and crushed and scalded the fireman and brakeman.[70]

Train-wrecking, whether real or imagined, also alarmed strike participants for broader cultural reasons. For many nineteenth century observers, such actions seemed to elevate the specific interests of the Knights above all other claims and thus to represent, like Gould's railway monopoly, a selfish force with little regard for the fate of individuals or the larger good.[71] Similarly, the large-scale intimidation and violence that strikebreakers confronted also troubled participants on both sides of the strike divide. Strikebreakers time and again testified to this before the congressional committee. They presented to the committee and had transcribed into the record the threatening notes that they had received and descriptions of the violence that they met with in the streets, on the trains, and in the shops and yards.[72] A considerable number of Knights shared their alarm and dismay and sought to separate the order from these tactics by blaming an uncontrollable minority within the order. Local leader J. H. Cooper, for instance, declared: "The first thing we want to do is to use brains instead of muscle. If I can persuade you to leave your engine or to leave any other vocation, if I talk to you, I have a perfect right to do so . . . but I have no right to use physical force." Cooper acknowledged that this outlook was not universally shared among strikers:

> Railroad men are not all saints and the men that worked for them, the blacksmiths and the laborers, are not all saints . . . . The gentleman has spoken here about there being bad men in the Knights of Labor. Great God, they are in the church. They are in the best of families. There are black sheep in all families and we can't keep them out; but we are banded together.[73]

Even some strikers who authored warning letters to strikebreakers betrayed ambivalence about the use of force, especially against men whom they knew. A March 22 letter to engineers and firemen implored that they remember their common bonds with Knights as citizens, workers, fellow men, and unionists at the same time they threatened bodily harm, apparently in the hope that their appeals would make violence unnecessary: "We warn you not to run trains out of Atchison. It is with regret we tell you, as we call you Brothers. If you do your life will pay the forfeit. Boys, we want to throw off the YOKE of SERFDOM and be FREE men like yourselves. Don't deny us what at one time you prayed for."[74] Other messages were cast more in the spirit of tipping off men in the line of fire rather than targeting an adversary. No explicit threat surfaces in an April 5 communication to engineers and firemen in Fort Worth. The author, "Your True Friend," begins, "You are respectfully requested to desist running trains" because to do so would "assist Jay Gould in his endeavors to crush the poor laboring men of the country who have created his millions of wealth." It then cautions, without apparent malice, "Your disinclination to follow the advice will be at your own peril. . . . [T]here may be danger ahead; beware of breakers."[75] The danger was real. An engineer, only two days prior had pulled a train out of Fort Worth with the help of a force of deputy sheriffs. Mysteriously, a woman had waved a red flag frantically in front of the engine as it left. Just outside of town, the deputies clashed with armed men in a melee that ended with several dead and wounded among both strikers and deputies.[76]

One might dismiss the frequent reports of union violence, which railway officials exaggerated in order to discredit strikers, and probably also because the specter of 1877 haunted them still. They consistently equated the disablement or destruction of property with violence, for example, and on occasion associated pro-strike figures with the turmoil of the Great Strikes of that year.[77] The fact remains that a major feature of the strike, sanctioned or not, was violence or the threat of violence. Individual strikebreakers were set upon along the Gould system, in their homes, on the streets, and at work, especially in East St. Louis. Although railway officials' charge that strikebreakers experienced a "reign of terror and absolute subjection" exaggerated events and ignored the disorder that railroad company policies and court orders wrought, other observers testified that civil authorities could not contain the violence and that retribution against strikebreakers was encouraged by Martin Irons, chief leader of DA 101.[78] Knights leaders and their allies explained these and other events by pointing to the larger context of brutality. Violence was a fact of life in railway work, as Marshall Knights leader C. A. Hall noted when questioned about deaths associated with a suspected train-ditching: "Engineers are killed very often when there is no strike on." The comment alludes to the high risks of injury and death that late nineteenth-century railroaders faced. This was an era of "carnage," to which management decisions regarding work pace and hours directly contributed.[79] The deployment of deputies and U.S. marshals was also brutal. Railroad-paid deputies carrying Winchester rifles lined the tops of trains, expelled strikers from the yards and shops, and forced back crowds with the butts of their weapons, and it was the "indiscreet and overbearing" approach of the U.S. marshals on the T&P that had incited mayhem in Fort Worth and elsewhere, one leader held. Another, the Judge Advocate of the Texas Knights of Labor, questioned the sincerity of those who loudly defended strikebreakers' freedom of contract but then quietly ignored "the power used by these corporations in using the United States Court to force free labor into worse than slavery." Similarly, "injustice and arbitrary power," which critics of the strike called on railroaders and their relations to endure in the interest of public commerce and public order, were a kind of violence, implied C. F. O'Leary, a De Soto Catholic priest who had "counseled peace" during the walkout. He reprimanded the committee, "Poverty and exasperation lead to demoralization . . .. To tell people to bear grievances is moralizing."[80]

These pro-Knights figures argued that, without recognition of the collective rights of railroad workers to organize, both individual rights and the broader "public good" suffered under the domination of the "arch-monopolist" Gould.[81] None went so far as to advocate violence, but clearly a significant number of Knights disagreed and saw violence as a means to secure communal goals. In this they met with considerable resistance, from strikebreakers and a large element of the Knights, many of whom condemned the use of force as bad strategy and poor principle. One explained to the congressional committee, "I considered it wrong and unbecoming a Knight of Labor . . . and . . . it was something for the railroad company to get a hold on us for."[82] Perhaps with this view in mind, many strikers relied on the mass action of crowds in their attempts to blockade freight traffic. While militant and combative, these measures did not usually involve physical violence against persons but simply the use of a crowd's large numbers to overwhelm guards and strikebreakers in order to disable, destroy, or seize the equipment necessary to run trains. Still, Knights parted ways over tactics here, too. Denison striker Elvis Roberts, the foreman of a labor gang, condemned "injuring property" but not "holding" it, while Knights leader George Bibb of Marshall, rejected not only threats against and assaults on strikebreakers and the imperilment of the traveling public and trainmen but also any interference with company property. The committee pressed him, should a strike simply entail that "the men shall be at liberty to walk out when they please?" Bibb answered affirmatively—this was the only rightful way to win a strike, even though, as he conceded, such a protest would not "do much good" where laborers were plentiful, desperate for work, and unorganized.[83]

In a way, George Bibb and like-minded Knights occupied one stretch of what was left of the middle ground in the aftermath of the 1886 Southwest strike, except the space that he staked out was a kind of no-man's land. In the tradition of antebellum "free labor" ideology, Bibb defended the right to strike, the use of moral suasion, and the principle that, ultimately, strikebreakers should be free to assume strikers' places uninhibited. Yet the injunctions' terms and the brotherhoods' stance had denied to Knights the use of non-violent moral suasion, and many of his fellow Knights had embraced militant seizure of railroad property and, some unknown number, physical violence.

New Questions for Labor Historians

By mid-April, the walkout was effectively over. Injunctions were in full force against strikers, freight trains were in motion, and state militia had suppressed both peaceable and violent union activity along the lines of the T&P and in East St. Louis, where deputies had exchanged fire with strike supporters on April 9, setting off an incendiary rampage against railway cars and yards in the city.[84] One approach to the strike might end here, with a focus on the mighty role of Gould and the courts in the defeat of the walkout and the rapid decline of the Knights' industrial unionism. However, this would miss an aspect of the story that mattered a good deal to Bibb and other participants. In the walkout's first phase, numerous brotherhood men, who traditionally were at pains to empathize with nonbrotherhood men, made an impassioned and determined effort to carve out with strikers some kind of accommodation on the basis of moral suasion. They did so because many railroaders were friends, neighbors, or acquaintances and part of a larger work culture. Most had worked under the pressures of the railroad companies' attempts to cut labor costs and to assume greater control of the workforce. The victory in 1885 over seemingly omnipotent forces demonstrated to Knights and brotherhood men the power of "free labor" as they understood it, but the situation changed rapidly in mid and late March. As skilled trainmen obeyed their union leaders, and as authorities moved in to protect both solvent and insolvent roads from even non violent protest, strikebreakers' numbers multiplied, and hostilities grew. Whichever position participants took, a considerable number arrived at, or tried to secure, a position somewhere between individualism and communalism, between freedom-of-contract on the one hand and large-scale, potentially deadly union violence on the other. In doing so, they drew on what many of them knew and shared in common—popular notions of manhood, older ideas about "free labor," and railroading culture, none of which offered clear answers in the end to the new reality that they confronted. By the strike's end, alliances, friendships, and neighborhood ties had been dealt a terrible blow, as had the cohesion and relevance of the broader culture that many unionists and strikebreakers shared.

The ambiguities present in strikers' and strikebreakers' positions and their search, particularly early on in the strike, from unequal positions of power, to work out some mutual solution suggest further research on these questions: To what extent did strikebreakers and strikers in other contexts share or reshape the freedom of contract ideal that judges embraced?[85] In the wake of the strike's defeat, what was the fate of the relationship between strikebreakers and former strikers, as they labored on the Gould system and other railways? Finally, what did it mean for strike participants to eschew the employment of violence in labor protest in a period in which lynching and domestic violence were common and typically not prosecuted? As Betsy Jameson, a historian of labor wars in the Colorado minefields, once commented, there is a

> larger picture of violence—work was violent (death by dynamite explosions); home and leisure could both be violent; labor, employers, and the state were all violent. The comparative perspective might help us both dissect a culture of normative violence, and also get us out of a dead-end debate about who was good or bad, who was the most violent, to the issues around which all sides mobilized, both peacefully and violently.[86]

There is social and cultural history to be told, in other words, about how Industrial Era labor protests unfolded, on both side of the strike divide, as working people sought to reconcile individualism and communalism in a context in which older notions of free labor were in crisis.

Notes

1. William M. Tuttle Jr., "Some Strikebreakers' Observations of Industrial Warfare," *Labor History* 7 (2) (Spring, 1966): 193–97 (quotation, 193).
2. Even some of the best histories of strikes use, without quotations, the derogatory term "scab," which connotes despicableness, treachery, and gutlessness, even as their authors deal in an otherwise balanced and insightful way with strikebreakers. A brief sampling: Richard L. Ehrlich, "Immigrant Strikebreaking Activity: A Sampling of Opinion Expressed in the National Labor Tribune, 1878–1885," *Labor History* 15 (4) (Fall, 1974): 529–42; Paul Krause, *The Battle for Homestead, 1880–1892: Politics, Culture, and Steel* (Pittsburgh: University of Pittsburgh Press, 1992); Sarah M. Henry, "The Strikers and Their Sympathizers: Brooklyn in the Trolley Strike of 1895," *Labor History* 32 (3) (Summer, 1991): 329–53; Michael Honey, *Southern Labor and Black Civil Rights: Organizing Memphis Workers* (Urbana, IL: University of Illinois Press, 1993); Ardis Cameron, *Radicals of the Worst Sort: Laboring Women in Lawrence, Massachusetts, 1860–1912* (Urbana, IL: University of Illinois Press, 1995). According to Karl Marx, the reserve army of labor is not comprised, for the most part of unemployable people, or produced periodically by market inefficiencies; it is a regular feature of an economy that requires labor competition in order to secure the command of employers over the workplace and thus to allow business to expand. See Alexander Keyssar, *Out of Work: The First Century of Unemployment in Massachusetts* (New York: Cambridge University Press, 1986), 69–75.
3. Stephen H. Norwood, *Strikebreaking & Intimidation: Mercenaries and Masculinity in Twentieth-Century America* (Chapel Hill: University of North Carolina Press, 2002), 7–12. Scholarly treatment of strikebreakers as a reserve army of labor is at times implicit. John W. Hevener, for example, discusses how during the early 1930s the forces of "hunger and military occupation" drove even pro-union coal miners of Harlan County, Kentucky, back to work, and Shelton Stromquist links the pattern of railway strikes in the late nineteenth century to the "shifting frontiers of labor scarcity" and the struggle between railway managers and workers to influence the supply of labor. John W. Heverton, *Which Side Are You On?: The Harlan County Coal Miners, 1931–1939* (Urbana, IL: University of Illinois Press, 1978), 46–51 (quotation, 49); Shelton Stromquist, *A Generation of Boomers: The Pattern of Railroad Labor Conflict in Nineteenth-Century America* (Chicago: University of Illinois Press, 1987), 57–58, 100–01, 127, 130–33, 268–69.
4. James R. Barrett, "Unity and Fragmentation: Class: Race, and Ethnicity on Chicago's South Side, 1900–1922" in Dirk Hoerder, ed. *Struggle a Hard Battle: Essays on Working-Class Immigrants* (DeKalb, IL: Northern Illinois University Press, 1986), 230–323; Ava Baron, "On Looking at Men: Masculinity and the Making of a Gendered Working-Class History" in Ann-Louise Shapiro, ed.

Feminists Re-Vision History (New Brunswick, NJ: Rutgers University Press, 1994); Alice Kessler-Harris, *Gendering Labor History* (Urbana, IL: University of Illinois Press, 2007).

5. Tuttle made a classic contribution with *Race Riot: Chicago in the Red Summer of 1919* (New York: Atheneum, 1970; reprint, University of Illinois Press, 1996). Other key works are: Eric Arnesen, "Specter of the Black Strikebreaker: Race, Employment, and Labor Activism in the Industrial Era," *Labor History* 44 (3) (Winter, 2003): 319–35; Warren C. Whatley, "African-American Strikebreaking from the Civil War to the New Deal," *Social Science History* 17 (4) (Winter, 1993): 525–58; James R. Barrett, *Work and Community in the Jungle: Chicago's Packinghouse Workers, 1894–1922* (Urbana, IL: University of Illinois Press, 1987); and Rick Halpern, *Down On the Killing Floor: Black and White Workers in Chicago's Packinghouses, 1904–54* (Urbana, IL: University of Illinois Press, 1997). The debate over race and labor relates to strikebreaking. Two good starting points are Eric Arnesen, "Up from Exclusion: Black and White Workers, Race, and the State of Labor History," *Reviews in American History* 26 (1) (March 1998): 146–74, and "Scholarly Controversy: Whiteness and the Historians' Imagination" in *International Labor and Working-Class History* 60 (Fall, 2001), and Peter Kolchin, "Whiteness Studies: The New History of Race in America," *Journal of American History* 89 (1) (June 2002): 154–73.

6. Robert Michael Smith, *From Blackjacks to Briefcases: A History of Commercialized Strikebreaking and Unionbusting in the United States* (Athens, OH: Ohio University Press, 2003), 7–14; Norwood, *Strikebreaking & Intimidation*; Joshua L. Rosenbloom, *Looking for Work, Searching for Workers: American Labor Markets during Industrialization* (New York: Cambridge University Press, 2002); Jerry Cooper, "The Army as Strikebreaker: The Railroad Strikes of 1877 and 1894," *Labor History* 18 (3) (Spring, 1977): 179–96. Army officers tended to defend the military's involvement in strike repression as a necessary protection of property and order.

7. H. M. Gitelman, "Perspectives on American Industrial Violence," *Business History Review* 47 (1) (Spring, 1973): 1–23.

8. Cameron, *Radicals of the Worst Sort*, 158; Timothy J. Minchin, "Torn Apart: Permanent Replacements and the Crossett Strike of 1985," *Arkansas Historical Quarterly* 59 (1) (Spring, 2000): 30–58, "Broken Spirits: Permanent Replacements and the Rumford Strike of 1986," *New England Quarterly* 74 (1) (March 2001): 5–31, "Permanent Replacements and the Breakdown of the 'Social Accord' in Calera, Alabama, 1974–1999," *Labor History* 41 (4) (November 2001): 371–96, and "'Labor's Empty Gun': Permanent Replacements and the International Paper Company Strike of 1987–88," *Labor History* 47 (1) (2006): 21–42; James Sidbury, *Ploughshares into Swords: Race, Rebellion, and Identity in Gabriel's Virginia, 1730–1810* (Cambridge, UK: Cambridge University Press, 1997), 95. An earlier piece on striker-strikebreaker interactions in mining is George B. Cotkin, "Strikebreakers, Evictions and Violence: Industrial Conflict in the Hocking Valley, 1884–1885," *Ohio History* 87: 140–50 (see *Ohio History* Online Archive, http://publications.ohiohistory.org/).

9. The quotation comes from Herbert Gutman's famous observation: "A central tension in all dependent groups over time has been between individualist (utilitarian) and collective (mutualist) ways of dealing with, and sometimes overcoming dependence and inequality." Herbert Gutman, *Power & Culture: Essays on the American Working-Class* (New York: Pantheon Books, 1987), 327.

10. See Theresa A. Case, *The Great Southwest Railroad Strike and Free Labor* (College Station, TX: Texas A&M Press, 2010).

11. Ibid.

12. Engineers were charged with the safety of the train across miles of track, its timely departure and arrival, and management of the locomotive's steam pressure. Firemen helped to control the production of steam by heaving just enough coal into the firebox and forcing enough water. See Paul Michel Taillon, *Good Reliable White Men: Railroad Brotherhoods, 1877–1917* (Urbana, IL: University of Illinois Press, 2009), 18; B. B. Adams, "The Every-Day Life of Railroad Men," in T. C. Clarke, ed. *The American Railway* (New York: Charles Scribner's Sons, 1889), 403.

13. *St. Louis Post-Dispatch*, March 6, 1886; *Investigation of Labor Troubles*, I, 401, 407, 449; *Dallas Morning News*, March 2, 1886.

14. Eric Arnesen, " 'Like Banquo's Ghost, It Will Not Down': The Race Question and the American Railroad Brotherhoods, 1880–1920," *American Historical Review* 99 (5)(December 1994): 1612–17; Stromquist, *Generation of Boomers*, 133; Donald McMurry, *The Great Burlington Strike of 1888: A Case Study in Labor Relations* (Cambridge, MA: Harvard University Press, 1956), 29–34.

15. *Locomotive Engineers' Monthly Journal* 19 (5) (May 1885): 275–76; *St. Louis Globe-Democrat*, March 6, 12, 1885; *Dallas Weekly Herald*, March 12, 1885.

16. *Investigation of Labor Troubles*, I, 176, 421, II, 84, 109; McMurry, *The Great Burlington Strike of 1888*, 34–36.

17. Letter from Knights in Moberly, MO, to Terence Powderly, September 23, 1885, and Jay Gould to Terence Powderly, October 11, 1885, Incoming Correspondence, Reel 10, Terence Vincent Powderly Papers, The American Catholic History Research Center and University Archives, Catholic University, Washington (cited hereafter as TVPP); *Investigation of Labor Troubles*, I, 155–56, 159, 161, 167, 218–19, 225–26, 335–36, 378–79, 434–35, 448, 450–51, 466–67, 478–79, 485–86, 553–56; *Dallas Morning News*, March 10, 1886.

18. *Fort Worth Gazette*, March 4, 1886; *Investigation of Labor Troubles*, I, 369. For a fuller explanation of anti-Chinese and ant-convict labor sentiment among strikers, see Theresa A. Case, "The Radical Potential of the Knights' Biracialism: The 1885–1886 Gould System Strikes and Their Aftermath," *Labor: Studies in Working-Class History of the Americas* 4 (4) (Winter, 2007): 83–107.

19. *Investigation of Labor Troubles*, I, 334–36.

20. E. T. Behrens to Ruth Allen, Box 2E302, Folder 11, Labor Movement in Texas Collection, Center for American History, University of Texas at Austin (cited hereafter as LMTC); *Investigation of Labor Troubles*, I, 355, 378, 440, 553 (quotation).

21. *Marshall Tri-Weekly Herald*, March 11, 1886; *Dallas Morning News*, March 11, 1886.
22. Colin J. Davis, *Power At Odds: The 1922 National Railroad Shopmen's Strike* (Urbana, IL: University of Illinois Press, 1997); Stromquist, *A Generation of Boomers*, 105, 109–11.
23. *Dallas Morning News*, March 11, 14 (6th quotation), 16, 1886 (1st and 2nd quotations); *St. Louis Post-Dispatch*, March 12 (3rd quotation), 13 (5th quotation), 15, 1886; *Atchison Daily Globe*, March 12, 13 (4th quotation), 1886.
24. *Investigation of Labor Troubles*, I, 310; *Dallas Morning News*, March 12 (quotation), 14, 16, 19, 1886; *St. Louis Post-Dispatch*, March 13, 1886.
25. *Dallas Morning News*, March 12, 1886.
26. *St. Louis Globe Democrat*, March 14, 1886.
27. *Investigation of Labor Troubles*, II, 84, 85, 111.
28. *Investigation of Labor Troubles*, I, 176, 178, 179, 614–15.
29. David Brody, "Free Labor, Law, and American Trade Unionism," 223 (quotation), and Leon Fink, "From Autonomy to Abundance: Changing Beliefs About the Free Labor System in Nineteenth-Century America," 126–30, in Stanley L. Engerman, ed. *Terms of Labor: Slavery, Serfdom, and Free Labor* (Stanford, CA: Stanford University Press, 1999).
30. *Dallas Morning News*, March 2, 5, 1886; *Missouri Republican*, March 5, 1886; *Investigation of Labor Troubles*, I, 343.
31. Strike opponents associated the disorder created by the walkout with racial disorder and feared that the former had contributed to the latter. Racial issues occupied a prominent place in the debates among Knights after the strike over whether they should mobilize on a biracial basis politically to seek reform. See Case, *The Great Southwest Railroad Strike and Free Labor*, 214–20.
32. *Dallas Morning News*, March 5, 6, 10 (2nd quotation), 12, 14 (1st quotation), 20, 1886; *Missouri Republican*, March 5, 1886.
33. *Dallas Morning News*, March 5, 7, 10, 1886.
34. *Atchison Daily Globe*, March 12, 13, 1886; *Dallas Morning News*, March 6, 8, 11, 12, 1886; *St. Louis Post-Dispatch*, March 16, 1886. Find examples of these early uses of physical force against strikebreakers in *Investigation of Labor Troubles*, I, 110, 150.
35. *Marshall Tri-Weekly Herald*, March 11 (quotations), 1886.
36. *Marshall Tri-Weekly Herald*, March 11; *Atchison Daily Globe*, March 14, 1886; Donald L. McMurry, "The Legal Ancestry of the Pullman Strike Injunctions," *Industrial and Labor Relations Review* 14 (2) (January 1961): 237–39.
37. *St. Louis Post-Dispatch*, March 15, 1886; Nick Salvatore, *Eugene V. Debs: Citizen and Socialist* (Urbana, IL: University of Illinois Press, 1982), 68–69, 74. In the walkout's aftermath, the brotherhoods experienced intense internal division, and the BLE met with defeat in the 1888 Burlington strike in part because embittered rank-and-file Knights acted as strikebreakers. See McMurry, *The Great Burlington Strike of 1888*.
38. *Investigation of Labor Troubles*, I, 349–50.

39. Maury Klein, *The Life and Legend of Jay Gould* (Baltimore, MD: John Hopkins University Press, 1986), 361–62; *Waco Daily Examiner*, April 2, 1886. Contrasting analyses of Gould's motivations can be found in Klein and in Case, *Great Southwest Railroad Strike and Free Labor*.

40. *St. Louis Post Dispatch*, March 15, 1886 (2nd quotation); *Dallas Morning News*, March 16, 1886 (1st quotation).

41. *Dallas Morning News*, March 21; *Investigation of Labor Troubles*, II, 305, 348; *Fort Worth Gazette*, April 7, 1886; *Marshall Tri-Weekly Herald*, April 1, 1886 (quotations).

42. *Waco Daily Examiner*, March 27, 30, 1886. See also the description of the situation in East St. Louis in the April 4, 1886, edition of the same newspaper.

43. *Investigation of Labor Troubles*, II, 224, 227; *Fort Worth Gazette*, April 5, 1886 (1st quotation); *Dallas Morning News*, March 18, 1886 (2nd quotation); *St. Louis Post Dispatch*, March 27, 1886.

44. Terence Powderly, *The Path I Trod: The Autobiography of Terence V. Powderly*, Harry J. Carman, ed. (New York: Columbia University Press, 1940), 123.

45. *St. Louis Globe Democrat*, March 25, 1886; *Atchison Daily Champion*, March 24, 1884; *Investigation of Labor Troubles*, II, 152, 383, 387–88. See "This is Your Box" sketch on p. 383.

46. *Investigation of Labor Troubles*, II, 78–79.

47. *Investigation of Labor Troubles*, I, 371, 372, 375, 376, 392–394; *Labor Enquirer*, March 20, 1886; Bureau of Labor Statistics and Inspection of Missouri, *Official History of the Great Strike of 1886 on the Southwestern Railway System* (Jefferson City, MO: Tribune Printing Co., 1887), 51.

48. *Investigation of Labor Troubles*, I, 378–79; quoted in Brody, "Free Labor, Law, and American Trade Unionism," 233.

49. *Investigation of Labor Troubles*, II, 310 (quotation).

50. *Investigation of Labor Troubles*, I, 412.

51. *Investigation of Labor Troubles*, I, 415–18.

52. The newspapers are the *Dallas Morning News*, *St. Louis Globe Democrat*, the *Atchison Daily Champion*, or the *Atchison Daily Globe*. Unfortunately, city directories do not exist for Denison, De Soto, and Marshall. Note that the congressional committee inconsistently asked witnesses for biographical information.

53. *Investigation of Labor Troubles*, I and II; U.S. Department of the Interior, Census Office, Tenth Census of the United States, 1880, in Heritage Quest Online, http://persi.heritagequestonline.com/hqoweb/library/do/census/search/basic; Taillon, *Good Reliable White Men*, 24–25.

54. *Investigation of Labor Troubles*, I and II; Tenth Census, 1880, in Heritage Quest Online, http://persi.heritagequestonline.com/hqoweb/library/do/census/search/basic; Adams, "The Every-Day Life of Railroad Men," 401–02; Stromquist, *Generation of Boomers*, xiii; Taillon, *Good Reliable White Men*, 24–26.

55. *Investigation of Labor Troubles*, I, 209–11, 432–33; *Dallas Morning News*, March 19 (quotation), 1886.

56. *Dallas Morning News*, March 7, 8, 1886; *Investigation of Labor Troubles*, I, 324–28, 371–78, 393–94, 407 (2nd quotation), 560 (1st quotation); *Missouri Republican*, March 5, 1886; *St. Louis Post-Dispatch*, March 8, 1886.

57. *Investigation of Labor Troubles*, II, 298–99, 394–95; *Dallas Morning News*, March 8, 1886. Strike towns in which Knights entered railroad grounds to seize, hide, or disable equipment include Atchison, Sedalia, Parsons, Denison, De Soto, Marshall, Whitesborough, Waco, Taylor, Big Springs, Mineola, Texarkana, and Alvarado. The list of arrestees overlaps a great deal with the list of strikers gathered from the testimony and newspaper reports.

58. *Investigation of Labor Troubles*, I, 132 (3rd quotation), 160 (1st quotation), II, 83 (2nd quotation).

59. *St. Louis Globe Democrat*, March 14, 1886.

60. *Investigation of Labor Troubles*, II, 316.

61. *Investigation of Labor Troubles*, I, 153.

62. *Dallas Morning News*, March 18, 19, 1886.

63. *Dallas Morning News*, March 18, 1886.

64. *Investigation of Labor Troubles*, I, 424–25.

65. For an explanation of the cultural significance that railroaders often attached to their occupation, see chapter two, "Labor Kinship" in Case, *Great Southwest Railroad Strike and Free Labor*, 45–70.

66. *Investigation of Labor Troubles*, I, 400, 415–18, 428; Paul Michel Taillon, "Culture, Politics, and the Making of the Railroad Brotherhoods, 1863–1916" (Ph.D. diss., University of Wisconsin at Madison, 1997), 48, 83 (quotations). For a gender analysis of the professional strikebreaking business in the first three decades of the twentieth century, see Norwood, *Strikebreaking and Intimidation*. Julia Guard questions the assumption that class concerns are the common ground for an otherwise divided workforce. See "Authenticity on the Line: Women Workers, Native 'Scabs,' and the Multi-Ethnic Politics of Identity in a Left-led Strike in Cold War Canada," *Journal of Women's History* 15 (4) (2004): 117–40.

67. *Investigation of Labor Troubles*, I, 617 (1st quotation), 388; Charles Maier, "The Realization of My Boyhood Dream," 24–26, Box 2E302, Folder 2, LMTC; *St. Louis Globe-Democrat*, March 26, 1886 (2nd quotation).

68. Cassity, *Defending a Way of Life*, 142–43. Knights in Holden, Kansas, denounced the alleged train-wrecking in Sedalia. See *Atchison Daily Champion*, March 26, 1886.

69. *Investigation of Labor Troubles*, II, 341–43.

70. *Dallas Morning News*, March 15 (quotation), 18, 19, 21, 1886; *Investigation of Labor Troubles*, I, 197–99, 230.

71. Melvyn Dubofsky, "The Federal Judiciary, Free Labor, and Equal Rights" in Richard Schneirov, Shelton Stromquist, Nick Salvatore, eds *The Pullman Strike and the Crisis of the 1890s: Essays on Labor and Politics* (Urbana, IL: University of Illinois Press, 1999), 166–67.

72. See, for example, *Investigation of Labor Troubles*, I, 134, 211, 315, 340, 374, 376, 377, II, 87, 105, 109, 149–50, 309, 383, 387–88, and *St. Louis Globe-Democrat*, March 16, 25, 26, April 29, 1886.
73. *Investigation of Labor Troubles*, I, 169–72.
74. *Investigation of Labor Troubles*, I, 200.
75. *Investigation of Labor Troubles*, II, 157.
76. *Investigation of Labor Troubles*, I, 490, 511, 533, II, 157; Ruth Allen, *The Great Southwest Strike* (Austin, TX: University of Texas Publications, 1942), 79–80.
77. *Investigation of Labor Troubles*, I, 493, 494, 503.
78. *Investigation of Labor Troubles*, I, 537–41, 562–63. An expanded analysis of the strike in East St. Louis can be found in Case, *Great Southwest Railroad Strike and Free Labor*, 197–200, 202.
79. *Investigation of Labor Troubles*, I, 357 (quotation); Mark Aldrich, *Death Rode the Rails: American Railroad Accidents and Safety, 1828–1965* (Baltimore, MD: John Hopkins University Press, 2006), 103–04.
80. *Dallas Morning News*, March 21 (2nd quotation), 22, 25 (1st quotation), 1886; *Investigation of Labor Troubles*, I, 470–71 (3rd quotation).
81. *St. Louis Globe-Democrat*, March 26, 1886.
82. *Fort Worth Gazette*, April 7, 1886; *Investigation of Labor Troubles*, I, 429.
83. *Investigation of Labor Troubles*, II, 131–33, 345–46. See also I, 541, II, 126, 259–60. Such mass actions were part of a long tradition of railway labor protest, although it is unclear how far back the debates over the limits of mass action go. See Shelton Stromquist, "'Our Rights as Workingmen': Class Traditions and Collective Action in a Nineteenth-Century Railroad Town, Hornellsville, N.Y., 1869–82" in David Stowell, ed. *The Great Strikes of 1877* (Urbana, IL: University of Illinois Press, 2008), 55–75.
84. See Case, *Great Southwest Railway Strike and Free Labor*.
85. Melvin Dubofsky asks a very similar question in "The Federal Judiciary, Free Labor, and Equal Rights" in Richard Schneirov, Shelton Stromquist, Nick Salvatore, eds *The Pullman Strike and the Crisis of the 1890s: Essays on Labor and Politics* (Urbana, IL: University of Illinois Press, 1999), an essay that in large part inspired my work here.
86. Betsy Jameson, October 14, 2002, H-Labor, Subject: "Violence and Taking Sides with Capital against Labor," http://www.h-net.org/~labor/ [Accessed: May 25, 2006].

CHAPTER THREE

Rethinking Working-Class Politics in Comparative-Transnational Contexts

Shelton Stromquist

The field of labor history, regarded by many in recent years as in crisis, stands at the cusp of a significant and invigorating redirection, comparable in some respects to the emergence of the "new labor history" from the institutional and intellectual moorings of the "old." Richard Ely and John R. Commons broke new ground in the study of labor during the decades around the turn of the nineteenth century, and their students and intellectual heirs carried forward the work of the "Wisconsin School" well into the post World War II era.[1] A "new labor history" that emerged from the path-breaking work of David Montgomery, Herbert Gutman, and David Brody refocused the study of workers on the structures, experience, and conflicts of daily life in the workplace and the community—what David Montgomery called "those daily experiences and visible social distinctions"—that bred class consciousness, ethnic working-class community, and a sharpened sense of the meaning of class, race, and gender as malleable constructions of social experience.[2] If our awareness of the relative significance and intersectionality of these identities has shifted in the last two decades, we have nonetheless continued to work largely within frameworks marked off by national boundaries and at least implicit assumptions of national exceptionality.[3] But these national boundaries are being breached from within and without. Like their colleagues in other subfields, labor historians have groped toward comparative points of reference and an awareness of transnational political and economic processes that have shaped outcomes, irrespective of national boundaries.[4] This essay examines the new directions in comparative and transnational labor history with particular attention to the practice of working-class politics locally and transnationally.

International and comparative labor history was hardly new at the end of the twentieth century. Comparativists had long since examined the rise and decline of the social democratic and cooperative movements, revolutionary syndicalism, and the mass strike in an international context. Indeed Commons' prize student, Selig Perlman, had compared the orientation of labor movements internationally in his quest for a "theory" of the labor movement that would explain what he perceived to be the American exception.[5]

A leading proponent of transnational and comparative history has for many years been the International Institute of Social History (IISG) in Amsterdam. Growing out of the history of its own collections—the records of European social democracy rescued from the clutches of the Nazis in the 1930s—the IISG became a primary center for initiative in the globalization of labor history scholarship. Its publications track the evolution of the field from multi-country studies to studies of comparative cases and transnational processes.[6] The Institute has continued to be a locus of innovation for transnational labor history, reorienting the field away from its traditional Euro-centric focus toward significant research and archival support for labor history in the "Third World."[7]

The practice of *transnational* and comparative labor history has taken significant turns in recent years. On the most basic level, labor historians have compared the working classes and labor movements of individual countries. Exemplary in this regard has been the work of Neville Kirk, whose explorations of the Anglo-imperial world have demonstrated, among other things, both working-class resistance to and collaboration in the British imperial project and the institutional legacies and inheritances that British workers diffused within that imperial world.[8] The collaboration of Canadian and Australian labor historians has produced the foundation for promising bipolar comparison of the processes of working-class formation in those countries.[9]

Fruitful multicountry comparisons of working classes in particular industrial sectors have also appeared. Here the work of Colin Davis on dockworkers in London and New York, Mary Hilson on Plymouth, England and Karlskrona, Sweden, and John Laslett on coal miners in Scotland and Illinois are especially noteworthy.[10] And, in some cases, such industrial comparisons have reached for a transnational or global scope that transcends specific locality or country comparisons. The essays on domestic labor, agriculture, coal mining, brick making, dock labor, and railway work in the IISG volume, *Global Labour History: A State of the Art* and Peter Linebaugh and Marcus Rediker's study of the maritime trades and laboring poor, slave and free, in the revolutionary Atlantic stand as important examples.[11]

Other areas of innovation in the past few decades have had a profound effect on studies of working classes globally. "Subaltern studies" emanating from South Asia opened new ways of conceptualizing the transnational relations of colonized and colonizer and have provided a model for social historians working "from the bottom up" to break the bounds of nation states. They have also contributed to a necessary re-imagining of working classes that embraces casual and informal sector workers, who have been critical to the expansion of the global manufacturing economy.[12] Historical comparisons of child labor transnationally have been relatively few. But, in the European context the comparative work of Hugh Cunningham has been pathbreaking, and recent studies have begun to challenge in a comparative context the conventional interpretive framework offered by "modernization theory."[13]

Studies of workers' migration and working-class internationalism have long histories that by definition have been transnational, though unevenly comparative.[14] But like migration, studies of the cross-fertilization of labor and socialist movements across borders and the hegemonic power of U.S. labor federations operating beyond their borders in the twentieth century have been the subject of renewed attention.[15]

A long-standing preoccupation of U.S. labor historians has been the albatross of Werner Sombart's provocative comparative question, "Warum gibt es keinen Sozialismus in den Vereinigten Staaten?" The paths around and through it have become diverse. Sean Wilentz suggested that a different, no less anticapitalist, republicanism characterized the dominant ideology of American workers, at least in the nineteenth century. Eric Foner raised the question of whether the United States was behind Europe in the development of social democracy or ahead in its demise. And, Katznelson and Zolberg asked "how many exceptionalisms?" might be needed to capture the politically diverse contexts of class formation in the industrializing world. While many historians are exasperated by what they regard to be an ahistorical effort to explain what did not happen, the Sombart question continues to be posed in both old and new, more rigorously comparative ways.[16]

Comparative Working-class Politics

The study of working-class politics has historically been constrained by the framework of the nation-state as the seemingly "natural" and inevitable vehicle by which workers might achieve greater public control of labor relations and the material circumstances and insecurities of workers' lives. But that national focus has been itself a historical artifact, the result, in part, of social democratic parliamentary aspirations to state power and ideological acquiescence to nationalism as an appropriate medium through which to legitimize workers' claims to power.[17] In recent decades the national locus of studies of labor politics has been challenged in three ways. First, building on older studies of the European left by G. D. H. Cole, Adolph Sturmthal, and others, a newer round of such studies has moved beyond surveys of national cases to conceptualize transnational politics in a continental context. Geoff Eley's transnational study of the European left and new scholarship on Latin American politics reflect such a development.[18] Second, a number of studies, in more rigorously comparative fashion, examine sets of paired national or local cases to uncover patterns of similarity and difference in political mobilization, ideological inclination, or tangible political outcomes.[19] Third, an emerging field of comparative working-class politics focuses on the municipality and its politics in a transnational context. Such studies break out of limitations of both the locality and the nation state as bounded worlds to suggest the vitality of the internationalist orientation of local political activism. Transnational studies of working-class movements such as the Knights of Labor and the Industrial Workers of the World contribute to such a reorientation.[20]

Despite such new directions in the comparative and transnational study of labor history, the field faces other challenges, and they are multifold. One of those challenges is reconceptualizing the relationship between the local, the national, and the international as a set of interlocking spheres of power and social action. Within this hierarchy of structures and political spaces labor historiography (like most historiography) has privileged the national, in relation to which both the local and the international have been viewed as peripheral. Certain features of our subject are inevitably local—the workplace, the community, the locally distinctive character of working-class culture—but the tendency for the "national" to override the local is often powerful. Yet much of the richest and most exciting labor history of the past generation in the United States has been rooted in community studies, the national and rarely transnational implications of which are at best implicit. An obvious exception might be Jefferson Cowie's, *Capital Moves*, where the interpretive spine of the work is both local and international. He examines Camden, NJ, Bloomington, IN, Memphis, TN, and Juarez, Mexico and the local impact of capital's transnationalization.[21] But for the most part we have failed to engage the concept of nationalism and the idea of the nation as a "construction" of specific historical and material circumstances.[22]

My own work, in seeking to resurrect the local (municipal) dimension of socialist politics *transnationally*, suggests that labor and socialist parties oriented to national parliamentary affairs and national party competition for power were in fact a contingent, historical construction, to some extent the product of the sea of nationalist ideology in which they swam and the nation-state vessels to which many leaders consigned their socialist identities.[23] While the evidence of an alternative, locally inspired internationalism abounds—a case in point being Broken Hill, New South Wales, Australia where a municipal movement grounded its local labor party activism in an internationalist context—labor and socialist parliamentarians in countries around the globe accepted the "nation" as the necessary and inevitable framework for [their] politics. In nationalizing politics, they marginalized local activists, a municipal socialist agenda, and a grassroots internationalism bred of common challenges posed by city life in a global industrial capitalist order.[24]

Eric Hobsbawm, Ernest Gellner, and Benedict Anderson, among others have focused attention on the bourgeois construction of the nation-state, a project by which elites attempted to navigate the social instability resulting from the rapid expansion of capitalism, the torrent of urbanization, and the social conflict such changes produced. An instrumentalist nationalism became, in Hobsbawm's phrase, an "invented tradition." As political theorist Umut Özkirimli observes, the capitalist social crisis "explains the importance of the idea of 'national community' which can secure cohesion in the face of fragmentation and disintegration caused by rapid industrialization." In short, he argues, during the volatile period from 1870 to 1914, the invented national community "was the main strategy adopted by the ruling elites to counter the threat posed by mass democracy."[25] One such threat came from the surging local movements pushing forward the expansion of local government services in ways that laid new claims on private property and challenged elite traditions of local governance. At the same time emerging labor and socialist party elites, in pursuit of access to centers of national power, adopted the "invented" nation as their primary sphere of political activity; in so doing they set up conflict within their own movements between local activists and the new parliamentary wings of their parties.[26] Much of the historiography of the social democratic left in this period has privileged the "national" and implicitly treated the "municipal" as secondary, if not peripheral.[27]

One of the challenges is to historicize the debate over the "national question" in the political practice of social democrats (c. 1890–1920) and in the subsequent historiography of social democracy. Social democracy, of the Second International variety, came of age with the high tide of late nineteenth-century nationalism, and aspiring social democratic politicians and theoreticians inevitably framed their project in national terms, however much they may still have gestured toward internationalist principles. Drawn to the quintessentially "modern" project of the bourgeois nationalists by their own positional struggles against socialist and anarchist "locals," social democratic leaders readily adopted the trappings of cosmopolitan moderns.[28] British labor parliamentarians fit this "modern" model perfectly; based on national political strategies they were detached from local constituencies to compete for seats for which they had no specific local claims.[29]

In the rise of social democracy the subordination and marginalization of local struggles to the agendas of labor and socialist parliamentary elites was widespread. Local activists challenged the parliamentarians over the place of municipal issues in their "fighting platforms." They resisted centralizing tendencies within the parties that undermined local control, and they remained wary of coalitional politics at the parliamentary level that grafted labor support onto liberal initiatives.[30] Some municipal activists continued to be fired by the radically inspirational history of the Paris Commune and the promise of a fundamental reconstruction of society from below.[31]

Localist politics within the emerging labor and socialist parties challenged the national framework of their respective movements with a different set of internationalist loyalties. This *localist internationalism* in the period I am considering (1890–1920) was fueled, for example, by transnational efforts of agitators such as Englishmen Tom Mann, Ben Tillett, E. R. Hartley in Australia, Michael Savage (and many others) who moved between Australia and New Zealand; the political sojourns of Christchurch's Jimmy Thorn in England, German Social Democrat Eduard Bernstein in London, Australian Claude Thompson and New Zealander Patrick Hickey in the United States, and Milwaukee socialist Walter Thomas Mills in New Zealand.

Bourgeois social reformers in the United States and elsewhere, as Daniel Rodgers has shown, built transnational networks of their own and, and as I argue elsewhere, seized the national mantle of reform as they sought to create a unifying, cross-class presence in civic life. While not aggressively or defensively nationalist (in the ways they would become with the outbreak of World War I), such reformers did invest national political communities with special meaning.[32]

Stefan Berger and Angel Smith have noted the commitment of social democrats to a "'great state' nationalism [that] lurked behind the internationalist rhetoric." They accepted the nation as the *natural* vehicle for democratic emancipation.[33] Even if their narratives emphasized the class character of the movement and its politics, they embraced with little question its national identity.[34] Historians of social democracy have likewise generally, though often unreflectively, adopted the national arena as the only political site worthy of close analysis. In so doing they have treated the municipality as marginal, at best a training ground for future parliamentarians.[35]

Imagining a counter-narrative requires a close reading of a different set of continuities. We might, for instance, trace the inspiration and impact of the Paris Commune on local socialist agitation, and examine more closely the political impact of the mass strikes of the 1880s and early 1890s across the industrializing world and the early optimism about the Second International, or we might consider the eruption of local municipal campaigns in the 1890s from which grassroots labor and socialist parties emerged, and then the continuing municipal activism within these movements with gradually increasing success in the period 1900–14.[36] During this same period parliamentarians contested for party leadership and asserted their national political agendas. The crisis of August 1914, of course, brought the nationalist-internationalist debate to the fore and splintered the socialist movement internationally along national lines but also within each country between local/anti-conscription forces and nationally aligned social democrats intent on power-sharing with liberal nationalists.[37]

Such an alternative narrative would place local cases within the context of an international movement not framed primarily by nation states. In the spirit of the "new labor history" the history of social democracy would require rewriting with closer attention to the grassroots political activism that addressed the day-to-day travails that workers faced in cities across the industrializing world. A vibrant socialist press and the international travels and exchanges of militants nurtured an organic internationalism that grew from such struggles. It survived the collapse of the Second International to fuel anti-conscription opposition to war-making national regimes.[38]

Although the precise timing and specific history varied from one municipality to another, similar patterns of local political activism can be observed in cities across the industrializing world: in Malmö and other Swedish cities, in manufacturing towns across the industrial North of Britain, in Vienna, Austria, Broken Hill (NSW), Brisbane, in Redfern and Glebe (Sydney), in Footscray, Fitzroy, Richmond, and Essendon (Melbourne), Australia, in Christchurch, Wellington, and Auckland, New Zealand, and in labor or socialist-oriented municipal administrations across a wide range of U.S. cities. The boundaries between municipal lib-labism and outright Labor Party activity in city politics were not always sharply drawn, and those politics advanced at different times under different labels.[39] Nonetheless, city affairs began to tilt under the influence of the political gravity labor brought to local politics. Sometimes the progress was more symbolic than real, or so incremental as to be barely discernible, but in other cases a minority labor interest in city council drew to its ranks around specific issues sympathetic liberal councilors and on occasion could constitute an effective, if ephemeral, majority. Labor's presence made a difference, if only by being able to shine the bright light of public attention into municipal affairs that had previously been shrouded from public view by an illusory consensus and arcane rituals and procedures of governance. What follows are a few case studies that highlight the birth pangs of a new labor and socialist municipal politics in an era of social democratic party building, burgeoning nationalism, and international crisis.[40]

Wellington: A Beachhead for Municipal Labor Politics

In New Zealand franchise reform opened the door at least partially in 1901 to participation of nonratepayers in municipal elections. And with that reform came the coalescence of what might be termed pre-party interest groups that focused on municipal issues and sought to recruit candidates sympathetic to their interests. In 1901, the Wellington Ratepayers' Association and the Wellington Progressive Municipal Association (PMA) each fielded slates for City Council, but both professed a desire to cooperate in preventing the intrusion of outright party politics into municipal affairs. The PMA supported for City Council two candidates associated with the labor movement, David McLaren and Alfred Hindmarsh. Of the two only McLaren, with close ties to waterfront workers' unions and a founding member of the New Zealand Socialist Party, was elected.[41]

Less than a year after being welcomed somewhat ambivalently by his fellow councilors, David McLaren, already a seasoned trade unionist not yet 30 years old, surprised his Council colleagues with an unprecedented proposal.[42] McLaren put before the Council a motion to appoint a special committee to "enquire into the existing provisions for the housing of the people within the city," adding that the Council might then be asked to take "such action . . . as may be deemed necessary."[43] Unable to come up with a good reason not to approve the motion, the Council appointed a "Housing of the Poor Committee," with McLaren as chair. And nine months later, with a completed housing census in hand, McLaren reported the results of the investigation to the Council. On behalf of his committee, he described the housing of the poor in Wellington as wholly unsatisfactory. McLaren managed to have the entire report, including a house-by-house inventory, transcribed into the minutes of the Council. The conclusion issued a ringing challenge.

> Having regard to the facts that a large proportion of the houses visited are unfit for habitation under conditions of cleanliness, decency, and health; that the rents charged are in excess of what the tenants are in a position to pay; that the existence of a large number of small houses at the rear of other buildings; [therefore] the existence of general bad conditions in many narrow lanes and the overcrowding of several dwellings make for the maintenance and increase of slum conditions.[44]

The final line of the report asked the Council to retain the committee "for the purpose of advising on the best means of improving the housing accommodations for the working class." Commissioning a report was one thing, but granting the committee power to lobby for remedies was quite another. Under duress, in order to get

Council acceptance of the report at all, McLaren substituted a more palatable alternative resolution—that the "facts as tabulated should receive serious consideration of the incoming Council with a view to improving the housing conditions of the working classes." Seconded by one of his opponents on the Council, the motion passed. Although the Council reappointed McLaren to the "Housing Committee" following his re-election the next month, the report lay dormant in the Council minutes, the subject of no further action.[45] With mixed results, McLaren had tested the limits of what a single labor councilor might do. He would continue to do so during the course of his municipal political career.

By the municipal election of 1903, the Progressive Municipal Association had disappeared as an interested party and in its place the New Zealand Socialist Party with support of the Wellington Trades and Labour Council sponsored the same two candidates, now running openly on a "labour platform." From this point, the axis of mobilization in municipal campaigns revolved more explicitly around labor's interests, increasingly with an explicit party identity.[46] Although only McLaren was returned to the Council, he continued to use his office to press the Council to open its affairs to public scrutiny. He put forward motions that would report the hours of employment of city laborers (successful), request the authority from Parliament to acquire the Wellington Gas Company (unsuccessful), initiate a study of the feasibility of a pension fund for city employees (successful), investigate concerns over building occupancy and overcrowding (unsuccessful), and provide better protection from inclement weather for tramway employees (successful).[47]

When various trades and labor councils formed the Independent Political Labour League (IPLL) in September, 1904 to push for labor representation independent of the Liberal Party in parliamentary and municipal elections, the Wellington branch moved aggressively to put forward a more ambitious labor slate, the so-called Labour Six, for City Council elections in April, 1905.[48] Within the broad contours of the IPLL "municipal platform," the several Wellington branches drafted their own program on behalf of the six labor candidates for Council. In the spirit of the strategy advocated by English municipal Labour Party activist E. R. Hartley during a subsequent New Zealand visit—that "socialists . . . must see that every step altering the material conditions for the better is a step forward"—the Wellington activists addressed the concrete needs workers faced.[49]

Fighting Municipal Platform

1 a. No further sale of municipal lands;
  b. The housing of the people at reasonable rents.
2 a. The establishment of abattoirs and workingmen's houses;
  b. The establishment of fruit, fish, vegetable and meat markets;
  c. The establishment of wood and coal depots;
3 The acquisition and extension of works for the manufacture of gas and electricity and the supply thereof as light and power.

4   All works to be performed by day labor, and trade-union rates of pay and hours to
     be observed.
5   The closing of shops on Saturday for the weekly half-holiday.
6   Free music in public places at suitable times.[50]

The "Labour Six" conducted a vigorous campaign of public speeches and mass
gatherings of voters. Even as they emphasized different aspects of the IPLL program,
they also repeatedly argued that their election would bring a different tenor to the
way the Council conducted the city's affairs. At the opening of the campaign, one of
the candidates, Mr. J. Brown, attacked "the fossilized idea that only businessmen
could govern the city." He noted labor representation on municipal bodies had grown
more common in "the Old Country" and should be emulated in New Zealand. At
another meeting Alfred Hindmarsh attacked the secretive methods of the current
Council and ridiculed its "business methods." It conducted virtually all business
behind a screen of committees whose work was not open to public scrutiny and the
committees had proliferated to a "ridiculous" extent. He argued that if the Council's
work were done with greater publicity, "the public would begin to take an interest in
the city's affairs." Indicting the Council for failing to take up municipalization of
tramways, the extension of municipal trading, and burying the McLaren report on
the condition of workers' housing, Mr. Brown also criticized the lax borrowing
methods of the city as typical of "the old party who had directed the city affairs for
so long."[51]
   The IPLL campaign for Wellington City Council in 1905 stressed the nonrevolu-
tionary character of its demands and its intention to bring better and more open
management to the city's business than the so-called business men had proved capable of doing. While arguing that their municipal platform served "the interests of
every class," they decried the antilabor bias of the current Council, its unwillingness
to deal fairly with tramway workers, and its exclusion of Councilor McLaren from
the Tramways Committee.[52]
   Despite their concerted campaign, only two of the six labor candidates were
elected. Alfred Hindmarsh now joined David McLaren in the effort to move city
governance toward greater responsiveness to labor's concerns.[53] During the campaign local socialists continued to debate the advisability of running candidates for
local office. At one open meeting in Socialist Hall, Mr. Wolstenholme criticized what
he called "Labour Misrepresentatives" because they ultimately served the capitalist
class. "Every measure of reform they advocated would bring greater security to
the capitalist." Instead, a straight-out campaign to abolish the capitalist class was
needed.[54]
   Between 1905 and 1912 Hindmarsh and McLaren served in the Wellington City
Council. Both also successfully ran for parliamentary seats. In Council they agitated
for a range of concerns that included a public fish market, revision of the residential
requirements for electors, the protection and improved pay for tramway workers,
and lower fares and better tram service for working class districts, while simultaneously contesting their own exclusion from key committees.

McLaren played a key role in settling a bitter Tramway strike in Wellington from January 31 to February 5, 1912, over the union workers' demand to dismiss an inspector for "want of tact" toward tramway employees under his charge. Despite initial hostility shown the strikers by a solid Council majority, McLaren, assisted in the later stages by Prime Minister Joseph Ward, crafted a carefully worded settlement that protected the strikers from victimization and insured the transfer of the inspector to a position where he would have no contact with the members of the Tramway Union.[55] Following this triumph, McLaren was elected Wellington's first labor mayor in the spring canvass that followed and served a single, one-year term before local elites regrouped to defeat him. Even as city government remained contested ground, socialists and labor party activists by 1912 found themselves increasingly preoccupied with their own internal political conflicts and polarization that stemmed from a series of bitter strikes.[56] Further gains for labor in the municipal arena would await the shifting political tides of the postwar period.

Wellington's municipal labor activists hardly operated in a vacuum. Working first under the fledgling New Zealand Socialist Party and later through the Independent Political Labour League, modeled directly on the Political Labor Leagues in the Australian states, they crafted a municipal platform that bore the hallmarks of widely circulating municipal platforms from cities in the United Kingdom, Australia and the United States They followed developments in the "old country," as candidate J. Brown termed the United Kingdom, and welcomed Bradford municipal socialist E. R. Hartley for an extended visit and consultation in the early 1910s. Milwaukee socialist Walter Thomas Mills arrived in New Zealand at a propitious moment and played a crucial role in forging a fragile political unity around a newly reformed New Zealand Labour Party in 1912. The Milwaukee socialists' victory in 1910 significantly enhanced Mills' credibility.[57]

Brisbane: Municipal Swamp in the Era Franchise Restriction

Not quite a year after the 1912 general strike in Brisbane, Australia that had ignited surprisingly broad working-class support behind the tramway workers' demand for higher wages, *The Daily Standard* expressed continuing frustration with Queensland's restrictive municipal franchise law. "A clean city still seems like a mystic dream in the far future. For we are sadly deficient in the first requisite, a clean franchise."[58] With a plural voting system favoring the city's largest ratepayers, Brisbane possessed in the eyes of labor activists a "nil" city government in which "[m]onopoly now claims the Divine Right to oppress the people." The editor noted that plural voting had disappeared in all "British communities" outside the state of Queensland. But in Brisbane and its neighboring municipalities,

[t]he big army of mosquito-bitten and fly-inoculated citizens look dumbly on, and have no power to lift a little finger in opposition to a continuance of a brand of civic "rule" which is a byword and a jest. They are helpless and cannot prevent the handing over of the government of our city to a small official bureaucracy.[59]

Nevertheless, despite the handicap of a highly restrictive municipal franchise and a pervasive sense that the municipal cause was "hopeless until the franchise is granted," the record suggests that elite control of Brisbane's local government did not go uncontested during the first two decades of the twentieth century. In part this stemmed from the growing voice and clarified agenda of local activists in the Queensland "Labor-in-Politics" conventions who from one year to the next pushed forward a municipal program.[60] But also, even under the franchise handicap, a solitary Council member, Thomas Wilson, reelected from 1905 to 1921 as alderman, and for one term in 1909 as Mayor, challenged the governing consensus on a number of key municipal issues and on rare occasions persuasively marshaled a fragile majority of other councilors in support of his positions.[61]

Wilson came to Council with working-class roots and "radical" inclinations. Hailing originally from Victoria, he learned sheep shearing in the Riverine District, New South Wales and worked as a copper miner in the Cobar field before settling in Brisbane. Finding time "to study local government," he ran successfully for alderman from Merthyr Ward in 1905 and thence served in City Council until 1921, including one term as Council-elected Mayor in 1909. He also entered Queensland parliament during the Ryan Labor government in 1916 and subsequently served as Minister for Public Instruction. For most of the period before franchise reform in 1920, Wilson served as a lone labor alderman before being joined in 1916 by Irishman and former Townsville railway worker J. T. McGuire (West Ward) and in 1917 by another transplanted Irishman, M. J. Barry (East Ward).[62]

From 1908 to 1920, labor's interest, largely put forward by Wilson, focused on several issues: contract versus municipal labor, municipal ownership of tramways, standardization and improvement of municipal wages, ward versus at-large representation, and expansion of the municipal franchise. Each of these issues became the focus of repeated and at times acrimonious debate. Most remained unresolved, though not without some incremental progress. Clearly fundamental franchise reform and implementation of labor's key demands would have to wait for the election of a labor majority in both houses of state government and the passage of the Local Government Act reforms in 1920.[63]

Despite indifferent support from the executive committee of the state parliamentary Labor Party, Labor-in-Politics conventions beginning at Rockhampton in 1907 and more decisively at Townsville in 1910 passed a substantial "Local Government Reform" platform, which went significantly beyond the routine call for a broadened municipal franchise. Addressing such issues as a Single Tax-style rating on unimproved land values (symptomatic of the widespread influence in labor circles of Henry George), abolition of contract labor on municipal works, the institution of trade union wages and the eight-hour day for city workers, free public baths, libraries and museums, public ownership of tramways and electric lighting, and city control of all parks and "commonages," the local branches moved the Queensland Labor Party more aggressively in the direction of a new municipal socialist politics, the outlines of which had emerged in industrial municipalities around the globe.[64]

The Brisbane City Council provides another window on the efforts of one labor representative to generate debate around key elements of labor's municipal program and in so doing to challenge the conduct of local government business more generally. On May 6, 1908, Alderman Wilson put forward a motion that a drainage works previously approved by the ratepayers should "be constructed by day labor." In the ensuing debate he noted that government was constructing railways with day labor and the work was "done quite as satisfactorily as by contract." The focus of debate shifted to the alleged higher cost of day labor in New South Wales. A move to refer the matter to committee for further study failed on the tie-breaking vote of Mayor Buchanan, and by the same margin Wilson's motion squeaked through. Clearly the issue was one on which he was able to mobilize a fragile majority. Just how fragile became apparent at the meeting on July 13 when Council rescinded by a single vote the adoption of its previous motion. But the matter refused to die. Wilson and his allies brought back his original motion for debate and a new vote in mid-August. Again the issue of comparative cost loomed large. Opponents of day labor offered an amendment whereby the City Engineer might submit a tender (a bid) along with interested private contractors. In a sign of another shift in the tide of debate that amendment failed to win a majority (one member abstaining). On Wilson's motion, the old majority of one reappeared and, at least for the time being, the city was empowered to undertake the work with its own day laborers.[65]

A persistent issue for Brisbane's Council revolved around another labor plank, support for which extended significantly into other constituencies. The Brisbane Tramways Company was managed by an expatriate American, J. S. Badger, whose notoriety grew over the years. In September 1910 Mayor Hetherington reported sympathetically to Council on a proposal from the Conference on Local Authorities that a commission be formed and invested with the authority to negotiate immediate purchase of the tramway lines or, alternatively, a renegotiation of the current franchise agreement on more favorable terms. Frustrated by the poor service and the failure of the company to extend lines into growing areas of the metropolitan district, a minority of Councilors pushed for municipalization. Unable to enlist state government behind the passage of the required statutory authority and deflected by Badger's alternative proposition for a renewal of the franchise that would include a municipal profit-sharing provision but leave private ownership in tact, the tramway issue circled again and again through Council business without resolution.[66]

The local reputation of Badger's tramway company hardly improved during 1912. His dismissal of tramway workers who challenged an order prohibiting the wearing of union buttons precipitated a general strike of more than a month's duration. Even though the brutal police repression visited on the strikers rested primarily at the doorstep of the Liberal Queensland government, local government found its own business disrupted for the month. To the deep displeasure of some Councilors, some municipal employees joined the strike, but city officials took no punitive action. The municipality distributed free flour to hard-pressed citizens, for which the Trades

Hall took credit, further irritating Council members. And the strike prevented the election of the Mayor for nearly a month.[67]

With Labor's political fortunes in Queensland improving in the years following the general strike and more directly with the election of T. J. Ryan's Labor government in 1915, Brisbane's municipalizers turned their attention again to new state legislation that would empower the city to purchase the tramways. With the legislation hamstrung in a divided parliament, little legislative progress was seen until 1920, and local municipalization was not finally achieved until 1923.[68]

Other labor issues also gained new steam with the election of a state Labor government. The Australian Workers' Union successfully petitioned the Industrial Court in Brisbane for a "Municipal Log" that would standardize wages in all municipalities of the South-Eastern Division of Queensland. The award advanced municipal wages by ten percent across the board despite the expressed opposition of some but not all Councilors.[69]

More longstanding and more contentiously resisted was labor's demand for franchise reform. In late 1915, at the behest of the Local Authorities Association of Queensland, the Brisbane Council resolved, with Thomas Wilson the sole dissenting vote, to oppose the Ryan government's proposal of adult suffrage in municipal elections. Despite T. J. Ryan's efforts Local Authorities reform remained hamstrung until labor majorities in both houses broke the logjam. With the passage of the Local Authorities Amendment Act of 1920, labor overcame the resistance and persistent lobbying of local councils in the Legislative Assembly.[70] With the municipal adult franchise achieved, local government in Brisbane and elsewhere in Queensland stood poised for a new era of local labor rule. The dogged and often beleaguered efforts of Thomas Wilson and his allies in the Labor Party to create political space for workers' interests in local government had borne fruit.

The war years saw the Labor Party in Brisbane and Queensland become a beacon of opposition to conscription and the war itself. Labor premier T. J. Ryan led the outspoken opposition to conscription in two national referenda in 1916 and 1917. Drawing inspiration as well from the opposition of American socialists and prominent British laborites, like Philip Snowdon and Ramsey MacDonald, Brisbane workers mobilized in massive numbers to defeat conscription and demand employment and relief from escalating prices. Patrick Hickey, an itinerant New Zealand labor agitator whose career had taken him to the hardrock mines of the western United States, to Blackball and Wellington, New Zealand, Melbourne and eventually to Brisbane, celebrated the Australian labor movement in 1918 as "one of the most inspiring in the world."[71]

Milwaukee's Municipal Socialists: Contesting for Power

Despite conditions that many observers regarded as significantly less auspicious for socialist success, labor and socialist activists in some municipalities in the United States forged municipal programs and conducted campaigns that paralleled those in

New Zealand and Australia, as well as Britain, Germany, and Sweden. Facing different impediments to victory, though generally not formal franchise restrictions on male voters, and with fewer entrenched "liberal" regimes, American socialists and urban populists in the early twentieth century achieved some dramatic political victories in a host of municipalities.[72]

The record of municipal labor and socialist electoral activity in the period from the mid-1890s through U.S. entry into World War I is deserving of more attention than it has received. Part of the explanation for historians' inattention is a Sombartian myopia that has produced a tendency to look only for "socialist" cases and, finding relatively few, to go on to other problems. Like the cases that I have discussed above, municipal reform politics in the United States was an untidy political stew. Labor's engagement with city politics frequently saw the construction of temporary pragmatic alliances between liberal reformers and working-class political activists within the partisan world of one or another major party on behalf of a municipal reform program that differed little from that put forward by socialists. In some cities—San Francisco, Cleveland, Toledo—labor and its allies formed the core of an enduring municipal reform politics. In others—Los Angeles, St. Louis, New York, Chicago—the periodic entry of Labor Reform or Municipal Ownership parties punctuated city politics. Furthermore, as many as 180 cities elected socialist administrations between 1911 and 1920. Milwaukee, of course, provides the outstanding example, but it hardly stood alone. Others included Schenectady, NY, Reading, PA, Flint, MI, Dayton, OH, Minneapolis, MN, Davenport, IA, and New Castle, IN. In Ohio alone, 29 cities elected socialist administrations during this decade. According to Richard Judd, the SPA estimated in 1911 that it had elected 1,141 socialists to local and state offices in 36 states and 324 municipalities. It won "majority control" that year alone in at least 23 cities.[73] The political mobilization and contestation around municipal issues in the United States was formidable and widespread.

Nonetheless, the record of municipal socialist success was nowhere more stunning than in Milwaukee. And that victory resonated throughout urban labor and socialist political movements worldwide. Over a period of two decades, the socialists in Milwaukee constructed a party of formidable strength in the municipal arena. Building on the city's Populist movement and Eugene Debs's Social Democracy of America, they had first become a political force with some presence during the 1890s. As the Social Democratic Party of Milwaukee (SDM), their electoral machine inspired the "constructivist" wing of the Socialist Party of America after 1901 and won the endorsement of the AFL-affiliated Milwaukee Federated Trades Council (FTC) in February, 1900. Despite optimism generated by the FTC's support, the SDM polled only 2,473 votes in the city election that year, a mere 29 votes more than in 1898, and failed to elect a single alderman.[74] But by the spring election of 1902, the socialists' fortunes began to ascend. With 8,400 votes, they claimed a sixth of the electorate. Doubling their vote in 1904, they elected nine aldermen to the Common Council.

Although the new socialist councilmen were a small minority in a City Council of 45 members, they demonstrated remarkable discipline and a willingness to challenge the established agenda and procedures by which Council conducted its business, a story with parallels to Wellington, Brisbane, and other municipalities around the world. Their nominees for president and clerk of the Council went down to defeat with only the support of the nine Social Democrats. Undeterred, they put forward a remarkable array of initiatives in the face of Democratic Mayor-elect David Rose's warnings about the use of "partisan tongue and partisan pen" and the duty of elected officials to be responsive to "the whole people rather than to party." At the second meeting of the Council, Frederic Heath, urged on by the Federated Trades Council, moved that City Council meetings henceforth be held at 7:30 p.m. rather than the customary 4 p.m. in order to facilitate workers' participation. The chair referred the motion to the Rules Committee, from which it failed to emerge. Reintroduced in early 1905 by another socialist, the proposal met the same fate.[75] Within their first six months on Council, the minority of nine socialists submitted motions for equitable expenditure for street repairs in the wards, for a municipal ice plant and coal and wood yard, to create space and speaker stands for open air meetings in public parks, to solicit bids for a long-promised children's "Isolation Hospital," to establish eight hours as the standard for all city work whether directly employed or on contract, and to seek state legislation to tax light, street railway, and telephone companies at the high rate established for railways. On all these initiatives, except the Isolation Hospital and the proposition to lobby for new tax legislation, the proposals disappeared into committee, were recommended for "indefinite postponement," or were eventually voted down on committee recommendation. Where votes were taken, the nine Social Democrats almost always stood alone.[76]

More complicated for the Social Democrats and their "non-partisan" opponents was the issue of municipalizing the electric light plant. In repeated referenda Milwaukee voters had asserted their support for a municipally owned electric utility. Democratic Mayor Rose acknowledged the mandate in his opening address to the Council. After rehearsing the results of the various votes taken, he said simply "It is now up to us to carry out the instructions of the people and build the plant." Doing so proved more difficult than it might have seemed. The Social Democrats' motion to appoint a committee of aldermen and experts to visit other municipal plants and develop a concrete proposal failed adoption. When a committee of aldermen and the City Engineer did eventually undertake the investigation, further action was again deferred. The socialist councilors repeatedly submitted petitions of citizens in support of erecting a municipal plant, but still the Council failed to act. Only with the election of a full socialist administration in 1910 would the city move forward after 15 years in which the public's desires had been "denied by the men who made the same perennial election pledge."[77]

The Milwaukee socialists' forward march continued in 1906 with the capture of five additional aldermanic seats, but victory came at a price. By 1908 the State of Wisconsin imposed an at-large municipal electoral process that saw an even larger socialist vote (nearly one-third) produce only nine aldermanic seats once again.[78]

Appealing to a broader social reform constituency, the Socialists rebuilt their strength at the ward level and made serious inroads into the Polish and Eastern European neighborhoods inhabited largely by new immigrant laborers and their families.[79]

The socialists had worked methodically and painstakingly for the victory in 1910 that would be theirs. Cleveland reformer Frederic Howe, visiting Milwaukee not long after the socialist success in 1910, observed that, "The Socialists have been represented in the Council for eight years [sic]. Since 1908 they have had a vigorous group of ten Aldermen [sic] who have given a suggestion of the honesty of the party . . . The public had grown accustomed to the name and the spectacle of Socialists in office." Milwaukee socialist leader Victor Berger put the case more simply: Milwaukee had become a "convinced Socialist city," its politics "saturated with Socialist doctrine."[80]

In the end, the Milwaukee Social Democrats won not by virtue of the support of middle-class social reformers but from their gains among immigrant workers.[81] Berger did not mince words, "our growth was not among the wards where independent voting is prevalent. Our great gains were among the Poles . . . And once they have voted the Socialist ticket, the workingmen never desert us."[82]

Milwaukee's Social Democratic Party stunned the nation and the world by electing a mayor, 21 of 36 aldermen, and 11 of 16 county supervisors. Also impressive was Victor Berger's election to Congress and that of 13 socialists to the state legislature. Both pragmatic and visionary, the SDM worked for urban home rule and immediate, tangible reforms, but the socialists also spoke of "the cooperative commonwealth as a guiding star" of their reform program.[83] Mayor-elect Emil Seidel mocked the inefficiencies of capitalism and advocated an expanded public sector. "See how easily we get along when the idea of profit is absent," he observed. They proposed an expanded public sector and largely succeeded in accomplishing it: municipal ownership of street cars and other city services, a city-owned terminal station, municipal baths, markets and cold storage plants, a public garbage disposal plant, a municipal ice plant, public works employment for the unemployed, free medical dispensaries and hospitals, an expanded system of parks and swimming pools, free textbooks, and the opening of schools as community social centers.[84] Having been burned by the advent of at-large elections in previous cycles, the socialists opposed at-large elections, short ballots, and commission forms of government. Berger in 1911 offered a devastating critique of the prescriptive political reforms offered by many progressives. Such reforms, he argued, "confuse the minds of the workers regarding the fundamental issue of today—the class struggle between the workers and owners. It tends to make workmen look to 'good men' and to reformed methods of election for relief, instead of working for a change of economic conditions." Speaking as a good machine politician, even if a socialist one, he astutely observed that political reforms were "not good mechanical devices for a democracy, for they limit the power of the people and tend to the establishment of an oligarchy."[85]

The Milwaukee socialists did not succeed themselves, in a pattern all-too-common in other cities as well, where competing parties temporarily fused in order to defeat the socialists. By 1916, now in the context of The Great War, the Social Democratic Party reasserted itself and elected as mayor Daniel Hoan, who had been

City Attorney in the first socialist administration. Despite their wartime travails Social Democrats would play a major role in Milwaukee municipal politics over the next 40 years.[86] They reconstructed the city's public space and culture in ways that made it, at least in some respects, a "workers' city."

Determined as Milwaukee's socialists were to achieve "socialism in one city," their vision was profoundly internationalist from the outset. Milwaukee's *Social Democratic Herald* reported extensively on the triumph of municipal socialists around the world. They welcomed countless international visitors intent on observing the results of this socialist breakthrough in a major American city. Emissaries like Walter Thomas Mills ventured forth to carry the message of their experience to New Zealand and elsewhere. The socialist press, including the German SPD periodical *Kommunale Praxis*, took up the Milwaukee story as an object lesson.[87]

Conclusion

The events in Wellington, Brisbane, and Milwaukee are instructive for a number of reasons. First, they suggest, as do the annals of municipal labor politics throughout the industrialized world in the early twentieth century, that despite its minority status labor came to exert a significant influence in local government by tearing away the mask of nonpartisanship and redefining how municipal business was conducted. Second, contestation of municipal elections by socialists grew more intense, spirited, and, by increments, successful over time. Third, labor's municipal program, honed through debates at party conventions and shaped by grassroots political activism, provided an agenda for labor councilors (and occasionally mayors) to reshape political debate and action around a set of issues to which labor was deeply committed. Lacking governing majorities in most instances, at least prior to the end of World War I, labor councilors could rarely claim outright victory, but their efforts did bring some changes in municipal affairs as they astutely assembled support for their program from sympathizers among liberals and independents.

The process of redefining the political space in cities was protracted and the impediments substantial. But in 1910, as a benchmark, Milwaukee's Social Democrats swept to municipal power in impressive fashion, their victory cause for celebration among municipal Social Democrats worldwide. In Christchurch and Wellington, New Zealand workers would elect labor mayors, though not a controlling majority of their councils. Labor Party activists in Brisbane would struggle on for nearly a decade in the face of severe franchise restriction, until a state Labor government in Queensland overcame the bitter opposition of the state's governing municipal elites to push through legislation guaranteeing one person-one vote in local contests. The significance of that measure would be evident as labor won power in both Brisbane and South Brisbane within a few years.[88] However briefly, the Milwaukeeans' victory suggested "American exceptionalism" of a different sort. Though driven from power two years later, they and their comrades in places like Christchurch, Wellington,

Brisbane, and scores of other municipalities around the world had begun a process of reclaiming cities in the name of their workers and reconstructing urban political space on a fundamentally more democratic basis.[89]

The city and its politics, then, provided a dynamic arena in which labor activists tested their mettle and honed their message, well aware that their efforts formed part of a broader international movement of municipal activists. Annual campaigns offered a medium for party-building and a training ground for party activists. The issues at stake had a tangible and immediate character that directly touched workers' lives. To raise those issues in the staid chambers of the "honourable" and grandly robed Councilors and "His Worship The Mayor" represented itself a victory of sorts and legitimation of a new politics that held the promise of more substantial victories in the future.

Notes

1. See Leon Fink, " 'Intellectuals' versus 'Workers': Academic Requirements and the Creation of Labor History," *American Historical Review* XCVI (1991): 395–421 on the intellectual origins of the Old Labor History, and a thoughtful intervention by David Brody, "Reconciling the Old Labor History and the New," *Pacific Historical Review* 62 (1) (February 1993): 1–18.
2. David Montgomery, *The Fall of the House of Labor: The Workplace, the State, and American Labor Activism, 1865–1925* (New York: Cambridge University Press, 1987), 2; for a different but complimentary emphasis, see Alice Kessler-Harris, "A New Agenda for American Labor History: A Gendered Analysis and the Question of Class," from the infamous Northern Illinois University "Synthesis" conference in 1984 and "Treating the Male as Other: Redefining the Parameters of Labor History" in her volume *Gendering Labor History* (Urbana, IL: University of Illinois Press, 2007)
3. See Aristide R. Zolberg, "How many exceptionalisms?" in Ira Katznelson and Aristide R. Zolberg, eds *Working-Class Formation: Nineteenth-Century Patterns in Western Europe and the United States* (Princeton: Princeton University Press, 1986), 397–456; Eric Foner, "Why is there no socialism in the United States?" *History Workshop Journal*, 17 (1984): 57–80; and Daniel T. Rodgers "American Exceptionalism Revisited," *Raritan* 24 (2) (Fall, 2004), 21–47.
4. Daniel T. Rodgers' *Atlantic Crossings: Social Politics in a Progressive Age* (Cambridge: Harvard University Press, 1998) was a pioneering work identifying transatlantic influences in realms of twentieth-century social reform. For a more general survey of historical trends in transnational scholarship, see *Rethinking American History in a Global Age*, Thomas Bender, ed. (Berkeley, CA: University of California Press, 2002); and Marcel van der Linden, "Transnationalizing American Labor History," *Journal of American History* 86 (3) (December 1999): 1078–92.
5. On the social democratic movement, see Georges Haupt, *Socialism and the Great War: The Collapse of the Second International* (Oxford: Clarendon Press, 1972);

G. D. H. Cole, *A History of Socialist Thought*, vol. 3, *The Second International, 1889–1914* (London: Macmillan, 1960. In other comparative vineyards, see Nikola Balnave and Greg Patmore, "'Practical Utopians': Rochdale Consumer Cooperatives in Australia and New Zealand," *Labour History (Australia)*, n. 95 (November 2008), 97–110 and special issue of *Labour History (Australia)* on cooperatives in Britain and Australia, n. 91 (2006); Andre Tridon, *The New Unionism* (New York: B. W. Huebsch, 1913); also Verity Burgmann, *Revolutionary Industrial Unionism: The Industrial Workers of the World in Australia* (New York: Cambridge University Press, 1995) on the IWW in Australia and the United States; Jürgen Kocka, ed., *Europäische Arbeiterbewegungen im 19. Jahrhundert: Deutschland, Österrecih, England und Frankreich im Vergleich* (Göttingen: Vandenhoeck & Ruprecht, 1983); and Selig Perlman, *A Theory of the Labor Movement* (New York: A. M. Kelley, 1970 [1928]).

6. See Marcel van der Linden and Jürgen Rojahn, "Introduction," and for example essays by Richard Price (Britain), Birger Simonson (Sweden), Klaus Tenfelde (Germany), Shelton Stromquist (U.S.), Lucy Taksa (Australia), and Erik Olssen (New Zealand) in *The Formation of Labour Movements, 1870–1910: An International Perspective*, 2 vols (Amsterdam: E. J. Brill, 1990) and Aad Blok, Keith Hitchins, Raymond Markey, and Birger Simonson, *Urban Radicals, Rural Allies: Social Democracy and the Agrarian Issue, 1870–1914* (Bern: Peter Lang, 2002). And more recently, Jan Lucassen, ed., *Global Labour History: A State of the Art* (New York: Peter Lang, 2006).

7. See Rana G. Behal and Marcel van der Linden, eds *Coolies, Capital and Colonialism: Studies in Indian Labour History* (New York: Cambridge University Press, 2006) and Arvind Das and Marcel van der Linden, eds, *Work and Social Change in Asia: Essays in Honour of Jan Breman* (New Delhi: Manohar Publishers, 2003).

8. See especially Neville Kirk, *Comrades and Cousins: Globalization, Workers and Labour Movements in Britain, the USA, and Australia from the 1880s to 1914* (London: Merlin Press, 2003) and *Labor and Society in Britain and the USA*, 2 vols (Aldershot: Scolar Press, 1994).

9. See special issue "Australia and Canada: Labour Compared," *Labour/Le Travail* 38 (Fall, 1996) and *Labour History (Australia)*, n. 71 (November 1996).

10. Colin J. Davis, *Waterfront Revolts: New York and London Dockworkers, 1946–1961* (Urbana, IL: University of Illinois Press, 2003), Mary Hilson; *Political Change and the Rise of Labour in Comparative Perspective: Britain and Sweden, 1890–1920* (Lund: Nordic Academic Press, 2006). See also the volume edited by Sam Davies, *Dockworkers: International Explorations in Comparative Labour History, 1790–1970* (Aldershot: Ashgate, 2000) and John H. M. Laslett, *Colliers Across the Sea: A Comparative Study of Class Formation in Scotland and the American Midwest 1830–1924* (Urbana, IL: University of Illinois Press, 2000).

11. See essays by Prasannan Parthasarathi (agricultural labor), Ratna Saptari (domestics), Jan Lucassen (brickmakers), Ian Phimister (coal mining), Lex

Heerma van Voss (dockworkers), Shelton Stromquist (railway workers) in Jan Lucassen, *Global Labour History: A State of the Art*; Peter Linebaugh and Marcus Rediker, *The Many-headed Hydra: Sailors, Slaves, Commoners and the Hidden History of the Revolutionary Atlantic* (Boston: Beacon, 2000).

12. See Dipesh Chakrabarty, *Provincializing Europe: Postcolonial Thought and Historical Difference* (Princeton: Princeton University Press, 2000); Daud Ali, "Recognizing Europe in India: Colonial Master Narratives and the Writing of Indian History," in Jeffrey Cox and Shelton Stromquist, eds *Contesting the Master Narrative: Essays in Social History* (Iowa City: University of Iowa Press, 1998), 95–130; Shahid Amin and Marcel van der Linden, eds *"Peripheral" Labour Studies in the History of Partial Proletarianization* (Cambridge: Cambridge University Press, 1997).

13. Hugh Cunningham, *Children and Childhood in Western Society since 1500* (London: Longmans, 1995); also Hugh Cunningham and Shelton Stromquist, "Child Labor and the Rights of Children: Historical Patterns of Decline and Persistence," in Burns Weston, ed. *Child Labor and Human Rights: Making Children Matter* (Boulder, CO: Lynne Rienner Publishers, 2005). For the traditional, Eurocentric modernization approach, see Clark Nardenelli, *Child Labor and the Industrial Revolution* (Bloomington, IN: Indiana University Press, 1990).

14. The vast literature on working-class migration has had a number of key pivot points. These include the linking of specific immigrant origins and destinations, for instance John Gjerde's, *From Peasants to Farmers: The Migration from Balestrand, Norway to the Upper Middle West* (New York: Cambridge University Press, 1985) and the examination of wider immigrant diasporas, as in Donna Gabaccia's *Italy's Many Diasporas* (Seattle, WA: University of Washington Press, 2000). A path-breaking overview of global migration processes was Frank Thistlethwaite, "Migration from Europe Overseas in the Nineteenth and Twentieth Centuries," in Rudolph Vecoli, ed., *A Century of European Migration* (Urbana, IL: University of Illinois Press, 1991). And also of note is the rising interest in what social scientists call the "transmigrant"; see Nina Glick Schiller et al., "From Immigrant to Transmigrant: Theorizing Transnational Migration," *Anthropological Quarterly* 68 (1995), 48–63. On working-class internationalism, see for instance, Marcel van der Linden, "The First International (1864–1876): A Reinterpretation," in *Transnational Labour History: An Exploration* (Aldershot: Ashgate, 2003), 11–21, and Tim Rees and Andrew Thorpe, eds, *International Communism and the Communist International, 1919–1943* (Manchester: University of Manchester Press, 1998).

15. For key documents in the forging of international networks, see Tom Mann, *The Labour Movement in both Hemispheres* (Melbourne: J. J. Miller, 1903) and Samuel Gompers, *Labor in Europe and America* (New York: Harper Bros, 1910). Also, Gregg Andrews, *Shoulder to Shoulder? The American Federation of Labor, the United States, and the Mexican Revolution, 1910–1924* (Berkeley, CA: University of California Press, 1991). For newer transnational studies of labor movements,

see Neville Kirk, "Transatlantic Connections and American 'Peculiarities':
Labour Politics in the United States and Britain, 1893–1908," and "The Australian
'Workingman's Paradise' in Comparative Perspective, 1890–1914," in *Comrades
and Cousins* 17–58, 59–148, and David Montgomery, "Workers' Movements
in the United States Confront Imperialism: the Progressive Era Experience,"
Journal of the Gilded Age and Progressive Era 7 (1) (2008): 7–42.

16. Werner Sombart, *Warum gibt es keinen Sozialismus in den Vereinigten Staaten?*
(Tübingen: J. C. B. Mohr, 1906); Sean Wilentz, "Against Exceptionalism: Class
Consciousness and the American Labor Movement, 1790–1920," *International
Labor and Working-Class History*, n. 26 (Fall, 1984): 1–24; Eric Foner, "Why is
there no socialism in the United States?"; Neville Kirk, "American 'Exceptional-
ism' Revisited: The Case of Samuel Gompers," *Socialist History* 16 (2000);
Seymour Martin Lipset and Gary Marks, *It Didn't Happen Here: Why Socialism
Failed in the United States* (New York: Norton, 2000); Ira Katznelson and
Aristide R. Zolberg, *Working-Class Formation: Nineteenth-Century Patterns in
Western Europe and the United States* (Princeton: Princeton University Press,
1986); Robin Archer, *Why is there no Labor Party in the United States?* (Princeton:
Princeton University Press, 2007).

17. The dominant influence of national studies of labor politics is striking. See, for
instance, the literature cited above on the Sombart question; also Bede Nairn,
Civilising Capitalism: The Beginnings of the Australian Labor Party (Canberra:
Australian National University Press, 1973); Herbert Tingsten, *The Swedish
Social Democrats: Their Ideological Development* (Totowa, NJ: Bedminster Press,
1973; orig. in Swedish, 1941); Carl Schorske, *German Social Democracy, 1905–1917:
The Development of the Great Schism* (Cambridge: Cambridge University Press,
1955); Dieter Groh, *Negative Integration und revolutionärer Attentismus. Die
deutsche Sozialdemokratie am Vorabend des Ersten Weltkrieges* (Frankfurt:
Propylaen, 1973); Henry Pelling, *A Short History of the Labour Party* (London:
Macmillan, 1965); Barry Gustafson, *Labor's Path to Political Independence: The
Origins and Establishment of the New Zealand Labour Party* (Auckland: Oxford
University Press, 1980).

18. Geoff Eley, *Forging Democracy: The History of the Left in Europe, 1850–2000*
(New York: Oxford University Press, 2000), and work on Latin America, includ-
ing Jorge Castañeda, *Utopia Unarmed: The Latin American Left after the Cold
War* (New York: Random House, 1993).

19. Stefan Berger, *British Labour Party and German Social Democrats, 1900–1931*
(Oxford: Clarendon Press, 1994); Madeline Hurd, *Public Spheres, Public Mores,
and Democracy in Stockholm and Hamburg, 1870–1940* (Ann Arbor: University
of Michigan Press, 2000).

20. My own work in progress, *Social Democracy in the City* makes the case for
such an orientation, as does recent work on the Knights of Labor (Kenneth Fones-
Wolf, Robert Weir, Francis Shor), the IWW (Verity Burgmann), and the Single
Tax, Bellamyite, and Fabian Socialist movements, on which Herbert Roth's

voluminous documentation for New Zealand and Australia sheds important light; see Herbert O. Roth Papers, Turnbull Library, Wellington, New Zealand.

21. Jefferson Cowie, *Capital Moves: RCA's Seventy Year Quest for Cheap Labor* (Ithaca, NY: Cornell University Press, 1999) and other examples of transnational firms, for instance, Greg Patmore's work on U.S. Steel in New South Wales, Colorado, and New Brunswick, "The Origins of Federal Industrial Relations Systems: Australia, Canada and the USA," *Journal of Industrial Relations* 51 (2) (2009): 151–72.

22. See local studies by James Barrett, *Work and Community in The Jungle: Chicago's Packinghouse Workers, 1894–1922* (Urbana, IL: University of Illinois Press, 1987); Michael Kazin, *Barons of Labor: The San Francisco Building Trades and Union Power in the Progressive Era* (Urbana, IL: University of Illinois Press, 1987); Richard Oestreicher, *Solidarity and Fragmentation: Working People and Class Consciousness in Detroit, 1875–1900* (Urbana, IL: University of Illinois Press, 1987); and Shelton Stromquist, *A Generation of Boomers: The Pattern of Railroad Labor Conflict in Nineteenth-century America* (Urbana, IL: University of Illinois Press, 1987) and more recent work. On the construction of the "nation" see Hobsbawm, *Nations and Nationalism since 1780: Programme, Myth, Reality* (Cambridge: Cambridge University Press, 1992); also Stefan Berger, *Writing the Nation: A Global Perspective* (Basingstoke: Palgrave Macmillan, 2007).

23. Ralph Miliband, *Parliamentary Socialism: A Study in the Politics of Labour* (London: Merlin Press, 1972); E. J. Hobsbawm and Terence Ranger, eds, *The Invention of Tradition;* Leif Lewin, *Ideology and Strategy: A Century of Swedish Politics* (New York: Cambridge University Press, 1988). See also Shelton Stromquist, "Thinking Globally, Acting Locally: Municipal Labor and Socialist Activism in Comparative Perspective, 1890–1920," *Labour History Review* 74 (3) (December 2009): 233–56. Also, Keith Laybourn, "The Rise of Labour and the Decline of Liberalism, c. 1890–1918," in Laybourn, *The Rise of Labour: The British Labour Party 1890–1970* (London: Edward Arnold, 1988).

24. See discussion below; also Pat Thane, "Labour and Local Politics: Radicalism, Democracy and Social Reform, 1880–1914," in Eugenio F. Biagini and Alastair J. Reid, eds *Currents of Radicalism: Popular Radicalism, Organized Labour and Party Politics in Britain, 1850–1914* (Cambridge: Cambridge University Press, 1991) and Shelton Stromquist, "A Politics for Every Day and Every Place: Labor Conflict and Political Experimentation at the Municipal Grassroots in the 1890s," unpublished paper, LAWCHA Annual Conference, Chicago, May 29, 2009.

25. See Hobsbawm and Ranger, eds, *The Invention of Tradition*, 264–303; Umut Özkirimli, *Theories of Nationalism: A Critical Introduction* (New York: St. Martin's Press, 2000), 117; see also Hobsbawm, *Nations and Nationalism since 1780: Programme, Myth, Reality*; Benedict Anderson, *Imagined Communities: Reflections on the Origin and Spread of Nationalism* (London: Verso, 1983, 1991); and Ernest Gellner, *Thought and Change* (London: Weidenfeld and Nicholson, 1964).

26. No contemporary observer seemed better attuned to these developments than Robert Michels, *Political Parties: A Sociological Study of Oligarchical Tendencies in Modern Democracy* (New York: Collier Books, 1962; orig. published in German, 1911).

27. See, for instance, Marcel van der Linden, "National Integration of European Working Classes," in *Transnational Labour History: Explorations*, 25, 29.

28. The persistence of localist alternative visions of political agency suggests the limits or at least the contested quality of such nationalist agendas. See for instance William Morris's *News from Nowhere* as an alternative to the "nationalist" vision of Edward Bellamy's *Looking Backward*. See also the important work of Canadian political scientist, Warren Magnusson, *The Search for Political Space: Globalization, Social Movements, and the Urban Political Experience* (Toronto: University of Toronto Press, 1996).

29. See, for instance, the political career of Keir Hardie, in Kenneth O. Morgan, *Keir Hardie: Radical and Socialist* (London: Weidenfeld and Nicholsen, 1975). Ramsey MacDonald's inquiry into the results of municipal campaigns in 1908 was clearly motivated by the strategic interests of a parliamentary-oriented party organization (see discussion below) Correspondence, re. Municipal elections, 1908–09, Labour Party Records, Peoples' Museum and Archives, Manchester.

30. Political Labor League, New South Wales, Executive Report for the Year 1901, New South Wales Political Labor League, John Dwyer Scrapbook (compiled by John Dwyer), Mitchell Library, Sydney; for municipal programs of the Swedish Social Democratic Party, see annual reports of the SAP, *Socialdemokratins Program, 1897 till 1990* (Stockholm: Arbetarrörelsens arkiv och bibliotek, 2001) and, for example, "Utkast till Arbetarepartiets Kommunalprogram," December, 1900 [ARAB]. Thanks to Klaus Misgeld, ARAB, for assistance. For the German SPD debates over the municipal program, see *Protokoll über die Verhandlungen des Parteitages der Sozialdemokratischen Partei Deutschlands*, München, September, 1902 (Berlin, 1902), 203–23, and *Protokoll über die Verhandlungen des Parteitages der Sozialdemkratischen Partie Deuschlands*, Bremen, September 1904 (Berlin, 1904), 290–304. See also Patrizia Dogliani, "European Municipalism in the First Half of the Twentieth Century: The Socialist Network," *Contemporary European History* II (4) (2002): 573–96. For further discussion of this phenomenon transnationally, see Stromquist, "Thinking Globally, Acting Locally."

31. See Georges Haupt, "The Commune as symbol and example," in *Aspects of International Socialism, 1871–1914: Essays by Georges Haupt*, Peter Fawcett, trans. (Cambridge: Cambridge University Press, 1986), 23–47.

32. Daniel Rodgers, *Atlantic Crossings*; Shelton Stromquist, *Reinventing "the People": The Progressive Movement, the Labor Problem, and the Origins of Twentieth-Century Liberalism*. As Berger observes for Britain, "the narrative construction of 'the people' was often used to defuse the disruptive potential of class and to unify the national narrative around issues of constitutionalism, freedom and individualism," "The Power of National Pasts: Writing National History in

Nineteenth- and Twentieth-Century Europe," in Stefan Berger, ed. *Writing the Nation: A Global Perspective* (Houndsmills, Basingstokes: Palgrave Macmillan, 2007), 42.

33. Stefan Berger and Angel Smith, "Between Scylla and Charybdis: Nationalism, Labour and Ethnicity across Five Continents, 1870–1939," in Stefan Berger and Angel Smith, eds *Nationalism, Labour and Ethnicity, 1870–1939* (Manchester: University of Manchester Press, 1999), 13.

34. Stefan Berger, "The Power of National Pasts," 42–43. Berger notes the "hyperna-tionalism of German *Volksgeschichte*, the intense patriotism of leading figures of the Annales school and the much commented on Englishness of the Webbs."

35. This tradition of national histories of parliamentary labor and socialist parties has deep roots going back to G. D. H. Cole and the Webbs in Britain, Robin Gollan, Bede Nairn, and John Rickard in Australia, David Shannon and Seymour Martin Lipset for the United States; Carl Schorske, Gerhard A. Ritter, and Jürgen Kocka for Germany, and for Sweden, Herbert Tingsten and Göran Therborn. In each national historiography some more recent work has exam-ined local politics but generally without attention to its internationalist dimen-sions. See, for instance, in Britain David Howell, *British Workers and the Independent Labour Party, 1888–1906* (Manchester: Manchester University Press, 1983), in Australia, Lucy Taksa, "Workplace, Community, Mobilisation and Labour Politics at the Eveleigh Railway Workshops," in Raymond Markey, ed. *Labour and Community: Historical Essays*, and in New Zealand, Erik Olssen, *Building the New World: Work, Politics and Society in Caversham 1880s-1920s* (Auckland: Auckland University Press, 1995).

36. On the Independent Labour Party in England—see Thompson's "Homage to Tom Maguire," and local studies of Bradford, Halifax, Huddersfield, Keighley and London; see also the radical municipalism in cities of New South Wales and Queensland, documented in the work of Ray Markey and Brad Bowden, or the local agitation of Axel Danielsson in Malmö, Sweden inspired by the utopian writer Herman Quiding.

37. See, especially, the work of Patrizia Dogliani, "European Municipalism in the First Half of the Twentieth Century," 573–96. For evidence from the fierce anti-conscription debates in Australia and New Zealand see, for instance, Australian Labor Party of the State of New South Wales, *Twenty-Seventh Annual Report, for the Year Ending, December 31, 1917* (Sydney: Worker Print, 1918), 4–16, and James Thorn, text of speech opposing conscription, delivered at the Globe Theatre, Auckland, December 10, 1916, in Herbert Roth Papers, "Pacifism in New Zealand," 82–213-04, Turnbull Library, Wellington, New Zealand.

38. One is struck by the abundant evidence from a place like the silver mining town of Broken Hill in a remote corner of New South Wales, whose workers elected a Labor municipal government in 1900, drawing inspiration from workers' municipal organizing across the globe, faithfully reported each week in their newspaper, *The Barrier Truth*, and whose bitter strike in 1908 drew the sustained

participation and arrest of British trade unionist, Tom Mann. Or, see the Milwaukee socialists' *Social Democratic Herald*, that in the years before and after the socialists' municipal triumph in 1910 carried internationalist reports of local municipal victories in far flung places across the globe. See, for instance, *Social Democratic Herald*, November 13, 1909, and July 15, 1911. Or, for a final example, the German SPD's municipal organ, *Kommunale Praxis*, whose annual reports similarly celebrated socialist municipal triumphs far beyond Kaiser Wilhelm's Reich. Anticonscriptionists in the warring states were profoundly aware of the efforts of comrades around the world. See, for example, "Snowdon's Great Speech Against Conscription," *Worker Print*, n.d., in Roth Papers, "Pacificism in New Zealand," 82–213-04, Turnbull Library, Wellington, New Zealand.

39. J. A. McCullough discussed the efforts to bring labor-leaning candidates more closely into the "Labour Party" fold in a series of letters, to Ramsey MacDonald, September 7, 1910, T. E. Taylor, November 7, 1910, and George Davis, November 7, 1910, J. A. McCullough Papers, Outward Correspondence, Canterbury Museum, Christchurch.

40. Additional cases are discussed in two of my other essays previously cited, "Thinking Globally, Acting Locally" (Sydney, New South Wales, Bradford and Halifax, England, Malmö, Sweden, and Stuttgart, Germany) and in "Claiming Political Space: Workers, Municipal Socialism and the Reconstruction of Local Democracy in Transnational Perspective," (Christchurch, New Zealand, Broken Hill, New South Wales, Manchester, England, Detroit, Toledo, and Cleveland, in the United States and Porto Alegre, Brazil).

41. George Michael Betts, "Participation in civic politics: a study of Wellington City Council and the part its elected Representatives and staff, together with the citizens, play in the decision-making Process," Ph.D. dissertation, Victoria University—Wellington, 1969, 716–18.

42. For a general overview of David McLaren's career, see "David McLaren, 1867–72? – 1939," (Kerry Taylor), *New Zealand Dictionary of Biography* vol. 3 (Auckland: Auckland University Press, 1996), 307–08; Erik Olssen, *The Red Feds: Revolutionary Industrial Unionism and the New Zealand Federation of Labour, 1908–14* (Auckland: Oxford University Press, 1988), 77–78.

43. Wellington City Council, Correspondence Files, "Notice of Motion," May 31, 1902.

44. Wellington City Council Minutes, March 30, 1903.

45. Wellington City Council Minutes, May 7, 1903.

46. George Michael Betts, "Participation in Civic Politics," 720–21.

47. Wellington City Council, Correspondence Files, Notices of Motion, August 28, 1903, June 27, 1904, September 7, 1904, May 13, 1905.

48. Herbert Roth Papers, Independent Political Labour League, Summary notes and newspaper clippings, "Political Labour League of New Zealand. A special general meeting of the Thorndon Branch" [c. 1905, no specific date], Turnbull Library, Wellington, New Zealand. See also George Michael Betts, "Participation in Civic Politics," 721–22.

49. Interview with E. R. Hartley, *Maoriland Worker*, May 24, 1912, quoted in George Michael Betts, "Participation in Civic Politics," 713.

50. Roth Papers, IPLL collection, newspaper clippings [c. 1905, no specific date]

51. Roth Papers, IPLL collection, newspaper clippings "The Mayoral Election. 'The Labour Six'," (c. 1905, no specific date].

52. Roth Papers, IPLL collection, newspaper clippings, "The Mayoral Election," "Labour and the City Council. Are 'Business' Councillors Biased?" [c. 1905; no specific date.]

53. Alfred Hindmarsh, a lawyer, had some association with the labor movement through serving as president of the Wellington branch of the Federated Cooks and Stewards Union and secretary of the Wellington Socialist Education League. From the late 1890s he had consistently challenged Liberal representation of labor and ran unsuccessfully for city council in 1901. From his election in 1905, he served until 1915. He was elected to Wellington South parliamentary seat in 1911 and held the position until his death in 1916. See *Dictionary of New Zealand Biography*, vol. 3, 222–23.

54. Roth Papers, IPLL collection, newspaper clippings, "The Municipal Elections," [c. 1905; no specific date.]

55. Wellington City Council Minutes, January 25, 31, 1912, 149–50; February 1–5 1912, 151–64.

56. See Roth Papers, McLaren biographical notes, Alexander Turnbull Library, Wellington; "David McLaren" (Kerry Taylor), *Dictionary of New Zealand Biography*, vol. 3, 307. For a discussion of the political turmoil within the labor and socialist left, see Barry Gustafson, *Labour's Path to Political Independence: The Origins and Establishment of the New Zealand Labour Party, 1900–1910*, and Erik Olssen, *The Red Feds: Revolutionary Industrial Unionism and the New Zealand Federation of Labour, 1908–14* (Auckland: Oxford University Press, 1988).

57. On the activities of E. R. Hartley in Australia and New Zealand, see Hartley Papers, West Yorkshire Archives Service, Bradford, England. The role of Walter Thomas Mills is discussed in Barry Gustafson, *Labour's Path to Political Independence* and in Herbert Roth's voluminous records of the "United Labour Party," Roth Papers, Turnbull Library.

58. *The Daily Standard* (Brisbane), January 17, 1913, p. 6.

59. Ibid. The structural and political limitations faced by "radical" labor in Queensland towns have been fruitfully explored by Bradley Bowden, "The Emergence of Labour Identity in a Queensland Town: Ipswich, 1861–1912," in David Palmer et al., eds *Australian Labour History Reconsidered* (Unley, SA: Australian Humanities Press, 1999), 92–101; also, Bowden, "'Some Mysterious Terror': The Relationship between Capital and Labour in Ipswich, 1861–96," *Labour History*, n. 72 (May 1997): 77–100.

60. See, for instance, Minutes of Labor-in-Politics Convention, 1905, 1907, 1910, 1913, John Oxley Library, Brisbane.

61. Gordon Greenwood and John Laverty, *Brisbane, 1859–1959: A History of Local Government* (Brisbane: Oswald Ziegler, 1959), 297.

62. F. J. Brewer and R. Dunn, *Sixty Years of Municipal Government* (Brisbane: H. Pole, 1925), 41, 12–13, 31. See also James Larcombe, *Labor's Ten Years Progress* (Brisbane, 1926). Gordon Greenwood and John Laverty, *Brisbane, 1859–1959*, 296–97.

63. Greenwood and Laverty, *Brisbane, 1859–1959*, 297; D. J. Murphy, ed., *Labor in Politics*, 211–12.

64. Minutes, Labour-in-Politics Convention, Townsville, May 16, 1910, John Oxley Library, Brisbane. During this same period, the Central Political Executive (CPE) of the Queensland Parliamentary Labor Party, May 1909 through July 1911, had no discussion of the agitation for Local Government planks in the party platform, though it did give passing acknowledgment to local branch discontent over the lack of local representation on the CPE. On the impact of Henry George's ideas in Australia, see Bruce Scates, *A New Australia: Citizenship, Radicalism and the First Republic* (Cambridge: Cambridge University Press, 1997).

65. Minutes, Brisbane City Council, May 6, July 13, and August 17, 1908, 58–59, 97, 113–14.

66. Minutes, Brisbane City Council, September 13, October 3, 1910, 95–96, 105; "Mayor's Report for 1911," 13–15; Minutes, April 29, May 3, 27, 1912, 20, 26, 31–32; August 25, 1913, 82–83; June 16, 1914, 60. On the early history of Brisbane's tramway service, see Greenwood and Laverty, *Brisbane, 1859–1959*, 280–82.

67. Minutes, Brisbane City Council, February 19, 1912, 160, 162–63, 166; March 6, 1912, 2. For an account of the general strike, see D. J. Murphy, 'The Tramway and General Strike, 1912," in D. J. Murphy, ed. *The Big Strikes: Queensland 1889–1965* (St. Lucia: University of Queensland Press, 1983), 117–31; also Ross Fitzgerald, *From the Dreaming to 1915: A History of Queensland* (St. Lucia: University of Queensland Press, 1982), 331–35.

68. Minutes, Brisbane City Council, September 27, 1915, 79; September 11, 1917, 87; March 8, 1920, 8. Greenwood and Laverty discuss the final resolution of the municipalization of Brisbane's tramways, 1920–23, in *Brisbane, 1859–1959*, 280–83. On the political context of the T. J. Ryan Labor government, see D. J. Murphy, "Queensland," in D. J. Murphy, ed. *Labor in Politics: The State Labor Parties in Australia 1880–1920* (St. Lucia: University of Queensland Press, 1975), 127–228.

69. Minutes, Brisbane City Council, December 13, 1915, 108; Mayor's Report, 1915, xxiii–xxiv; Mayor's Report, 1916, xvi–xvii.

70. Minutes, Brisbane City Council, November 8, 1915; September 25, 1916, 85; December 13, 1920. See Greenwood and Laverty, in *Brisbane, 1859–1959*, 297–99.

71. D. J. Murphy, *T. J. Ryan: A Political Biography* (St. Lucia, Queensland: Queensland University Press, 1975): "Ryan defies Hughes," *The Australian Worker* (Sydney), November 30, 1917, p. 6; P. H. Hickey, *Solidarity or Sectionalism? A Plea for Unity* (Brisbane: Worker Newspaper Proprietary Limited, 1918), 19; see also Erik Olssen,

"Patrick Hodgens Hickey, 1882–1930," *Dictionary of New Zealand Biography*, www.dnzb.govt.nz, 3pp (accessed June 30, 2009).

72. The term "urban populists," although not widely used in the early twentieth century is meant to denote a whole variety of working-class based urban political movements that aimed to construct a program similar in most respects to those of municipal socialists and labor parties in other parts of the world. See, for example, Daniel J. Johnson, " 'No Make-Believe Class Struggle': The Socialist Municipal Campaign in Los Angeles, 1911," *Labor History* 41 (1) (2000): 25–45; Georg Leidenberger, " 'The Public is the Labor Union': Working-Class Progressivism in Turn-of-the-Century Chicago," *Labor History* 36 (2) (1995): 187–210; John Enyeart, *The Quest for "Just and Pure Law"*; Shelton Stromquist, "The Crucible of Class: Cleveland Politics and the Origins of Municipal Reform in the Progressive Era," *Journal of Urban History* 23 (2) (January 1997): 192–220 and Robert Bionaz, "Streetcar city: popular politics and the shaping of urban progressivism in Cleveland, 1880–1910," unpublished Ph.D. dissertation, University of Iowa, 2002.

73. Richard W. Judd, *Socialist Cities: Municipal Politics and the Grass Roots of American Socialism* (Albany: SUNY Press, 1989), 19. See also James Weinstein, *The Decline of Socialism in America, 1912–1924* (New York: Vintage, 1967).

74. *Milwaukee Journal*, March 24, April 4, 1900.

75. Minutes, Milwaukee Common Council, April 25, 1904, 20; January 9, 1905, 1295.

76. Minutes, Milwaukee Common Council, May 31, July 11, 25, October 24, November 14, December 12; February 6, 20, 1905, 213, 392–93, 515, 936, 1039–40, 1136, 1142–3; 1411–12, 1427.

77. Minutes, Milwaukee Common Council, April 19, July 25, September 19, October 31, 8, 1904, 461, 759, 982; April 19, 1910, 5–6.

78. On the Milwaukee socialists' alliance with the Populists, see Leon Fink, *Workingmen's Democracy* (Urbana, IL: University of Illinois Press, 1982), 204–11, Frederick I. Olson, "The Milwaukee Socialists, 1897–1941," unpublished Ph.D. dissertation, Harvard University, 1952, 28–38, and on the formation of the Social Democratic Party see Olson, 39–53, Marvin Wachman, *History of the Social-Democratic Party of Milwaukee, 1897–1910* (Urbana, IL: University of Illinois Press, 1945), 13–29 and Sally Miller, *Victor Berger and the Promise of Constructive Socialism, 1910–1920* (Westport, CT: Greenwood, 1973).

79. *Social Democratic Herald*, March 7, 1908, quoted in Wachman, *History of the Social Democratic Party of Milwaukee, 1897–1910*, 64. For discussion of 1906 and 1908 campaigns, see Wachman, 58–65, Olson, "The Milwaukee Socialists, 1897–1941," 155–60.

80. Frederic C. Howe, "Milwaukee, A Socialist City," *The Outlook*, June 25, 1910, 414, 416–17.

81. The Milwaukee socialists' campaign tactics are covered in Wachman, *History of the Social Democratic Party of Milwaukee, 1897–1910*, 62; A. W. Mance, *History*

of the Milwaukee Social-Democratic Victories (Milwaukee, WI: Milwaukee Social-Democratic Publishing Co., 1911), 15–18; and Robert Lewis Mikkelsen, "Immigrants in Politics: Poles, Germans, and the Social Democratic Party of Milwaukee," in Dirk Hoerder, ed. *Labor Migration in the Atlantic Economies* (Westport, CT: Greenwood Press, 1985), 289–90; see also Robert Mikkelson, *The Social Democratic Party of Milwaukee, Wisconsin: A Study of Ethnic Composition and Political Development* (Oslo: Mars, 1976.)

82. Mikkelsen, "Immigrants in Politics," 289–92.

83. Wachman, *History of the Social Democratic Party of Milwaukee, 1897–1910*, 70–73.

84. Howe, "Milwaukee, A Socialist City," 416, 420–21. *History of Milwaukee Social-Democratic Victories* (Milwaukee: Social-Democratic Herald, 1911), 50–52.

85. Frederick I. Olson, "The Milwaukee Socialists, 1897–1941," 115. See also Sally M. Miller, "Milwaukee: Of Ethnicity and Labor," in Bruce M. Stave, ed. *Socialism and the Cities* (Port Washington, NY: Kennikat, 1975), esp. 51–54.

86. For a study that emphasizes the resiliency of Milwaukee's Social Democratic politics in a very different era, see Eric Fure-Slocum, "The Challenge of the working-class city: recasting growth politics and liberalism in Milwaukee, 1937–1952," unpublished Ph.D. dissertation, the University of Iowa, 2001.

87. *Social Democratic Herald*, November 7, 1908; *Kommunale Praxis* (Berlin), 13 Jahrgang, Nummer 38/39, September 20, 1913, 1235–45.

88. R. J. Brewer and R. Dunn, *South Brisbane: From Its Inception in 1888 to Its Absorption in Greater Brisbane on October 1st 1925* (Brisbane: H. Pole, 1925), 7–12; Greenwood and Laverty, *Brisbane, 1859–1959*, 301–03.

89. See, Warren Magnusson, *The Search for Political Space*, 164–65, 167 and David Harvey, *Spaces of Hope* (Berkeley, CA: University of California Press, 2000), 177, 238–40. The construction of this new municipal labor and socialist politics is the subject of my book-length work in progress, *Social Democracy in the City: Class Politics and Social Reform in Comparative Perspective, 1890–1920*.

CHAPTER FOUR

No Common Creed: White Working-Class Protestants and the CIO's Operation Dixie[*]

Elizabeth Fones-Wolf and Ken Fones-Wolf

In May 1945, the United Methodist Church's *Social Questions Bulletin* looked forward to a "new social climate" in the postwar South. Jack McMichael, head of the Methodist Federation for Social Service, pointed to the campaign against the poll tax in Georgia, the opposition of key Methodists to the "unhuman and unbrotherly" regime of Jim Crow, and the work of Methodist layman and CIO labor leader William Mitch in fighting segregation in Alabama. This last example was crucial; one church leader remarked to McMichael, "If the CIO is doing these things, it sort of seems to put the churches on the spot."[1] Not to be outdone, even some Baptists demonstrated support for a new South. In 1946, a group created a new journal, *Christian Frontiers: A Journal of Baptist Life and Thought*, which declared that November: "Welcome Labor Unions!" Reflecting on the CIO's Southern Organizing Campaign (or Operation Dixie), the journal editorialized that if unions helped workers achieve equality with employers, "Out of the balance for power will come collective bargaining and with collective bargaining [will come] approximate justice."[2] At least some Christians in the immediate postwar years expected the CIO to usher in a new era of social and economic justice for the South.

Evidence that there were pockets of growing Protestant support for labor and civil rights in the 1940s defies the conventional wisdom of labor historians. Right-wing Protestant groups that relentlessly red-baited and race-baited the CIO, frightening workers precisely because unions threatened to upend the region's social and racial status quo, loom large in the scholarship on the southern labor movement. Popular religious sentiment, historians argue, ran resolutely in support of a regime that rested on low wages and racial inequality. In the prevailing narratives, the closer one gets to individual congregations in the postwar era, the more virulent the defense of the southern way of life.[3] What, then, accounts for the optimism of many liberal Protestants that the South was ready for a new day? And what accounts for their absence in the historical record?

Part of the difficulty in reconciling this apparent contradiction reflects the reluctance of most labor historians to examine the centrality of religion in working-class life. Trained in "a materialist conception of historical change" that owes much to

British Marxism, even the best American labor historians have often omitted spiritual influences from their analyses.[4] For some of the earliest scholars of the working class, religion served as an impediment to workers understanding their class interests, either dividing workers of different faiths, serving as a tool for the upwardly mobile, or numbing them to their exploitation. Others followed the example provided by E. P. Thompson and Herbert Gutman more than four decades ago, examining how Christianity infused the rhetoric and writings of nineteenth-century labor activists and provided "a postmillennial Christian justification" for their actions. Yet, both groups tended to ignore how beliefs and devotion "framed the consciousness" of average working people. Rather than grapple with the messiness of spiritual convictions, scholars typically reduced religious experience to an explanation of either conservative or radical actions.[5]

Within the last decade, labor historians have advanced more nuanced interpretations. Scholars tackling a variety of topics and time periods—Kimberley Phillips, Joe Creech, David L. Chappell, and Richard J. Callahan, Jr—have benefited from the insights of religious scholars and anthropologists who seek to examine "how particular people, in particular places and times, live in, with, through, and against the religious idioms available to them in culture."[6] The possibilities of such approaches are certainly evident in the new work of Jarod Roll. Experiencing the dramatic transformation of rural life in the boot heel of Missouri in the early twentieth century, black and white farmers, sharecroppers, and tenants gravitated to Pentecostal, Holiness and other fundamentalist churches, which bolstered a range of political responses, from Garveyism to the Klan. But these poor, rural farm people continually reoriented their religious values amid ongoing change to the point where "the children of white supremacists and black nationalists came to protest together on the roadsides in 1939."[7]

Roll's approach is suggestive for the study of white Protestant millhands in the postwar South. Variously depicted by labor historians as either intolerant or fatalistic, their evangelical religion invariably hindered activists trying to unite workers as a class.[8] Despite scholars' sympathetic treatment of black Christianity, the religion of poor whites garners few admirers.[9] One problem with the existing scholarship, particularly as it relates to the white working class, is that it tends to treat popular Christianity in the South as a stagnant force in a region experiencing extraordinary social change. The Depression and war years witnessed extreme poverty and hardship, an exodus from rural agriculture, an expansion of urban manufacturing, a leap in union membership, and the incursion of the federal government into the social and political milieu of the region. Moreover, military service and the presence of military training bases in the region challenged the racial norms of many black and white southerners.[10] Not surprisingly, southern churches also experienced significant upheaval. Some denominations revitalized their social consciences during the Depression and grew closer to northern churches; others turned inward, finding stability in traditional religious values. Meanwhile, there was explosive growth in Holiness, Pentecostal, and fundamentalist churches in the 1930s, as well as in Bible institutes, evangelical radio programs, and itinerant revivalists.[11] Many southerners felt their spiritual world was in just as much turmoil as their earthly one.

Labor historians have been slow to analyze how white, working-class southerners experienced this spiritual turbulence.[12] How did faith influence attitudes about expanding government, labor conflict, racial boundaries, and secular political and social movements? It is true that in many cases popular religion generated a fierce defense of the existing social order. The emphasis on local autonomy, Biblical authority, traditional theology, and premillenialism created in many southern Protestant churches a powerful influence against organized labor's association with class conflict and collectivist liberalism. But social and religious upheaval also created spaces where dissident voices clamored for change. Competing against the *Old Fashioned Revival Hour* and the fundamentalist sermons of such preachers as J. Harold Smith were the prophetic gospel teachings of radicals like Claude Williams, Don West, and the Fellowship of Southern Churchmen. Followers of these radical versions of Protestantism organized black and white tenant farmers along the Mississippi River, coal miners in Appalachia, and textile and tobacco workers in the Piedmont during the 1930s and 1940s.[13]

In short, there were multiple Protestant creeds in the South, each with devoted white, working-class adherents. Moreover, the ways in which they lived their religion did not necessarily advance either a pro-union or anti-union agenda. The challenge for the CIO was to construct a campaign that captured some of the hope of prophetic Christianity without alienating those who clung to more conservative religious beliefs. With this in mind, Operation Dixie recruited Protestant activists and employed ordained ministers to interpret the campaign for the South's white evangelicals.[14]

This essay examines the intersection of Protestantism and a key working-class social movement in the postwar South. It will consider the CIO's attempt to embrace evangelical Protestantism in its campaign as well as the consequences of the shifting denominational and theological loyalties of southern workers in this crucial era. More importantly, this essay will explore the impact of evolving evangelical Protestantism on the attitudes of the white workers as they grappled with the meaning of the CIO's challenge to the social order of southern society. Sorting out the incongruities of southern Protestantism in the decade after World War II helps explain the high hopes of the CIO as well as the considerable barriers it faced in constructing a new social order.

Southern Protestantism in a Time of Change

Religious faith was one of the primary ways that many poor southerners sought to understand the upheavals of the 1930s and 1940s. The Depression triggered a mass exodus from southern rural society that only accelerated during World War II. Meanwhile, the New Deal, which identified the South as the nation's number one economic problem, left a spotty record in the region. Employers successfully beat back most union drives and maintained their low-wage regime. The war years were more successful, bringing 800,000 new industrial jobs and some pockets of union success as a result of the Fair Employment Practices Commission and the National War Labor Board.[15] As they moved from the countryside to industrial towns and mill villages, migrants carried values nurtured by popular evangelical Protestantism. Although there were variations, rural evangelicals held strong beliefs about the importance of God's grace, redemption through faith, the necessity of bearing witness, and the Bible as the sole religious authority. Many southerners also believed in the worldly presence of Satan and that mankind was "regressing toward the imminent end of the world."[16] For some, the existence of communism and the challenge to segregation were evidence of this regression.[17] Hard times reinforced this spiritual side, especially among those who worshipped outside the mainline Protestant denominations. In fact, the greatest growth occurred among the Holiness, Pentecostal, and fundamentalist churches, suggesting a changed religious order.[18]

Transformations in Protestantism both reflected and contributed to an altered religious landscape in the postwar South. One example that provides insight into broader patterns of regional change is Gaston County, North Carolina, an area made famous by Liston Pope's study of its 1929 textile strike. Most Gastonians in the 1920s went to a Protestant church; 88 percent worshipped in three southern denominations, the Methodist Episcopal Church South, the Presbyterian Church in the United States, and the Southern Baptist Convention. During the 1930s, however, white millhands began to move to newer Holiness and Pentecostal churches. Twenty one of the 24 churches established in the mill villages in the 1930s were outside the mainstream.[19] Nor were the changes limited to what Pope called the "newer sects." Fast forward another decade, and one sees a marked shift from the Methodists to the Baptists. While most white churchgoers in Gaston County remained in one of those two denominations, Methodists dropped from 26 to 19.5 percent while Baptists increased their share by a similar amount. Baptists were the only mainstream denomination to expand in the mill villages of Gaston County. It was also the mainstream denomination that most closely resembled the primitive church—autonomous local bodies of saved individuals free from ritualized worship and hierarchy.[20]

Listening to the voices of white working people can make religious beliefs seem almost serendipitous. For some the choice of church was simply a matter of location. Growing up in Rock Hill, South Carolina, Eva Hopkins's family, like many others, did not have a car. On Sunday, "You went to the church that was closest to you." Ethel Faucette recalled that her mill village "Didn't have but one" church, and "most everybody here on the hill went to this little church." Mary Thompson was even more blunt; her community "didn't have any recreation, only what the church put out."[21] It was also true that in some mill villages the company employed not-so-subtle pressures to attend the church it financed. In Burlington, North Carolina, James Pharis remembered that "If you didn't belong to the Hocutt Memorial Baptist Church over here, you didn't get along too well in the Plaid Mill."[22]

Even workers who made choices often made them without reference to creeds or theology. Eva Hopkins became a Baptist after attending Methodist churches in her youth. When asked why, she stated: "Well, I don't know, I went down there to visit, and I liked the preacher. I liked the sermons he preached better, and I enjoyed the Sunday School class and the teachers, the way they taught and all, more. I just really enjoyed it more, so that's where I went." Flake and Nellie Mae Meyers switched from a Lutheran to a Methodist church because their children had friends there. Theology appeared to have little impact to the Meyers: "like we all say, the church is not going to save you; it's the way you live. One denomination's no better than the other."[23]

Increasingly during the 1930s and 1940s, however, working-class whites felt that the creeds and the practices of the church they attended mattered. Ila Dodson remarked on her switch from a Baptist church to a Pentecostal Holiness church: "There was boys come over here from the Holmes Bible College. . . . preaching Holiness, and we just liked it." Hoy Deal, who worked in Piedmont lumber and glove factories, felt uncomfortable in the Lutheran Church because of its concentration on the catechism. He became a Baptist after listening to the local preacher. To him, "if a man ain't going to preach the word of God, why, he ain't got no business in the pulpit." Deal also regularly listened to radio preachers who testified; "that's one thing that any Christian is supposed to do when they get a chance, to witness to anybody about the Savior."[24] Even many who clung to mainline churches found ones that fit particular needs. Alice Levitt recoiled against mill village Holiness preachers, but her Methodist church adopted the practices of rural folk religion. Anyone who had "been in another Methodist church," she asserted, would be surprised by hers "because they have all that [spontaneous witnessing and testifying]. We all stand up and read the Bible in church. . . . It's like old-timey," she claimed.[25]

Working-class whites gravitated toward congregations that resembled primitive Christianity. The Depression and war years witnessed a surge of sects with antimodernist outlooks—Old Regular and Primitive Baptists, Nazarenes, Assembly of God, Holiness and Pentecostal churches, and independent fundamentalist churches. These churches imposed strict standards of behavior, rejected hierarchies, and insisted on the autonomy of their congregations. They also adopted rituals like footwashing, as well as spontaneous sermons and ecstatic services. But as Alice Levitt's Methodist congregation exemplified, currents of folk religion reached many mainline churchgoers.[26]

Many scholars, both then and today, dismiss the turn to popular religious beliefs during hard times as escapist, fatalistic, and otherworldly; such convictions diverted the poor from attending to the tasks of improving their conditions. However, believers were hardly out of touch with reality. Belief in God's grace, the hope of salvation, and even the worldly presence of Satan, "all had real and precise psychological and social functions," according to historian Wayne Flynt. Their practices and faith were reassuring in difficult times; they allowed the emotional release of "resentments and fears" and brought "calm as well as excitement."[27] For one rural-born white, church was a place "where you meet God, where for a little while you find Him and keep Him, where He tells you that it's all right, and it's going to be all right, and that no matter what, you'll come out on His side." Textile worker Louise Jones's faith was critical in surviving hard times: "God helped us through. He's been with us all the time. I give God credit for being what I am and having the life I've had, and helping me all of my life."[28]

Popular, Pentecostal, and folk religious beliefs could also be more than practical coping mechanisms. In places like Harlan County, Kentucky, many Pentecostal miners felt that their faith gave religious sanction to the United Mine Workers. Lay preachers, like Findlay Donaldson, who made his living as a miner, could assert: "A man who won't support his children [by supporting the union] is worse than an Infidel, and there is no place for that man but Hell." Social activist Myles Horton discussed the paradox of "mountain religion." He noted that unpaid preachers would "preach on Sunday, this fundamentalist religion, then go out on the picket line all week." Meanwhile, "preachers in the cities were talking liberal theology, liberalism, all the modern . . . interpretations of religion, yet they would side" with the coal operators.[29]

Similarly, sharecroppers and tenants joined the Southern Tenant Farmers Union in Alabama, Mississippi and Arkansas in part because organizers like Claude Williams and Howard Kester, divinity students of Vanderbilt's Social Gospel teacher Alva Taylor, brought a prophetic Christianity along with radical political affiliations to the rural struggle. Kester was a Socialist; Williams worked closely with the Communist Party at various times. Their interpretation of the Bible as a "continuous record of revolutionary struggle" meshed with the message of many sharecropper-ministers who were in the same straits as their congregations.[30] These individuals plumbed the radical implications of religious faith. Don West, yet another of Taylor's students, grew up in poverty in the mountains of North Georgia. Like Williams, West flirted with membership in the Communist Party, but he also spoke to miners, tenants and sharecroppers in the language of an Appalachian Primitive Baptist. Even in the 1950s, West still commanded a loyal following from white workers who worshipped at an independent Pentecostal church in Dalton, Georgia, until his political positions were exposed.[31] Southern whites could take a variety of messages from the emotional but theologically conservative folk religion in the 1930s and 1940s.

One reason that prophetic ministers like West and Williams succeeded was their understanding of rural Christianity. Their Vanderbilt mentor, Alva Taylor, praised their acceptance of the newer sects. Writing to Williams, Taylor asserted that "the mountain preachers have agreed with you regarding the sincerity of their Pentecostal preaching brethren. Now if we could induce the more highly educated men in our mountains to adopt your method rather than one of criticism and denunciation, we would get somewhere."[32] Through the radical, prophetic People's Institute of Applied Religion, which Williams created in 1940 to recruit "leaders from the people to preach and practice the Gospel of the Kingdom of God on earth," he trained effective labor organizers—people like Harry Koger of the Food, Tobacco and Agricultural Workers. Williams taught Koger to embrace the spirituality of southern workers but link it to "a God who wants them to get their bellies full of food" and "a Jesus, who much to their surprise, is actually interested in them having a more abundant life here on Earth and not merely 'pie in the sky' after they get up to that gold-paved city."[33]

In the aftermath of World War II, however, the prospects of radical, prophetic religion diminished. The horrors of the war and the prospects of a new Cold War with the Soviet Union gave even many proponents of social Christianity pause. Church-labor cooperation confronted a newly re-energized spirit of anticommunism, which helped reshape American Protestantism, particularly in the South. Increasingly, adherence to evangelical, sectarian, and fundamentalist creeds imparted certain habits of thought and behavior that had consequences for social movements. First was their commitment to live a "separated life." Convinced that their nation was rejecting God, many evangelicals distanced themselves from the world's values and tried to live as Bible-believing Christians. This included strict standards of behavior regarding sex, alcohol, dress, and profanity. One staunchly Baptist North Carolina mill worker recalled a man who left his church because "he said it wasn't right to cook and eat in the church." Another noted that his conversion to Pentecostalism required him to refrain from cursing, drinking, and smoking. "We're not of this world," he added, and "we are not supposed to participate in anything of this world."[34]

A second important change was the adoption of dispensational premillenialism. Dispensationalists professed a popular premillenialist belief that world conditions would inevitably degenerate until Christ returned to establish his kingdom through a rapture that could occur at any moment.[35] For many southerners, the Depression, World War II, and escalating tensions with the Soviet Union confirmed their interpretation of the end times. Religious magazines noted the "remarkable growth of those sects which represent radical mysticism." In trying to explain this phenomenon, one minister recognized that dispensationalists had the ability to impart the sense of urgency to their evangelicalism. "What they have to preach greatly matters and it matters *now*. . . . The end of the age is approaching."[36] The Depression and war shook the postmillennial optimism of many. Meanwhile, churches that preached dispensational messages and fundamentalist values brought the Holy Spirit into the lives of southern white workers and enabled them to take charge of their destiny.[37]

Southern Protestant Churches and Labor's Gospel

The shifting terrain of southern Protestantism had important repercussions for the ways working-class whites felt about the CIO's organizing drive inaugurated in 1946. Labor historians have focused on only one particular aspect of the relationship between religion and Operation Dixie, its difficulty confronting well-funded groups delivering antiunion messages tinged with popular Christianity. David Burgess, an ordained minister and CIO organizer, briefed the U.S. Senate in 1950 on the use of ministers and publications paid for by employer organizations to propagandize against unions. Included were Parson Jack Johnson's *Gospel Trumpet* and Sherman Patterson's *Militant Truth*, which mysteriously appeared in the mailboxes of workers just prior to NLRB elections and linked the labor movement to "godless Communism." Other examples included ministers who preached sermons claiming that CIO stood for "Christ Is Out" or that it was the "Mark of the Beast" as revealed in the Book of Revelations. Popular radio ministries, bankrolled by right-wing groups, also denounced unions in apocalyptic terms.[38] For evangelical Protestants who believed that the spread of communism and interracialism were examples of Satan's work, such charges might appear credible, however much we might dismiss them.

Southern Protestantism was more complex, however, and the Cold War context was not the only factor influencing working-class Protestants. Building upon the Christian social activism sparked by the Depression, the CIO cautiously hoped for more support. Southern Baptists gave encouraging signs by adopting a resolution in favor of collective bargaining and in denouncing the Ku Klux Klan. The denomination's most liberal wing even welcomed Operation Dixie. Labor also expected backing from the region's second largest denomination, the Methodists, following a merger with the more liberal northern Methodists in 1939. In addition, the CIO recognized that the Southern Conference for Human Welfare attracted numerous liberal Christians, and that the Fellowship of Southern Churchmen was revitalizing its labor committee under the direction of David Burgess.[39] Although the CIO sought to maintain distance from groups allied with Leftists, its leaders saw signs of a new day dawning in southern Protestantism.

More pervasive, and probably more representative of the vast majority of southern white Protestants than either vigorous opposition to or support for unions, were subtle religious hurdles that the CIO needed to overcome. While many churches had accepted the need for collective bargaining, they expected unions to respect local culture, which included fear of outsiders and the expanding powers of the federal government.[40] These were matters that touched a nerve for southerners concerned about the changes that already threatened the religious liberty of southern churches. They pointed to the Methodists' merger, which caused turmoil and defections. Stirrings of North-South unification among Baptists and Presbyterians frightened many, especially those of fundamentalist persuasion who felt that northerners would force racial accommodation, liberal politics, and a modernist theology on the South.[41] Although the Methodists and Presbyterians had become progressively more middle class in composition, the Baptists continued to be by far the most popular denomination with the white working class. Equally disturbing for southern evangelicals were the efforts of northern mainline Protestants to control religious radio broadcasting. They resented the liberal Federal Council of Churches for successfully keeping fundamentalist, Bible-oriented programs off the airwaves.[42]

Evangelical Protestants in the South, led by Baptists and Presbyterians, also strongly opposed the Federal Council's efforts to unite churches across creeds.

One minister asserted that the Council "sails under the old flag of evangelical Christianity, but in it are all the modernists and skeptics of the churches, and they are in control." In July 1946, the *Southern Presbyterian Journal* editorialized: "We do not believe that a theological outlook which makes 'electives' of the infallibility of the Bible, the virgin birth, the miracles, the bodily resurrection and the blood of atonement, can beget a true effective Christian leadership."[43] Southern Baptists deplored the Federal Council's efforts to "prescribe a common creed, or form of church government, or form of worship." So adamant were some Baptists against ecumenical infringements that in 1949 they considered banning anyone who affiliated with a state or local council of churches from eligibility to serve on Baptist boards or agencies.[44] Equally hostile was the young National Association of Evangelicals, which included Holiness and Pentecostal groups like the Church of God and the Nazarenes, churches that were growing rapidly among the southern poor. Evangelicals cautioned that the Federal Council, which was rooted in the Social Gospel, was actually a "socialistic religious 'front organization'" for communistic groups that threatened the nation's churches. The National Association of Evangelicals singled out such groups as the Methodist Federation for Social Service, the National Religion and Labor Foundation, and the CIO, which advocated doctrines not "in accord with the Word of God."[45]

Thus, when the CIO began its campaign in 1946 it needed not only to confront the antiunion rantings of hate-sheets like *Militant Truth* but also to calm the fears of many antimodernist southern white Protestants. To accomplish these tasks, the CIO formed a Community Relations Department, led by active laypersons John Ramsay and Lucy Mason. Mason was from a long line of prominent Episcopalian ministers, descendants of Virginians George Mason and John Marshall. She had worked with the YWCA and headed the National Consumers League in New York before returning south to help the CIO organize in 1937.[46] Ramsay was a devout Presbyterian layman whose spiritual example had spearheaded United Steelworker organizing drives in Bethlehem, Pennsylvania, and at Armco Steel in Kentucky.[47] The CIO also had religious people in a number of other key positions in the South. Franz Daniel, who trained to be a minister at Union Theological Seminary before embarking on a career in labor, headed up the SOC in the Carolinas.[48] Charles Webber, a Methodist preacher trained at the Boston University School of Theology, joined the labor movement in 1943, leaving behind a career as a minister, professor, and social activist. During Operation Dixie, Webber organized for the Amalgamated Clothing Workers of America and became President of the Virginia CIO.[49] Finally, David Burgess, a Congregational minister, joined the Operation Dixie staff in 1947, working as an organizer and political activist in South Carolina, Virginia, and Georgia.[50]

Operation Dixie organizers coping with hostility from ministers or laypeople routinely turned to these individuals for assistance. However, in contrast to the prophetic ministers like Don West and Claude Williams who stitched radical messages into the tapestry of rural folk religion, the CIO's Protestants tended to be dismissive of charismatic churches and their theologies. Lucy Mason was an Episcopalian, Webber a Methodist, Ramsay a northern Presbyterian, Burgess a Congregationalist and Daniel a Unitarian Universalist. These were mainstream northern churches, some considered nonevangelical by many southerners. These were also churches that were losing ground in the South, particularly among workers who had migrated from the countryside and those who worshipped in mill villages.

Critically, the CIO's religious activists misjudged what would appeal to southern white Protestants. For example, Ramsay, Mason and Burgess developed and distributed thousands of copies of pamphlets, such as *Religion Speaks to Labor* or *Trade Unions and Preachers*, to attract workers and community leaders. However, these tracts relied on statements from the national bodies of mainstream denominations or on statements from the Federal Council of Churches.[51] Many local ministers viewed such literature negatively, believing that the true mission of religion was to "win men to Christ" not to social movements.[52] Endorsements from the Federal Council rarely elicited the desired response. For example, in Operation Dixie's early years, Presbyterians were embroiled in a debate over whether or not to continue its association with the Council for both social and theological reasons. Presbyterians critiqued the Council's positions on the virgin birth and the "old-fashioned substitutionary doctrine of the Atonement," as well as on racial intermarriage, socialized medicine, and the Fair Employment Practices Commission. CIO emissaries, claiming the Council's endorsement while trying to organize workers, thus identified organized labor with an unpopular ally. In Mecklenburg County, North Carolina, Chattanooga, Tennessee, and Rock Hill, South Carolina, Presbyterian laypeople rejected both the Federal Council and CIO organizers who professed "so much that is unscriptural and wrong."[53]

Among Southern Baptists the CIO's efforts were equally problematic. The CIO's religious activists thoroughly misunderstood Baptist creeds. At the very outset of Operation Dixie, the CIO distributed the pamphlet entitled "The Church and the CIO Must Co-operate." Immediately, Baptists took issue. Richmond, Virginia's *Religious Herald* objected to the notion that it was necessary for Baptists to support a social movement even if it aimed to bring about a "more abundant life." The idea that the pamphlet would instruct Baptists about what they "must" do was evidence of just how little the CIO knew about Southern Baptists' regard for individual freedom and congregational autonomy. The *Religious Herald* editorialized that the "only imperative for the Christian Church is to preach the Gospel of Christ to men everywhere."[54] Numerous articles in the Southern Baptist press agreed with another minister who wrote that "the church should not be pro-capital or pro-labor in its sympathies. It must retain both groups within its fellowship and make its ministry vital for both."[55] In situations where conflict arose, many Baptists looked at organized labor as the instigators. According to Lucy Mason, in one South Carolina textile town, a Baptist preacher's wife "demanded that the young organizer in charge in that town (a good Methodist) and I leave— truly said she, 'We are not paying any attention to anything you say, we don't believe it, you can't do any good by staying, so please just get out.'"[56]

Mason compared the enmity of the Baptists with a growing tolerance from the Church of God and Pentecostal Holiness churches. She found it "curious that the opposition we once had from the little new sects . . . has died down and we have little of it," she wrote in 1946; "Often union chaplains, fellow working men in the same plant and belonging to the union, come from these sects, while relatively few of them belong to the more prosperous churches."[57] But Mason also knew that the impression existed that these sects were opposed to labor. In 1948 she wrote to Church of God minister John C. Jernigan: "Many of your members have asked me to get something from their Church that could be included in whatever I may print in the future—something positive, commending unions." Most were unwilling to comply. A year later, Mason noted that the Church of God, the Pentecostal Holiness Church, and the Assembly of God would state only that the ban on membership in "secret societies" did not apply to participation in unions where it was necessary for retaining employment or where it was "in association with a legal effort on the part of labor, to prevent oppression and injustice."[58] Franz Daniel and David Burgess did not share Mason's optimism; they were certain that these churches were arrayed against organized labor, mired in unenlightened ideas and fatalistic thinking. Despite the occasional preacher friendly to the CIO, most sects avoided large institutions and impersonal aggregations, which they interpreted as racing "toward outright socialism."[59]

Interestingly, radicals Claude Williams and Don West seemed better able to develop relationships with members of the sects than were the CIO's religious activists, at least until their association with communists became public knowledge. Their success with sects derived, at least in part, from their emphasis on grassroots control as well as on a message that unions were a vehicle for God's deliverance in the struggle between rich and poor.[60] In contrast, the CIO's Community Relations Department had less success making contact with the preachers of the Nazarenes, the Church of God, or the Pentecostal Holiness churches. Its staff routinely visited clergy at the start of a union organizing drive, but reports of the department's contacts show that it concentrated on mainstream Protestant ministers. Undoubtedly, some of that bias resulted from the religious affiliations of CIO personnel, but some also resulted from the greater availability of ministers who were paid, full-time clergy. Many preachers in the smaller sects had day jobs, often in the factories where their congregations worked.[61]

Perhaps most disappointing for Operation Dixie, its religious activists proved incapable of winning unconditional support from the Methodists, a denomination with millenarian traditions. The second largest denomination in the region, Methodists offered a liberal theology and a hierarchy that supported social action, but these characteristics actually eroded its working-class base in the conservative South. Nevertheless, one of the CIO's best spokespersons for cooperation between religion and labor, Charles Webber, was a Methodist preacher. During the 1930s, Webber spent a year organizing clothing workers in Richmond. Later, he served as the Methodist Federation for Social Service field secretary from 1937 until 1943, when he rejoined the Amalgamated Clothing Workers in Virginia. Within two years, Webber was elected President of the Virginia CIO.[62] Webber's pedigree did not guarantee him success with Methodists in the South. In 1946, the *Methodist Advocate* demanded that Webber surrender his credentials as a Methodist minister if he continued as Virginia CIO president and director of its Political Action Committee. Despite holding an appointment as "chaplain to organized labor" from Methodist Bishop G. Bromley Oxnam, Virginia Methodists found Webber's activities "exceedingly embarrassing," particularly his opposition to Senator Harry F. Byrd. Webber's credentials became a source of considerable debate, eliciting antagonism from laymen in neighboring states, until Oxnam finally withdrew the appointment.[63]

White, Working-Class Faith and Operation Dixie

Southern white workers filtered union messages, as well as the conflicts they witnessed, through their religious cultures. Despite denominational differences, most southern churches shared some basic tendencies, one of which stressed congregational autonomy.[64] Consequently, local ministers and laypeople exerted a good deal of sway over the beliefs of workers. Even in the more hierarchical Methodist Church, Bishop Oxnam found local ministers making pronouncements that ran counter to "the official position of the church" on matters such as labor's right to organize. Oxnam interceded, "making bold to send an inquiry" for facts when informed that a Cherryville, North Carolina, Methodist minister signed a letter urging members to vote against the CIO. Oxnam found the minister's actions reprehensible, but ultimately had to admit that the matter was "quite beyond the realm" of his authority.[65]

At the start of organizing drives, the CIO typically surveyed the attitudes of local clergy. In these surveys, it found local ministers who were sympathetic to labor's message, some who knew very little about unions, as well as some who were hostile. It is difficult to detect any consistent denominational pattern; Methodist, Baptist, Church of God, Nazarene, Presbyterian, and other ministers could be found in each category. But these surveys captured sentiments at the beginning of the organizing drives, before the issues of union representation became contentious.[66] In one of the earliest campaigns, in Kannapolis, North Carolina, CIO staff member Ruth Gettinger talked with six Baptist clergy. The three most likely to help labor had been workers or had family in the mills, although one noted that "he could not preach labor unions from the pulpit." Two others promised Gettinger, a Southern Baptist herself, to study the issues and to consider attending future meetings bringing together ministers and labor people. One asked more pointed questions about whether the CIO "tolerated communists" in its organization and "how we would handle the Negro situation." While he said "that every sincere religious person would uphold anything that benefited the working man," this minister was guarded about unions and "not entirely unbiased on the racial question."[67] Of course, a survey conducted during a contentious campaign probably would have elicited different responses, particularly since southern churches put a premium on community harmony.

Ministers who supported unions did so for many different reasons. In some cases, experience with industrial work was key. John Ramsay enlisted the aid of a Baptist minister who had formerly worked at a plant in Radford, Virginia, and "would like to work there for the union." Many sympathetic clergy combined ministerial duties with factory work. In Elizabethtown, Tennessee, CIO director Paul Christopher relied on a "Missionary Baptist preacher" with a little church who was also "a good union member" at North American Rayon.[68] For others, it was the composition of the church body. One Concord, North Carolina, minister preached to an "entire congregation" of mill workers. As a result, the CIO found that "he preaches a good sermon and is a very likable, human person" who was "greatly in favor of our organization." In Macon, Georgia, a Disciples of Christ minister counseled members of his flock on the picket line: "As a disciple of Jesus Christ, I am concerned about you as a brother—I am concerned about your family and hunger and shelter and clothing."[69] A few changed their minds after earlier experiences. Ruth Gettinger met a "fiery" Church of God evangelist who came to support unions because of the inspiring example of a coal mine organizer.[70]

Congregations that contained both workers and management people, however, often put ministers in a difficult position. Methodist laymen in Lawrenceburg, Tennessee, objected to CIO criticism that the church's failure to join with unions meant that it "has failed throughout these centuries to instill the teachings of Christ into the fabric of society." In Rock Hill, South Carolina, elders of a Presbyterian church in which many supervisors worshipped rejected CIO organizer David Burgess's application for membership. When the minister was seen having lunch with union activists, "leading church officials" told him, "We think you're seeing too much of that CIO union organizer."[71] Similarly, in Easley, South Carolina, Baptist church officials asked a "fine young union man to resign as superintendent of the Sunday School—he could not teach there because no CIO member can 'go to heaven.'"[72]

Some pro-union ministers defied the pressure to reject the CIO. The Rock Hill minister warned about seeing too much of a CIO organizer replied that if he "is as evil as you say, that's where I should be spending my time. Our task is to save the sinners, not the righteous!" He also demanded that the congregation admit Burgess to membership or look for another minister.[73] The CIO, in turn, tried to recognize its obligation to supporters. Lucy Mason warned Memphis CIO leaders that if her friend Sam Howie opened "his church to unions, as he wishes to do, organized labor should surely support him. He will have attacks from industrialists and business men and will find it hard to keep his church going unless unions stand solidly with him."[74] Other ministers were not so fortunate. Rev. Arthur Hyde wrote John Ramsay that his interest in the CIO "proved my undoing in Rome [Georgia]." Pro-union preacher John B. Isom resigned from his Baptist church in Spartanburg, South Carolina, "convinced that the working people of the South will never have the freedom to support a minister with a sensible and helpful religious outlook until they are organized into strong and dependable unions."[75]

Clergy opposed to unions also had an assortment of reasons, but most are refracted through the lenses of Operation Dixie organizers. Ruth Gettinger found one North Carolina Methodist minister "rabidly anti-union. He had all the old ideas of violence and strikes being associated with unionism." A young Baptist minister in Morristown, Tennessee, was "ambitious," and thus antiunion, according to Lucy Mason.[76] Typically, Mason and Gettinger made such cryptic assessments as: "individualist and non-cooperative," "innocent concerning unions," or "stupid man." They often put clergy in the antiunion column if they had career aspirations or if they hoped to build a new church. Similarly, the CIO expected less from ministers whose congregations included mill owners or "management men."[77] Most typical were the ministers who listened attentively but were unlikely to take a stand on either side. Lucy Mason met with a Baptist publication editor in Greenville, South Carolina, who was "a sensible, liberal old gentleman with whom [she] had a good talk. But he can't tackle these mill village men," she asserted.[78]

Occasionally antiunion clergy cited previous experiences to justify their opposition. Rev. Walter Cooley, a Methodist pastor at Great Falls, South Carolina, wrote Operation Dixie director George Baldanzi about why he opposed the CIO. He had formerly been a minister at Ware Shoals and at Lyman, sites of South Carolina CIO campaigns that ended badly for the union and the workers. Twice Cooley had witnessed the CIO convince workers to walk out on good jobs only to call off the strike and leave "them to root hog or die." In Lyman, when Cooley advised against the strike, the workers "turned against me. I lived to see the horror of my prophecies enacted before my very eyes: People turned out of their homes, hunger and deprivation, spreading of hate, families divided," all leading to lawlessness and even murder.[79] Over a decade, CIO defeats meant that many ministers despaired of seeing yet another organizing drive.

Intimidation from employers and local law enforcement officials undoubtedly played a role. In Cuthbert, Georgia, police told a Methodist minister to stop allowing unions to meet in his church. When he replied that people had a right to join unions, the police warned that "he was liable to wake up one morning to find everything burnt up around here." In Great Falls, South Carolina, "all the ministers in town were called over to the Company office for a meeting." One Nazarene minister "stayed an hour after the others left" to make a special recording against the union. That Sunday, the Church of God minister told his congregation that "members could not belong to the CIO."[80] Employer opposition to organizing drives convinced some ministers to take sides. One CIO organizer complained of a Nazarene preacher in Norwood, North Carolina, who was part of a group threatening violence to union organizers. "I believe when you saw him he assured you he would remain neutral," the organizer wrote John Ramsay, but "he has become an accessory to violence," and is now "a king pin in this whole affair."[81]

Effective intimidation, especially amid the growing Cold War tensions, often involved charges that supporters of the CIO were communists or that they hoped to upset the racial status quo, charges that frequently overlapped. The "hate sheets," like Sherman Patterson's newspaper, *Militant Truth*, tried desperately to fan the flames of racial prejudice with claims that unions would replace white workers with blacks. In the tobacco factories of Winston-Salem, North Carolina, fears about eliminating racial job categories mingled with a religious justification of segregation: "That was just the way God had created the world, that white people made cigarettes and the black people made chewing tobacco." Whites who joined the union found themselves "completely isolated and ostracized," facing accusations that they supported un-American and un-Christian doctrines that filtered down from the communist-sympathizing CIO.[82] Ironically, the more CIO spokespersons sought to distance Operation Dixie from any taint of leftism, the more they called attention to unions that had communist leaders, thereby adding weight to the charges. Many workers who heard CIO radio speeches concerning efforts to defeat communist-led unions probably had difficulty differentiating militant messages from radical ones.[83]

Workers made pragmatic assessments of potential gains in concert with their religious beliefs, especially in the piedmont and upland South where textile workers were Operation Dixie's primary target. Millhands who joined the union, like "hardshell" Baptist George Dyer, believed that "the union organizer helped the people in people's work." A Church of Christ member in Elizabethtown, Tennessee, became a union activist because she thought "the people benefited from it." Baptist Eva Hopkins joined the union because it promised better wages and working conditions; her company "wouldn't let you raise the windows, [and] it was so hot." When her co-workers went on strike, "people that belonged to the union, they had a community house up here. They would take the union dues that you'd pay, and buy food" and take care of one another.[84]

But pro-labor workers expected unions to share their religious concern for a religious ideal of community harmony, one which united believers rather than pit Christians against one another. Methodist Pauline Griffith supported labor "if it's done right," but not "if they have some hotheads in there that causes trouble." One Bible-believer worried about cases when unions "go to the extreme with it; cause trouble and don't benefit nobody." James Pharis, a good Christian, was union president *and* a loyal company man. He complained when the union sent a "radical" speaker who ran down the company. Pharis "just got right up there on the stand. I told him, I says, 'Wait a minute. You're on the wrong track here. You ain't going to make no hit with the people here.' "[85]

For other Christian millhands, religious values dictated suspicion about outside organizations, particularly when they threatened to divide congregations over secular conflicts. During the 1949–50 strike in Spartanburg, South Carolina, Sunday morning services turned the Second Baptist Church into warring factions that actually drove many from membership.[86] Evangelical churches constantly reminded their congregations that "being yoked with unbelievers" was unchristian and harmful to God's work. Unions were thus unwelcome intruders. Methodist George Elmore "didn't want to see that outside crowd come in there and taking dues from them that basically didn't give a damn about the good will of the people." Ethel Faucette, a Baptist, felt union people "came in from somewhere else, and I don't know who they was." Kasper Smith, who had participated in the 1934 general textile strike, turned his back on unions after joining the Church of God. His congregation kept earlier rules opposing labor activities: "We're not allowed to participate in a strike. The Bible speaks on all that," he claimed. When reminded about the 1934 strike, Smith replied: "I couldn't do that now. And, well, see, I joined the union before I joined the church. I haven't joined no other organizations *since*."[87]

Southern evangelical churches also stressed autonomy and freedom, values that working-class followers felt were at times endangered by unions. For example, when shirt workers in LaFollette, Tennessee, won a union contract, the company elimi- nated the workers' morning prayer meeting. Many millworkers believed that union contracts ended the informal culture of the shop floor, and resulted in more rigid work rules and standards. Josephine Glenn, a Baptist, enjoyed working "just about like we wanted to, as long as we stayed at work;" Eula Durham, who regularly attended mill village churches and revivals, felt she could "go outdoors when I get ready and come in when I please." Neither one wanted to give up this freedom for a contract, fearing that "you'd have to come up to their standards."[88] Methodist Flake Myers hated the idea that a union could "come in and tell you what to do," while Murphy Sigmon asserted: "The union has got laws, too, to go by, and if I'm working with the plant, I just don't feel like I can satisfy both" the union and the company.[89]

Workers also weighed the possibility of defeat against the improvements that they had experienced since the 1930s. Although southern wages lagged behind northern counterparts, most saw a significant improvement in their standard of living. For instance, one Methodist millhand believed that most "were satisfied as it was," and thus immune to union appeals. For Flake Myers, union sympathizers were "mostly drifters, people that was all the time groaning."[90] However, such sentiments were typically combined with fear and a history of defeat. Emma Whitesell ignored union appeals "'cause it was kind of scary," and Mareda Cobb refused "because I always knew that North Carolina [workers] would never stick" to organized labor. CIO organizer Scott Hoyman recalled the impact of earlier failures, particularly 1934, on the postwar campaign: "Oh God. They remembered it in the organized plants, but they really remember it in the unorganized plants."[91]

Memories of previous defeats mixed with and even reinforced the notions of many millhands that it was a religious duty to work hard. Mary Thompson, a fre- quent attendee at Holiness tent meetings read "in the Bible that people is supposed to make their living by the sweat of their brow." Tessie Dyer, raised a hardshell Baptist, crossed the picket line because "I was supposed to go to work, and I was going."[92] Other workers, like the ones at J. P. Stevens Company in Roanoke Rapids, worried that unions put too much emphasis on promises to improve wages. Millhand Leonard Wilson believed it unfair "to God and our country for the unions to insist on raising the prices of everything that is made" by demanding increases. In fact, he felt that "it is against God's will for the unions to preach more and more money, for First Timothy 6:10 tells us that the love of money is the root of all evil."[93]

Conclusion

While some workers felt that there was no contradiction between Operation Dixie's goals and a concern for Christian brotherhood, for others there was a gap between the values and ideas promoted by the CIO and those that arose from postwar southern Protestantism. Demonstrations of solidarity, the mechanics of collective bargaining, and the potential for conflict at times deviated from the freedom, autonomy, and community harmony that southern white Protestants desired in their churches. Furthermore, antiunion forces in the South did their best to associate the organizing campaign with a godless communism, with northern notions of race relations, and with intrusive and hierarchical institutions that would dictate changes in southern culture. White, Protestant workers thus measured the potential gains from union representation against the dangers inherent in disrupting the status quo, but their calculations did not occur in a vacuum. The devastation of a depression and world war bolstered a premillenial outlook that stressed individual salvation, the failures of previous organizing drives encouraged satisfaction with the gains already made, growing Cold-War fears cautioned against joining unions that harbored communists, and CIO support for interracial unions increased concern for the survival of white privilege. The fact that these factors were intertwined with changes in southern Protestantism added to their power.

Of course, southern Protestantism, by itself, did not doom Operation Dixie. Rather, the campaign disappointed for a variety of reasons—improvements in wages, the CIO's decision to target the most defiant industrialists, poor organizing strategies, the passage of the Taft-Hartley Act, the racism of white workers, the bureaucratic nature of the CIO, the structure of southern industry, and anti-communist hysteria all contributed to its defeat.[94] Still, the impact of evangelical Protestantism on southern white workers needs to be considered as an independent variable, helping shape their receptiveness to Operation Dixie's message. Their religious beliefs braced a culture that made them wary of the new social climate that these "northern" unions promised to deliver. Contributing to that culture were the most virulent sorts of red-baiting and race-baiting found in publications like *Militant Truth* or *The Gospel Trumpet*. Because they were so inflammatory and because they provide an easy explanation for the CIO's failure, labor historians have focused on them, neglecting other religious developments in the South. It is thus difficult to reconcile the optimism that organizers felt about the possibilities for religious support in the postwar South. Moreover, by emphasizing the most reactionary variants of southern Protestantism, historians also ignore the richness and complexity of the religious values of southern white workers.

At the time, while organizers recognized the importance of religion for Operation Dixie, they did not appreciate the intricacies of southern evangelical Protestantism. Instead, the CIO misconstrued what it would take to build upon the pockets of pro-union Christianity in the region. Few union organizers understood Pentecostalism, premillenial dispensationalism, or the finer points of Southern Baptist beliefs. The prophetic radicals who most closely echoed the accents of southern evangelicalism could not harmonize for very long their communist associations and the loyalties of Bible-believing Christians. And even those more mainstream union activists who had strong Protestant connections were tied to creeds that were out of touch with the religious changes taking place in the South. These same problems continued beyond labor's campaign and helped smooth the way for white, working-class Protestants to become a key bloc in modern conservatism. When Operation Dixie professed Christianity's support for collective action, fair employment practices, or expanded government regulation in southern communities, it was as if they were preaching from a different Bible. If labor historians are to penetrate the mind of white, southern workers, they cannot afford to make the same mistake.

Notes

* The authors would like to thank Eric Arnesen, Wayne Flynt, Bob Korstad, Joe McCartin, Steve Rosswurm, David Watt, and the editors of this volume for helpful comments on this project.
1. Jack R. McMichael, "The New Social Climate in the South," *Social Questions Bulletin* (May 1945): 4–5.
2. "Welcome Labor Unions!" *Christian Frontiers* (November 1946): 277–78.
3. Timothy J. Minchin, *What Do We Need a Union For?: The TWUA in the South, 1945–1955* (Chapel Hill, NC: University of North Carolina Press, 1997); Barbara S. Griffith, *The Crisis of American Labor: Operation Dixie and the Defeat of the CIO* (Philadelphia, PA: Temple University Press, 1988); David S. Burgess, *Fighting for Social Justice: The Life Story of David Burgess* (Detroit: Wayne State University Press, 2000); Robert Rogers Korstad, *Civil Rights Unionism: Tobacco Workers and the Struggle for Democracy in the Mid-Twentieth Century South* (Chapel Hill, NC: University of North Carolina Press, 2003); Stetson Kennedy, *Southern Exposure* (New York: Doubleday & Co., Inc., 1946); Lucy Randolph Mason, *To Win These Rights: A Personal Story of the CIO in the South* (New York: Harper, 1952); Jane Dailey, "Sex, Segregation, and the Sacred after *Brown*," *Journal of American History* 91 (June 2004): 119–45; *Politics and Religion in the White South*, ed. by Glenn Feldman (Lexington, KY: University Press of Kentucky, 2005); Andrew M. Manis, *Southern Civil Religions in Conflict: Black and White Baptists and Civil Rights, 1947–1957* (Athens, GA: University of Georgia Press, 1987).
4. James R. Barrett, "The Blessed Virgin Made Me a Socialist: An Experiment in Catholic Autobiography and the Historical Understanding of Race and Class," in Nick Salvatore, ed., *Faith and the Historian: Catholic Perspectives* (Urbana, IL: University of Illinois Press, 2007), 139.
5. An excellent survey of the literature on this literature is contained in Robert Wuthnow and Tracy L. Scott, "Protestants and Economic Behavior," in Harry

Stout and D. G. Hart, eds, *New Directions in American Religious History* (New York: Oxford University Press, 1997), 260–95. See also Herbert Gutman's pathbreaking essay, "Protestantism and the American Labor Movement: The Christian Spirit in the Gilded Age," *American Historical Review* 72 (1966): 74–101; and E. P. Thompson, *The Making of the English Working Class* (New York: Vintage, 1966). For an astute critique, see Nick Salvatore, "Herbert Gutman's Narrative of the American Working Class: A Reevaluation," *International Journal of Politics, Culture and Society* 12 (1988): 64–66 (quote from p. 66).

6. Robert A. Orsi, "Everyday Miracles: The Study of Lived Religion," in David D. Hall, ed., *Lived Religion in America: Toward a History of Practice* (Princeton: Princeton University Press, 1997), 7. Examples include: Kimberley L. Phillips, *Alabama North: African-American Migrants, Community, and Working-Class Activism in Cleveland, 1915–45* (Urbana, IL: University of Illinois Press, 1999); David L. Chappell, *A Stone of Hope: Prophetic Religion and the Death of Jim Crow* (Chapel Hill, NC: University of North Carolina Press, 2004); Joe Creech, *Righteous Indignation: Religion and the Populist Revolution* (Urbana, IL: University of Illinois Press, 2006); Richard J. Callahan, Jr, *Work and Faith in the Kentucky Coal Fields: Subject to Dust* (Bloomington, IN: Indiana University Press, 2009).

7. Jarod H. Roll, "Road to the promised land: rural rebellion in the New Cotton South, 1890–1945" (Ph.D. dissertation, Northwestern University, 2006), 25. See also Erik Gellman and Jarod H. Roll, "Owen Whitfield and the Gospel of the Working Class in New Deal America, 1936–1946," *Journal of Southern History* 72 (May 2006): 303–48.

8. See especially, Griffith, *Crisis of American Labor*, chapter 7; Minchin, *What Do We Need a Union For?*, 47.

9. Wayne Flynt, "Religion for the Blues: Evangelicalism, Poor Whites, and the Great Depression," *Journal of Southern History* 71 (February 2005): 6–7.

10. Bruce J. Schulman, *From Cotton Belt to Sunbelt: Federal Policy, Economic Development, and the Transformation of the South, 1938–1980* (New York: Oxford University Press, 1991); James C. Cobb, *The Selling of the South: The Southern Crusade for Industrial Development, 1936–1980* (Baton Rouge, LA: Louisiana State University Press, 1982); Jennifer Brooks, *Defining the Peace: Race, World War II Veterans, and the Remaking of Southern Political Tradition* (Chapel Hill, NC: University of North Carolina Press, 2004).

11. Joel A. Carpenter, *Revive Us Again: The Reawakening of American Fundamentalism* (New York: Oxford University Press, 1997); William R. Glass, *Strangers in Zion: Fundamentalists in the South, 1900–1950* (Macon, GA: Mercer University Press, 2001); Grant Wacker, *Heaven Below: Early Pentecostals and American Culture* (Cambridge, MA: Harvard University Press, 2001); Joel L. Alvis, *Presbyterians and Race: Southern Presbyterians, 1946–1983* (Tuscaloosa, AL: University of Alabama Press, 1994).

12. Historians of Catholic workers have done much better. See, Neil Betten, *Catholic Activism and the Industrial Worker* (Gainesville, FL: University Presses of Florida, 1976); Mel Piehl, *Breaking Bread: The Catholic Worker and the Origins of Catholic Radicalism in America* (Philadelphia, PA: Temple University Press, 1984); Kenneth J. Heineman, *A Catholic New Deal: Religion and Reform in Depression Pittsburgh* (University Park, PA: Pennsylvania State University Press, 1999); Evelyn Sterne, *Ballots and Bibles: Ethnic Politics and the Catholic Church in Providence* (Ithaca, NY: Cornell University Press, 2003); and the work of Steve Rosswurm, *The FBI and the Catholic Church, 1935–1962* (Amherst, MA: University of Massachusetts Press, 2009).

13. Roll, "Road to the Promised Land"; James Lorence, *A Hard Journey: The Life of Don West* (Urbana, IL: University of Illinois Press, 2007); David L. Chappell, *A Stone of Hope: Prophetic Religion and the Death of Jim Crow* (Chapel Hill, NC: University of North Carolina Press, 2004); Anthony P. Dunbar, *Against the Grain: Southern Radicals and Prophets, 1929–1959* (Charlottesville, VA: University of Virginia Press, 1981).

14. Elizabeth Fones-Wolf and Ken Fones-Wolf, "Sanctifying the Southern Organizing Campaign: Religious Activists in the CIO's Operation Dixie," *Labor: Studies in Working Class History of the Americas* 6 (February 2009): 5–32.

15. Schulman, *From Cotton Belt to Sunbelt*, 14–15, 22–31, 56–60, 82; "Labor in the South," *United States Department of Labor Bulletin No. 898* (Washington: GPO, 1947), 170–73; Pete Daniel, *Lost Revolutions: The South in the 1950s* (Chapel Hill, NC: University of North Carolina Press, 2000), chapter 1; James N. Gregory, *The Southern Diaspora: How the Great Migrations of Black and White Southerners Transformed America* (Chapel Hill, NC: University of North Carolina Press, 2005).

16. Robert Coles, *Children of the Crisis, Volume II; Migrants, Sharecroppers, Mountaineers* (Boston, MA: Little, Brown and Company, 1971), 578–617; Loyal Jones, *Faith and Meaning in the Southern Uplands* (Urbana, IL: University of Illinois Press, 1999); Jeannette Keith, *Country People in the New South: Tennessee's Upper Cumberland* (Chapel Hill, NC: University of North Carolina Press, 1995).

17. For the importance of anti-communism in the minds of evangelical Protestants, see William Martin, *With God on Our Side: The Rise of the Religious Right in America* (New York: Broadway Books, 1996), 29, 33–35.

18. Carpenter, *Revive Us Again*, 31–32; Robert T. Handy, "The American Religious Depression, 1926–1935," *Church History* 29 (March 1960): 3–16.

19. Liston Pope, *Millhands and Preachers: A Study of Gastonia* (New Haven, CT: Yale University Press, 1942), 98–103; Kenneth K. Bailey, *Southern White Protestantism in the Twentieth Century* (New York: Harper & Row, 1964), 2.

20. National Council of the Churches of Christ in the U.S.A., *Churches and Church Membership in the United States*, Series C, No. 31 (New York: NCC, 1957), table 77; Pope, *Millhands and Preachers*, 103; Glass, *Strangers in Zion*, chapter 5;

H. B. Cavalcanti, "God and Labor in the South: Southern Baptists and the Right to Unionize, 1930–1950," *Journal of Church and State* 40 (Summer, 1998): 639–60.

21. Eva Hopkins interview with Lu Ann Jones, March 5, 1980, Southern Oral History Project, University of North Carolina, Chapel Hill (hereafter SOHP); Ethel Marshall Faucette interview with Allen Tullos, November 16, 1978 and January 4, 1979, SOHP; Mary Thompson interview with Jim Leloudis, July 19, 1979, SOHP.

22. James Pharis interview with Cliff Kuhn, July 24, 1977, SOHP.

23. Hopkins interview; Flake and Nellie Mae Meyers interview with Pat Dilley, August 11, 1979, SOHP.

24. Ila Hartsell Dodson interview with Allen Tullos, May 23, 1980, SOHP; Hoy Deal interview with Pat Dilley, June 17, 1974, SOHP.

25. Alice P. Levitt interview with Jim Leloudis, July 18, 1979, SOHP.

26. Flynt, "Religion for the Blues," 10–13; Glass, *Strangers in Zion*, 27–32.

27. Flynt, "Religion for the Blues," 11–12.

28. Coles, *Children of the Crisis*, 578–617 (quote from pp. 584–85); Louise Jones interview with Mary Frederickson, October 13, 1976, SOHP.

29. Alessandro Portelli, *The Death of Luigi Trastulli and Other Stories: Form and Meaning in Oral History* (Albany, NY: State University of New York Press, 1991), 226–27.

30. Mark Fannin, *Labor's Promised Land: Radical Visions of Gender, Race, and Religion in the South* (Knoxville, TN: University of Tennessee Press, 2003), 293; Mark Naison, "Claude and Joyce Williams: Pilgrims of Justice," *Southern Exposure* 1 (1974), 44–48; Roll, "Road to the Promised Land," 214–17.

31. Lorence, *A Hard Journey*, 4–5, 154–58; Flamming, *Creating the Modern South*, 293–99. Also, see the important new work, Callahan, *Work and Faith in the Kentucky Coal Fields*.

32. Alva Taylor to Claude Williams, March 25, 1944, box 3, folder 7, Claude Williams Papers, Archives of Labor and Urban Affairs, Wayne State University, Detroit, Michigan (hereafter Williams Papers).

33. Harry Koger to Williams, January 7, 1945, box 14, folder 5, Williams Papers; Robert H. Craig, *Religion and Radical Politics: An Alternative Christian Tradition in the United States* (Philadelphia, PA: Temple University Press, 1995), 164.

34. Deal interview; Mimi Conway, *Rise Gonna Rise: A Portrait of Southern Textile Workers* (Garden City, NY: Anchor Books, 1979), 171; Carpenter, *Revive Us Again*, 58, 64, 69.

35. Gary Dorrien, *The Remaking of Evangelical Theology* (Louisville, KY: Westminster John Knox Press, 1998), 28–29; Carpenter, *Revive Us Again*, 70–75; Glass, *Strangers in Zion*, 19–21.

36. Anton T. Boisen, "What War Does to Religion," *Religion in Life* 14 (Summer, 1945), 389–400; Charles S. Braden, "What Can We Learn From the Cults?" *Religion in Life* 14 (Winter, 1944), 59; Randall J. Stephens, *The Fire Spreads:*

Holiness and Pentecostalism in the American South (Cambridge, MA: Harvard University Press, 2008), 234.

37. Samuel S. Hill, *One Name but Several Faces: Variety in Popular Christian Denominations in Southern History* (Athens, GA: University of Georgia Press, 1996), 81.

38. David Burgess, "The Role of the Churches in Relation to the C.I.O. Southern Organizing Drive," undated typescript [12 pages], in box 1556, folder 16, John Ramsay Papers, Southern Labor Archives, Georgia State University (hereafter Ramsay Papers). Of course, the Operation Dixie Papers and the Ramsay Papers are rife with examples that historians have used when studying particular locations. See also Jonathan Gentry, "'Christ is Out, Communism is On': Opposition to the Congress of Industrial Organization's 'Operation Dixie' in South Carolina," *Proceedings of the South Carolina Historical Association* (2003): 15–24.

39. William Holmes Borders, "The Spiritual and Economic Basis for Democracy in the South," *Christian Frontiers* (April 1947): 114–20; Lee Sheppard, "Industrialization of the South," *Christian Frontiers* (April 1947): 164–66; Egerton, *Speak Now Against the Day*, 422–29; Nelle Morton to David Burgess, February 15, 1945, Morton to Burgess, April 30, 1945, and *Fellowship of Southern Churchmen Newsletter*, June 1945, all in box 1, Fellowship of Southern Churchmen Records, Southern Historical Collection, University of North Carolina, Chapel Hill, NC (hereafter FSC Records).

40. Joseph Fletcher, "Collectivism: Problem for Christian Ethics," *Religion in Life* 20 (Autumn, 1951): 483–505; John F. Duffy, Jr, "Communism Rejected by American Workers," *Christianity and Crisis*, May 30, 1949, 67–70.

41. Bailey, *Southern White Protestantism*, 126–29. See also Peter C. Murray, *Methodists and the Crucible of Race, 1930–1975* (Columbia, MO: University of Missouri Press, 2004) and Alvis, *Presbyterians and Race*; and John Lee Eighmy, *Churches in Cultural Captivity: A History of the Social Attitudes of Southern Baptists* (Knoxville, TN: University of Tennessee Press, 1972).

42. Tona J. Hangen, *Redeeming the Dial: Radio, Religion, and Popular Culture in America* (Chapel Hill, NC: University of North Carolina Press, 2002), 104–05.

43. Robert L. Vining, "Comments on the Federal Council of Churches," *Southern Presbyterian Journal* (December 1943): 3; Vining, "Is the Federal Council Evangelical?" *Southern Presbyterian Journal* (May 1945): 22–25; "Protestants-Catholics and Communism," *Southern Presbyterian Journal* (July 15, 1946).

44. Porter Routh, "Facts About the National Council of Churches," undated typescript, box 53, folder 32, Clifton Judson Allen Papers, Southern Baptist Library and Archives, Nashville, TN (SBLA); Handwritten observation of Clifton J. Allen on National Council of Churches, n.d., box 53, folder 75, Allen Papers; Southern Baptist Convention Executive Committee Files, box 3, folder 25, AR 627–1, SBLA.

45. R. L. Decker, "What the NAE Is and What It Is Doing," *United Evangelical Action* (April 15, 1948): 5–6; Wacker, *Heaven Below*, 194–95; Carpenter, *Revive Us Again*, 141–60; George Washington Robnett, "Communism a Threat to America's Churches," *United Evangelical Action* (August 1, 1949): 3–4; George Holwerda, "Christian Principles and Labor Organizations," *United Evangelical Action* (February 1, 1949): 5–6, 8–9, 21.

46. Michael Sloan, "A Misguided Quest for Legitimacy: The Community Relations Department of the Southern Organizing Committee of the CIO During Operation Dixie, 1946–1953," MA thesis, Georgia State University, 2005; Mason, *To Win These Rights*; John A. Salmond, *Miss Lucy of the CIO: The Life and Times of Lucy Randolph Mason* (Athens, GA: University of Georgia Press, 1988).

47. Elizabeth Fones-Wolf and Ken Fones-Wolf, "Conversion at Bethlehem: Religion and Union Building in Steel, 1930–42," *Labor History* 39 (1998): 381–95.

48. Unidentified clipping, November 21, 1954, box 6, folder 27, Franz Daniel Papers, Archives of Labor and Urban Affairs (ALUA), Wayne State University. See also his job application for Field Representative, War Production Board, 1942, box 5 folder 4, Daniel Papers.

49. "Biographical Sketch of Charles C. Webber," typescript in box 14, UAW Public Relations Department Records, ALUA; Charles Webber, "Chaplain to Organized Labor," *Zion's Herald*, October 23, 1946, 1011, 1021, 1025.

50. Burgess, *Fighting for Social Justice*, 73–103; Mason, *To Win These Rights*, 182–83.

51. *Religion Speaks to Labor*, undated pamphlet in ODP, reel 43; David S. Burgess, *Trade Unions and Preachers* (Chapel Hill, NC: Fellowship of Southern Churchmen, n.d.).

52. R. W. Childress to David Burgess, undated, C. E. Derby to Burgess, August 26, 1946, Roy D. Coulter to Burgess, November 1, 1946, all in box 4, FSC records.

53. See, for examples, Mary Byrd to Samuel McCrea Cavert, March 25, 1947; Walter Lingle to Cavert, April 17, 1947, Alfonso Johnson to Federal Council of Churches, June 24, 1947, T. B. Jackson to Federal Council of Churches, August 1, 1947, George Crosby to Federal Council of Churches, August 31, 1947, and I. M. Bagnal to Cavert, September 8, 1947, all in RG 18, box 20, folder 11, National Council of Churches Records, Presbyterian Historical Society, Philadelphia, PA (hereafter NCC Records).

54. *Religious Herald* (August 15, 1946): 11. See also Ralph A. Phelps, Jr, *Tangled Threads: A Study of People in Need* (Atlanta, GA: Home Mission Board, Southern Baptist Convention, 1950), 53–56; and Keith Cameron Wills, "Southern Baptists and Labor, 1927–1956," Th.D. dissertation, Southwestern Baptist Theological Seminary, 1958.

55. *Christian Index* (Atlanta) (April 11, 1946): 4, 11.

56. Lucy Mason to Dr Bernard C. Clausen, September 14, 1946, ODP, reel 63; Cavalcanti, "God and Labor in the South," 639–60.

57. Mason to Clausen, September 14, 1946; Mason to Cameron Hall, August 30, 1946, ODP, reel 63. For the lifting of the ban by the Church of God, see Michael Szpak, "Removing the 'Mark of the Beast': The Church of God (Cleveland, Tennessee) and Organized Labor," *Labor's Heritage* (Summer, 1991): 46–61.

58. Mason to Rev. John C. Jernigan, June 28, 1948, ODP, reel 63; "Memorandum by Lucy R. Mason on attitude towards organized labor by Church of God," Assembly of God, and Pentecostal Holiness Church, May 14, 1949, ODP, reel 64.

59. Burgess, *Fighting for Social Justice*, 48–51, 76–78; Franz Daniel to John Ramsay, March 30, 1950, box 1568, folder 152, Ramsay Papers. For Pentecostal opposition to large institutions, see Wacker, *Heaven Below*, 194–95.

60. Flamming, *Creating the Modern South*, 291.

61. One systematic use of these reports that agrees with our assessment is found in Sloan, "A Misguided Quest for Legitimacy," 46–47.

62. Information on Webber comes from correspondence in the Methodist Federation for Social Action Records, boxes 4 and 7, United Methodist Archives, Drew University, Madison, NJ; *Richmond News Leader*, December 5, 1945; Charles C. Webber, "Chaplain to Organized Labor," *Zion's Herald*, October 23, 1946, 1011, 1021, 1025.

63. "Asks Webber Surrender Credentials," *Zion's Herald* (June 19, 1946): 588; "Labor Chaplain," *Zion's Herald* (July 24, 1946): 712; "An Important Committee," *Zion's Herald* (October 2, 1946): 949; "Chaplain to Labor Causes Dispute," *Zion's Herald* (September 3, 1947): 848; "Tenn. Methodists Anti-Communist," *Zion's Herald* (October 8, 1947): 965.

64. Samuel S. Hill, Jr, *Southern Churches in Crisis* (New York: Holt, Rinehart and Winston, 1966), 74–77.

65. G. Bromley Oxnam to Rev. Bishop Costen J. Harrell, May 23, 1953, box 1557, folder 24, Ramsay Papers. The Lutherans also investigated one of their ministers who signed the letter. See *The Lutheran*, March 25, 1953, 8–9.

66. For just a few of the many examples, see Lucy Mason to Franz Daniel, September 14, 1946, in ODP, reel 63; and Mason memos on Cuthbert, Georgia, Summer 1947; on Pell City, Alabama, July 19–20, 1948; on Morristown, Tennessee, September 19–24, 1948; on Hogansville, Georgia, October 4–6, 1949, all in ODP, reel 64.

67. Ruth Gettinger to William Smith, July 23, 1946, box 1566, folder 132, Ramsay Papers.

68. Ramsay to John Riffe, July 25, 1951, box 1562, folder 94; Paul Christopher to Ramsay, September 2, 1952, box 1568, folder 159, Ramsay Papers.

69. Ruth Gettinger to William Smith, July 23, 1946, box 1566, folder 132; "Radio script," undated typescript (ca. 1952), box 1560, folder 65, Ramsay Papers.

70. "Report" of Ruth Gettinger on Pickens, South Carolina, 1952, in box 1568, folder 153, Ramsay Papers.

71. *Zion's Herald* (May 8, 1946): 448; Don McKee, "Organizing Southern Textile Workers: Early Days with the CIO," p. 109, typed manuscript in box 8, Don McKee Papers, Southern Labor Archives, Georgia State University, Atlanta, Georgia.

72. Lucy Mason to Franz Daniel, September 14, 1946, ODP, reel 63.
73. McKee, "Organizing Southern Textile Workers," 109.
74. Mason to William E. Henderson, undated [ca. 1947], ODP, reel 38.
75. Arthur Hyde to Ramsay, October 2, 1951, box 1563, folder 99; John B. Isom to Ramsay, July 3, 1951, box 1568, folder 153, Ramsay Papers.
76. Gettinger to William Smith, July 23, 1946, box 1566, folder 132; "Report on Morristown, Tennessee," by Lucy Mason, September 19–24, 1948, box 1559, folder 52, Ramsay Papers.
77. See the reports and correspondence cited in note 68, above.
78. Mason to Franz Daniel, September 14, 1946, ODP, reel 63.
79. Rev. Walter Y. Cooley to George Baldanzi, ca. November 25, 1950, ODP, reel 64.
80. Lucy Mason to Turner L. Smith, August 1, 1947, ODP, reel 63; Franz Daniel to John Ramsay, March 3, 1950, box 1568, folder 152, Ramsay Papers.
81. Joel Leighton to Ramsay, June 13, 1947, box 1566, folder 132, Ramsay Papers.
82. "Southern Industrialists Attack Churches by Fanning Race, Religious Prejudice," *Alabama News Digest* (March 14, 1947); Mary Robertson interview with Jacquelyn Hall, August 13, 1979, SOHP; Korstad, *Civil Rights Unionism.*
83. "Radio: Winston-Salem, New Year— 1950," typewritten script, ODP, reel 64; "Mine-Mill Clean Up Campaign," typewritten radio script #4, Station WAPI, Birmingham, AL, box 1562, folder 94, Ramsay Papers; Cary Joseph Allen, Jr interview with Rosemarie Hester, April 3, 1980, SOHP; Pharis interview.
84. George and Tessie Dyer interview with Lu Ann Jones, March 5, 1980, SOHP; Christine and Dave Galliher interview with Jacquelyn Hall, August 8, 1979, SOHP; Hopkins interview.
85. Pauline Griffiths interview with Allen Tullos, May 30, 1980, SOHP; Jefferson M. Robinette interview with Cliff Kuhn, July 1977, SOHP; Pharis interview.
86. G. C. Waldrep, III, *Southern Workers and the Search for Community: Spartanburg, South Carolina* (Urbana, IL: University of Illinois Press, 2000), 166.
87. George R. Elmore interview with Brent Glass, March 11, 1976, SOHP; Faucette interview; Kasper Smith quoted in Conway, *Rise Gonna Rise*, 171.
88. Minutes of ACWA Local 95 (Southeastern Shirt Co.), July 11, 1945, in box 58, folder 23, Amalgamated Clothing Workers of America Records, Kheel Labor Management Documentation Center, Cornell University, Ithaca, New York; Durham interview; Josephine Glenn interview with Cliff Kuhn, June 27, 1977, SOHP.
89. Myers interview; Mareda Sigmon Cobb interview with Jacquelyn Hall and Patty Dilley, June 16 and 18, 1979, SOHP.
90. Eunice Austin interview with Jacquelyn Hall, July 2, 1980, SOHP; Myers interview. For an elaboration of this argument, see Minchin, *What Do We Need a Union For?*
91. Emma Whitesell interview with Cliff Kuhn, July 27, 1977, SOHP; Mareda Sigmon Cobb interview with Jacquelyn Hall and Patty Dilley, June 16 and 18, 1979, SOHP; Scott Hoyman interview with Bill Finger, July 16, 1974, SOHP.

92. Mary Thompson interview with Jim Leloudis, July 19, 1979, SOHP; Tessie Dyer interview with Lu Ann Jones, March 5, 1980, SOHP.
93. Wilson quoted in Conway, *Rise Gonna Rise*, 153.
94. For a sampling of the best overviews on the various causes of Operation Dixie's failure, see Goldfield, *Color of Politics*, 243–46; Griffith, *Crisis of American Labor*, 161–76; Minchin, *What Do We Need a Union for?*, 26–47; Honey, "Operation Dixie," 216–44; Bryant Simon, "Rethinking Why There Are So Few Unions in the South," *Georgia Historical Quarterly* 81 (Summer, 1997): 465–84; and Zieger, *CIO*, 227–41.

CHAPTER FIVE

A. Philip Randolph, Black Anticommunism, and the Race Question

Eric Arnesen

Over the past few decades, scholars of American labor and civil rights have shared a foundational premise concerning the contribution of the Left to the cause of racial equality in the mid-twentieth century. At a time when the Republican and Democratic parties either ignored black concerns or actively supported Jim Crow, the Communist Party stood out for the forthrightness of its opposition to racial discrimination, disfranchisement, lynching, and economic exploitation. In the years after World War I, Glenda Gilmore has recently argued, the "presence of a radical Left . . . redefined the debate over white supremacy and hastened its end. . . . It was the Communists who stood up to say that black and white people should organize together, eat together, go to school together, and marry each other if they chose."[1] The party's stance took concrete form in its efforts to build trade unions. Through its position on the "Negro question" and its commitment to organizing workers inside and out of basic industry, the party "played a critical role in broadening and diversifying the base of the organized working class," in Shelton Stromquist's view; the "Left changed the face of the organized American working class."[2] Left-led unions, this school of interpretation insists, forged an impressive civil rights unionism that married workplace and community concerns by pursuing racial equality on the shopfloor, in the labor movement and labor market, and in municipal, state, and federal politics. The party, the unions it influenced or dominated, and those in its broader orbit—what has been called the "Black liberal-left alliance," the "Negro People's Front," or "Black Popular Front"—engaged in "an uncompromising struggle for equal rights" whose agenda embraced not only "civil and political rights" but "social and economic rights" as well, long before the onset of the "classic stage" of the civil rights movement in 1955–56.[3] Indeed, proponents of the concept of the "long civil rights movement" like Jacqueline Dowd Hall have made the persuasive case that the Montgomery Bus Boycott hardly inaugurated the civil rights crusade. Rather, decades before Montgomery, they insist, activists built a national movement rooted in the "liberal and radical milieu" of the Great Depression that was "not just a precursor of the modern civil rights movement. It was its decisive first phase."[4]

That the Communist Party and its sympathizers played important roles in the labor and civil rights movement is beyond question. What is open to debate is the nature of their contribution and the merits—or historical accuracy—of the largely uncritical portrait revisionist historians have painted of that contribution. There is more than a little romanticization in revisionist scholars' treatment of the party's race work in the labor movement and broader community. One might speculate that their reluctance to interrogate the party's record too closely may stem from identification with their protagonists' purported antiracism and hostility to economic inequality under capitalism or a desire to create uplifting or even "useable" historical narratives. But it also reflects a broader phenomenon among revisionist historians of American communism: the tendency, as Theodore Draper once put it, to write "about Communists-without-communism."[5] The discomfort with exploring explicit political doctrines or a belief that radical ideology is less important than radical commitment has long characterized much of the revisionist literature. Today, the historians of the "long civil rights movement," who draw extensively from that work, have adopted this orientation.

A. Philip Randolph, a central figure in the twentieth-century crusade for racial equality and labor rights, would have been perplexed by the revisionists' romantic portrait or the long movement scholars' highlighting of the Communist Left's contributions. A committed African-American socialist and labor organizer who had worked side-by-side with Communists during the Popular Front, Randolph concluded that the party was not only *not* in the vanguard for civil rights, it constituted a genuine threat to the civil rights cause and the security of all Americans, black and white. From 1940 onward, he engaged the party in a war of words; denouncing its practices and beliefs, he, in turn, was denounced for his anticommunism and "reformist" approach. On what grounds did Randolph criticize the party? What, precisely, does that critique tell us about the party's race work? And what light can it shed on the findings of revisionist scholars? This essay explores the anticommunism of Randolph to challenge the often uncritical revisionist interpretation of the Communist Party and the long civil rights movement scholarship that shares its assumptions.[6] At a minimum, it suggests that revisionists and long movement scholars need to take the black anticommunist critique more seriously, address the inconsistencies in the party's record, and pay greater attention to the multiple and competing strains of black activism from the 1930s to the 1950s. The point is *not* to replace a romantic picture of the black Communist Left with one of the black anticommunist left. Rather, it is to better appreciate the complexities of the history of civil rights, labor, and radicalism in the United States.

Taking the podium in the U.S. Department of Labor auditorium in late April 1940, the president the National Negro Congress (NNC), A. Philip Randolph, threw down a gauntlet in what he realized was a futile battle for the organization's soul. After three days of speeches and resolutions, there was little question for Randolph that the assembled delegates had moved the NNC far from its original mission. Only four years old at the time, the Congress had initially represented a heterogeneous collection of African-American organizations and viewpoints; members had been united in their commitment to political nonpartisanship and independent action, on the one hand, and to militancy and aggressive grassroots organizing, on the other. Now, the Congress had lost much of its ideological diversity. Numerically dominated by members of the American Communist Party, the NNC jettisoned its initial independence and voted to affiliate with the Congress of Industrial Organizations (CIO) labor leader John L. Lewis's Labor's Non-Partisan League. Worse, from Randolph's perspective, its delegates lined up squarely behind the current policy line of the Communist Party, lambasting President Franklin Roosevelt for his retreat from the New Deal's social programs and his embrace of militarism. Accordingly, they vowed to fight to keep the United States from entering what they now termed an imperialist war raging in Europe. Much to Randolph's chagrin, the convention's script appeared to have been written in the Communist Party's headquarters, if not in Moscow.

Now it was Randolph's turn. The 51-year old activist harbored few illusions about what his speech could accomplish; he was facing, in historian Mark Naison's words, "a stacked deck."[7] Basking in the glow of winning union recognition for Pullman porters in 1935 and securing a first-ever contract with the Pullman Company just two years later, Randolph had been catapulted into front-page prominence in black America, dubbed by journalists as the "major Negro prophet in the realm of labor organization" and the "ranking hero of the race."[8] On this April day, however, Randolph disappointed, even angered, many of the assembled delegates. His stern words about the NNC, its dominance by the party, and the moral equivalence of communism and fascism elicited hisses and catcalls of "traitor" from party members and fellow travelers. It was as if Randolph had thrown "a bombshell into the Congress," recalled Howard University professor Ralph Bunche. After 15 minutes, a general "exodus" had begun; by the time Randolph finished his address, two-thirds of the delegates' seats in the auditorium were empty.[9]

Randolph anticipated that his carefully chosen words would meet with widespread disapproval from a majority of the 1,700 delegates. The speech frontally challenged the beliefs of many of those assembled, a significant number of whom were white. Beginning on common ground, he touched upon the world crisis, labor's divided house, and unemployment, before taking aim at the congressional Dies Committee for undermining civil liberties. "Without the right, freely to express one's opinions, wrong as well as right," Randolph intoned, "a democratic society cannot long endure."[10] It was a calculated charge, for what was damning about the Dies committee was applicable to the Communist Party and the Soviet Union. Minutes later, Randolph would make the connection explicit: Not just totalitarian Nazi Germany but Communist Russia too was a place "where freedom of speech, press and assembly, the foundations of democracy, are suppressed." Like Japan, Russia was "a dictatorship . . . with no concern" for its people's rights. The American Communist Party came in for specific condemnation. The CP was, he intoned, "unsound and disastrous in tactic, strategy and allegiance to the Soviet Union"; its policies and programs "are as fitful, changeful and unpredictable as the foreign policy and line of

Moscow." For "anyone to take the position that the Negroes should place their fortunes at the feet of the Communist Party, which is subject to such violent and far-
reaching shakeups, a party which lacks stability of purpose, and serves an alien
master, is passing strange."[11]

The source of Randolph's vehement denunciation was the party's 1939 *volte
face* on antifascism and the threat posed by Nazi Germany. After several years in
the forefront of antifascist struggles in the United States, the party reversed course
overnight with the unexpected signing of the Hitler-Stalin Pact. The party that had
promoted aggressive struggle against fascism abroad and support for the New Deal
at home instantly morphed into a body promoting left-wing isolationism in the now
renamed inter-imperialist conflict in Europe and expressing hostility to Roosevelt
the "warmonger" and those who supported him. The collaborative Communists of
the Popular Front, pledged to work harmoniously with all "progressive forces," had
given way to cadre who now turned sharply critical of any who stood in their way.[12]
The abrupt shift stunned the party's membership, many of whom registered their
dismay and disappointment by dropping away in large numbers. For those who
remained, however, the defense of the Soviet fatherland became all-important and
they adjusted their strategies accordingly. For Communist members of the NNC,
this meant a wholesale transformation of the organization they had contributed so
significantly to building. The NNC dropped its antifascism and support for Franklin
Roosevelt and the New Deal and, at the 1940 convention, denounced the president
and vowed to fight to keep the United States out of the European war. The "Yanks
Are Not Coming," they forcefully declared.[13]

Randolph's speech and the delegates' hostile response marked the end of his ten-
ure in the NNC and, arguably, the beginning of the end of the Congress. Randolph
declined to stand for reelection, paving the way for the unanimous elevation of Max
Yergan, a former YMCA official and NNC vice president in the CP's camp, to that
office.[14] (Yergan, a "rank neophyte," Bunche later remarked caustically, could "only
parrot the slogans laid down in the party tracts.")[15] With few exceptions, the NNC's
transformation was received poorly among nonparty activists and editors in America's heterogeneous black communities. Black newspapers that had once viewed the
Congress favorably now unleashed a torrent of criticism. "We think it a travesty that
the congress did so foolish a thing as to endorse communism and denounce the
New Deal," grumbled the *Washington Afro-American*. "With all its faults, the New Deal
is American, while communism is an alien doctrine which stands in considerable
disrepute in the eyes of rich and poor alike, and we believe that the colored group
has difficulties enough, trying to solve its own problems without hanging another
millstone around its neck."[16] The *Amsterdam News* condemned the Communists for
making a "political football" out of the NNC: John Davis had "patted Soviet Russia
on the back and slapped the Allies in the face," vitiating "any good it might have been
able to do for the disfranchised voters, the dispossessed sharecroppers and the inse-
cure citizens."[17] The meeting, in the view of the Urban League's Lester Granger,
"marked the passing of the Congress from any effective role as a coordinating agent

serving the Negro population." Ralph Bunche concurred: the NNC had "dug its own grave," leaving it "reduced to a Communist cell."[18] As it turned out, the NNC did not entirely vanish from the protest scene and its remaining left-wing members remained active, particularly on the local level.[19] But the vision of a broad-based and diverse alliance of religious, civil, and labor groups was a permanent casualty of the take over. For all practical purposes, the once credible and effective NNC was reduced to a shell of its former self.

That prospect, however, lay in the near future. The Communists who had steered the NNC down the path laid down by the new party line cheered the outcome. "All true fighters for Negro rights and genuine friends of Negro liberation cannot but greet enthusiastically the decisions" of the third NNC gathering, insisted Theodore R. Bassett in the pages of the party's theoretical journal, *The Communist*; the convention marked an "enormous step forward in the centuries-old struggle of the Negro people." As for Randolph, the NNC's first and only president to date, his departure was greeted on the order of good riddance. His convention speech, which "bristled with the most vicious and provocative anti-working class, anti-Communist, anti-Soviet slanders," filled the audience with "uneasiness, consternation and disgust." No longer speaking was the African-American labor leader of old, Bassett declared; Randolph's words were "of the frightened Negro petty bourgeoisie, chattering with fear, pleading for mercy before the white master. They were the words of treacherous Social-Democracy." The old, progressive Randolph had exited stage right; "only a hollow mockery remains." Swelling "the chorus of Rooseveltian and Wall Street warmongers," he was guilty of inciting "war against the Soviet Union."[20]

Over the course of the next year, Randolph launched a new campaign free of all Communist involvement—the March on Washington Movement—to combat discrimination in the armed forces and rapidly expanding defense industries. The party would have none of it. Hammering away at the former NNC president, the *Daily Worker* complained in February 1941 that Randolph was exhibiting a "mighty strange way of fighting for his people" by seeking to "hog-tie the Negro people to the war chariot" of FDR. Claiming (misleadingly) that he had surrendered in the fight against discrimination in defense industries and had abandoned the antilynching and anti-poll tax campaigns, the party press insisted that "Randolph does not speak for the Negro people." Later that month, the harangue continued, with the *Daily Worker* editorializing that Randolph and the NAACP's Walter White were giving "lip-service to the fight against 'defense' discrimination" as a "smokescreen for their war-mongering and red-bating." To African-American Communist William L. Patterson, Randolph was just the new public face for a "Negro reformism" that had "almost become thoroughly discredited" with the "label of Uncle Tom." "Negro labor must show its contempt for Randolph's Social-Democratic surrender," he insisted. "Thus it will help the Negro people to see the poisonous role of Negro reformism and Social Democracy." Not to be outdone, the future New York City Communist councilman Ben Davis, Jr labeled White and Randolph the "faithful lackeys" of the war-mongers whose actions would dispatch the "needs of the Negro people . . . down the hatch."[21]

Randolph's resignation, his scathing critique of the Soviet Union and its American followers, and the NNC's effective take-over by the Communist Party bring into stark relief the CP's record on race, civil rights, or, as it was then called, "the Negro question." Before the 1970s, many scholars hostile to the Communist Party would have largely agreed with Randolph, taking a dim view of the party's civil rights activities (and everything else about it too). Over the past generation or so, historians more sympathetic to the party have offered an alternative perspective that views the party's involvement in civil rights campaigns and its cultivation of black membership in a most favorable light. In their view, anticommunism—to the extent they have explored it—was a blunt weapon cynically deployed by opponents of black rights to discredit progressive reform. To their credit, revisionists have provided us with detailed accounts of the many campaigns waged by party members against racial discrimination at the grassroots level. In doing so, however, they have sidestepped key aspects of the anticommunist scholars' charges *and* the voices of contemporary African-American opponents of the party like Randolph.

As a means of initiating a reexamination of the party, race, and civil rights, the 1940 NNC convention is a convenient starting point, raising uncomfortable issues that many historians favorable to the party have shied away from answering. In placing the needs of the Soviet Union at the head of its agenda, party supporters at the NNC's 1940 meeting significantly undermined an organization they had been instrumental in founding. In this, and in other instances, the party's record appears spottier than revisionist historians have suggested. Randolph's critique of the party for its devotion to the totalitarian Soviet Union, lack of internal democracy, and willingness to sacrifice black interests on command from the Comintern invite us to reconsider the party's actual record on race and its treatment by revisionists.

Randolph's political bona fides lent legitimacy to his critique of the party, at least to many interested in the fate of civil rights, by the World War II years.[22] Born in 1889 in Crescent City, Florida, Randolph migrated to New York, immersed himself in the world of socialist politics, and edited the radical *Messenger* magazine. An opponent of World War I, he quickly came to be seen as the most "dangerous Negro in America," in the words of one government official. From the mid-1920s to mid-1930s Randolph led a successful union campaign among Pullman porters, serving as the president of the Brotherhood of Sleeping Car Porters (BSCP) through the 1960s.[23] From his union base, Randolph undertook wide-ranging campaigns against racial inequality. Following his departure from the NNC, his frustration with persistent discrimination during the U.S. preparation for war prompted him to launch the March on Washington Movement in early 1941.[24] His threat to bring 100,000 blacks to the nation's capital to protest discrimination in employment and the armed forces pressured President Franklin Roosevelt to create by executive order the Fair Employment Practice Committee (FEPC). During the war, Randolph led numerous demonstrations and protests against segregation. His efforts made his a household name in black communities across the country. By 1942, he had become the "foremost race leader" of black Americans, in one black journalist's words.[25]

Randolph emerged by 1940 as an unrelenting anticommunist whose objections to the party were rooted in fundamental ideological disagreements and on first-hand experiences with CP members. His conflicts with the party reached back several decades. During the political upheavals that led to the formation of communist parties in many parts of the world in the immediate post-World War I period, Randolph remained firmly in the Socialist Party camp. By 1923, he dismissed the Communists as "utterly devoid of any respect for fact, truth, or honesty." "Negro Communists are a menace" to "the workers, themselves, and the race," declared an unsigned article in the pages of his journal, the *Messenger*, in 1923. "Why? Because they are disruptionists, seeking with irrational and romantic zeal to break down the morale, to confuse the aims and ideals of the New Negro Liberation Movement." Their policies and tactics were "utterly senseless, unsound, unscientific, dangerous and ridiculous," leaving the *Messenger* to speculate that they were "either lunatics or agents provocateurs, [or] stool pigeons." But whether "paid tools" or "mere ignorant, credulous fanatics, believing that they are serving a holy cause," the Communists were dangerously preaching "doctrines of extremism" calculated to attract persecution. "Their preachments and antics about r-r-r-e-volution, the Third Internationale, the dictatorship of the proletariat," mocked the *Messenger*, "are so inane and childish that they would be amusing were they not so tragically disastrous." Later that year, the *Messenger* put forward the theme of foreign control—one that Randolph would return to repeatedly in his subsequent denunciations of the party—ridiculing the "Communist brethren" in the minuscule African Blood Brotherhood for their "obedience to the edict of Moscow" and for advancing the "gospel of St. Zinoviev of the Third International of Soviet Russia." When the CP formed the American Negro Labor Congress in 1925, the *Messenger* complained of its lack of independence, for the "source of its influence and control, its backing, is the Communists of Russia" whose purpose, it accurately observed, was the disruption of labor movements in Europe and the United States. Their "tactics are foolish, silly, dangerous and calculated to provoke unnecessary persecution," the *Messenger* concluded. For black workers in America to have their policies "dictated in Soviet Russia by persons and groups who know nothing about Negroes" would create an "impractical and ridiculous spectacle."[26]

Communists reciprocated the animosity. Castigating Randolph for leading the BSCP "into the hands" of the AFL's leadership, whose "many betrayals of the Negro workers" Randolph knew only too well, the party condemned him for calling on "tools of the bosses to lead the porters away from struggle." But it was more the Communists' actions than their words that caused Randolph grief. Particularly aggravating was the party members' practice of stationing themselves in different parts of meeting halls, the better to "introduce confusion." Testifying at a congressional hearing on Communist propaganda in 1930, Randolph recounted party efforts to "penetrate the various divisions" of the BSCP "with a view to either capturing the organization or wrecking it." It was only because he was familiar with their "strategy, motivity, [sic] and technique" that he was able to instruct BSCP organizers to "drive them out" and have "absolutely nothing to do with them." The porters' union succeeded. "We routed them," Randolph reported with satisfaction. "They do not molest us any more."[27]

It was the formation of the NNC in 1935–36 that drew Randolph into a pragmatic, and ultimately short-lived, alliance with the far left. The NNC garnered support from a wide swath of the civil rights community, ranging from black trade unionists, community activists, women's clubs, Communists, and disgruntled NAACP members advocating a greater focus on labor issues. Uniting the coalition was the desire to pursue a more confrontational form of grassroots protest, support black trade unionism, and foster closer relations between black and white labor activists. From the outset, however, critics called the NNC's political complexion into question. While black ministers kept aloof because of the new body's ostensible coolness to religion, black educator and writer Kelly Miller was disturbed by the "spirit of radicalism" that "predominated throughout the proceedings. The reds, the socialists and communists were everywhere in ascendancy, either in number or indominitable purpose, or in both," he complained.[28] Randolph, the new association's president, took considerable pains to distance its radicalism from communism while simultaneously defending the organization's membership. The charge of Communist domination was "entirely false and entirely without foundation," he responded. While the Congress was an ecumenical body open to people of all political persuasions, Communists included, no group controlled its agenda. Randolph offered no apology for the NNC's willingness to accept CP members into its ranks; indeed, he made clear his determination to "go down fighting for the rights of any Negro to exercise his Constitutional right as a free man, to join the Communist party or any other party he may choose to join, for to deny him this right is to reduce him to a slave." The CP was a "legitimate political party" and its members were "not criminals." It was common practice for opponents of black rights to label as communist those who fought for social justice. "It's gotten to be a regular indoor sport now to damn most movements and individuals who resolutely and aggressively fight for human and race rights and the rights of workers and minority groups by branding them as 'red,'" he forcefully concluded.[29]

Over the next four years, the NNC threw itself into a variety of grassroots campaigns, with its diverse membership providing crucial community support for CIO organizing campaigns and sponsoring antilynching and other conferences. The suspicions of its critics notwithstanding, neither the tone nor substance of the NNC's struggles could be attributed to Communist domination. Years later, in 1950, Randolph recalled that he was "familiar with the fact that the National Negro Congress had Communists in it and that they would naturally seek to shape and control its policy." Although his "feeling was that that could be prevented," he was wrong: Serving as president of the BSCP meant that he had "limited time to work" for the NNC. Randolph's inability to devote his "full time to break the grip of the communists on the Congress" allowed them to establish "control and domination"— to "run riot"—with the NNC. At what point he arrived at this conclusion is not clear.

But as long as his goals and those of the CP coincided in the joint project of building the NNC, there was little overt friction.[30]

When their goals diverged, as they did in 1939–40, their political marriage of convenience ended in acrimonious divorce. With the party's switching its Popular Front stance against fascism for an anti-imperialist, class-war one, common ground gave way. For Randolph, the break was bitter and permanent. Over the next two decades or so, he carried out his own rhetorical and organizational cold war against Communists. His founding in 1941 of the March on Washington Movement (MOWM) to challenge the blatant discrimination in defense industries and the military was premised on his belief in Communist duplicity. Determined to avoid a repeat of the 1940 NNC debacle, Randolph declared the MOWM open only to African Americans and off-limits to Communists. Initially, he need not have worried. The party's members unleashed their own counterattack on Randolph for fanning the flames of war. After the Nazi invasion of the Soviet Union prompted another line change, CP-ers opposed the MOWM's aggressive pursuit of black rights as disruptive of the war effort. After the war, the party hammered away at various civil rights efforts by Randolph and other noncommunists. Right-wing social democrats were advancing "reactionary policies" under a "barrage of 'super-militancy,' of radical-sounding and 'socialist' phraseology," complained Ben Davis in 1947. At times, these "fakers . . . like Randolph . . . mix mysticism and confusion with reactionary bourgeois Negro nationalism . . . Right-wing Social Democracy is a conscious force for disunity among the Negro people." Randolph's 1948 campaign to desegregate the armed forces came in for particular criticism. As black Communist Harry Haywood memorably put it, it was an attempt to win equal rights for blacks to serve as "cannon fodder in the execution of Wall Street's imperialist program" and an endorsement of the "Truman-Marshall plan of world domination in exchange for 'equal rights.'" This was nothing but a "flagrant betrayal of the American Negro" and the "millions of colored peoples throughout the world now rising to throw off the yoke of colonial enslavement of which American finance capital . . . has become the chief mainstay."[31]

Randolph's critique of the party from 1940 onward rested on the twin foundations of principle and personal experience. "I consider the Communists a definite menace and a danger to the Negro people and labor," he explained, "because of their rule-or-ruin and disruptive tactics in the interests of the totalitarian Soviet Union."[32] There was no getting around the fundamental dividing line represented by attitudes toward the Soviet Union. To Randolph, the Soviet Union was a "death prison where democracy and liberty have walked their last mile and where shocking blood purges wipe out any and all persons who express any dissenting opinions from those of Dictator Stalin."[33] To a writer sympathetic to the party, Randolph shot back that "while no one is more aware of the shortcomings of American democracy than I am," the simple fact was that "there is NO democracy at all in Communist Russia." Any critic of Stalin's policies would be the "unhappy victim of a savage and brutal blood purge, and in the lingo of the American gangster, 'rubbed out', exterminated, killed forever and ever."[34] Before the NNC delegates assembled in 1940, Randolph denounced the country they so prized as sharing with Nazi Germany a totalitarian character, where all of the "foundations of democracy" were suppressed. As if that weren't enough, the post-pact territorial expansion of both nations—the "imperial invasions and conquests by Hitler and Stalin in the Baltic and Scandinavian Republics"—were but "proof as strong as Holy Writ, that democracy and the totalitarian governments are incompatible and exclusive forces." Like Japan, the Soviet Union was not merely a dictatorship but an "imperial power" that sought "the extension and expansion of its power over weaker peoples, regardless of color." None of this was to excuse the "long, tragic history of the fingers of England and France dripping with the blood of black, yellow and brown colonials," those imperialist nations the party was fond of condemning after the pact. Randolph was more than willing to admit that England and France, "like Japan and Russia, are empires that subjugate and do not liberate weaker peoples," holding down "by bayonet and sword" millions of their "dark colonials" as slaves.[35] Randolph's anti-Stalinism did not lead him toward an uncritical embrace of the Allies, before, during, or after World War II; rather, he was, and remained, a fierce critic of European colonialism. But his antifascism, the political sensibility that animated tens of thousands during the brief Popular Front years, remained intact when the Communists discarded theirs on orders from Moscow.

The American party's fealty to the Soviets was an inexcusable failing, Randolph incessantly maintained following the break in 1940. Unlike other political parties in the United States, the CP was responsible "to an alien country . . . Its boss is the Comintern in Moscow."[36] Whatever good works they might be engaged in, he explained in 1948, the "Communists in the U.S.A. owe allegiance to and carry out the mandates of Soviet Russia and the interests of Russia are not always in harmony with the interests of America."[37] Nor in the interests of blacks. "It is a matter of common knowledge that the Communists would sacrifice America, the Negro people and heaven and earth for Soviet Russia," Randolph concluded in 1942.[38] Randolph expressed genuine revulsion at the notion, advanced by the Communists in 1940 and again in 1950, that should war break out between the United States and the USSR, black Americans would refuse to fight against the Soviets. Anyone "who says the American Negro would not fight for the United States in a war with Russia simply does not know the Negro," he said in a denunciation of remarks by actor and singer Paul Robeson in 1950.[39] "Whatever may be the limitations and racial problems of the United States," Randolph's union organ, The Black Worker, editorialized toward the end of World War II, "the basic interests of the Negro are tied up with the rise or fall of his country, the U.S.A. If the United States goes down, the Negro will go down."[40]

Finally, decades of personal experience with party members led Randolph to conclude that since emancipation, no movement constituted a "graver danger to the Negro and labor than the Communist Party" and its "varied and various front organizations and transmission belts." The Randolph of the 1940s, even more than the Randolph of the early 1920s, feared the party as a "sinister menace."[41] Revelations that agents of Soviet espionage in Canada had managed to steal atomic secrets only raised the stakes even higher: What a "notorious Communist Spy Ring" could do north of the border, Randolph presciently predicted, "they will do in the U.S.A. Protestations of Communists to the contrary are meaningless. Lying, deceit, fraud, misrepresentation, slander, libel, pretense and hypocrisy are, according to the high priests of Communists [sic] doctrine and strategy, such as the great Lenin, articles of Communist faith. Truth is discounted and sneeringly branded as a bourgeois prejudice and weakness."[42]

What was to be done about the threat posed by the party? Randolph adopted a civil libertarian stance that put him at odds with more conservative anticommunists. He minced few words in his condemnation of the House Un-American Activities Committee, J. Edgar Hoover and the F. B. I., or the "McCormick-Patterson–Hearst Press" which would, he believed, "left unchecked, thoroughly totalitarianize our American Republic, leaving not a single vestige of our Bill of Rights."[43] The "wild-eyed, super-patriots" composing the "forces of reaction" in the postwar era "would burn down the temple of democracy in order to get rid of a few Communist rats," he predicted.[44] Opposed to the government's loyalty oaths and the "fascist forces that would enact legislation to outlaw the Communist Party," Randolph instead advocated freedom of assembly for all groups, Communists included. The "best antidote for communists in America and the world," he advised, was to "make the democratic process work."[45] To prohibit the "advocacy of varying political, economic and social ideas relating to forms of society is to eliminate the free play of thinking." There could be "no free speech, freedom of the press or assembly for republicans or democrats, if Communists are denied the same rights."[46]

While he opposed the enactment of repressive laws against the party, Randolph did not believe that Communists should have *carte blanche* to pursue their campaigns unchallenged. He exposed Communist efforts to infiltrate his own union's ranks, praised steelworker president Philip Murray for barring party members from holding union office, and extolled the UAW's Walter Reuther for the "strength and force" of his "able fight against communists." In calling for a unification of the AFL and CIO in 1948, Randolph concluded that no substantive differences divided the rival federations, because both were "together in their opposition to communists."[47] Randolph took his gospel of anticommunism on the road, lecturing countless black religious, civic, and fraternal organizations against what he termed the "Number One Enemy of the Negro people."[48]

As the Cold War at home and abroad deepened, the accumulated weight of the party's recent history—particularly its shifts in line and periodic sectarian spasms— diminished its standing.[49] The brief against domestic communism was further augmented by stories of black CP-ers who defected. Celebrated novelist Richard Wright is a case in point. "For God's sake, let's quit. I've had it," Wright reportedly told his wife Ellen in 1942. His growing dissatisfaction was rooted in the party's "unconditional support" for the war. Biographer Hazel Rowley argues that Wright initially withdrew quietly from the party's various activities, concerned about drawing the attention of the War Department if he voiced criticisms of the war. But two years later, he went public with a two-part essay in *The Atlantic Monthly* entitled "I Tried To Be A Communist." To a New York *Herald Tribune* interviewer, Wright complained about the "distinct and lamentable regression" by the party on racial issues. Its members were "narrow-minded, bigoted, intolerant, and frightened of new ideas which don't fit into their own." According to Rowley, Horace Cayton allowed Wright to compose one of his *Pittsburgh Courier* columns for him. Under Cayton's signature, Wright continued his public denigration of his former comrades. "One wonders what Communists really believe today about the Negro," Wright/Cayton pointedly asked. "Without even an iota of apology, [black Communist New York City councilman] Ben Davis urges Negroes to donate blood to the jim crow blood bank. . . . When the history of the Communist relationship to the Negro during this war is written," he concluded, "Communists will have a lot to answer for."[50]

Wright obviously hadn't felt that way during the 1930s when he joined the Communist Party. During the Great Depression, the CP had earned a reputation for forthright action on behalf of African Americans. Even those contemporaries unsympathetic to the party had to concede its often impressive role in fighting the manifestations of racism, not just in the larger society but in its own ranks as well. "Should Black Turn Red?" the conservative black educator Kelly Miller asked rhetorically during the depths of the Great Depression in 1933. Insisting that communism was "not native to American soil nor indigenous to the American spirit," Miller had to admit that communism's "apostles" tried to practice what they preached, were not frightened by the "stigma of social equality," staged parades protesting outrages committed against African Americans, and invited "persecution and imprisonment in the Negro's behalf."[51] Only the Communists "offer the Negro full equality within their ranks," Asbury Smith concurred that same year in the pages of *Opportunity*, a journal of the Urban League that in no way could be described as radical. "The white and Negro Communists march side by side. They eat and sleep together, and nowhere is any distinction made between them." The contrast with other movements was evident: "Today no group except the Communist group is willing to put into immediate operation the gospel principle that 'there is no Greek or barbarian, no bond or free, no male or female, but we are all one in Christ Jesus.' Communistic practice of racial equality appeals to all of us who feel the injustice of racial discrimination."[52] Few non communist observers feared that Communist ideology was proving attractive to black Americans. Rather, it was Communists' behavior that won them praise, even from skeptics. Their "relentless and spectacular struggles" on behalf of the Scottsboro boys and their efforts "to secure equal justice and living wages" have "tended to capture the imagination and win the sympathy and respect of thousands of colored citizens," the black weekly the Detroit *Tribune Independent* concluded in 1934.[53] Although black voices of praise, either cautious or enthusiastic, diminished by the 1940s, the party's earlier engagement with civil rights had earned it a positive reputation that persisted regardless of its later policy turns.

There is little question that the CP made the oppression of black Americans central to its agenda at a time when few other largely white groups took cognizance of it. The Comintern's Sixth World Congress signaled the party's prioritization of "the Negro question" and its embrace of blacks as agents of revolutionary transformation. Although the party's new "Black Belt Thesis"—which viewed blacks as a "nation within a nation" and advocated black self-determination in the South—won it few African-American converts, its commitment to making the "Negro problem . . . part and parcel of all and every campaign conducted by the Party"[54] represented a new departure for the left. During the party's sectarian, ultra-left "Third Period" which lasted up to 1935, its public embrace of black rights and social equality and members' willingness to place themselves at physical risk on behalf of blacks caught the attention and won the admiration of a growing number of black Americans. The party's role in the Scottsboro case may have served to alienate black liberals, but it also linked the party with the militant defense of oppressed blacks in the popular imagination.[55] During the Popular Front years (1935–39), party members shed their sectarian skin, ceased denouncing liberals and socialists as "social fascists," donned the cloak of Americanism, and worked tirelessly to build broad-based alliances to support the New Deal and oppose fascism. Contemporary critics of the party were not convinced of the party's sincerity or trustworthiness, even during the Popular Front.[56] But increasingly, the party's identification with anti-racism and liberalism won it praise from those who sought similar ends. " 'The Reds' won the admiration of the Negro masses by default," sociologists Horace Cayton and St. Clair Drake explained. "They were the only white people who seemed to really care about what happened to the Negro."[57]

In recent decades, revisionist historians on the left have meticulously reconstructed the CP's track record of accomplishment, commitment, and courage in the struggle for black rights, contributing to the party's rising reputation among many in the professoriate (if not the broader public). More than a few historians of labor and the African-American experience have embraced a positive—and in some instances glowing—portrayal of the party on matters of race and racial equality. "[W]hatever its programmatic and practical lapses," Bryan Palmer concludes, it is "striking how much US history in the 20th century that is associated with eradicating racism is inextricably entwined with the Communist Party." To Michael Honey, it was the CP's "unprecedented activity in support of black self-determination and labor rights that established much of the groundwork for an ongoing civil rights and labor alliance in the South."[58] The record is clear to political scientist Michael Goldfield: CP-led unions "engaged in significant racially egalitarian struggles on behalf of their African-American members"; more "inclusive and egalitarian" than non-left unions, they provided "the seeds for both interracial solidarity and civil rights struggles."[59]

Scholars, of course, have not always embraced a flattering portrayal of Communists on the race question. To some degree, revisionists have responded to an earlier view of the CP as cynically manipulating the otherwise valid grievances of African Americans. At the height of the Cold War, writers in the orthodox/ traditionalist camp viewed the party's race work, just as they viewed all of the party's efforts, in a negative light. The most detailed and influential accounts on this subject came from sociologist Wilson Record, whose *The Negro and the Communist Party* (1951) and *Race and Radicalism: The NAACP and the Communist Party in Conflict* (1964) informed the subsequent orthodox interpretation. Record exhaustively chronicled the multiple changes in the party's line and the rise and disappearance of its many pro-black/civil rights organizations; throughout, he insisted that the Comintern set American party policy and that changes in its line produced sharp reversals in CP practice and argument. A sharp critic of racial inequality in the United States, Record acknowledged that "despite the monolithic character of the Party structure, it should be recognized that there are many individual Communists who are consistently concerned with winning full equality for Negroes"[60] and who were "primarily motivated in the beginning by the desire to 'do something' about segregation and discrimination per se." But when the party line inevitably changed, many such members simply withdrew. Ultimately, Record concluded, the party's race work was never an end in itself but always grounded in an "overriding logic"—the "premise that whatever serves the interest of the 'workers' fatherland' is *right*—for the Negro and the human race."[61] Unlike many of the revisionists who followed decades later, Record paid close attention to Communists' actual words and analyses.

Even today it is impossible to consider any aspect of the Communist Party on the race question without walking into a historiographical minefield. Valuations of the party's race work rest, in part, on assessments of the party's fundamental character. Revisionists of the past generation have emphasized the party's indigenous radicalism which, if not free from Moscow's direction, nonetheless exhibited a substantial degree of autonomy and represented the genuine aspirations of countless American radicals. They have resolutely rejected what they consider to be the traditionalists' reduction of the CP's history to totalitarianism and Soviet domination, denial of any meaningful distinction between party leaders and the rank and file, and failure to recognize the party's grassroots accomplishments. In revisionist Randi Storch's words, the anticommunist historians remain guilty of ignoring the "complexity of communist activity" and "neglecting communists' day-to-day civil rights activity."[62]

For their part, anticommunist traditionalists continue to view the party's race work as determined in its broadest outlines by Moscow and ultimately manipulative and insincere. Moreover, they have ceded little ground to revisionists, rejecting arguments that party membership was neither monolithic in outlook nor motivation, that mechanical notions of totalitarianism and Soviet domination do not capture the party's broader culture, and that the party and its culture were part of a genuine, indigenous American radicalism. To the traditionalist scholars, revisionists continue to draw unwarranted distinctions between the party's leadership and rank and file.[63] With the Venona decryptions and documents from the former Soviet archives revealing Moscow's heavy hand and financing, not to mention the extensive espionage activities undertaken by American party officials, the traditionalists declared themselves the victors in the historiographical war.[64] The interpretive gap between the two camps remains large.

My concern in this essay is with the revisionists, who have produced the richest studies of the party's programs against racial inequality. In the pages that follow, I ask a number of related questions: To borrow Storch's question, have pro-party scholars been comparably guilty of "neglecting" complexity and avoiding too close scrutiny of "communists' day-to-day civil rights activity"? To what extent have revisionists addressed the anticommunists' central charges? There is no question that historians Robin D. G. Kelley, Michael Honey, Rick Halpern, Gerald Horne, Martha Biondi, Glenda Gilmore, and others have produced carefully researched accounts of the CP's race work and of individual Communists who exhibited dedication in the face of adversity and repression.[65] But revisionists have evaded the substance of the critique put forth not only by traditionalist scholars but also by anticommunist activists like Randolph.[66] Historians who lavish praise on the party's race record have shied away from close scrutiny of those aspects of the party's activities that contemporaries complained about or that potentially reflect negatively on the party—including its various white chauvinism trials, its involvement in the Scottsboro case (which critics charge involved the party's exploitation of the defendants for its own benefit and the mismanagement of funds), its takeover of the NNC, or its hostility to the World War II-era March on Washington Movement.

Their avoidance is facilitated by their minimizing of the formal political dimension of the Communist experience. As Joshua Freeman recently observed, his students today, "following the lead of the New Left historians they read, sympathetically view the Communist Party as a benign organization of ultraliberals."[67] In fact, revisionists seem to have reversed historian Robert Zieger's characterization of the party: "Communism was, after all, a disciplined international movement, not merely a collection of progressive-minded individuals."[68] In revisionists' hands, the politics of communism takes a distinct back seat to dedication and militancy. "The pull towards social history can sometimes diminish the significance of formal communist affiliations," Geoff Eley aptly wrote in 1986, "leading in extreme cases (mainly in the literature of the CPUSA) to a history of communism with the Communism left out."[69] If the "Communist" character of the Communists is downplayed, then it is relatively simple to dodge the question of the consequences of Communist policy on local Communists' work. In the remaining section of this essay, I approach this issue from two interconnected angles: first, through a brief examination of the CP and its race policies in one specific historical context, World War II, and second, through an exploration of revisionist historiography's treatment of the "significance of formal communist affiliations," the "party line," and their consequences.

Nowhere is the revisionists' reluctance to address the anticommunists' arguments more evident than in their treatment of the party's civil rights work during the World War II years. With the signing of the Nazi-Soviet pact in 1939, the party instantly repudiated its antifascist program and threw its energies wholeheartedly into a peace movement aimed at keeping the United States out of the growing conflict. The "Negro people are saying: we shall not die in the war of American imperialism," thundered John P. Davis in retort to Randolph's anti-CP speech at the

1940 NNC meeting. Just weeks before the Nazis invaded the Soviet Union on June 22, 1941, then-party member Richard Wright explained that the European conflict was "Not My People's War." In Chicago, local party activist and NNC organizer Ishmael Flory explained that "battle for full citizenship of the Negro people is a battle against the Roosevelt foreign policy and its supporters."[70]

Once the Nazis invaded the Soviet Union in 1941, the party reversed course yet again. The inter-imperialist war backed by Wall Street warmongers instantly became a "people's war," for, in the minds of party members, the German attack had "changed the character of the war."[71] The "great mass of Negroes now know that this is *their* war," claimed party leader Doxey Wilkerson. An Axis victory would "plunge the Negro people into a fascist slavery far worse than their forefathers ever knew."[72] ("I do declare!" the poet Langston Hughes, who had earlier broken with the party, privately remarked upon hearing the news of the Nazi invasion. This would "no doubt make the Communist Party change its line again. Strange bedfellows! But it's more like Ringling's flying trapezes.")[73] Revisionists readily admit that the party's sudden antiwar stance in 1939, followed almost two years later with its sudden pro-war stance, bewildered its followers. These shifts, Robert Korstad notes, "alienated many of its former allies." They "were alternately energizing and debilitating for the Communist movement, and inspired, among some, distrust about the reliability of the left," Martha Biondi observes. But the *consequences* of these shifts, beyond allusions to distrust and alienation, have been peripheral to the revisionists' analyses. Biondi herself argues that the "left's appeal" to blacks flowed from "its willingness to engage in an uncompromising struggle for equal rights."[74] The party, it seems, remained in the vanguard for the fight for black equality.

Or did it? This is, ultimately, an empirical question with implications for our understanding of the party's record on race. Contemporaries themselves were not of one mind on the question. In December 1944, the monthly *Negro Digest* posed the matter starkly in a roundtable debate on "Have Communists Quit Fighting for Negro Rights?" Although a slim majority of those polled in the journal's coast-to-coast canvas of black opinion believed that the party had not abandoned its militant fight, a significant minority believed it was now less outspoken on blacks' behalf to avoid embarrassing the Roosevelt administration.[75] The *Digest* opened its pages to three black Communists who defended the party's record. William L. Patterson countered that the very question—raised by the forces of reaction to set back black advances and reduce black support for the party—revealed an "abysmal ignorance of Communist philosophy or to consciously seek to deceive people, or both." New York City's Communist councilman Benjamin A. Davis, Jr described the party's "self-sacrificing support" of the country as the "greatest service that can be contributed to Negro rights." Finally, the CP's former vice presidential candidate James W. Ford simply equated the war against fascism with the fight for African-American rights. Blacks understood that the "two are inseparable," for an Axis victory would rob both the "American nation and the Negro people of independence and democratic gains."[76]

Answering the abandonment question in the affirmative, iconoclastic black writer George Schuyler dismissed all Communist efforts on blacks' behalf. Communists, he proposed, had "not quit fighting for Negro rights because they never began." It fell to sociologist and columnist Horace Cayton to lay out the substantive case against the party. Whereas party members maintained an "uncompromising position against discrimination" in the 1930s, their wartime behavior was marked by a lack of aggressiveness in the fight for Negro rights. Their obsession with promoting national unity led them to counsel minority groups to subordinate their agendas to the larger task at hand. What Communists gave was "verbal approval" to blacks' struggles, not organized support. The wartime gains blacks had won could be attributed to the NAACP, the Urban League, and other groups, not the Communist Party. It was Cayton's impression that the party had "misjudged the situation," for "more aggressive action for Negro rights would have indeed aided the war effort."[77]

In the end, it was Cayton, not the black Communist defenders of the party's record, who would have the last word on the subject. In less than a year, Communists would come to embrace Cayton's critical position following yet another change in line. Interpreting the letter published by French Communist Jacques Duclos in April 1945 as Soviet instructions, they jettisoned their general secretary Earl Browder as a "social-imperialist," "enemy of the working class," and "apologist for American imperialism," formally reestablished the Communist Party (which Browder had just transformed into the Communist Political Association), and renounced what they termed "Browderism." A more militantly anti-capitalist stance and an undisguised hostility to what they now called America's "swaggering militarism" came to characterize the party's rhetoric.[78] The new line was accompanied by a reassessment of their recent past. In their retrospective critique of Browderism, party members stridently denounced their inadequate wartime handling of the race question. James W. Ford confessed his "grave" error in creating the illusion among blacks "of expectation of democratic rights gratis from Roosevelt and the Democratic party." Party journalist George Lohr concluded that having become "smug and complacent," the party had "committed many tactical errors" on the race question. H. V. Saunders admitted that the party's revisionism "weakened the whole struggle for the emancipation of the Negro people," while Thelma Dale acknowledged that the win-the-war-at-all-costs approach had produced the illusion, held by Communists, that "Negroes would *automatically* win their rights through all-out support of the war effort." This led to a "soft-pedaling" of the "fight against the inferior status of Negroes in the armed forces." The Communists' "politically phlegmatic position" was "untenable." Lest there be any misunderstanding, Dale concluded by insisting that "Never again must we allow a situation to develop in which Social-Democrat and Trotskyite demagogues can assume leadership of important struggles in the Negro movement." In some quarters, this auto-critique of wartime practices only reinforced the image of the party as willing to place Soviet foreign policy before the interests of those it purported to support.[79]

Could the party's auto-critique be trusted as a reliable assessment of its own failures? Maurice Isserman suggests not. "Ironically," he argues, "the Communists themselves played an important role in creating this interpretation [of abandonment of blacks] when, in the aftermath of Browder's downfall in 1945, they searched their wartime record for evidence of the negative effects of 'revisionism'" and repudiated it accordingly. Their opponents may have dismissed the party's wartime condemnations of Jim Crow as little more than "empty rhetoric," but Isserman concludes that the party, whose policies "proved an inadequate response to the black community's demands for redress of long-standing grievances," had not abandoned "the struggle for black rights during the war." Rather, it "forced that struggle into narrow channels."[80]

There is much in the pages of the revisionists' scholarship to support Isserman's argument—at least to a degree. Alex Lichtenstein, for instance, has demonstrated the indispensable role of party activists in building the CIO in Florida. The party's win-the-war stance did not slow efforts to organize the burgeoning shipyards in Miami, Tampa, and Jacksonville, led by the indefatigable Charles Smolikoff, a CP-member and organizer for the Industrial Union of Marine and Shipbuilding Workers of America [IUMSW]. Smolikoff and the IUMSW aggressively addressed black workers' needs by developing black rank-and-file leadership, integrating black stewards into the union's executive board, and appointing black representatives to grievance and negotiating committees. Rick Halpern and Roger Horowitz have established the positive role played by Communists in the Packinghouse Workers Organizing Committee/United Packinghouse Workers of America during the war, while Michael Honey has chronicled the workplace accomplishments of leftwing unionists in the segregationist stronghold of wartime Memphis. Full support for the war effort did not lead to a halt in either union organizing or support for civil rights.[81]

But the second part of Isserman's argument—that the party "forced that struggle into narrow channels"—has received considerably less attention from revisionists. In each example above, party members in positions of union leadership tried hard to keep workers on the job, discouraging or opposing strike activity. Smolikoff later boasted that "there has not been a single CIO strike in Florida," an achievement that, Lichtenstein concludes "accommodated both the nation's wartime mobilization and the CP line." In Memphis, strikes presumably declined in number following the Nazi attack on the Soviet Union. Black workers chafed at discriminatory treatment and wages, but the left-led United Cannery, Agricultural, Packing, and Allied Workers of America (UCAPAWA) balked at direct action. "When the black workers did strike," Honey mentions in passing, "the company, with the support from the War Labor Board and union officials, fined and suspended their leaders." In 1943, a spontaneous walkout by 160 black workers was ended only when the business agent of UCAPAWA issued "threats and fines" against them, leaving their grievances about their exclusion from higher-paying job classifications unaddressed. Left-wing union organizers "urged the blacks to put off action on job classification until after the war," advice that did little to quell their agitation.[82] Rick Halpern found that in

Chicago, packinghouse organizers in the party engaged in a difficult "balancing act." To their credit, leftists pursued antidiscrimination contract clauses and used the federal Fair Employment Practice Committee (as did Smolikoff in Florida) to pursue blacks' job rights. But party-reinforced constraints closed off certain avenues of protest. Although union officials "displayed considerable tolerance of rank-and-file self activity," aware that they were sitting on "a tinder box," Halpern found, they nonetheless supported wartime curbs on shop floor activity.[83]

These examples do not speak of an outright abandonment of black rights during the war; even with the prioritization of uninterrupted war production, party activists pursued a modified civil rights agenda. But what were the consequences of party members' directing black grievances and civil rights issues into the "narrow channels" Isserman identified? In Chicago, the CP's embrace of a prowar stance after the Nazi invasion of the Soviet Union reflected poorly on the party. The "first great wave of dissatisfaction with the Communists swept through the ranks of Negro intellectuals and Race Leaders" who felt that Communists' endorsement of "national unity" meant that they were being advised "to moderate their demands for full equality," St. Clair Drake and Horace Cayton found. "[C]harges were hurled that 'the Reds' are selling out the Negroes." Although Drake and Cayton did not fully agree with that claim, they did note the moderation of the party's earlier role: "The Communists feared that mass demonstrations might hurt morale of the Negro soldiers fighting in a coalition war beside the Soviet Union"; they "insisted that defeating Hitler came first" and that "Negro demands should be couched in 'win the war' terms," which many race leaders objected to. Black rank and filers in the labor movement "saw that while 'the Reds' played down mass action they continued to fight for Negro rights *within* the labor unions, and tried to inject the issue of Negro rights into the political coalitions they formed . . . The Communists were still preaching BLACK AND WHITE UNITE, but in a more quiet fashion than during the stormy Thirties, and with less emphasis upon Negro mass action."[84] The wartime experience suggests that the praise accorded the party on its race record requires qualification.

Contemporaries on the democratic left did not hesitate to ask tough questions. Observing party members' attacks on their own wartime behavior after the war, Randolph must have felt vindicated. The "Communists opposed the fight for jobs for Negroes . . . on the grounds it would hold up war production of munitions for Soviet Russia," he charged in November 1945. Their "greatest contribution to the Negro" during the recent war had been attempts to "disrupt sound Negro movements . . . While the Negroes were marching and fighting all over the country for fair employment practices in war plants, the Communists were denouncing such activities as Fascist, demanding that racial discrimination be overlooked in the interest of war production."[85] What Randolph had in mind was the Communists' coolness, and at times hostility, to his March on Washington Movement, before and after the Nazi invasion of the Soviet Union. Party members charged that its all-black membership policy (designed, in large part, to avoid the fate of the NNC by reducing the threat of Communist infiltration) was a chauvinistic slap in the face of white allies designed to foster ill will, while Randolph's relentless challenges to the Roosevelt administration's racial policies weakened the war effort. Randolph offered only "defeatist, anti-war leadership," party leader Doxey Wilkerson complained in 1943. The BSCP leader's "program of Roosevelt-hating war obstruction," blasted the *California Eagle*, a paper sympathetic to the Communists, put Randolph on the "road to treason of the nation and betrayal of his people."[86]

Randolph spoke from the heart in castigating the party for what he saw as its obstructionism, but his dogged anticommunism prevented him from recognizing the genuine contributions CP-ers made during wartime in building industrial unions and, within limits, supporting civil rights. The shipyards of Florida and the San Francisco Bay area, the packinghouses of Chicago, and the factories of Memphis were obviously not in Randolph's line of vision. Rather, his eyes were fixed on national politics and organizational campaigns. There, he found much in the party's stance wanting. "Although Negroes are still the victims of lynchings, white Primaries, the Poll Tax, mob law and sharecrop exploitation, and are Jim-Crowed and treated like second-class citizens," he complained in the pages of the *Black Worker* in 1942, "the Communists advise them to submerge and forget their grievances and abandon their right [sic—read 'fight'] for their democratic rights for a SECOND FRONT and the salvation of Soviet Russia."[87] After Hitler invaded Russia, he explained after the war, all that mattered for the Communists was "winning the war."[88] As bad as it was, the party's retreat on the civil rights front wasn't what offended Randolph the most. He considered the Nazi-Soviet Pact to be "the blackest page in the history of the USSR" and the CPUSA's reflexive anti-war protests to be "the blackest page in the history of American Communists." Posing as the "Messiah of the Negro," the Communists had "deserted and betrayed the cause of the Negro."[89] Some things Randolph would never forget—or forgive.

In contrast, revisionist historians have. If the party's record was perhaps not nearly as weak as Randolph—and party leaders—claimed it was, neither was it as positive as revisionist historians maintain. But why have revisionists been so reluctant to pose critical questions or to address squarely the respective charges of Moscow's domination of the party, the impact of changes in the party line, or evidence of back-pedaling on race? Their evasion may stem from their rejection of the anticommunists' portrait of a monolithic Communist movement directed from Moscow which erases any meaningful distinction between the party rank and file and its top leaders, denies significant agency to party activists, and dismisses Communists' good work in the realms of race and labor as cynical manipulations of various constituencies. It may also reflect a persistent infatuation with a left tradition that, however flawed, is believed to have embodied real hope for black equality at a time when few other groups in American society did.

Revisionist treatments of the party share the assumption that formal party ideology mattered less to individual Communists than did the causes the CP embraced or the broader political sensibility it sustained. "For many on the left,"

Robert Korstad writes, "the Popular Front had less to do with these twists and turns in the Party line than with a sea change in American political culture."[90] Michael Honey similarly contends that workers in Memphis "joined the Communist party not so much out of ideological conviction but because it offered them an active organizational vehicle at a time when few others existed." Goals, not explicit ideology, were what mattered. Many of the "most active organizers during the popular front era paid little attention to whether a person actually was or was not a member of the Communist party," he concludes, for "people worked together around goals that they could all agree upon and did not debate the finer ideological questions."[91] Black socialists like Randolph and Crosswaith, black conservatives like George Schuyler and C. W. Rice, black liberals like Walter White, Roy Wilkins, Clarence Mitchell, and Edith Sampson, black Catholics like Theophilus Lewis, black trade unionists like Willard Townsend and Maida Springer, and Trotskyites like Herbert Hill (white) or C. L. R. James (black) would not have recognized the Communists they encountered in their daily lives in this revisionist portrait, at least not by the 1940s.[92]

These revisionists' assumptions appear more as articles of faith than empirically demonstrated facts. In his valuable assessment of the historiography of American communism, Bryan Palmer offers an observation that pertains directly to the literature on the CP and race. Revisionist scholarship is characterized by an "avoidance of specific issues of theory and programmatic direction," he recently suggested. "With the turn to a social history of rank-and-file experience, characteristic of the intellectual climate of the 1970s"—which I would add, persists to this day—"questions of leadership and of ideas assumed, initially at least, an almost inconsequential status." The downgrading of the status of ideas in revisionist analyses has led to a "dearth of interpretive commentary in the writing on the US left" on the "important, if problematic role of Stalinism." The reluctance to "grapple openly with Stalinism's forceful historical presence" is no minor problem, rendering it difficult to understand "specific parts of the left experience" for the simple reason that "Stalinism matters in what happened to 20th-century American radicalism."[93] It certainly mattered to noncommunist and anticommunist radicals in mid-twentieth century America; in many instances, it mattered a great deal.

That "the American communists loyally followed the Kremlin's directives had crucial political consequences and cannot be dismissed as a figment of Cold War ideology," argues Manfred Berg in his study of the NAACP. But revisionists who portray Communism largely as a "progressive grassroots movement for social justice" (in Berg's words)[94] and downplay the party's subservience to the Soviet Union are ill-equipped to recognize those consequences, particularly the role played by the CP itself in its own destruction. Historian Adam Fairclough's implicit challenge to revisionist interpretations is worth quoting at length: It is difficult to see how the CP, "even in the absence of government repression, could have avoided isolation and decline," he argues. "In some ways, the Communist Party was its own worst enemy. The party's secrecy, tactical inconsistency, and ideological rigidity alienated most of its supporters and many of its members. At a time when Stalin was erecting police states in Eastern Europe, blockading West Berlin, and intensifying repression inside the Soviet Union, the CPUSA's steadfast allegiance to Moscow made the party a moral leper." As for the party's erstwhile allies, many liberals who had "gladly worked with the Party during the halcyon days of the Popular Front could no longer stomach associating with Communists. Postwar anticommunism was not merely a right-wing plot to discredit the Left: it was also a genuine defense of democratic ideals."[95]

That was certainly how Randolph and numerous other noncommunist progressives would have seen it. That their critique of the party prefigured the one later advanced by the traditionalist anticommunist scholars should not be cause for dismissing it out of hand as opportunistic, conservative, or anti-civil rights. Nor did their alternatives always bear fruit. The progress of Randolph's own crusades on behalf of racial equality in the United States proved painfully slow, his organizational efforts often stalled, and his leadership style was over-centralized and at times ineffective. Ultimately, his ardent hostility to Communism precluded his recognizing the real contributions of his opponents on the left. If he missed the truth of Communists' commitment and contributions—which, at times, were substantial—he realized a separate truth that a party dedicated to the defense of dictatorship and subordinated to a foreign power could not bring about permanent or desirable change for African Americans—or any Americans.

Revisionist historians may not accept Randolph's ultimate moral and political indictment of the Communist activists whose dedication and accomplishments they choose to celebrate. But they might fruitfully listen to the critique of the party whose support for the goals of ending racial discrimination and inequality was not enough to offset its frequently destructive tendencies and the genuine harm it did to those with whom it disagreed. Communists' flaws were not incidental but constitutive of their politics, at all levels of the party, at least for those who chose to remain in its ranks. Coming to terms with the party's uneven role in civil rights history requires us to take seriously the pragmatic, political, and ethical critiques lodged by anticommunist progressives. It should also prompt those exploring the "long civil rights movement" to recognize that the record of their protagonists on the Communist left was far more complicated and—at times—even harmful to the cause of racial equality. The "far grayer picture"[96] that emerges is one that more accurately accounts for the specific trajectory of civil rights struggles and the larger tragedy of the American left.

Notes

1. Glenda Elizabeth Gilmore, *Defying Dixie: The Radical Roots of Civil Rights, 1919–1950* (New York: W. W. Norton & Co., 2008), 6.
2. Shelton Stromquist, "Introduction: Was All (Cold War) Politics Local?" in Stromquist, ed., *Labor's Cold War: Local Politics in a Global Context* (Urbana, IL: University of Illinois Press, 2008), 8.

3. Martha Biondi, *To Stand and Fight: The Struggle for Civil Rights in Postwar New York City* (Cambridge: Harvard University Press, 2003), 6; Biondi, "How New York Changes the Story of the Civil Rights Movement," *Afro-Americans in New York Life and History* 31 (2) (July 2007): 17.

4. Jacqueline Dowd Hall, "The Long Civil Rights Movement and the Political Uses of the Past," *Journal of American History* 91 (4) (March 2005): 1235, 1245.

5. Theodore Draper, "Life of the Party," *New York Review of Books* (January 13, 1994).

6. On the implications of the "long civil rights movement" scholarship, see Eric Arnesen, "Reconsidering the 'Long Civil Rights Movement,'" *Historically Speaking* X (2) (April 2009): 31–34.

7. Mark Naison, *Communists in Harlem During the Depression* (Urbana, IL: University of Illinois Press, 1983), 296.

8. "Stanley High, 'Black Omens,' *Saturday Evening Post* (June 4, 1938): 38.

9. Brian Urquhart, *Ralph Bunche: An American Life* (1993; rpt. New York: W. W. Norton & Company, 1993), 93–94; Ralph J. Bunche, "Extended Memorandum on the Program, Ideologies, Tactics and Achievements of Negro Betterment and Interracial Organizations: A Research Memorandum," in Carnegie-Myrdal Study, The Negro in America. Research Memorandum for use in the preparation of Dr. Gunnar Myrdal's *An American Dilemma*, 1940, pp. 71–74, reel 1; Earl Ofari Hutchinson, *Blacks and Reds: Race and Class in Conflict 1919–1990* (East Lansing, MI: Michigan State University Press, 1995), 182.

10. A. Philip Randolph, "The World Crisis and the Negro People Today" [n.p., 1940], 9.

11. Randolph, "The World Crisis and the Negro People Today," 11, 14, 18, 19. In equating Nazi Germany with the Soviet Union, Randolph drew upon arguments common in anti-Stalinist circles after the Pact. See William L. O'Neill, *A Better World: The Great Schism: Stalinism and the American Intellectuals* (New York: Simon and Schuster, 1982), 45–46.

12. Maurice Isserman, *Which Side Were You On?: The American Communist Party During the Second World War* (Middletown, CT: Wesleyan University Press, 1982); O'Neill, *A Better World*, 13–42; Guenter Lewy, *The Cause That Failed: Communism in American Political Life* (New York: Oxford University Press, 1990), 60–65.

13. Pat Toohey, "Greater Attention to the Problems of the Negro Masses! Speech Delivered at the Meeting of the National Committee, Communist Party, U.S.A., February 19, 1940," *The Communist* XIX (3) (March 1940): 280. Also see Theodore R. Bassett and A. W. Berry, "The Negro People and the Struggle for Peace," *The Communist* XIX (4) (April 1940): 320–35.

14. "Communism Causes Split in Congress," *Chicago Defender* (May 4, 1940): 1, 2; 'Foe of Reds Quits Negro Leadership," *New York Times* (April 29, 1940): 17. The fate of the NNC has received insufficient attention from historians, yet many concur that the 1940 organizational coup proved fatal to the Congress. See Hilmar Ludvig Jensen, "The Rise of an African-American Left: John P. Davis

and the National Negro Congress," Ph.D. dissertation, Cornell University, 1997, 517; Urquhart, *Ralph Bunche*, 94. Lawrence S. Wittner concludes in contrast that the NNC's history "cannot be understood solely by reference to Communism." Wittner, "The National Negro Congress: A Reassessment," *American Quarterly* 22 (1970): 901.

15. Bunche, "Extended Memorandum," 82; Jonathan Scott Holloway, *Confronting the Veil: Abram Harris Jr., E. Franklin Frazier, and Ralph Bunche, 1919–1941* (Chapel Hill, NC: University of North Carolina Press, 2002), 190.

16. "Whither the Negro Congress?" Washington *Afro-American* (May 4, 1940): 16.

17. "Negro Congress," *Amsterdam News* (May 11, 1940).

18. Lester B. Granger, "The Negro Congress—Its Future," *Opportunity* XVIII (6) (June 1940): 164; Bunche, "Extended Memorandum," 82.

19. Erik Gelman, "'Carthage Must be Destroyed': Race, City Politics, and the Campaign to Integrate Chicago Transportation Work, 1929–1943," *Labor: Studies in Working-Class History of the Americas* 2 (2) (Summer, 2005): 100; Beth Tompkins Bates, *Pullman Porters and the Rise of Protest Politics in Black America 1925–1945* (Chapel Hill, NC: University of North Carolina Press, 2001), 145; Bates, "A New Crowd Challenges the Agenda of the Old Guard in the NAACP, 1933–1941," *American Historical Review* 102 (2) (April 1997): 372; John Baxter Streater, Jr, "The National Negro Congress, 1936–1947," Ph.D. dissertation, University of Cincinnati, 1981, 293; Hutchinson, *Blacks and Reds*, 188; Carol Anderson, "From Hope to Disillusion: African Americans, the United Nations, and the Struggle for Human Rights, 1944–1947," *Diplomatic History* 20 (4) (Fall, 1996): 552–53.

20. Theodore R. Bassett, "The Third National Negro Congress," *The Communist* XIV (6) (June 1940): 542, 548.

21. "Not the Voice of the Negro People," *Daily Worker* (February 10, 1941); "A Step That Leads to Surrender," *Daily Worker* (February 22, 1941); William L. Patterson, "A. Philip Randolph Can't Sell This War to Oppressed, Jim Crowed Negro People," *Daily Worker* (March 3, 1941); Ben Davis, Jr, "Reformist Walter White 'Protests'—But Really Backs FDR's Jim Crow War Program," *Daily Worker* (March 12, 1941); Herbert Garfinkel, *When Negroes March: The March on Washington Movement in the Organizational Politics for FEPC* (1959; rpt. New York: Atheneum, 1969), 48–53.

22. On Randolph's life, see Jervis Anderson, *A. Philip Randolph: A Biographical Portrait* (1973; rpt. Berkeley, CA: University of California Press, 1986); Paula F. Pfeffer, *A. Philip Randolph, Pioneer of the Civil Rights Movement* (Baton Rouge, LA: Louisiana State University Press, 1990); Cynthia Taylor, *A. Philip Randolph: The Religious Journey of an African American Labor Leader* (New York: New York University Press, 2006); Andrew Edmund Kersten, *A. Philip Randolph: A Life in the Vanguard* (New York: Roman & Littlefield, 2006); Eric Arnesen, "A. Philip Randolph: Labor and the New Black Politics," in Arnesen, ed., *The Human Tradition in American Labor History* (Wilmington, DE: Scholarly Resources, 2003), 173–91.

23. On Pullman porters, see: Beth Tompkin Bates, *Pullman Porters and the Rise of Protest Politics in Black America*; William H. Harris, *Keeping the Faith: A. Philip Randolph, Milton P. Webster, and the Brotherhood of Sleeping Car Porters, 1925–37* (Urbana, IL: University of Illinois Press, 1977); Eric Arnesen, *Brotherhoods of Color: Black Railroad Workers and the Struggle for Equality* (Cambridge, MA: Harvard University Press, 2001).

24. Arnesen, *Brotherhoods of Color*, 181–202; Garfinkel, *When Negroes March*; Merl E. Reed, *Seedtime for the Modern Civil Rights Movement: The President's Committee on Fair Employment Practice, 1941–1946* (Baton Rouge, LA: Louisiana State University Press, 1991).

25. Joseph D. Bibb, "Randolph Arrives," *Pittsburgh Courier* (July 11, 1942); "A. Philip Randolph—Our New Leader," *Minneapolis Spokesman* (July 17, 1942) (reprinting an editorial from the *Philadelphia Tribune*); L. Baynard Whitney, "Randolph Heads List, to Receive Award; March Biggest News," *Houston Informer* (January 10, 1942); H. George Davenport, "A. Philip Randolph Looms High as Negroes Foremost Leader," Seattle *Northwest Enterprise* (September 29, 1943).

26. "The Menace of Negro Communists," *The Messenger* V (8) (August 1923): 784; "The Sanhedrin," *The Messenger* V (1) (October 1923): 830; "The American Negro Labor Congress," *The Messenger* VII (8) (August 1925): 305; Harris, *Keeping the Faith*, 24–25.

27. "Pullman Porters Situation Desperate," *Liberator*, July 20, 1931; Randolph Testimony at Hearings before a Special Committee to Investigate Communist Activities in the United States of the House of Representatives, Seventy-First Congress, 2nd Session. "Investigation of Communist Propaganda," Part III, Vol. 1, July 15 to July 23, 1930 (Washington D.C.: U.S. Government Printing Office, 1930), 243–44, 249–50; Harris, *Keeping the Faith*, 114–15.

28. "Miller Says Spirit of Radicalism Was Major Factor of Meet," *Pittsburgh Courier* (March 7, 1936). On the NNC's formation, see: "Toward Negro Unity," *The Nation* CXLII (March 11, 1936): 302; Lester B. Granger, "The National Negro Congress: An Interpretation," *Opportunity* XIV (5) (May 1936): 151–53.

29. A. Philip Randolph, "Randolph Says Race Congress Not Communist," *Chicago Defender* (February 29, 1936).

30. Bates, "A New Crowd," 360–70; Cicero Alvin Hughes, "Toward a Black United Front: The National Negro Congress Movement," Ph.D. dissertation, Ohio University, 1982; Randolph to Ernest Angell, November 1, 1950, in *The Papers of A. Philip Randolph* (Bethesda, MD: University Publications of America, 1990), reel 23.

31. Benjamin A. Davis, "Build the United Negro People's Movement," *Political Affairs* XXVI (11) (November 1947): 1004; Harry Haywood, *Negro Liberation* (1948; rpt. Chicago: Liberator Press, 1976), 211; John Pittman, "Negro Workers Test Allies by Action against Jimcrow," *Workers Magazine* XV (36) (September 3, 1950): 5.

32. "A. Philip Randolph Tells . . . 'Why I would Not Stand for Reelection as President of the National Negro Congress,'" *American Federationist* (July 1940). An almost

identical statement appears as A. Philip Randolph, "Why I Would Not Stand for Re-Election for President of the National Negro Congress," *Black Worker* (May 1940): 1, 4.

33. "A. Philip Randolph Tells . . . 'Why I would Not Stand for Reelection.'"

34. A. Philip Randolph, "Reply to Lucius C. Harper—Randolph Hits Critics In Negro Congress Affair," *Chicago Defender* (May 25, 1940) (reprinted in pamphlet, "The World Crisis and the Negro People Today" [1940; n.p.]).

35. Randolph, "The World Crisis and the Negro People Today," 11, 14.

36. "Communists: A Menace to Black America," *Black Worker* (November 1945): 1; also see Randolph, "The Menace of Communism," *American Federationist* (March 1949): 19.

37. "Wallace for President," *Black Worker* (February 1948): 6. Its title notwithstanding, the BSCP rejected Wallace's candidacy. Also see "A. Phillip Randolph Charges Wallace Led By Reds; Attack Jim Crow in UMT, Draft," *Negro Labor News* (April 17, 1948).

38. A. Philip Randolph, "Editorial: The Communists and the Negro," *Black Worker* (July 1942): 4.

39. "Randolph Fires New Broadside at Robeson, Progressives, Reds," *Pittsburgh Courier* (February 4, 1950); Randolph, "The World Crisis and the Negro People Today," 20.

40. "Communists: A Menace to Black America," *Black Worker* (November 1945): 4.

41. "The Danger of Communists and Communism to Labor and the Negro," *Black Worker* (December 1948): 5; Randolph, "One Union's Story," 22.

42. "U.S.A. against U.S.S.R.," *Black Worker* (July 1948): 3.

43. "U.S.A. Against U.S.S.R.," *Black Worker* (July 1948): 3.

44. A. Philip Randolph, "The Problem of Communists," *Northwest Enterprise* (June 4, 1947).

45. "Labor Today," *Black Worker* (May 1948): 3.

46. Randolph, "The Problem of Communists."

47. "Labor Today," *Black Worker* (May 1948): 3.

48. A. Philip Randolph, "Editorial: The Communists and the Negro," *Black Worker* (July 1942): 4; "Warns Race Against Communism," Norfolk *Journal and Guide* (December 21, 1946); "Randolph Warns Students Against Totalitarianism," *Northwest Enterprise* (December 11, 1946).

49. See Frank R. Crosswaith, "Communists and the Negro," *Interracial Review* XVI (11) (November 1943): 166–68.

50. Hazel Rowley, *Richard Wright: The Life and Times* (New York: Henry Holt and Company, 2001), 263–64, 252–54; Richard Wright, "I Tried to Be A Communist," *The Atlantic Monthly* (August 1944): 61–70 and (September 1944): 48–56; New York *Herald Tribune* statement quoted in Rowley, *Richard Wright*, 291; Horace Cayton, "The Communists," *Pittsburgh Courier* (August 26, 1944), quoted in Rowley, *Richard Wright*, 292.

51. Kelly Miller, "Should Black Turn Red?" *Opportunity* XI (11) (November 1933): 328; "K. Miller Says Communism No Negro Remedy," Seattle *Northwest Enterprise* (March 22, 1934).

52. Asbury Smith, "What Can the Negro Expect from Communism?" *Opportunity* XI (7) (July 1933): 211.

53. Editorial: "Communism and Colored America," Detroit *Tribune Independent* (March 10, 1934).

54. Quoted in Sterling D. Spero and Abram L. Harris, *The Black Worker: The Negro and the Labor Movement* (1931; rpt. New York: Atheneum, 1969), 419.

55. On Scottsboro, see Dan T. Carter, *Scottsboro: A Tragedy of the American South* (1969; rpt. Baton Rouge, LA: Louisiana State University Press, 1979); James A. Miller, *Remembering Scottsboro: The Legacy of an Infamous Trial* (Princeton: Princeton University Press, 2009).

56. On the party and race from the late 1920s through 1939, see Harvard Sitkoff, *A New Deal for Blacks: The Emergence of Civil Rights as a National Issue*, vol. I: *The Depression Decade* (New York: Oxford University Press, 1978), 139–68; Naison, *Communists in Harlem*; Robin D. G. Kelley, *Hammer and Hoe: Alabama Communists During the Great Depression* (Chapel Hill, NC: University of North Carolina Press, 1990).

57. St. Clair Drake and Horace R. Cayton, *Black Metropolis: A Study of Negro Life in a Northern City*, vol. 2 (1945; rpt. New York: Harcourt, Brace & World, 1970), 736.

58. Bryan D. Palmer, "Rethinking the Historiography of United States Communism," *American Communist History* 2 (2) (2003): 146–47; Michael Honey, *Southern Labor and Black Civil Rights; Organizing Memphis Workers* (Urbana, IL: University of Illinois Press, 1993), 118.

59.. Michael Goldfield, "Race and the CIO: The Possibilities for Racial Egalitarianism During the 1930s and 1940s," *International Labor and Working-Class History* n. 44 (Fall, 1993): 23, 27. Not all historians place left-led unions in the forefront of struggles for equality. See the qualifications raised by Alan Draper, "The New Southern Labor History Revisited: The Success of the Mine, Mill and Smelter Workers Union in Birmingham, 1934–1938," *Journal of Southern History* LXII (1) (February 1996): 87–108; Judith Stein, "The Ins and Outs of the CIO," *International Labor and Working-Class History*, no. 44 (Fall 1993): 53–63.

60. Wilson Record, *The Negro and the Communist Party* (1951; rpt. New York: Atheneum, 1971), 292–93, 296; Wilson Record, *Race and Radicalism: The NAACP and the Communist Party in Conflict* (Ithaca, NY: Cornell University Press, 1964). Sharing Wilson's perspective are Nathan Glazer, *The Social Basis of American Communism* (New York: Harcourt, Brace & World, 1961), 169–81; David A. Shannon, *The Decline of American Communism: A History of the Communist Part of the United States since 1945* (New York: Harcourt, Brace and Company, 1959), 58–67.

61. Record, *The Negro and the Communist Party*, 288.
62. Randi Jill Storch, "Shades of Red: The Communist Party and Chicago's Workers, 1928–1939," Ph.D. dissertation, University of Illinois at Urbana-Champaign, 1998, 237. Also see Storch, *Red Chicago: American Communism at Its Grassroots, 1928–35* (Urbana, IL: University of Illinois Press, 2007).
63. John Earl Haynes, "The Cold War Debate Continues: A Traditionalist View of Historical Writing on Domestic Communism and Anti-Communism," *Journal of Cold War Studies* 2 (1) (Winter 2000): 87; Haynes and Klehr, "The Historiography of American Communism," 65.
64. See Haynes, "Cold War Debate Continues," 76–115; John Earl Haynes and Harvey Klehr, "The Historiography of American Communism: An Unsettled Field," *Labour History Review* 68 (1) (April 2003): 61–78. On Venona and Soviet espionage, see John Earl Haynes, Harvey Klehr, and Alexander Vassiliev, *Spies: The Rise and Fall of the KGB in America* (New Haven, CT: Yale University Press, 2009); Ted Morgan, *Reds: McCarthyism in Twentieth-Century America* (New York: Random House, 2003), 225–34, 291–93; Maurice Isserman, "Guess What—They Really Were Spies," *Forward* CII (January 29, 1999): 11; Ellen Schrecker and Maurice Isserman, "The Right's Cold War Revision," *Nation* 271 (4) (July 24, 2000). On the fate of black communist Lovett Fort-Whiteman, a founder of the American Negro Labor Council in 1925 who later died in a Soviet gulag, see Harvey Klehr, John Earl Haynes, and Kyrill M. Anderson, *The Soviet World of American Communism* (New Haven, CT: Yale University Press, 1998), 218–27; Gilmore, *Defying Dixie*, 153–54.
65. Rick Halpern, *Down on the Killing Floor: Black and White Workers in Chicago's Packinghouses, 1904–54* (Urbana, IL: University of Illinois Press, 1997); Honey, *Southern Labor and Black Civil Rights*; Biondi, *To Stand and Fight*; Gilmore, *Defying Dixie*; Gerald Horne, *Communist Front? The Civil Rights Congress, 1946–1956* (Rutherford: Fairleigh Dickinson University Press, 1988). Also see Nell Irvin Painter, *The Narrative of Hosea Hudson: His Life as a Negro Communist in the South* (Cambridge: Harvard University Press, 1979).
66. A different revisionist approach was that of Mark Naison, whose pioneering 1983 *Communists in Harlem* never lost sight of the political dimension of the communists' politics and did not shy away from confronting and interrogating the consequences of the party's changing line. More recently, Vernon L. Pedersen has argued that the CP "was not the first or only organization to speak out against racism, and its record is not as unblemished" as revisionists claim. Vernon L. Pedersen, *The Communist Party in Maryland, 1919–57* (Urbana, IL: University of Illinois Press, 2001), 5. Two recent, important contributions that seriously explore the contours of black anticommunism are William A. J. Cobb, "Antidote to Revolution: African American Anticommunism and the Struggle for Civil Rights, 1931–1954," Ph.D. dissertation, Rutgers University, 2003 and Daniel W. Aldridge III, "A Militant Liberalism: Anti-Communism and the

African American Intelligentsia, 1939–1955" (paper delivered at the American Historical Association meeting, January 2004).

67. Joshua B. Freeman, Review of Robert W. Cherny et al., eds, "American Labor and the Cold War: Grassroots Politics and Postwar Political Culture," in *Labor: Studies in Working-Class History of the Americas* 2 (3) (Fall, 2005): 141.

68. Robert Zieger, *The CIO 1935–1955* (Chapel Hill, NC: University of North Carolina Press, 1995), 256.

69. Geoff Eley, "International Communism in the Heyday of Stalinism," *New Left Review* 157 (May/June 1986), quoted in Palmer, "Rethinking the Historiography of United States Communism," 151. Also see Eric Arnesen, "Race, Party, and Packinghouse Exceptionalism," *Labor History* 40 (2) (1999): 209; Arnesen, "Class Matters, Race Matters," *Radical History Review* no. 60 (Fall, 1994): 230–35.

70. Davis quoted in Wittner, "The National Negro Congress," 899; Richard Wright, "Not My People's War," *New Masses* 39 (June 17, 1941): 3; Ishmael P. Flory, Letter to the Editor: "What the People Say: Fight for Negro Rights," *Chicago Defender* (June 31, 1941).

71. "Why This Is Our War: An Editorial," *New Masses* (July 8, 1941): 3, cited in Garfinkel, 45.

72. Doxey A. Wilkerson, "The Negro in the War," *New Masses* 49 (December 14, 1943): 18. Also see Doxey A. Wilkerson, "Freedom—Through Victory in War and Peace" in Rayford W. Logan, ed., *What the Negro Wants* (Chapel Hill, NC: University of North Carolina Press, 1944), 197.

73. Hughes quoted in Arnold Rampersand, *The Life of Langston Hughes*, Vol. II: *I Dream A World* (New York: Oxford University Press, 1988), 24.

74. Robert Rodgers Korstad, *Civil Rights Unionism: Tobacco Workers and the Struggle for Democracy in the Mid-Twentieth-Century South* (Chapel Hill, NC: University of North Carolina Press, 2003), 147; Biondi, *To Stand and Fight*, 6; Honey, *Southern Labor and Black Civil Rights*, 143, 6.

75. Wallace Lee, "Have Communists Quit Fighting for Negro Rights?" *Negro Digest* (December 1944): 56.

76. William Patterson, "No," *Negro Digest* (December 1944): 57–60; Benjamin A. Davis, "No," *Negro Digest* (December 1944): 64–66; James W. Ford, "No," *Negro Digest* (December 1944): 68–70.

77. George Schuyler, "Yes," *Negro Digest* (December 1944): 60–64; Horace R. Cayton, "Yes," *Negro Digest* (December 1944): 66–68.

78. Quotes from Harvey Klehr and John Earl Haynes, *The American Communist Movement: Storming Heaven Itself* (New York: Twayne Publishers, 1992), 103. On the party's shift, see Isserman, *Which Side Were You On?*; James Barrett, *William Z. Foster and the Tragedy of American Radicalism* (Urbana, IL: University of Illinois Press, 1999), 222–25.

79. James W. Ford, "Revisionist Policies Weakened Struggles for Negro Rights," *Daily Worker* (June 25, 1945); George Lohr, "Negro Struggle Weakened by

Revisionism," *Daily Worker* (July 17, 1945); H. V. Saunders, "Struggle for Negro Liberation," *Daily Worker* (July 23, 1945), all cited in Record, *The Negro and the Communist Party*, 229; Thelma Dale, "Reconversion and the Negro People," *Communist* XXIV (10) (October 1945): 896–97, 901; "Speech by Doxey A. Wilkerson," *Political Affairs* XXIV (7) (July 1945): 619–21; Irving Howe and Lewis Coser, *The American Communist Party: A Critical History* (1957; rpt. New York: Frederick A. Praeger, 1962), 414, 416.

80. Isserman, *Which Side Were You On?*, 141–43,169.
81. Alex Lichtenstein, "Exclusion, Fair Employment, or Interracial Unionism: Race Relations in Florida's Shipyards During World War II," in Glenn T. Eskew, *Labor in the Modern South* (Athens, GA: University of Georgia Press, 2001), 135–57. Rejecting the common "morality tale" versions that pit forward-looking party members against more racist CIO leaders—or vice versa—in the postwar era, Lichtenstein finds a "far grayer picture," with "few angels on either side." Alex Lichtenstein, " 'Scientific Unionism' and the 'Negro Question': Communists and the Transport Workers Union in Miami, 1944–1949," in Robert H. Zieger, ed., *Southern Labor in Transition, 1940–1995* (Knoxville, TN: University of Tennessee Press), 58–85, especially 59–60.
82. Honey, *Southern Labor and Black Civil Rights*, 199–201.
83. Halpern, *Down on the Killing Floor*, 182, 214–15.
84. Drake and. Cayton, *Black Metropolis* 2: 740.
85. "Communists: A Menace to Black America," *Black Worker* (November 1945): 5.
86. Doxey Wilkerson, "The Negro in the War," *New Masses* 49 (December 14, 1943): 18; "Randolph Marches Against War Effort," *California Eagle* (July 15, 1943).
87. A. Philip Randolph, "Editorial: The Communists and the Negro," *Black Worker* (July 1942): 4.
88. "The Danger of Communists and Communism to Labor and the Negro," *Black Worker* (December 1948): 5.
89. "Communists: A Menace to Black America," *Black Worker* (November 1945): 4.
90. Korstad, *Civil Rights Unionism*, 147.
91. Honey, *Southern Labor and Black Civil Rights*, 127–28.
92. F. Crosswaith, "Communists and the Negro," *Interracial Review* XVI (11) (November 1943): 166–68; Kenneth Robert Janken, *White: The Biography of Walter White, Mr. NAACP* (New York: The New Press, 2003), 149–59, 301–23; Roy Wilkins with Tom Mathews, *Standing Fast: The Autobiography of Roy Wilkins* (New York: Penguin Books, 1982), 158–61, 190, 205–06, 210–11; "Townsend Tells Why He Thinks Communists are Dangerous to Us," *Chicago Defender* (March 15, 1938); Herbert Hill, "The Communist Party—Enemy of Negro Equality," *Crisis* 58 (6) (June–July 1951): 365–71, 421–24; George S. Schuyler, "The Negro and Communism," *Interracial Review* XIX (4) (April 1946): 54–55; C. W. Rice, "As I See It: Communists Pushing Plans to 'Take Over' the 'Black Belt' of East Texas; Labor Unions Used as 'Trojan Horse' in Plan," *Negro Labor News* (August 23, 1947); Yevette Richards, *Maida Springer: Pan-Africanist and International*

Labor Leader (Pittsburgh, PA: University of Pittsburgh Press, 2000), 37, 47–52; Denton L. Watson, *Lion in the Lobby: Clarence Mitchell, Jr.'s Struggle for the Passage of Civil Rights Laws* (New York: William Morrow and Company, 1990), 98; Helen Laville and Scott Lucas, "The American Way: Edith Sampson, the NAACP, and African American Identity in the Cold War," *Diplomatic History* 20 (4) (Fall, 1996): 565–90; Theophilus Lewis, "Plays and A Point of View: Illusions of Negro Pinks," *Interracial Review* XX (9) (September 1947): 142–43; Joseph V. Baker, "The Radicals Take the Low Road," *Negro World-Statesman* VII (4) (June 1947): 8–9.

93. Palmer, "Rethinking the Historiography of United States Communism," 151, 147, 143.
94. Manfred Berg, *"The Ticket to Freedom": The NAACP and the Struggle for Black Political Integration* (Gainesville, FL: University Press of Florida, 2005), 137; Berg, "Black Civil Rights and Liberal Anticommunism: The NAACP in the Early Cold War," *Journal of American History* 94 (1) (June 2007): 75–96.
95. Adam Fairclough, *Better Day Coming: Blacks and Equality, 1890–2000* (New York: Penguin Books, 2001), 215–16; Berg, *"The Ticket to Freedom,"* 139.
96. Lichtenstein, "'Scientific Unionism' and the 'Negro Question,'" 59–60.

CHAPTER SIX

The Contextualization of a Moment in CIO History: The Mine-Mill Battle in the Connecticut Brass Valley during World War II*

Steve Rosswurm

By 1942, the conflict between the two opposing factions within the Waterbury International Union of Mine, Mill & Smelter Workers (Mine-Mill) locals had been going on for more than a year. Little news of it, though, had reached the public and few outside each group's leadership and their most active followers had much of an idea of what was happening. That began to change in September, 1942, however, as the anticommunist group sought to have the Mine-Mill convention pass a constitutional amendment barring members of the Communist Party of the United States (CPUSA) from holding union office. Dennis McGrath, the Catholic president of Scovill #569, convinced his local to instruct its delegates to support this anticommunist resolution and another one stripping the Mine-Mill president of his control over organizing. When #569's convention delegates did not vote for either, its membership refused to accept their report. The local's secretary-treasurer told a newspaper that this disapproval showed that the membership did not "want the Communist Party to get control of labor units here." The Mine-Mill organizing staff responded with charges of red-baiting and disrupting the war effort.[1] Several days of wrangling in the newspapers ensued.

Things changed dramatically when McGrath telephoned Father Joseph H. Donnelly, the young assistant pastor of St. Thomas in Waterbury, asking for his help. Donnelly's bishop, with whom he consulted, "agreed that I should help them." The resulting statement appeared in the *Waterbury Democrat* on October 1.[2] Its publication initiated a public battle between anticommunists, opposed to Mine-Mill President Reid Robinson, and those led by communists, Robinson supporters, that went on until mid-January, 1943. It was then that the anti-Robinson group forced Philip Murray, CIO president, to facilitate the changes in Mine-Mill personnel that his left-wing opponents thereafter referred to as the "Pittsburgh Purge."

In several ways, the characteristics of this battle between CIO communists and anticommunists defy the familiar patterns charted in the existing historical literature.

First, since this confrontation occurred during the World War II alliance of the US and USSR, the federal government did not directly or indirectly support the anticommunists, as it did so effectively, in so many ways, in the postwar period.[3] Patriotic rhetoric, then, was on the side of the communists, not their opponents. Second, there is no evidence that any employer in Waterbury intervened in this conflict. This was a battle within the working class and its allies. Third, perhaps because they do not fit easily into existing narrative frameworks, historians have paid little attention to these events.[4]

The main conclusions of this chapter—as well as the assumptions that undergird its research and conclusions—find no easy resting place in the reigning historiography. The primary field that it speaks to—labor history—is one that seldom takes seriously the religious values of working people. This bracketing of working-class religiosity is a common denominator of historians who have little else in common.[5] The study of communism and anticommunism—one of the subordinate fields in which this story intervenes—almost always begins with the assumption that there can be no legitimate motivation for any anticommunism, let alone the working-class variety. It more often than not makes heroes of the left and villains of their opponents.[6] The story of the conflict within the Mine-Mill union in Waterbury challenges this dichotomous paradigm.

This chapter argues that Waterbury workers were anticommunist, at least in part, because of their Catholicism. This account of the conflict in Waterbury, then, not only takes seriously these workers' values, but also puts aside the Manichean focus found in such earlier studies in its exploration of the complicated nature of working-class identities that contributed to their political stand. The Waterbury working class was, as far as it can be discovered, limited and parochial in their world-view and willing to remain passive onlookers at much of what went on around them.

Father Donnelly, however, was far from a passive bystander. Yet there has been relatively little written on the Catholic labor priests, like him, who were integral to the organization and institutionalization of the CIO. Historians of U.S. Catholicism have been no more interested in working-class issues than labor historians have been in religion generally and Catholicism particularly.[7] Donnelly, though, is the key to the story presented here for several reasons. The priest never controlled the action in Waterbury, but most of what took place there makes no sense without understanding what he did and what he thought he was doing. His personal correspondence, moreover, provides an almost day-to-day insider's account. As with the Waterbury working class, though, he is not the hero of the story. As the following demonstrates, he was duplicitous, directly intervened in internal union affairs, and apparently utilized the racism and sexism of working-class white males in his cause. Donnelly, finally, may well have intensified their quiescence.

The study of U.S. communism, as distinct from the literature on communism and anticommunism, is yet another historiographical field within which this chapter rests uneasily. If one includes in this camp historians like Bryan Palmer and Geoff Eley, it is traditionalist in its assumption that communists (both members and fellow-travelers of the CPUSA) were not just cutting-edge liberals: They operated within a Marxist-Leninist organizational framework and milieu that stipulated—if not demanded—a commitment both to secularism and the Soviet Union.[8] Because the events in Waterbury occurred during the formal friendship of the United States and the USSR, the communists readily avoided some the dilemmas presented by their allegiances, but others, as we will see, could not be escaped. Yet communists are not the antiheroes of this piece. Their accomplishments in Waterbury, let alone their monumental work in building many of the CIO's most important unions, cannot—and should not—be underestimated.

The dispassionate analysis this chapter offers produces a decidedly complex reconstruction of what went on in the Brass Valley during these crucial months: More voices are heard and more motives discovered as the diversity of working-class beliefs and politics are illuminated. That illumination reveals the inability of communists to understand the way workers really were: a misunderstanding that was one of the main reasons their organizing agenda in Waterbury and elsewhere floundered.

This chapter has two sections. The first narrates the events in Waterbury from October, 1942 through April, 1943. The second focuses on the analysis of what happened. In the conclusion, I return to the main themes and arguments.

I

Waterbury was a factory city within a heavily industrialized state. With a population of almost 100,000 in 1940, it was Connecticut's fourth largest city, ranking second, behind Bridgeport, in manufacturing. The end point of a long circuit of capitalist production—and its concomitant exploitation of humans and nature—that included Arizona, Montana, Chile, the Tri-State Region, Pennsylvania, and New Jersey, Waterbury was the largest brass manufacturer in the country.[9] As such, it anchored the industrial region that ran along the Naugatuck River from Torrington on the north to Ansonia on the south. About 50,000 male and female brass workers lived in what became known as the "Brass Valley."[10] In addition to industrial products, they made buttons, hook and eyes, pins, clocks, buckles, and dozens of other items: Waterbury, people said, "had something on everyone."[11] Most of the machinery for making these things was fabricated locally, so significant foundries and machine companies grew up in the area.[12]

It also was an immigrant and Catholic city. About one-third of the population in 1920 was foreign-born: Italians ranked first, followed, in order, by Irish, Lithuanians, and Russians. African-Americans had been living in Waterbury since the seventeenth-century; more recent immigrants arrived from the South. More than 70 percent of Waterbury's population was Catholic. In 1942, at least seven, possibly eight parishes were territorial; the remaining national: three Italian and one each of Lithuanian, Polish, and German.[13]

CIO unionists faced a daunting task when they began their organizing drive in 1936, the year the first Mine-Mine local in Waterbury, #251, was chartered. First, the three major brass manufacturers, American Brass, Chase, and Scovill employed thousands, but many of their employees labored in relatively small and fragmented workplaces. Second, competing hierarchies and overlapping identities of race, sex, ethnicity, and skill existed within and outside of the plants. The combination of the fragmented workplaces and the competing identities created particularities that presented significant obstacles to the broad working-class unity necessary to create industrial unions. Third, brass manufacturers, especially the big ones, like Scovill, but also the smaller ones like Waterbury Buckle, practiced an extensive and intensive paternalism that, from all appearances, won the loyalty of many. Fourth, the CIO organizers, led primarily by those born and bred in Waterbury, lacked any sort of union experience. Finally, they were working far from the center of Mine-Mill's main constituency—Western lead, zinc, and copper miners—and its union headquarters in Denver, Colorado.

Local #251 never completely overcame these obstacles, but did win some significant victories. In 1937, there were sit-down strikes at Waterbury Battery and Benrus Watch; the following year, workers at Waterbury Buckle struck. Mine-Mill's most important triumph came at American Brass where, after strikes in 1936 and 1937, it won an election in 1938. It also soon came to represent the company's plants in Torrington and Ansonia. Mine-Mill, moreover, was a political presence in the Brass Valley.[14]

By early 1940, if not before, Mine-Mill's drive in Waterbury, though, had stalled. The union had been successful in organizing smaller integrated companies, like Waterbury Button and Manufacturers Foundry, but had relatively little success at the largest ones. There had been sporadic, unsuccessful organizing efforts at Chase, but #251 put most of its effort into vainly trying to spread its organization at Scovill beyond its Oakville Pin unit and Main Plant Power House, where it gained early negotiating rights. The contract at American Brass, moreover, was much of a chimera: #251 had fewer than 100 members out of 4,000 when it won its election and was having trouble moving outside its original areas of strength.[15]

Those critical of the leaders of #251 were convinced that they should have accomplished considerably more in Waterbury than they had. William Stanton, who would become a key pro-Robinson supporter at Chase, argued vigorously during an interview with the 1942 investigatory committee that this failure was due primarily to "a handful, a clique, running things, with nobody else having much to say."[16] John Driscoll, the undisputed leader of #251, responded that he, in its organizing efforts, was following the policy laid out by Mine-Mill's national leadership and that he had not had the financial help the task required.[17] No matter who was right, it is evident that Driscoll and other local leaders never developed a strategy to overcome the divisions within the Waterbury working class, to engage the energy of large numbers of the rank-and-file, and to disrupt the web of loyalty between the companies and their employees.

Two decisions by Reid Robinson, Mine-Mill's president, seem to have been perfectly calculated to cope with the situation in the Brass Valley in 1940. First, he committed considerable financial resources to completing Mine-Mill's organizing drive there. Second, he decided that talented and experienced organizers from outside Mine-Mill were necessary for success. He chose to do so despite the union's constitutional provision that organizers ought to be hired as much as possible from inside the union.

Mine-Mill kicked off the new drive with a rally in Waterbury on May 28, 1941 that was the union's first all-city gathering. About 800 workers heard Robinson's rousing speech that committed the International's "full resources" to organizing the Brass Valley and pointedly noted that his audience's "most powerful weapon would be the total organization of the valley, rather than action by single plants." Driscoll then introduced Don Harris, who, although on the CIO's payroll and assigned to Delaware, had been brought to Connecticut at Robinson's request to head up the drive.[18]

Harris brought a wealth of experience to his work in the Brass Valley. He had served on the Packinghouse Workers Organizing Committee (PWOC) in Iowa, Nebraska, and Chicago, rising to the position of Assistant National Director by 1938. In August, 1939, he, along with other CP members who worked for PWOC, lost his job when Van Bittner purged the Committee: Harris and "his circle" had tried to recruit packinghouse workers into the CP and paid the price with this firing. Harris also had let go several staff members who opposed "his efforts to control" his district and replaced them with "well-known Communists," something Bittner would not allow to stand.[19]

Harris' arrival in Waterbury originated the sharp departure of the next year-and-a-half of organizing from what had gone on previously in the Brass Valley town. First, he hired four new staff members. The three who came from the Valley had picked up a good deal of experience since 1936. One of them, Mike Barkauskas, a Lithuanian, reflected Harris' appreciation of ethnicity, for he was to serve as the "union interpreter."[20] The fourth organizer that Harris appointed, Lowell Hollenbeck, was a communist and while the anticommunists in the union had no complaints against Barkauskas and the other organizers from the Valley, they lodged plenty against Hollenbeck.[21] Second, Harris established "volunteer organizing staffs" for Scovill and Chase and set up a competition for those signing up the most new members. Third, he established a divisional competition for #251's already existing units; those who enrolled 85 percent of their potential membership would receive a banner. Fourth, plans were made to work through the various "church, fraternal, and language groups" in the city. Fifth, newspapers would be published for both the drives. Finally, the radio would be used extensively.[22]

Nothing better typified this drive than the gathering Mine-Mill held on July 27, 1941 to celebrate the fifth anniversary of #251's founding and to announce the winners of the organizing competition. A caravan of more than 300 cars, stretched "in an unbroken two-mile rolling chain" and "[d]ecorated with bunting and CIO banners and piloted by three sound trucks," drove around the brass plants, through the working-class neighborhoods of Waterbury, and wound up at Quassapaug Park, where 5,000 "brass workers and their families" waited.[23] There, the crowd heard several speakers, including Donnelly and an Episcopalian priest, and witnessed the awarding of the prizes to those who had signed up the most new members. Harris announced the immediate beginning of a new six-week competition.

Organizing at Chase and Scovill peaked at about the same time. From June through September, 1942, Mine-Mill won elections in the former's three main Waterbury divisions. In August, it did the same for the latter's main plant as well as a smaller one outside the city. Mine-Mill, meanwhile, had been organizing elsewhere in Connecticut. From July through September, 1942, it had won 11 elections throughout the state.[24] The Brass Valley had gone Mine-Mill and Waterbury was its anchor.

These successes, associated in everyone's mind with Harris, coincided with or precipitated the increasing disaffection of John Driscoll with Robinson and his administration. Driscoll, born in Waterbury, with two degrees from Wesleyan and a year of Harvard Law School, came to prominence in 1936 and 1937, during the earliest days of Mine-Mill organizing in the Brass Valley. At the time of Harris' arrival, he not only was the undisputed labor leader in Waterbury, but also a force in the Connecticut CIO. He had been a firm and publicly identified Robinson supporter until the 1941 convention, when a combination of personal and political developments drove a wedge between the two. Many of Waterbury's convention delegates came home, in the words of William Moriarity, a key anticommunist leader, determined to "clean house." The "battle lines were drawn."[25]

The friction between the Harris and Driscoll groups, which actually began during the convention as news of its proceedings filtered back to Waterbury, increased almost weekly from September, 1941 on. It did not impede the organizing efforts and seldom, if ever, came to the public's attention, but there does not seem to have been anything connected to union affairs that did not wind up being part of the factional battle. By late winter, 1942, the situation had become bad enough that Mine-Mill's executive board sent an investigatory committee to the Brass Valley, where it interviewed the membership for almost two months. Instead of resolving the problem, its work—also marred by deep disagreement—only served to signal how divided Mine-Mill was.[26]

All the evidence indicates that this factional struggle largely took place at the level of the leadership, not the rank-and-file. With that in mind, then, here is how the factional situation stood in September just before Donnelly entered the fray. The pro-Harris/pro-Robinson group first came from previously unrecognized or inactive members who rose through the organizing in 1941 and 1942 at Chase and Scovill; some of them nursed grievances against #251—often interwoven with more personal animosity toward Driscoll and his lieutenants—for expending too many resources on its core and not enough on organizing new locals. The second group of men came from the American Brass plants in Ansonia and Torrington and had a similar set of complaints as the first. The third consisted of those suitably impressed with the Harris group's organizing achievements. Waterbury's #251 provided the core of the pro-Driscoll and anti-Robinson forces, but they also picked up several key leaders, like John Mankowski, from Ansonia and other outlying towns, whose opposition to Harris outweighed all other concerns. To the degree that ethnicity played a role, Driscoll's supporters seem generally to have been Irish and Eastern European while Italians sided with Harris.[27]

The reason Dennis McGrath, Scovill's president, went to Donnelly in September, 1942 rather than to another priest in his search for help in fighting the communists was simple: He had no choice. Driscoll had failed to gain the public support of any religious figure in Waterbury, but Harris, who had learned how significant such support could be in his years in Chicago, already had set about rectifying the situation by reaching out to Donnelly.[28] At the huge CIO rally in Waterbury at the end of July, 1941, Donnelly joined an Episcopalian priest in praising Mine-Mill's organizing efforts. Urging his listeners to join the CIO, he told them that unions were "not only American," but also "Christian." "Recognize your dignity as men of God," he told them, "recognize your dignity as workingmen."[29] In May, 1942, as the drive at Scovill heated up, Donnelly used the occasion of a membership meeting to attack those who would not join the union. According to a newspaper account, he "likened" them to the "fellow who is willing to ride, but won't share the cost of the fare." Workers, according to Donnelly, had not just the right, but also the "duty" to the union.[30] Donnelly's public support of the union made him the obvious choice for McGrath to approach for help in fighting the communists within the Mine-Mill locals. If McGrath could get this vocal priest on his side in the fight, he would have a significant advantage.

Donnelly, the son of Irish immigrants, was born in Norwich, Connecticut. Ordained in 1934, his first post, at which he served until 1944, was St. Thomas in Waterbury. He then was chaplain of Highland Heights, New Haven's Catholic orphanage, until 1958. This position permitted him to devote most of his energies to the Diocesan Labor Institute and other labor activities. He became auxiliary bishop of Hartford in 1965 and was extremely active in the California farm workers' battles. Cesar Chavez did a reading at Donnelly's funeral mass.[31]

Donnelly's response to McGrath's request took the form of an October 1 newspaper attack on the local and national communists in Mine-Mill. In it, his commitment to the CIO rang out loud and clear. "If we have any hope of building a better world after the war," he asserted, "the organization of the workingman must be the first step. That is the official teaching of the Church." He had supported the organizing in the Brass Valley factories in the past and still did, but Mine-Mill was an "unhealthy" union. Using the Dies Committee's investigations as evidence, Donnelly argued that since it was "Communist-controlled and Communist-dominated," Mine-Mill was a "menace to our democratic institutions." He urged Robinson to withdraw Harris and his organizers if they could not put aside their "political theories." Donnelly acknowledged that he was endangering the CIO drive in Waterbury, but considered the communist threat serious enough to require action. He urged workers to join Mine-Mill and "fight to build it on principles that are truly American and truly Christian. Fight to build a clean and wholesome union organized for the benefit of the workers and not for the benefit of a few misleaders who put political considerations ahead of the welfare of the members."[32]

Donnelly seems to have been primed for this battle. First, he believed that the moral, social, and religious crises that he described in his sermons and talks in the late 1930s and early 1940s, which originated, he sometimes argued, in shifting gender relations, and other times, in international communism, demanded one's participation: "We must take sides. We must either gather with Christ or scatter—we must be either with him or against him—we must be either on the Cross as other Christs or under it as executioners."[33] Second, Donnelly began collecting information on how to set up and run a labor school six months or so before McGrath contacted him.[34]

The October 1 newspaper article was just the beginning. His correspondence with Father John M. Hayes, at the Social Action Department (SAD) of the National Catholic Welfare Conference, produced not only excellent advice from Hayes and others, like John Brophy, the CIO's Director of Industrial Union Councils and Industrial Unions, but also alerted James B. Carey, the CIO Secretary-Treasurer, and Murray to the Mine-Mill conflict.[35] With his bishop's permission and support, the priest also established the Diocesan Labor Institute, a set of state-wide labor schools that emulated those which labor priests and CIO activists had been running across the country since the mid-1930s.[36] Waterbury's branch opened at the end of October. Moreover, Donnelly used his political and ecclesiastical connections to gain secret information that could be used against Harris and his allies. None of this evidence appeared publicly, but the cleric undoubtedly used it to good effect in the numerous meetings he had with anticommunist leaders.[37]

The pro-Harris and Robinson supporters responded in several ways to Donnelly's charges of communism. They counterattacked by arguing that their opponents' accusations were undermining the unity essential to Mine-Mill's efforts to defend its membership. In so doing—here was a theme the Robinson administration stressed long before this and long after—the anticommunists were playing the boss' game of divide and conquer. The pro-Harris and Robinson supporters also charged the anticommunists with impeding the war effort with their divisiveness: These attacks were "blows at America's war efforts. They were sabotage. They aid Hitler and only Hitler."[38] They moreover criticized Donnelly's use of the Dies Committee's findings: Everyone, they argued, knew how much antilabor bias was embedded in them. Robinson personally continued these themes in a "surprise" visit to the Brass Valley: Government officials had praised his union's war efforts and Murray had acclaimed him by name.[39] Robinson also issued a charter to a new local that had just won recognition and joined his supporters for a widely publicized testimonial dinner.

The race between Robinson and Driscoll for the Mine-Mill presidency, which officially had begun with their nomination at the 1942 convention, raised the stakes in the Brass Valley as locals chose sides amid the continuing communist vs. anticommunist clash that periodically surfaced in the local newspapers. Several newly organized Mine-Mill locals endorsed Robinson, but the only large ones to do so were American Brass in Torrington and Chase in Waterbury.[40]

It was at Chase where the real battle between the communists and anticommunists played out. The pro-Harris forces had been easily defeated at Scovill, whose president's plea had pushed Donnelly into action. It was not so simple at Chase, which had been organized by Harris' people, led by Lowell Hollenbeck, who had experience with the PWOC in Kansas and Mine-Mill on the West Coast. Stanton, whose anti-Driscoll sentiments we already have seen, headed #565; he was a local man, whom the other side first snubbed and then dismissed as of little importance. Donnelly, therefore, focused his efforts there. If he won at Chase, Harris and Robinson were done in the Brass Valley.[41]

By mid-November—meetings with Donnelly had begun the previous month and petitions calling for the withdrawal of Harris and Hollenbeck and the resignation of #565 officers had been circulating in the plants for weeks—anticommunist rank-and-filers at Chase were "awake" and "rallying to the cause."[42] A group at the Chase Rolling Mills, Donnelly noted, was "piping hot."[43] The Waterbury priest would have preferred to have worked in conjunction with Murray, but several letters went unanswered, various lobbying efforts ignored, and Murray had "brushed off Driscoll quite lightly" at the CIO convention, so Donnelly and his people must have decided they were on their own.[44]

Things came to a head at Chase's monthly membership meeting on December 6, when the membership was to vote on its executive board's request for the resignation of #565's pro-Harris officers.[45] According to a local newspaper, everything went exactly as planned, but Donnelly's account tells us how wrong that report was.[46] After "three weeks of meeting and planning," 300 "boys" went "down there" and "threw all our planned parliamentary practice out of the window and just took over." Someone "hollered that it wasn't constitutional." To which "the boys" responded that "that was the way" Harris' people "taught them to run a meeting." Several days later, about 50 men, after removing the financial records, "closed and padlocked" the #565 office. A week or so later, two leaders took the union's letterhead and seal from Harris' office.[47]

In the jockeying for position that went on for the next month or so, the anti-Robinson group clearly won. They consolidated their hold over the Brass Valley—only one significant local, in Torrington, remained out of reach—established "Save the Union," whose goal was to unite antiadministration Mine-Mill locals across the country, and responded vigorously to one of Robinson's emissaries, and even more dramatically to Robinson himself when he visited the state.[48] Most important, they extracted a promise from Carey and Allan Haywood, CIO National Director of Organization, to remove Harris and Hollenbeck.

The final show-down came in Pittsburgh in January, but it was not Robinson and his opponents who tangled, but rather Save the Union and Murray.[49] Coming in well-prepared with a clear-cut set of demands, 16 Save the Union delegates not only refused to accept Murray's pleas to drop the whole issue, but walked out on him on the morning of January 20. The same thing happened again later in the afternoon despite Carey's entreaties and assertion that they were not listening to "reason." Moriarity, their elected spokesman, responded: "There is no reason, it's either right or wrong, it either is or isn't . . . We're not going to take it. If you don't have any better solutions than speeches; then we're going to go back."[50] The Save the Union delegates took the next train home.

Things changed over the next several days as Save the Union's confrontational tactics paid off. First, six Mine-Mill Executive Board Members "lined up against Robinson," calling Connecticut and telling the leaders of Save the Union that they would "talk business." Second, Carey also telephoned and "said that he was appointed by Murray to get the parties together." On January 25, Save the Union returned to Pittsburgh and a Waterbury newspaper headline read "Murray Seeking Truce in Feud."[51]

The Mine-Mill Executive Board's nearly week-long meeting in Pittsburgh resulted not in the "unconditional surrender" that Save the Union wanted, but it was "definitely a victory."[52] The Board asked the CIO to place an administratorship over District 6, the Mine-Mill administrative unit of which the Brass Valley was a part. All organizers in the District had to submit their resignations so it could choose which ones to fire. Several Party members, including Robinson's assistant and a close advisor, also were discharged. When Harris, who was on the CIO's payroll, refused to obey Haywood's order to leave Connecticut, he was fired. Every organizer to whom Save the Union objected was let go.

As those familiar with the nooks and crannies of CIO history know, this was not the end of the Brass Valley's conflict with the Mine-Mill leadership. Despite the CIO administrator's best efforts, over the space of five months or so, to establish the basis for a lasting peace in Connecticut and Mine-Mill, nothing ever approached normal again.[53] In 1947, most of the Brass Valley locals seceded from Mine-Mill. They eventually wound up in the UAW after short stints as an independent entity and as part of the Shipbuilders.

II

This, then, is a succinct re-telling of the battle between the communists and anticommunists that went on in Waterbury from October, 1942 through January, 1943. How we are to understand its primary actors is the issue to which we now turn our attention. One of the few things that Murray, acting through Carey, refused to do in the face of Waterbury's intransigence, was to overturn the 1942 election that continued Reid Robinson's presidency of Mine-Mill. The Connecticut anticommunists were convinced he was the source of their trouble, so we will begin with him.

Robinson served as secretary and head of the Butte local before being elected president of Mine-Mill in 1936 when he ran against a member of the Communist Party. The CP was soon backing him, though, since his popularity made such a move its only option: "We're going to support you," a CP functionary told him, "you son of a bitch, because we can't beat you."[54] From his side, opposed by many on the Executive Board, some of whom were quite ineffective and insular in their concerns, Robinson found himself increasingly relying upon the CP; at some point, he committed completely to the alliance.[55]

Within the next several years, Robinson appointed four CP members to his staff in Denver. Ben Riskin, who came first, served as his Director of Research. Then arrived Harold Rossman (Editor of Publications), Howard Goddard (Director of Organization), and Harold Sanderson (Assistant to the President). Each not only was extremely competent, but also brought with him a wealth of experience and a set of networks.[56] It was during meetings with these men that Robinson surely appointed Harris and his staff who came from outside the union; all of them were either in the CP or very close to it.[57]

Though the internal workings of the Robinson-CP alliance are impossible, at this point, to get at in any detail, one perspective is that they each made a deal with the devil. The CP had to know—or soon would—that Robinson, while dedicated, courageous, and fearless, also was erratic and impulsive. He periodically went on drinking binges and liked to gamble.[58] He, in turn, had to realize—or soon would—that he was more or less turning Mine-Mill over to outsiders. The denouement came in 1947 when the CP forced him to resign after continuing anger and resentment about his efforts to borrow money from a company executive—which surfaced shortly after that attempt in August, 1945—made his position increasingly untenable. (Robinson had to ask for the loan, according to the FBI, because he had gambled away an advance from the CIO for an official trip to Europe.[59]) Maurice Travis, another CP member, replaced him as president.

It is impossible to say exactly how the political affiliation of Harris and his staff affected the day-to-day organizing in the Brass Valley, but one bit of evidence suggests the symbiotic and self-serving relationship between the CP and its Mine-Mill members. In late August, 1942, Harris met with Isadore Wofsy, a CPUSA functionary who would become one of its "financial chiefs" by 1954, to arrange for publicity in *News of Connecticut* pertaining to the drive at Scovill: The news story not only would provide publicity for the Robinson administration and the Harris group, but it also would feature a picture of Al Skinner, the communist organizer who had come to Mine-Mill from the Die Casters.[60]

How should we analyze Donnelly's actions? The priest's public interventions helped establish the context in which Harris and his organizers were isolated and unable to capitalize on their tremendous organizing achievements. Donnelly, though, went considerably further than this. His caucus meetings with Chase and Scovill workers clearly played a significant role in their ultimate victory. Moreover, he may have done ghostwriting for them.[61] Finally, the Waterbury cleric used his Catholic connections to gain access to Murray and Carey, acquire intelligence reports on his opponents, and hook into a national anticommunist network that offered advice and help.[62]

In so doing, Donnelly violated a guiding principle of Catholic CIO activists: No outside intervention in the internal affairs of a union. This policy originated from several sources: First, there was an acute awareness that Catholic activity *qua* Catholic activity might well precipitate, even among potential allies, an anti-Catholic backlash. Second, one of Catholic laborites' best objections to left involvement with the trade unions was that it involved discussion of union affairs with outsiders: To do that very thing was to undermine the critique. The Detroit Association of Catholic Trade Unionists (ACTU), developing intellectually and politically in the pressure cooker of the UAW battles of the late 1930s, best articulated and implemented this policy.[63]

Donnelly contravened yet another principle of Catholic laborism: The best way to deal with communism in the CIO was not through mere denunciation—the "negative" way—but by the creation of leaders, whether Catholic or not, capable of providing the guidance and vision necessary to implement social Catholicism—the "positive" way. To focus entirely upon excoriation might well get rid of communists, but would leave the rank-and-file in the hands of those unqualified to lead. The SAD's Monsignor John A. Ryan and Father Raymond McGowan had been the primary architects of the positive policy.

Hayes, well aware of these rules, tried to steer Donnelly away from focusing his attacks on communists as communists. First, he specifically urged him to avoid using the Dies Committee because "he has been wrong so often that he is rather easily discredited."[64] Paul Weber, Newspaper Guild officer and Detroit ACTU leader, put it more strongly. Using Dies, he wrote Donnelly, "prejudiced" his case. Because of his "falsely blackening the characters of many legitimate people," Dies had "destroyed any confidence which anticommunists in the CIO ever had in him." We "have a standing rule," Weber concluded, "never to use Dies Committee evidence in any way for that reason."[65] (When Robinson finally replied directly to Donnelly's charges, he responded exactly as Weber suggested he would: "I trust that union people know what the Dies Committee is."[66]) Second, using conversations with Brophy as a point of reference, Hayes strongly encouraged the Waterbury priest to criticize Harris, with whom Hayes was familiar because of his years in Chicago, for the ways in which the wartime alliance between the United States and the USSR impinged upon his responsibilities as a trade unionist.

Donnelly never publicly used the Dies Committee as a source after the October 1 statement, but beyond that, he seems to have ignored Hayes' advice. It is possible that Hayes may have moderated Donnelly's anticommunism, but there is no direct evidence of it. Donnelly stressed throughout the battle that he was not attacking unionism *per se* nor was he urging Mine-Mill members to desert their locals or the CIO, but bread-and-butter trade-union issues—despite the availability of several significant ones[67]—do not seem to have ever been a significant part of his attack on Harris and his organizers. It is no wonder, then, that Donnelly seems to have wanted to forget this phase of his long history as a social activist, focusing instead on the

Diocesan Labor Institute, which concentrated on training "sound" labor leaders, and on his support of the Farm Workers.[68]

Hayes had two different, but related, reactions to Donnelly's way of fighting the CP. On the one hand, he apparently modified—or at least, couched in more sophisticated ways—SAD thinking about anticommunism. Hayes seems to have learned the fruitfulness and the necessity of combining anticommunism with what he considered sound unionism.[69] On the other, he expressed public and private ambivalence about the violence used to gain control of #565.[70] As to the revolt and the way it was conducted, his unease led him to characterize it in a way with which few in Waterbury would have agreed. In a SAD publication whose readership was limited to clerics, Hayes noted that Donnelly had "helped instigate" the anticommunist movement, but "[f]ortunately, the revolt is built on additional charges—mismanagement of union affairs. This is the only sound tactic."[71]

The results, though, in the end were what most concerned Hayes. Father John Cronin S.S. had been waging a similar battle in the Baltimore shipyards. In mid-December, after hearing about the take-over of #565, Hayes wrote Donnelly, giving him news about Cronin's activity: "This sounds very conservative in comparison with the Waterbury system. In any case, if we get results[,] we shall be satisfied."[72] This pragmatic emphasis on results—it was the ends, not the means that counted—would turn out to be the Church's primary attitude and *modus operandi* in the battle against communism.

The antipathy of the Waterbury working class for Harris and his organizers as communists is quite understandable since communism—in theory (Marxism) and in practice (the USSR)—violated their deepest religious and political commitments. This hostility, though, from all the available evidence, was laced with anti-Semitism, racism, and sexism. There is little doubt that their leadership saw itself as policing the borders of the Waterbury body politic in all of these complex and, in some instances, quite ugly ways.

Harris was the perfect target. That he was an outsider and brought others with him undergirded much of the distrust and hostility directed toward him and his staff.[73] The intensity of this localism had been visible months before Harris' arrival when Mine-Mill organizers Jack Flaherty and Tommy Ray, both hired from the National Maritime Union staff and both on the left, had to leave town because of so much animosity.[74] Shortly after his arrival in the Brass Valley, "a campaign of ridicule against" Harris "sprang up" in Ansonia because of his lack of work experience in the brass industry. It went, according to one local unionist, like this: "What does Harris know about organizing brass. He is a packinghouse worker. He may know how to organize porkchops, but not a damn thing about organizing brass." He was referred to as "Mr. Porkchop," not Harris.[75]

Harris' opponents "red baited" him with increasing ferocity as the months went on. Large doses of anti-Semitism accompanied it. Harris was a "Jew," the story went, and "Weissman, the attorney for the Company [Waterbury Clock] was a Jew, and that they got their heads together and sold us down the river."[76] A key anticommunist leader, Mike Barkauskas, not only "red baited but was Jew baiting as well" at Oakville Pin.[77] At membership meetings, Harris was not only "red-baited" and "Jew-baited," but also "called a 'nigger lover.' "[78]

Everything about Ann Brown, a Harris-appointed union organizer, seems to have challenged Waterbury workers' sense of themselves. That Harris hired her from the outside angered those who thought preference should be given to local candidates. That she was single led to gossip about her behavior. The International Ladies Garment Workers, her opponents discovered, had fired Brown, who worked, as Harris noted, "under the 'handicap' of being of Jewish origin."[79] Once the Scovill drive, for which Brown had been specifically hired, was over, she resigned her staff position and got a job at Benrus Watch. Local #251, which was the original Mine-Mill outpost in Waterbury and therefore the foundation of the anti-Robinson forces, refused her a union card, however, because there was "some motive outside of applying for membership in Local 251."[80]

Perhaps the best evidence about the way these anticommunists perceived these outsiders lies in the material Donnelly collected. Ben Rubin was identified as a "little Jew" and "Fitch" as "a colored boy with one of the longest police records in Waterbury." Harris "has a woman here he calls his wife—Shirley," while Hollenbeck "had a woman in town who was common property—Called her his wife." The latter attended the Soviet American Friendship Congress in New York "with the colored boy Fitch"; she also "boasted that she was a friend of Pretty Boy Floyd's wife." Finally, Donnelly's notes identified Henry Horwitz, Mine-Mill's publicity directory in the Brass Valley as a "clever Jew."[81] This information, amplified and elaborated upon, undoubtedly spread throughout Waterbury and from there to Ansonia and Torrington through the myriad gossip networks and rumor mills for which there is abundant evidence.[82]

The part that the "rollers" played in the defeat of the Robinson forces tells us more about the Waterbury working class. Plant managers seem to have been successful in replacing the crucibles of the casters—those who actually made brass out of copper and zinc—with electric furnaces. They apparently, though, had little success in de-skilling the rollers, who performed the next step in the process: turning the brass bar into shapes that could be further processed.[83] Because it was so highly skilled and took so long to learn, rollers were well paid and had a degree of control over their work. If Russell Sorbin's experience with American Brass was typical of Scovill and Chase's rolling departments, the Irish also predominated.[84]

It was the men at Chase Rolling Mills, where less than 500 worked, who responded to the gendered call to action that Donnelly made in mid-November: "The boldness of this group [communists] is appalling. And the indifference of the Waterbury workingmen is appalling. What are these workingmen going to do about it? Do they run blood or water in their veins?"[85] The "Chase men," the priest noted the same day his article appeared, were "piping hot." The "rollers from the mill" wanted to beat up Hollenbeck, take him to Donnelly, and "make him confess he is a communist."[86] The cleric did not specifically name the rollers as those who took over the #565 meeting in December, but there is little doubt that they were the ones who were—he repeated the same phrase—"piping hot."

There is considerable evidence that this period of intense conflict did little to activate, let alone politicize, the Waterbury working class. First, even during the long string of Mine-Mill victories in 1942, substantial numbers stayed at home or voted against the union in two significant cases. At Scovill, Mine-Mill won by a wide margin (4,892 to 1,325), but with the addition of those who did not vote (906), it faced the prospect of winning over more than 2,000.[87] At Chase's Waterbury Manufacturing plant, Mine-Mill won 1,139 to 441, but about 600 did not vote; about 1,000, then, still remained outside the union umbrella.[88] Second, the evidence, scant as it is, for attendance at meetings of #565, the huge Chase local, indicates that few bothered to participate. In early October, 1942, a resolution endorsing Robinson for Mine-Mill president passed 45 to 5. There were more at the climatic December 6 meeting, but the single recorded vote was 112 to 35.[89] Third, few bothered to vote in the Mine-Mill presidential election. Robinson defeated Driscoll 563 to 229 at Chase, but thousands were eligible to vote. At Scovill, Driscoll won 280 to 136, but again, thousands could have voted. Only in #251, the original Mine-Mill outpost in Waterbury and Driscoll's home base did voters turn out; he won here, 2,450 to 84.[90] A January 10, 1943 meeting of all the Connecticut Mine-Mill locals with Robinson attracted just 359; among them were 115 from Chase, 90 from #251, and 50 from Scovill.[91]

It is hard to avoid characterizing Waterbury workers as quiescent in everything except their unshakeable and stolid hostility to outsiders and communists. As Moriarity, as solid a trade unionist as there was in the Brass Valley, remembered about this period: "It wasn't hard to get people to vote for the union, but it was hard to get them to become members, be active, and pay dues on a regular basis."[92] Helen Johnson, who worked at Scovill, remembered it much the same way: "We had them in and out. They wanted something, they needed a grievance, they'd join. Then they'd drop out again."[93] The union shop was not won at the "major brass plants" until the 1950s.[94]

These sorts of shortcomings extended well beyond Waterbury to include Mine-Mill's executive board, comprised of district directors elected by the membership. It had an anti-Robinson majority until the mid-1940s, but seldom united around any particular issue or perspective. In the one case that it did—the firing of Harold Rossman as newspaper editor—anti-Semitism muddied the waters; another CP member replaced him.[95] In the 1942 election, Robinson faced not just Driscoll, but also another candidate, James Byrnes, a Butte "old-timer;" they, of course, split the opposition ballots.[96] A close reading of Mine-Mill's internal political life during this period strongly supports Bert Cochran's assertion that this anti-Robinson majority on the Mine-Mill executive board was a "disunited, jealous-ridden, opportunist group."[97]

III

Several conclusions of this story will not surprise many. First, CP cadre were excellent organizers, not always the best, but very, very good. They had a wider per-spective on the world than most working-class people, perceived the need for unity in practical and realizable ways, and saw connections and relationships that others missed. By 1941, moreover, many had much experience doing exactly the kind of organizing that needed to be done in Waterbury. Second, the Catholic Church was firmly committed to the CIO and anticommunism. Both had been abundantly clear since the mid-1930s when the Church made its turn to its Catholic working-class constituents. When forced to choose between the two, however, Donnelly was will-ing to risk the CIO's fragile achievements. In so doing, moreover, the labor priest helped drive out those very organizers who might have been able to produce more organizing gains in Waterbury. That he ignored trade-union issues in this battle, moreover, impeded the development of a group of local working-class activists who could have learned a good deal from such a conflict. Third, most of the Waterbury working class, helped (if not led) by the Church, decisively rejected these CP organiz-ers and their politics. It was not just that they were outsiders—this was bad enough—but the CP cadre violated virtually—in reality or fantasy—every value held dear by Waterbury's laboring people. At one level of analysis, the organizers represented a force of modernity that the Brass Valley defeated. This conflict, moreover, was inter-woven with racism, sexism, and anti-Semitism.

Other conclusions, though, will stand out. First, the relative passivity of Waterbury's working-class rank-and-file is at least a bit surprising, especially to those who see this whole period as one of broad and sustained popular upheaval. How common this was throughout the nation is still a question, but an argument has been made that it was far more prevalent than most now think.[98] Second, Waterbury's anticommunist working-class leadership was particularly resolute and determined. Less impressive than the seizure of the December 6 meeting—this was, after all, the kind of physicality upon which these men thrived—was the creation of "Save the Union" and forcing Carey and Murray to meet with them in Pittsburgh. Led by Moriarity, they stood down both men and forced Murray, the CIO President, to lend himself to a solution they found satisfying. This was a remarkable achievement by men, who by all accounts, had never before left Connecticut.

Third, Murray's caution throughout all of this is noteworthy. The pressure from the communists and the Catholics had been there from the beginning and increased over time, but Murray continually tried to avoid doing what either side wanted. Once Save the Union walked out on him, though, he did not have much choice: He apparently acted in such a way so as the Mine-Mill executive board, which could never agree on anything, voted in favor of doing virtually almost everything that Waterbury wanted, except that is, to remove Robinson: That would have been going too far.[99]

Finally, perhaps what is most surprising is how mistaken communists were in their understanding of what was happening and what had happened in Waterbury. Like most historians after them, they never realized who had defeated them in Waterbury.[100] It was not the Catholic Church or the ACTU or Murray or Driscoll. It was the working class and its rock-solid commitment to a set of values that the communists and their allies—past and present—could not understand and respect, but could only caricature or condemn. Some of these were spiritual, some political; many praise-worthy, others mean, prejudiced, and reactionary. All were deeply held.

If this story and analysis of what happened in Waterbury during these few months is on the mark, it suggests the need to go beyond, as I indicated in the introduction, much of the existing historiography on many different topics, particularly the relationship between Catholicism and the CIO and the CPUSA and the CIO. It especially suggests the necessity of studying the U.S. working class as it was, not as we sometimes think it ought to have been.

Notes

* I am grateful to Dawn Abt-Perkins, Wendy J. Ohman, and the editors of this volume for helpful readings of earlier drafts.
1. "Delegates Report Refused by Local," *Waterbury Democrat* (hereafter WD) (September 28, 1942): 16; "Scovill Brass Workers Union Opens Attack," *WD* (September 28, 1942): 1, 4.
2. Donnelly to Hayes, October 3, 1942; "Rev. Joseph F. Donnelly Defends Scovill Union Officers, Scores Leftists," *WD* (October 1, 1942): 4; Donnelly to Hayes, October 3, 1942, SAD, box 8, folder 24.
3. Ellen Schrecker, "McCarthyism and the Labor Movement: The Role of the State," in Rosswurm, ed., *The CIO's Left-Led Unions* (New Brunswick, NJ: Rutgers University, 1992), 139–57.
4. For the only sustained discussion, see Vernon H. Jensen, *Nonferrous Metals Industrial Unionism (1932–1954): A Story of Leadership Controversy* (Ithaca, NY: Cornell University, 1954), 89–107; Jeremy Brecher, Jerry Lombardi, and Jan Stackhouse, comps and eds, *Brass Valley: The Story of Working People's Lives and Struggles in an American Industrial Region* (Philadelphia, PA: Temple University, 1982), 172–76. Also see Harvey Levenstein, *Communism, Anti-Communism, and the CIO* (Westport, CT: Greenwood, 1981), 66, 170, 272. Pace Levenstein, Monsignor Charles Owen Rice was not involved in the battle.
5. For example, David Montgomery, *The Fall of the House of Labor: The Workplace, the State, and American Labor Activism, 1865–1925* (New York: Cambridge University, 1989) and Robert Zieger, *The CIO, 1935–1955* (Chapel Hill, NC: University of North Carolina, 1995).
6. For example, Daniel Sidorick, *Condensed Capitalism: Campbell Soup and the Pursuit of Cheap Production in the Twentieth Century* (Ithaca, NY: Cornell University, 2009) and Elleen Baker, *On Strike and On Film: Mexican-American*

Families and Blacklisted Filmmakers in Cold War America (Chapel Hill, NC: University of North Carolina, 2007). On these issues more generally, see: Leslie Woodcock Tentler, "On the Margins: The State of American Catholic History," *American Quarterly* 45 (1) (March 1993): 104–27; Tentler, "Present at the Creation: Working-Class Catholics in the United States," in Rick Halpern and Jonathan Morris, eds, *American Exceptionalism? US Working-Class Formation in an International Context* (London: St. Martin's, 1997), 134–57; Joseph A. McCartin, "Estranged Allies on the Margin: On the Ambivalent Response of Labor Historians to Catholic History," *U.S. Catholic Historian* 21 (2) (Spring, 2003): 114–20; James P. McCartin and Joseph A. McCartin, "Working-Class Catholicism: A Call for New Investigations, Dialogue, and Reappraisal," *Labor* 4 (1) (Spring, 2007): 99–110; Richard Gid Powers, *Not Without Honor: The History of American Anticommunism* (New York: Free Press, 1996); Eric Arnesen, "No 'Graver Danger': Black Anticommunism, the Communist Party, and the Race Question," *Labor* 3 (4) (Winter, 2006): 13–52; Kenyon Zimmer, "Premature Anti-Communists?: American Anarchism, the Russian Revolution, and Left-Wing Libertarian Anti-Communism, 1917–1939," *Labor* 6 (2) (Summer, 2009): 45–46.

7. "Robert Zieger's History of the CIO: A Symposium," *Labor History* 37 (1996): 157–88; Michael Denning, *Cultural Front: The Labor of American Culture in the Twentieth-Century* (London: Verso, 1996); James Hennesey, *American Catholics: A History of the Roman Catholic Community in the United States* (New York: Oxford University, 1981); James T. Fisher, *Communion of Immigrants: A History of Catholics in America* (New York: Oxford University, 2000).

8. Randi Storch, *Red Chicago: American Communism at its Grassroots, 1928–1935* (Urbana, IL: University of Illinois, 2007), 2–4; Arnesen, "No 'Graver Danger,'" 33–38, 47–52; Palmer, "Rethinking the Historiography of United States Communism," *American Communist History* 2 (2) (December 2003): 143, 147, 151; Geoff Eley, "International Communism in the Hey-Day of Stalin," *New Left Review* no. 157 (January–February, 1986): 92.

9. See the very useful mapping of this circuit in *CIO News* (Mine-Mill edition) (February 19, 1940): 4–5 (hereafter *CION (M-M)*. For Anaconda's particular circuit, see Isaac F. Marcosson, *Anaconda* (New York: Dodd, Meade, 1957).

10. "Prairie Fire of Organizations Sweeps Brass Valley As Drive Hits Strike," *CION (M-M)* (August 11, 1942): 2.

11. Mary Procter and Bill Matuszeski, *Gritty Cities* (Philadelphia, PA: Temple University, 1978), 230.

12. This paragraph, as well as the next, draws from *Brass Valley* and Cecelia Bucki, *Metal, Minds, and Machines: Waterbury at Work* (Waterbury, CT: The Society, 1980).

13. Parish Reports, 1942, Hartford Archdiocesan Archives (HAA); *Religious Bodies: 1926. Volume I, Summary and Detailed Tables* (Washington, D.C.: Government Printing Office, 1930), 565.

14. *Brass Valley*, 162, 160, 159, 162, 164; Driscoll, "Waukegan NLRB Win Cracks Brass Center," *People's Press* (Mine-Mill) (May 28, 1938): 1; "Three Brass Locals," *CION(M-M)* (December 18, 1939): 1.

15. *Brass Valley*, 162.

16. "Statements by Bill Stanton, George Miller and Henry Kleist, Chase Brass and Copper Workers Union #565 (Supplement to the records because of omissions in earlier transcript)," Western Federation of Miners/International Union of Mine, Mill, and Smelter Workers (hereafter WFM/M-M), box 300, folder Connecticut 1942, University of Colorado, Boulder. Many of those in Driscoll's leadership group came out of Oakville Pin.

17. "Interview with John Driscoll," ibid. Also see "Interview with Frank Delmonaco and Edward Lynch," March 27, 1942, ibid.

18. "Brass Workers' Mass Mtg Cheers Plan for Valley Drive," *CION(M-M)* (June 2, 1941): 8.

19. FBIHQ 100–38112, 122–370; New Haven Report, December 2, 1942, 100–108, 199-124; R. H. Simons, Special Agent in Charge, to J. Edgar Hoover, December 12, 1942, 100–108199-132; Simons to Hoover, January 12, 1943, 100–108199-[?]; New Haven Report, January 26, 1943, 100–108199-[?]; Shelton Stromquist, *Solidarity and Survival: An Oral History of Iowa Labor in the Twentieth Century* (Iowa City, IA: University of Iowa, 1993); Roger Horowitz, *"Negro and White, Unite and Fight": A Social History of Industrial Unionism in Meatpacking, 1930–1990* (Urbana, IL: University of Illinois, 1997), 127–28 (quotation). Compare this version of Harris' firing with Rick Halpern, *Down on the Killing Floor: Black and White Workers in Chicago's Packinghouses, 1904–1954* (Urbana, IL: University of Illinois, 1997), 192, 194. All FBI files were obtained by the author through the Freedom of Information and Privacy Act.

20. "Hard-Hitting Quartet to Spark Valley Drive," *CION(M-M)* (June 9, 1941).

21. FBIHQ 100–1803; New Haven Report, December 2, 1942; Simons to Hoover, December 14, 1942, 100–108199-[?]; New Haven Report, January 26, 1943.

22. "Volunteer Force Swings into Brass Valley Campaign," *CION(M-M)* (June 9, 1941): 1, 8.

23. "Waterbury Union Takes Over Town in Monster Anniversary Celebration," ibid. (August 4, 1941): 1, 12.

24. *CION (Michigan)* (October 2, 1942): 12.

25. "Interview with William Moriarity," 7, 9, HCLA. For Driscoll's side of the split, see "Report of John J. Driscoll, Delegate to 38th Convention, IUMM&SW," August 22, 1941, WFM/M-M, box 34, folder 17; "Interview with John J. Driscoll," WFM/M-M, box 300, folder Connecticut 1942; "Driscoll Oral History," May 14, 1970, HCLA.

26. Besides, WFM/M-M, box 300, folder Connecticut 1942, see Angelo Verdu, "To the Officers and Executive Board Members of the IUMM & SM," n.d. and Robinson to All Executive Board Members, April 24, 1942, WFM/M-M, box 29, folder 2.

27. This is based upon an immersion in numerous sources.
28. "Driscoll Oral History," 13; "Volunteer Force Swings Into Brass Valley Campaign," *CION(M-M)* (June 9, 1941): 1, 8.
29. "Waterbury Union Takes over Town in Monster Anniversary Celebration," *CION(M-M)* (August 4, 1941): 1, 12. Donnelly received permission from his bishop before speaking at the rally.
30. "Priest Lauds Scovill Local," *Union* (May 18, 1942): 7.
31. "Biographical Information on the Most Reverend Joseph F. Donnelly, D.D.," November, 1973, HAA; Patrick W. Gearty, "Diocesan Labor Institute, Diocese of Hartford," M.A. thesis, Catholic University of America, 1947.
32. "Revd. Joseph F. Donnelly Defends Scovill Union Officers, Scores Leftists," *Waterbury Democrat* (WD) (October 1, 1942): 4.
33. "And where in the future . . . ," Sermon Book (1937–40), Joseph Donnelly Papers (JDP), Box 8, HAA. This sermon book and another, dated 1935–59, are the best sources for Donnelly's understanding of what was going on in the world. Also see box 10, folder Social Action (1940–55).
34. William J. Smith to Donnelly, April 7, 1942, John P. Delaney to Donnelly, April 20, 1942, JDP, box 15, folder 1941–43, HAA.
35. The correspondence between Donnelly and Hayes can be found in: National Catholic Welfare Conference/United States Catholic Conference Collection, Social Action Department (SAD), box 8, folder 24, Catholic University of America Archives; JDP, box 15, folder 1941–43. These letters provide the basis for generalizations in the text unless otherwise noted.
36. Joseph M. McShane, "A Survey of the History of the Jesuit Labor Schools in New York: An American Social Gospel in Action," *Records of the American Catholic Historical Society* 102 (1991): 37–64; Rosswurm, "The Catholic Church and the Left-Led Unions: Labor Priests, Labor Schools, and the ACTU," in Rosswurm, ed., *The Left-Led Unions* (New Brunswick, NJ: Rutgers University, 1992), 119–37; Mathew Pehl, "Remaking of the Catholic Detroit Working Class," *Religion and American Culture* 19 (1) (2009): 37–67.
37. For at least some of the information that Donnelly gathered, see JDP, box 14, folder Communism. For its collection, see Donnelly to Hayes, October 16, 1942, November 14, 1942, SAD, box 8, folder 24; Anthony J. Scanlon to Donnelly, November 24, 1942, JDP, box 21, folder Personal Correspondence (laity).
38. "Chase Local Heads Attack Statements," *WD* (October 2, 1942): 1, 4.
39. "Unions Divided on Presidency," ibid. (October 10, 1942): 9.
40. Donnelly to Hayes, October 10, 1942; "Reid Robinson Carries Chase," *WD* (November 16, 1942): 7; "Torrington Board," *The Union* (January 25, 1943): 3.
41. "Statements by Bill Stanton, George Miller and Henry Kleist, Chase Brass and Copper Workers Union #565 (Supplement to the records because of omissions in earlier transcript)," "Interview with John J. Driscoll," "Statement by Lowell Hollenbeck," WFM/M-M, box 300, folder Connecticut 1942.

42. Donnelly to Bishop Maurice McAuliffe, November 15, 1942, JDP, box 15, folder 1941–43.

43. Donnelly to Father John M. Hayes, November 14, 1942.

44. For the letters to Murray, see Donnelly to Hayes, November 14, 1942; Donnelly to Murray, November 9, 1942. For the lobbying efforts, carried on through Hayes, see Donnelly's correspondence with him; for the dismissal of Driscoll, see Donnelly to Hayes, November 11, 1942. Murray's letter to Donnelly, December 3, 1942, JDP, box 15, folder 1941–43, confirmed the latter's sense that he and his group were on their own.

45. "CIO Membership Facing Revolt," WD (December 7, 1942): 7.

46. Donnelly to Hayes, December 9, 1942, SAD, box 8, folder 24. The official account, #1565 Minute Book, December 16, 1942, 45–47, Archives of Labor History and Urban Affairs (ALHUA), Walter P. Reuther Library, Wayne State University, does not mention any of the conflict discussed in Donnelly's letter.

47. "Drastic Action Taken by Chase CIO Members," WD (December 9, 1942): 2; "Union Leaders Under Arrest," WD (December 16, 1942): 1, 4.

48. "Save the Union," WFM/M-M, box 163, folder 5.

49. For the pre-Pittsburgh meetings and the demands, see "Resolution Establishing Rank-And-File Councils of IUMMSW," SAD, box 41, folder Priest Worker—Miscellaneous. Donnelly sent this document to Hayes in his letter of January 16, 1943. In this account of the Pittsburgh Purge, I am working from three sources: "Interview with William Moriarity," 12–15, HCLA; Donnelly to Hayes, January 31, 1943: "From Unidentified Man [Nathan Witt] to Roy Hudson," January 26, 1943, attached to E. E. Conroy, Special Agent in Charge, February 6, 1943, 100–108199-[?]. Jensen's discussion is quite thin: Nonferrous Metals Industry Unionism, 101–02.

50. "Interview with William Moriarity," 14, HCLA.

51. Donnelly to Hayes, January 31, 1943; WD (January 25, 1943): 3.

52. Donnelly to Hayes, January 31, 1943.

53. "Report of Robert J. Davidson, Regional Director, CIO, Cincinnati, Ohio as Administrator of District 6, International Union of Mine, Mill & Smelter Workers, CIO," WFM/M-M, box 300, folder Connecticut 1942.

54. Reid Robinson Interview, March 28, 1955, Theodore Draper Papers, box 15, folder 33, Manuscript, Archives, and Rare Book Library, Woodruff Library, Emory University; "Interview with Reid Robinson," December, 1969, 24–25, HCLA.

55. "Interview with Robinson," 22–26; Draper interview with Robinson.

56. See the following for their political affiliation: Riskin: Draper interview with Robinson; Cleveland Report, 11/23/42, FBI 100–11687-13; Ralph Rasmussen testimony, Hearings before the Subcommittee to Investigate the Administration of the Internal Security Act and Other Internal Security Laws of the Committee of the Judiciary. United States Senate. 82nd Congress. Second Session on Communist Domination of Union Officials in Vital Defense Industry—International Union

of Mine, Mill, and Smelter Workers. October 6, 7, 8, and 9, 1952 (Washington, D.C.: Government Printing Office, 1952), 143 (hereafter *Senate Hearings*). Rossman: Rasmussen, *Senate Hearings*, 147. Goddard: George Knott testimony, March 20, 1957, *Records of the Subversive Activities Control Board, 1950–1972* (Frederick, MD: University Publications of America, 1988), reel 54, 658 (hereafter only reel number and page). Sanderson: Draper interview with Robinson; Knott, reel 54, 658–59; Kenneth Eckert testimony, reel 54, 893, 896, 899, 920, 923, 925.

57. Henry Horwitz: Knott, reel 54, 656; New Haven Report, January 26, 1943; Jack Flaherty: Rasmussen, *Senate Hearings*, 144; JDP, box 14, folder Communism; New Haven Report, January 26, 1943; Ann Brown: JDP, box 14, folder Communism; Brown, "The Life of a Woman Labor Organizer by One of Them," *Union* (April 13, 1942): 5; New Haven Report, January 26, 1943. Several organizers from the Die Casters, who arrived late in the conflict, also were in the CP: Al Skinner, Eckert, *Senate Hearings*, 48–49; Knott, reel 54, 661; Eckert, reel 54, 899, 920, 921; Irving Dichter, Eckert, *Senate Hearings*, 48–49; Knott, reel 54, 661; Eckert, reel 54, 901, 937.

58. For Robinson's work with the CP, see: Draper interview with Robinson; Eckert testimony; Knott testimony; Cleveland Report, November 23, 1942, FBI 100–11687-13; Cleveland Report, January 18, 1944, FBI 100–7602-404; E. E. Conroy, SAC New York, to Director, February 14, 1944, FBI 100–7602-415; San Diego Report, September 16, 1952, FBI 100–12875-124; "From Unidentified Man [Nathan Witt] to Roy Hudson"; *Official Proceedings of the . . . Convention of the International Union of Mine, Mill and Smelter Workers, 1941*, 386 (hereafter *1941 Convention*); Kent Hudson, "Mine-Mill: The Voices from the Mountains," Ph.D. dissertation, Union Institute and University, 1979. Robinson told Draper that Sanderson knew "more about [the] inner workings of the union than other single individual," but his HCLA interview is very disappointing in this regard. For Robinson's drinking, gambling, and fist fights, see: *1941 Convention*, 370, 450; San Diego Report, September 16, 1952; "Interview with Sanderson," 38–39.

59. San Diego Report, September 16, 1952.

60. Simons to Director, FBI, October 30, 1942, 100–108199- [?]; David J. Garrow, *The FBI and Martin Luther King, Jr. From "Solo" to Memphis* (New York: W. W. Norton,]1981), 41. Labor's Non-Partisan League published this newspaper. The FBI, Simons to Director, November 10, 1942, 100–108199- [?], asserted that everyone in its employ was in the CP except for David Hedley, who also was at the meeting with Harris and Wofsy. Headley, according to the Bureau, could not join because he was a British citizen.

61. JDP, box 14, folder Communism.

62. The main source here is the correspondence between Hayes and Donnelly, but also see: Paul Weber to Donnelly, November 4, 1942, Detroit Association of Catholic Trade Unionists Collection (DeACTU), box 21, folder Mine-Mill 1942–1947, ALHUA; Scanlon to Donnelly, November 24, 1942; Cronin to

Donnelly, October 13, 1942, K. A. Slocum to Donnelly, May 31, 1943, Donnelly to McAuliffe, November 15, 1942, JDP, box 15, folder 1941–43.

63. Paul Weber, "Memorandum to ACTU-New York re Intro-Union Organization, n. d. DeACTU, box 2. folder New York, 1939–43. This policy, of course, underwent revision and amplification as the Detroit ACTU implemented its "conference" policy.

64. Hayes to Donnelly, October 13, 1942.

65. Weber to Donnelly, November 4, 1942, DeACTU, box 21, folder Mine-Mill, 1942–47.

66. "Robinson Repudiates Charge of Communism," WD (January 16, 1943): 7.

67. The most significant issue, as discussed in the investigatory committee's records, was a contract Harris negotiated at Lux in which he apparently gave away double time on Saturday and Sundays.

68. Donnelly skipped over the October 1 newspaper article and moved directly from the original visit from the Mine-Mill anticommunist to the founding of the Diocesan Labor Institute in an oral history done in 1970 and in a 1971 or 1972 untitled and undated document; "Interview with Joseph Donnelly," May 15, 1970, HCLA; JDP, box 10, folder Social Action, 1956–74. Also see *Brass Valley*, 173.

69. *Social Action Notes for Priests (SAN)* February, March, 1943.

70. Hayes to Donnelly, December 15, 1942, JDP, box 15, folder 1941–1943; *SAN*, November–December, 1942.

71. *SAN*, January, 1943.

72. Hayes to Donnelly, December 15, 1942. For Cronin's activity in Baltimore, see Joshua B. Freeman and Rosswurm, "The Education of an Anti-Communist: Father John F. Cronin and the Baltimore Labor Movement," *Labor History* 33 (2) (Spring, 1992): 217–47.

73. For hostility toward them as outsiders, see "Interview with Bronislaus Vaiciulis—Chairman of Oakville Pen Unit of Local 251," "Statement of Mario Vigezzi," "Interview with Don Harris," "Statement by Lowell Hollenbeck," "Waterbury—Local 251," WFM/M-M, box 300, folder Connecticut, 1942.

74. "Interview with Don Harris" "Statement by Jack Flaherty," "Statement of Mario Vigezzi," "Interview with John J. Driscoll," WFM/M-M, box 300, folder Connecticut 1942. Flaherty soon returned to Waterbury.

75. "Statement of Mario Vigezzi," ibid. There is no indication that "Mr. Porkchop" was being used derisively because of Harris' staff job.

76. "Statement by Samuel Cipriano," WFM/M-M, box 300, folder Connecticut 1942. Also see "Meeting with the Lux Clock Unit, 568," April 16 [1942].

77. "Statement by Lowell Hollenbeck," ibid.

78. "Statement by Henry Rapuano," ibid.

79. "Interview with Dorothy Dunne," ibid.; Donnelly to Hayes, November 14, 1942; "Interview with Don Harris," ibid.

80. Brown to Robinson, November 26, 1942, attached to Robinson to Brown, November 4, 1942, ibid., box 34, folder 17.

81. JDP, box 14, folder Communism.
82. See generally WFM/M-M, box 300, folder Connecticut 1942, but particularly the interviews with Dunne and Cipriano. Henry McCormack repeated story after story, but under close questioning, backed away from virtually each one, "Interview." For a discussion of a similar dynamic, see Gerald Zahavi, "Passionate Commitments: Race, Sex, and Communism at Schenectady General Electric, 1932–1954," *Journal of American History* 83 (2) (September 1996): 534ff.
83. The most accessible description of brass-making is in *Brass Valley*, 43–48, but also see Bucki, *Metal, Minds, and Machines* and *Seven Centuries of Brass Making* (Bridgeport, CT: n. p., 1920).
84. *Brass Valley*, 70, 171. For rollers more generally, especially see *Seven Centuries*, 56–61.
85. "Reverend Joseph F. Donnelly Flays Brazenness of Red Party Personnel in City," *WD* (November 9, 1942): 10.
86. Donnelly to Hayes, November 14, 1942.
87. "It's Big!," "MMSW Wins Scovill Election! 31 of 34," *Union* (August 17, 1942): 5; (August 24, 1942): 5.
88. *CION (Michigan)* (September 25, 1942): 12; "Third Chase Election Will be Held September 9th," *Union* (August 31, 1942): 10.
89. #1565 Minute Book, October 4, December 6, 1942; "Robinson at Scovill CIO Session," *Waterbury Republican* (October 5, 1942) (clipping), WFM/M-M, box 163, folder 5.
90. "Reid Robinson Carries Chase's," *WD* (November 16, 1942): 7.
91. "Representation Wtby Meeting Jan 10–43," WFM/M-M, box 163, folder 5; "Showdown Looms in CIO Union's Dispute Tomorrow," *WD* (January 9, 1943): 1.
92. Quoted in *Brass Valley*, 167.
93. Ibid. Johnson, however, then argued that this made the shop stewards do their job.
94. Ibid., 167.
95. *1941 Convention*, 625–704. It was Graham Dolan who replaced Rossman in September, 1941: Eckert, *Senate Hearings*, 51; Eckert, reel 54, 923; Knott, reel 54, 658.
96. Jensen, *Nonferrous Metals Industrial Unionism*, 98.
97. Cochran, *Labor and Communism: The Conflict that Shaped American Unions* (Princeton: Princeton University, 1977), 150.
98. Melvyn Dubofsky, "Not so 'Turbulent Years': Another Look at the American 1930s," *Amerikastudien* 24 (1979): 5–20.
99. For one explanation of the Board's actions, see James Leary to Chelsey Smothermon, March 3, 1943, WFM/M-M, box 301, folder 9. For another example of Murray's caution, see Rosswurm, "The Wondrous Tale of an FBI Bug: What it Tells Us About Communism, Anti-Communism, and the CIO Leadership," *American Communist History* 2 (1) (2003): 3–20.
100. For example, see: *Records of the Subversive Activity Control Board*, reel 54, Witt: 470–82, 487–91, 614; "Interview with Robinson," 37, 38.

CHAPTER SEVEN

Organizing the Carework Economy: When the Private Becomes Public

Eileen Boris and Jennifer Klein

Carrying oversized pennies and chanting, "Stop the Cuts," women and men in wheelchairs rolled through the streets of Springfield, Illinois on November 17, 1992. The Republican governor had vetoed cost of living and back pay for the personal attendants who made it possible for disabled people to remain in their own homes rather than face institutionalization. In response, 200 workers, consumers (as militant independent living activists named themselves), and advocates rallied on the capitol steps to end such "Follies." Charged Bessie Coleman, the President of Service Employees International Union (SEIU) Local 880, "Home care . . . costs the state less than half of what it pays for nursing home care, and yet, when it comes to slashing budgets the Governor and General Assembly go for the 'Penny Wise Pound Foolish' approach . . . "[1] Through such public performances, poor African American and Latina women bore witness to their struggles for dignity and found their voice through a union that mobilized in the community.

Two weeks later, the crowd returned to celebrate their successful lobbying of the legislature to restore client hours and worker wages.[2] Better care, the union had argued, depended on better jobs; both required political clout. For the next decade, the state refused to engage in collective bargaining or sign a contract, and yet these well-organized home attendants won wage increases, grievance procedures, and other demands. Their yearly trip to the legislature and direct-action political tactics illustrate the organizing strategies of a new carework unionism that relied on coalition politics and depended on government funding during the last decades of the twentieth century. Cleaners and carers for the welfare state, these low-paid women have stood at the vanguard of labor resurgence.

Broad trends in U.S. social policy over the latter half of the twentieth century fostered the creation of new occupations, funded by the state, and new opportunities for union organizing by formerly invisible workers. Home aides and attendants engage in intimate labor—bathing, dressing and undressing, cooking meals, cleaning clothes, and providing emotional support—performed mostly in domestic spaces, but they belong to a labor market sustained by public institutions: the welfare office, public hospital, state department of rehabilitative services, and various agencies for the aged. While the United States never implemented a social insurance or dedicated program for long-term care at home, it used public welfare, especially Medicaid, to fund the provision of care. That the United States relied primarily on means-tested social services available only to the poorest people fundamentally shaped the entire labor market for care, whether "public" or "private," no matter how much we assume that middle-class people can just go out and hire someone to look after their loved ones.

Even though they funded the service, state and local governments denied home care workers the status of employee, decade after decade. Instead, governments claimed that workers were independent providers or that the receivers of care were their employers. When home attendants tried to unionize along with other public employees, as they did in New York during the 1960s, local and state governments quickly sought to distance themselves even further from the employment relationship by contracting out the service to vendor agencies or redefining the mode of payment. Hence the structure of the job, as well as its location in the home, generated new barriers to unionization. Neither public employment nor private service, combining aspects of health care and household labor, home care existed in the shadows of the welfare state.

Yet the very nature of the labor also created unique hurdles for organizers. The actual labor process is relational, creating interdependence. Such work consists of more than tasks completed; it doesn't produce something that can be quantitatively measured, or easily represented in the GNP. Essential to the job is emotional labor, affection, and building trust. Workers cannot simply go on strike and leave clients who are unable to get out of bed. After spending many hours, weeks, even years with a client, the job may end suddenly with the death of the person cared for. Part of these workers' struggle involves establishing the legitimacy of care itself in a way that defies our most taken-for-granted definitions of work as production.

This sort of reevaluation of care and its worth has broad implications. Over the last half-century, a carework economy has developed out of the long shift of household work into service jobs—a movement from unpaid to paid labor and from personalism to contract—that intensified with the spurt of labor force participation by married white women. Families increasingly sought other women to take up the slack. They hired immigrant and U.S.-born women of color not only to clean their houses and care for children but to assist elderly and ill people, tasks once associated with unpaid labor of mothers and wives within families. Personal and domestic labor expanded into an array of specialized occupations, including home aide, personal attendant, and childcare worker. During this same period, the health sector became a major engine of overall economic growth. With the development of more outpatient services, the discharge of patients from hospitals earlier and sicker, and the increasing emphasis on deinstitutionalization in the last quarter of the twentieth century, home aides became a vast subsidiary workforce for the medical and long-term care system.

These jobs are also increasingly important because they cannot be offshored. Wherever capital may migrate globally to produce goods or provide technical services, care work stays home. Moreover, waves of new immigrants continually replenish these jobs. Home care's demographics reflect the migrant flows of this era's global economy: the workers are Latin American, Chinese, Vietnamese, Filipina, Eastern European, African, and Caribbean. Consequently, women's labors—once considered outside of the market or at the periphery of economic life—have now become the strategic sites for worker struggle and the direction and character of the American labor movement. By the late twentieth century, SEIU had claimed the place that the United Automobile Workers (UAW) occupied during the mid twentieth century as the major organizing and political force among wage earners.

Since the late 1970s, hundreds of thousands of black, Latina, and immigrant women, like those protesting in Illinois in 1992, have demanded recognition for the worth of their caring for elderly and disabled people as well as more funding of services for their clients.[3] Just as industrial unionism emerged in the 1930s as the structural response to mass production, an expanding carework economy compelled a reawakening labor movement to rethink questions of strategy and structure, "industry" and the state, labor value, and the employment relation. Organizing low-waged workers in dispersed locations, many of whom lacked the legal status of employee, required unions to think outside the box of the National Labor Relations Act with its format of signing up members, holding an election over representation, gaining certification, and then bargaining with an employer. Further, the location of home care as part of a state-funded health and medical sector also shaped union approaches. Unions like SEIU had to confront a fundamental strategic question: how to build a labor movement of poor people in a service so completely dependent on state funding. As workers and unions reformulated who constituted their movement, they had to build concepts and strategies reflective of the increasingly complex interpersonal relations essential to care work. Home care workers and their allies among consumers had to challenge representations of self-sacrificing workers and helpless consumers, as well as the stigmatization of dependency, whether on other human beings or the state. They had to find local unions willing to forge new solidarities.

Labor of Care

Very little scholarship exists specifically on paid home care and what does addresses contemporary concerns. Sociologists and economists celebrate the major union victory of California's In-Home Supportive Service (IHSS) workers in 1999, discuss home care as women's work, explicate conflicts between consumers and workers in the struggle to preserve such programs in face of budget deficits, and debate the unionization strategies of the turn of the twenty-first century—all without much historical perspective.[4] Gerontology experts write regularly on the subject of long-term care policies; rarely do workers enter their picture, except as problems for clients and states. Accepting policymakers' jeremiads of labor shortage at face value, this literature has not sought to explain why home care is a lousy job or states' role in perpetuating it as such.[5] Legal scholars, in contrast, seek to explain the standing of home care in employment law in order to change it.[6] In providing the first history of home care as an occupation, we not only shift the feminist focus to paid careworkers but illuminate the making of home care into a low-waged occupation in which the racial division of labor has remained fixed for decades.

Historians, on the other hand, have recovered changes and continuities in household labor, domestic service and family care. They consider the impact of demographic, technological, and policy change on housework and childcare and illuminate the dynamics of class and race inequalities between women.[7] Further, feminist scholars have de-naturalized the presumption that women should tend to those needing care, either out of love or from an inclination to serve others, no matter how poorly paid.[8] They have produced a rich interdisciplinary literature on the labor of care.[9] Seeking to capture the experience as well as the meaning of care, ethnographers describe the interaction between caregivers and receivers.[10] Political economists and sociologists trace a new global care deficit in which women leave their own children in the Philippines or Mexico to tend families in the United States.[11] Some theorize about women's propensity for an ethic of care, turning carework into a special form of labor. Others reject relegating care to a separate sphere and see no inherent reason to avoid its commodification: unwaged tending, they argue, is not necessarily better than purchased services.[12]

Finally, a robust literature on nursing captures the professionalization of this women-dominated field, the impact of feminism, and the growth of unionization. Much as nurses' professional associations defined their field by marginalizing aides and attendants, nursing historians have reinforced this invisibility by writing them out of their story.[13] Home care aides also make a minor appearance in studies of hospital workforces, the service sector, and public employment.[14]

To understand both the political economy of home care and organizing by workers, we need to look first at home care's hybrid structure: part domestic service, part health care. Though federal policies shaped its contours, implementation occurred on the local level and in light of state governments and their budget allocations. Given the workings of federalism, then, a national overview is not enough to understand home care. Thus we focus on those places with robust or illustrative programs—like New York, Illinois, and California—to chart this history.

The Emergence of an Occupation

Home care as a distinct occupation emerged in the crisis of the Great Depression to meet both welfare and health imperatives. One strand took shape as work relief for unemployed women who previously labored in domestic service. Private welfare agencies and social work professionals in centers of immigrant populations like New York, Philadelphia, and Chicago had initiated homemaker services in the early twentieth century for "a very limited task: the replacement of the sick mother in the household."[15] With the New Deal, state funding began to play a significant role in formulating a new occupation that helped poor families and individuals with medical emergencies, chronic illness, and old age, while curtailing the costs of institutionalization.[16] State and local governments would provide state support to one group of needy Americans—women with children—through employing another needy group—poor, unemployed women—as "substitute mothers." Government employed homemakers directly through the Works Progress Administration (WPA); it also financed private efforts and demonstration projects.

Relieving public hospitals of long-term elderly and chronically ill patients became the other origin of state-supported home-based care. The WPA also initiated programs to move such people out of the hospital and give them the necessary assistance to become "independent" at home. These programs often called the workers housekeepers, reflecting the nonmedical designation of service workers in hospital settings. In either case, social workers within welfare agencies oversaw the provision of care as a service for indigents.

The workforce resembled that of domestic service: middle-aged African American women, most of whom were or had been married, and supported family members. They were experienced housekeepers who could "handle things on [their] own initiative under economic conditions resembling those in the patients' households," reported the WPA. At a time when private household laborers could receive not much more than car fare home, WPA homemakers earned the prevailing relief rate for the unskilled.[17] A murky line separated visiting housekeeper from domestic servant. Whether working as a homemaker or housekeeper for children or the aged, the worker cleaned, cooked, laundered, helped with bathing and dressing, and provided sympathy and comfort. She was not a nurse, but social workers in the U.S. Children's Bureau and its network of family agencies hoped she would be more than a maid. By the end of the WPA in 1942, some 38,000 housekeeping aides in 45 states and the District of Columbia had assisted needy families.[18] Over the next half-century, similar women would move in and out of home care, hospital and nursing home work, private household labor, and public assistance.

While New Dealers developed home care as a form of relief, for both providers and receivers, they ignored it as a job. When the Democratic Congress passed old age insurance, unemployment benefits, collective bargaining, minimum wages, and maximum hour limits, it excluded nurse companions, homemakers, and other in-home care workers from coverage.[19] As employees of nonprofits, most nurses and health aides also fell outside the law. The formulators of Social Security, as well as family law administrators, claimed it impossible to account for work done in the home. The long refusal of courts to apply labor law within families or to familial-like relations, as with farm hands and domestic servants, impeded the regulation of home care.[20] That some states, notably California, in time would reimburse family members for home care further confused the legal status of this labor. The preponderance of racial minorities undergirded and reinforced the devaluation of the work.

The New Deal left a three-fold legacy, which persisted through the rest of the century. Although tied to the medical sector, states would pay for home-based care through welfare agencies but often with federal funds. Second, policy experts and welfare administrators saw female public assistance recipients as a ready supply of labor for home care. And, third, the exclusion of home attendants from national wages and hours laws remained in place for the next seven decades. Though first focused on families with children, with the growth of old-age insurance after World War II, homemaker services eventually came to prioritize support for the elderly, a group of voters privileged by the American welfare state over other recipients of social assistance.

The Significance of Welfare Funding

Although begun as emergency relief, home care services received new impetus after World War II, again from varying needs: a focus on rehabilitation after the war, concerns about chronic illness, welfare dependency, worries about the re-employment of women, and a rising elderly population. A handful of cities, including New York, Cleveland, Chicago, and Washington, D.C., continued WPA housekeeper services.[21] Policy innovations to keep seniors and disabled people in the community found a labor force in poor single mothers being pushed from welfare to "work." Home care further grew in the postwar period as both an expansion of the hospital and an attempt to free hospitals from direct care of charity patients and people with chronic illnesses. By the early 1960s, over 300 programs existed in 44 states, the District of Columbia, and Puerto Rico, the vast majority under private social welfare auspices, with the largest public programs in New York City and Chicago.[22]

With war's end, the network of welfare professionals around the U.S. Children's Bureau eagerly sought to create and define a new occupation—a job that took place in the home but performed the public work of the welfare state.[23] North Carolina created a model program under its director of welfare, Ellen Winston, who became the first U.S. Commissioner of Welfare in 1962. Typically, the service grew through demonstration projects funded through Social Security's child welfare grants, and reflected local conditions, which in North Carolina meant that it maintained segregation. Winston and her crew were New Deal liberals. Responding to the state's history of race and class, homemaker advocates insisted that they were "not furnishing a housekeeper." Their support allowed black homemakers to refuse tasks. Thus, Mrs Walker, who worked in High Point and Greensboro, replied to the lady who ordered her to clean a long-neglected closet "that she was going to help the woman to get well so that she would be able to do this task for herself."[24] The director of North Carolina's Division of Services for the Aged praised homemakers for "the caring ingredient that makes the difference."[25] Nonetheless, deep racial associations of domestic work and care would remain, with clients and their families referring to home care workers as domestics for the rest of the century.

New York City's Department of Welfare offered the most successful model of a public homemaker service that directly employed homemakers, worked closely with private social welfare agencies like Jewish Family Services, secured federal funds, and expanded from child to elder care. It sought to train workers through a Homemaking Center, which taught cleaning, laundry, cooking, sewing, and bedside and child care. Recruited from families on public assistance, homemakers cared for others from the same class. From 1945 until the 1970s, they belonged to a booming municipal public sector, even though their actual workplace was in client homes.[26]

New York defined its homemakers as public employees with limited Civil Service protections. They could receive pensions, health benefits, vacation time, and sick leave.[27] Unlike a typical domestic, city homemakers officially worked a 40-hour week. Advancement in annual salary was possible within a narrow range.[28] By 1960, 135 women worked on the staff of the department; in October 1963, after increased federal funding, the numbers jumped to 263 full-time workers, covered by a collective bargaining contract with the American Federation of State, County, and Municipal Employees (AFSCME). Homemakers still earned just a bit above minimum wage, with the top annual salary reaching $4,580.[29]

As with the WPA, rhetoric about "mature women" and their "richness of experience" dominated personnel discussions. So did their status as welfare recipients. The Cook County Bureau of Public Welfare was typical in deploying women on Aid to Dependent Children (ADC; later AFDC).[30] Its caseworkers talked of the "honesty, reliability, good morals, industry, cooperation, adaptability and understanding of human behavior" expected from homemakers. Descriptions of "high standards" were meant to give the work and the workers dignity and respect, but they also reflected long-standing discourses about black women, especially those who would enter other people's homes, that invoked old fears about servants, disease, and contagion. Worker manuals emphasized simple outfits, daily hygiene, and regular physical check-ups to assuage clients and the general public more than to protect workers.[31]

Illness-specific charities or service agencies, such as the New York Cancer Committee working with Montefiore Hospital, also sent homemakers to patient residences.[32] Hospital affiliated programs presented a competing model, defined and dominated by medical professionals.[33] As the director of Montefiore explained, its pioneering Home Care program was "primarily an effort to extend the hospital's facilities into the community and to take the home under its wing."[34] Doctors would lead a team to extend care to the "ward home."[35] Although housekeepers' home visits were far more regular than those of nurses or doctors, their labor was, for the most part, invisible, treated—like other forms of domestic or care work—as informal, voluntary, and open-ended. The medical staff assumed "the housekeeper was usually available to provide extra assistance in the event of emergency."[36] Untrained, she stood outside of the medical team, as a provider of services whose value commercial insurers found impossible to calculate and thus ineligible for reimbursement.

Fighting Poverty through Home Care

The War on Poverty in the 1960s provided new vehicles for the state to expand the home care labor market. Once again, this time under the umbrella of antipoverty policy, the state set terms that maintained a racialized, gendered occupation. The 1962 Public Welfare Amendments to the Social Security Act asked public welfare departments to identify services that would "restore families and individuals to self-support" and "help the aged, blind, or seriously disabled to take care of themselves."[37] This emphasis on services and self-support required a labor force that could undertake such tasks. As Wilbur Cohen, Assistant Secretary of HEW, argued, public welfare departments "should directly utilize significant numbers of Negro women as trained homemakers."[38] The new Office of Economic Opportunity (OEO) in 1964 created programs for AFDC recipients to meet the labor shortage in service occupations, especially health and child aides, home attendants, and homemaker aides, programs classified by the U.S. Department of Labor as similar to domestic service.[39] "In the 'war on poverty'," wrote the first U.S. Commissioner of Welfare, Ellen Winston, "homemakers have a crucial role."[40] OEO grants to local job training projects redirected "manpower" policy toward training paraprofessionals in human service fields. Especially through the New Careers program, administrators sought to place the poor as workers within the expanding welfare state itself.[41] Yet for those directed into jobs associated with domestic work or family care, the new career turned out to be a lot like the old one. Most jobs were temporary and peripheral to major service functions. They were "low-paying, low-status, dead-end." Movement up the health care services hierarchy was impossible. Although purportedly a solution to welfare dependency, employment as a home health or homemaker aide kept women working but poor.[42]

New York City took advantage of War on Poverty funding by creating a Housekeeping Aide Project.[43] These new "housekeepers" would work with elderly and disabled clients. In contrast to Department of Welfare homemakers, housekeepers were not city employees. Who employed them and thus provided proper compensation, Social Security deductions, and worker compensation remained unclear. Realizing that housekeepers received none of these benefits, New York State ruled in 1969 that the city could not label them independent contractors but had to contract through vendor agencies, which would then become the employer.[44]

State Expansion, Home Care Devolution

Great Society programs for the elderly significantly solidified dependence on low-wage labor. The Older Americans Act of 1965 promised the elderly "equal opportunity to the full and free enjoyment" of everything from decent housing and employment to health services.[45] Through a new Administration on Aging, it distributed grants for community-based services. Private agencies, such as the Community Council of Greater New York, soon received funding for "home help personnel" to relieve a shortage in health and welfare paraprofessionals by connecting private vendors with public agencies.[46] At the end of the project, it claimed to have tripled the number of homemaker-home health aides, a new designation for the job that more accurately reflected its hybridity.[47] In Oregon, activist seniors used Area Agencies on Aging, another outcome of such legislation, to organize a powerful movement that expanded housekeeping and aide services, meals-on-wheels, and other community-based programs.[48]

Even more transformative for the delivery and politics of home health care were the Social Security Amendments of 1965: Medicare and Medicaid. The new Medicare program (Title XVIII) provided the elderly with hospital insurance and partially subsidized medical insurance. Following hospitalization, it also would pay for limited in-home "professional" services, such as skilled nursing or physical therapy, as authorized by a physician and supervised by a registered nurse or therapist. Home health aides as paraprofessionals could deliver some services but only as long as the patient's primary need was for skilled medical care.[49]

Owing to those limitations, it was the companion Medicaid program (Title XIX) that became a more significant source for long-term care. For those elders identified as "functionally disabled," it offered medical assistance through community health or welfare agencies. Physicians could prescribe in-home health services to any person who would be eligible for nursing homes. Unlike Medicare, prior hospitalization was not required. Soon Medicaid would become the main funding source for nursing home care, but it also created a window through which states could provide indigent and low-income elders and disabled people in-home support.[50]

In the early 1970s, New York City redefined home care yet again, in particular to shift the burden onto the federal tab. In order to access Medicaid funds, this time it devised the Home Attendant Service for more severely functionally limited, usually older, clients in need of greater personal care. Since Medicaid had no spending caps and paid half of the cost, upon approval by federal authorities in 1973, the City began to transfer more and more of its elderly caseload to this program.[51] Nonetheless, those who did the work saw through such reorganizations. As Brooklyn home care aide Elizabeth Johnson declared, "they say . . . that they are different jobs, but that is not true because I am a home attendant and I do a housekeeper's job too."[52]

The reclassification resulted in marked deterioration in the conditions of labor. Barred from receiving overtime, repeated investigations found that home attendants made less than the minimum wage.[53] No one knew how many hours attendants worked, since the client paid the worker from her own benefits check. Every audit, whether conducted by a public or private agency, found "inordinate delays and errors in payment," with workers who waited weeks or even months for their wages. Elderly and disabled clients used their own social security to pay attendants; some workers hid that they had to apply for public assistance. With deteriorated working conditions in the 1970s, clients found themselves with untrained, unprepared caretakers, who rapidly left. Additional worker abuse followed from lack of precise job specifications, so that clients threatened attendants with loss of their job unless they washed outside windows or did the laundry of the entire household.[54]

These conditions failed to deter policymakers who sought to end women's dependency on public assistance. At the very same moment investigations reported extensive labor violations in New York City's Home Attendant Service, public officials argued for using such jobs to "break" poor women's dependency on AFDC. They predicted savings of $3 million yearly "from decreased public assistance costs." Once again, welfare administrators would rehabilitate poor women of color through low-paying jobs in domestic labor.[55]

By the late 1970s, the job of homemaker-home health aide stood on the lowest rungs of both health care and service labor. Yet it had become essential to the privatizing welfare state. The deliberate exclusion of home care workers, even those employed by vendor agencies, from the Fair Labor Standards Act (FLSA) further casualized the work. In 1974, Congress finally placed private household workers under the wage and hour law. The legislation, however, left the door open for the Department of Labor to exempt home care workers by redefining them as elder "companions"—seen as casual, temporary workers like a friendly neighbor or babysitter. This determination that home care would be low-paid, low-cost, labor somehow reassured governments that herein lay the answer to several welfare problems: overcrowding of public hospitals, rising cost of nursing homes, an aging population, and public refusal to spend tax dollars on "welfare."

After 1976, the home health care sector entered a phase of significant growth that as yet is unabated. The number of agencies certified to deliver Medicare or Medicaid home health services mushroomed. Unlicensed agencies proliferated, which indirectly gained government reimbursement by contracting with certified agencies—mainly to provide homemaker and personal care services. In 1980 Congress opened the door to for-profit agencies to provide Medicare-funded home care services. With this growth, the home health sector became the home health industry. For-profit agencies jumped ten-fold in the first half of the 1980s, capturing 30 percent of the market by 1986. The Bureau of Labor Statistics estimated that the number of paid homemaker, personal care attendant, and home health aide positions jumped from under 2,000 positions in 1958 to 60,000 in 1975, to over 350,000 in the late 1980s; nor did this include many of the aides employed as independent providers. The expansion of their numbers was critical to the whole enterprise: without an aide who helps with daily tasks of living, most clients would have to leave their homes. By the beginning of the twenty-first century, home care was one of the fastest growing, but poorest compensated, occupations.[56]

Consequences: Home Care Workers Organize

Even as the welfare state location of the labor devalued the workforce, it opened up a new site of social and political struggle. State policies set the possibility for a new careworker unionism that brought together workers, consumers, and voters to demand better wages and better care. Home care unionism originated in social justice movements for domestic workers' recognition, rights, and dignity in New York and California. It became tied to service sector unionism in New York and hospital worker organization in New York and San Francisco. It gained momentum through the community organizing of groups like ACORN (Association of Community Organizations for Reform Now), most successfully in Chicago. Activism among receivers and providers of home care made this "invisible workforce" visible. Success depended on a combination of grass-roots mobilization and political lobbying, tactics that social scientists consider typical of different types of unionism—social movement unionism and political unionism. Organizing reflected local conditions. Yet in each struggle, unionists confronted the tangle of policies that had obscured the employment relationship.

The rights of poor women as both clients of and workers for the welfare state defined this struggle. In developing two different delivery systems for home care, a private agency system paid through state contracts for the elderly and an independent contractor system for people with disabilities, Illinois contained in one state both structures that unionists faced in varying degrees elsewhere. While SEIU began its efforts in New York City in the late 1970s and achieved its greatest gains in California in the late 1990s, what happened in Chicago powerfully illuminates the tangle of public and private forces against which home care organizing occurred. Given the structure of home care, it was never enough just to win collective bargaining rights with individual vendor agencies. To make economic gains, the union had to go to government. But with Reagan Era assaults on public benefits and government employees, turning to the state for economic rights was no easy matter. Emerging in the 1980s, the political unionism of Chicago's Local 880 would require innovative tactics and new allies. What began as a militant, anticapitalist, and community organizing movement paved the way for adaptive strategies for union growth in an increasingly hostile antilabor climate.

Illinois initially ran its home care program out of public welfare, assisted by Area Agencies on Aging.[57] In 1979 it established the Community Care Program in the Department of Aging, which contracted with a wide-range of non- and for-profit agencies to offer homemaker and housekeeping services to those over age 60. Workers became employees of vendors, who relied upon the reimbursement rate they obtained from the state. People under 60 received similar assistance from the Department of Rehabilitative Services (DORS), funded in good part after 1984 by Medicaid. In keeping with the ethos of independence, DORS relied on a different mode: clients hired their own provider, who could be family or friends, but DORS claimed to be co-employer and it set wages—for most of the decade at the minimum wage. Workers had no hospital or medical insurance, paid vacation, compensated sick days, life insurance, or compensation for time spent traveling to and from clients' homes, often on long bus and subway rides.[58]

ACORN came to town to change all of this in 1983, planting a branch of its United Labor Unions (ULU), what became SEIU Local 880. Key ACORN leaders and rank-and-filers had come out of the welfare rights movement. Like other radicals of the period, they had developed a sectoral analysis that linked low-waged workers with those on public assistance, including poor single mothers. The ACORN model tied together workplace issues, such as wages and working conditions, with community ones, such as struggles over housing, banking, and living wage campaigns. Union organizing was one part of a broader mobilization against poverty. ULU/880 used direct action and political lobbying with agency-by-agency bargaining. It would pressure the legislature to increase the rate given to vendors and then demand that the vendors pass on some of the increase to the workers. It built power by recruiting members through door-to-door canvassing, house meetings, and developing leaders for specific actions. From the get go, it mobilized members for electoral campaigns to gain access to political power.[59] It would "*build an organization* first" that could maintain itself during workplace campaigns that could take years. Members paid dues from the moment they signed up, well before the union had a contract or certification; for people who made little, paying over that few dollars a month cemented organizational loyalty.[60]

In its successful drive against National Home Care Systems, a domestic temp agency formerly named McMaid, Local 880 honed its tactics: recognition actions, member bargaining, direct action, political lobbying and pressure, and strategic use of consumer "choice." With a cadre of just 15–20 paid up members, out of a total workforce of about 225, the union made its presence known. In October 1983, the organizing committee led by employees Irma Sherman, Doris Gould, and Juanita Hill showed up at the company on pay day, "fired up," and gathered around them workers willing to listen. Beginning with testimonials of mistreatment and disrespect, they declared it was time for a union and marched into the offices chanting, singing, and demanding a meeting with the boss. When the executive director came out, Sherman announced their union, ULU 880, and asked him to sign a "Recognition Agreement." The boss declined, called the police, and retreated to his office amid louder chants. But the workers had made their union public.[61]

With this agency, the union won its election fairly quickly, but contract bargaining turned into trench warfare that led it to combine the militant direct action of welfare rights—showing up en masse at the owner's plush suburban estate and pinning a notice on his door—with political unionism, as Local 880 creatively deployed tactics that blurred the public and private domains. Workers turned their relationship with consumers and the state to their advantage. They raised the specter that they would ask their clients to transfer to another agency. In the carework sector, moving consumers to another agency had a similar impact to a strike, without leaving those cared for stranded. The union then gambled on calling an actual strike, which required notice to the State Department of Aging as well as the company. National Home Care now faced the prospect that the state would drop it as a problematic contractor and decided to settle. Local 880 won a union shop, paid holidays and vacations, a grievance procedure, a health and safety protective clause, and a "Dignity and Respect" clause.[62]

In this case, the company recognized that settlement with the union could bring it more state contracts; it agreed to union demands as long as the union helped secure more state resources. Most agencies, even nonprofits like the YWCA, preferred to fight the union and drag out the NLRB process through legal suits over unit size or employee status. But they fought the union at a cost. After an eight-year battle against SEIU, plagued by low service ratings, one national chain lost its contract. Boasted the union, this "is just the ending we wanted to show employers what we can do to a company that fights its employees' right to organize right up to the Supreme Court, loses there, spends hundreds of thousands on legal fees and goes out of business anyway." The union helped to move former employees to union shops "where they keep their seniority, get benefits and don't have to go back down to minimum wage!"[63]

Recalcitrant public officials also proved fair game. When Secretary of Labor Lynn Martin visited Chicago in May 1991, Local 880 greeted her with the sign, "We Do our Job. You Do Yours. Enforce Minimum Wage Laws!" Members assembled at the Federal Building to seek an audience with the woman overseeing the FLSA because they weren't being paid for time taken to travel between clients. Martin dismissed their complaints as a state issue, but her refusal to meet with the union failed to deter publicity.[64] Under the auspices of Local 880, this demonstration—and other campaigns to raise wages, like "Give Me Five, So We Can Survive"—brought lobbying into the streets. Such performances had a double goal: to solidify the identity of unionists and win attention to the issue at hand.

Thousands of Chicago-area home care workers did not work for vendor agencies; they were DORS independent providers. The long struggle to gain recognition of DORS as the employer of attendants, and hence responsible for collective bargaining, underscores the ways that state structuring of home care, while placing roadblocks in front of unionization, also provided an avenue for obtaining those intermediate victories important for member morale. In 1985, the State Labor Relations Board determined that DORS and individual clients were co-employers. The state set the terms of employment, including salaries, service contract plan, and assessment, and processed the payroll. It withheld FICA, unemployment, and worker compensation. Clients had "the sole responsibility to hire, dismiss, train, supervise and discipline workers," even if state counselors advised them in this process, and supervised daily routine. Without jurisdiction over the clients as employers, the State Board refused to treat attendants as public employees. This determination made the union's claim for a Chicago and Cook County bargaining unit moot.

The union proceeded with its organizing project anyway. Whatever the formal status of the personal attendants, their names and addresses were available from the state comptroller's office. Local 880 organizers combed through all the checks written under the program and painstakingly built the list. DORS workers joined the fabric of the union, participating in membership meetings, fundraising events, canvassing, legal actions, and lobbying days. They led a legislative campaign for a Homecare Workers' Bill of Rights.[65]

Local 880 also mobilized a wide network of political friends to pressure the agency. In 1986, for example, Carol Moseley Braun, then Assistant Majority Leader of the State House, pressed SEIU's case to the DORS director through a letter formulated by the Local. Repeating the union's grievance—abysmal pay, late paychecks, and lack of bargaining recognition, she captured the contradiction at the center of home care: "it seems that as a department delivering basic human services to the disabled in order that they may retain their dignity, it is not too much to ask that you treat the attendant-housekeepers with the same dignity and respect for their human rights."[66] Between 1985 and 1990, through member lobbying and political clout, the union managed to win wage hikes to $4.50 an hour and eliminate underpayments.[67]

Relying on the insider clout of other SEIU officials with the governor, Local 880 gained dues check off and a "Meet and Confer" agreement in October 1990. The union, in theory, could now meet and confer with the state about wages, hours, and working conditions.[68] In reality, DORS administrators only would deal with grievances and the issuance of checks.[69] The "Meet and Confer" was a breakthrough, but it was no union contract and it needed perpetual renewal. It offered an institutional foothold, while the union kept its sights on the horizon and built for some day in the future when a majority of workers would become members. A new governor, however, could take away what the old one had given.

Dependence on the state budget posed specific challenges to clients and workers alike. In the economic downturn of the early 1990s, Illinois cut services to elderly and disabled clients, hurting home care workers in the process. Waiting lists for homemakers and attendants soared, with DORS refusing new applicants. Administrators feared the reaction of "national militant and conservative disability and gay communities," as its director confessed; with "another budget reduction these groups [like ADAPT (Americans Disabled for Attendant Programs Today) and ACT-UP] could take the concept of Illinois being a 'target state' one step further and make Jim Edgar a 'target Governor.'" ADAPT fulfilled that fear by launching confrontational protests in Chicago. Disability rights activists filed a lawsuit, with the result that a federal court prohibited "the state from denying eligible Medicaid recipients in-home services," forcing the department to open up its applications six months later.[70]

When the federal minimum wage rose in 1991, Illinois home care workers found themselves squeezed between the state and the vendors; they would only gain if the state increased vendor reimbursements.[71] DORS workers again had to seek legislative remedies, an uphill battle amid a new recession. Hostage to budget negotiations, they had to await back pay at the end of late budgets. The union held on for another ten years; workers paid their dues, attended meetings, built the union—still without recognition. Finally, through financial and ground support for the Democratic gubernatorial candidate in 2004, a labor-friendly governor came into office and

through executive order formally recognized SEIU Local 880 as the collective bargaining agent for these workers.[72] Within months, the state legislature codified his
executive order into law.[73]

California and the Growth of Careworker Unionism

The problem of the independent provider stymied unionization in other states, most
notably California. In 1973 activists in the independent living movement won a new
In-Home Support Services program (IHSS), which gave them the right to hire and
fire individual attendants. Most IHSS aides became independent contractors. Yet,
since the state paid for the service, home care aides existed in a legal limbo. Where
were workers to turn to negotiate for better pay, health insurance, and more regular
hours? For the next 20 years, California unions engaged in legal and political battles
over who would serve as the employer for collective bargaining purposes. Whether
the organizing originated with public worker locals, hospital worker locals, nursing
home or domestic worker organizations, they deployed the tactics of community
organizing and public sector or political unionism—constant membership meetings,
neighborhood social events, numerous demonstrations, and political education.
Ultimately, it seemed only legislative mandates and increased funding could improve
conditions. To achieve that, workers had to join with consumers to win new legislation. SEIU leaders recognized they had to step outside of the typical adversarial
stance because homecare relied on a "unique relationship between the homecare
workers and their 'boss' the homecare consumer."[74] Some militant disability activists
remained skeptical, charging that unions saw "attendant services as a lucrative area
in which to organize previously unorganized workers."[75] They feared that union concern for wages and working conditions would inhibit their ability to control their
own care. An attendant was a component of autonomy and control: an aid, like a
wheelchair, to help the consumer with daily activities. To forge a successful alliance
with independent living adherents, SEIU gave up the right to strike and accepted
consumer-direction of workers.

Helping along the coalition was a common enemy: politicians from both parties
used IHSS as an easy target during yearly battles over the state budget. After Proposition 13 in 1978, California required a two-thirds majority to pass fiscal measures,
often delaying passage of its budget. Legislators constantly proposed to reduce IHSS
funding, cap worker wages, cut family providers, restrict the service to the most
impaired, and limit client hours. A political game unfolded in which governors could
appear tough and avoid asking for "new revenues," but also look compassionate
because, after all the commotion, they would restore what amounted to a small percentage of the state's budget to avert "human tragedy."[76]

In the 1990s, a coalition of disability groups, senior citizens, and unions created
enough political leverage to win an institutional means to enable unionism and
collective bargaining: a public authority. At the county level, a newly created public
authority would set the IHSS wage for home care providers and provide a central

registry to locate the homecare workforce. Hence, the public authority could function as the employer with which to bargain; it also provided for consumer in-put and direction. Such a settlement opened the way to county-by-county union organizing, with the first success coming in the more liberal Bay area.

Reflecting its particular mixture of progressive politics, community involvement, and labor culture, San Francisco developed the best conditions for home care workers in the country. In May 1995, the city voted for a public authority that would be independent of the supervisors and accountable to the consumer groups. SEIU Local 250, a long-standing hospital and nursing home workers union, stepped up it efforts to organize home attendants. With a strong, militant on-the-ground presence in hospitals and nursing homes, Local 250 had earned the city's respect through years of supporting local issues and working in healthcare coalitions. That year the union gained card check from the San Francisco IHSS Consortium and the first pay raise in 20 years. Then, in the largest union representation election in San Francisco in recent years, 5,600 independent providers voted to join Local 250 in the Spring of 1996, bringing the union's overall membership to over 40,000. Sensitive to the interpersonal dynamics of the carework economy, all parties then underwent training in "interest-based" bargaining to proceed in a nonadversarial manner, and in 1997, San Francisco became the first California county to sign a union contract.

Given the inter-dependence of care work, attendants were not the only ones at the table. "Consumers should focus on how to 'use' the strength of union rather than fear its influence," advocates advised, but they also shrewdly recognized the need to give consumers a voice.[77] What resulted, organizer Karen Sherr explained, "was more of a social contract—about living together in society—it was about the further organization of society, about political aims and alliances" that would enhance the "vested interest in a continuous and well-qualified care program" by the workers, clients, community, and state social services.[78] Within a decade, with continuous improvement in wages and health benefits, economist Candace Howe found, turnover among San Francisco's IHSS workers decreased by nearly a quarter. Wages became the highest in the state in home care, along with Santa Clara, topping $10 an hour.[79]

The local's well-organized hospital and nursing home workers integrated the home-based workers into all aspects of a participatory, democratic culture within the union: shop stewards, member organizers, elected bargaining committees, leadership committees, and elected executive board. In turn, they stuck together, developing an identity as care-workers who worked at different nodes along a medical care-long-term care spectrum. As home care worker, union steward, and bargaining committee member Danny Villasenor explained, he learned through his participation in the union that "I was always a health care worker but I never realized it."[80] Home aide and union activist Lola Young developed an even deeper, broader identity; rejecting a bureaucratic designation as personal assistants, she told us: "I'm nobody's gopher. . . . I'm a care worker."[81]

In L.A., home care workers and consumers finally won a public authority at the end of the century and in 1999, 74,000 home attendants voted to join SEIU, the largest single winning union drive since the sit-down strikes of the Great Depression. It was a stunning victory; low-paid women workers, many of them immigrants or women of color, shone as the new face of labor. Here, however, they remained in a union of low-waged home care and nursing home workers, not joined with hospital workers. On their own, home care workers in this sprawling metropolis, with the largest IHSS caseload, could not ultimately muster enough political power to push wages much above the minimum.

* * *

The California union campaigns built alliances, stepped outside the NLRB framework, organized tens of thousands of workers, and created new institutional state structures that enabled the union to represent workers on a sectoral, rather than worksite, basis. These tactics subsequently were imitated across the country from Oregon to Maryland. But because the arrangements for home care have varied by time and place, no single term captures the full range of organizing strategies for this workforce. These unions engaged in political unionism, because they had to influence the state; social movement unionism, because they depended on mobilizing clients and communities; and service sector unionism, because they helped create this new epicenter of organized labor. As a whole, it is perhaps most constructive to see these new trends as "careworker unionism": a solidaristic attempt to move the labor of care away from its marginalized status to recognize its centrality to the contemporary political economy.

Careworker unionism arose to improve the conditions of workers whose job mitigates the inevitable dependencies of the human condition. But as a nation, we take careworkers for granted. We seek respect and dignity for aging and disabled people but not for those who make it possible for them to live in the community. This contradiction at the heart of paid carework has intensified amid the decline of both employee benefits and social entitlements, especially those relating to health care and retirement. Home care itself remained as intensely political as ever: in 2007 the Supreme Court reinscribed these laborers as outside the nation's primary wage and hour law when it upheld their classification as elder companions, reaffirming their place at the margins of recognized employment. Fiscal crisis has called into question union reliance on legislative payback as well as state reliance on Medicaid to fund such services. Though home care workers entered the twenty-first century with unions and collective bargaining rights, most still lived in or just above poverty. Will the nation find the political courage to guarantee a right to care and affirm the respect and dignity of those who care? Recognizing our human interdependence then might become another name for solidarity.

Notes

1. Unless directly quoted, we are drawing upon our book manuscript, *Caring for America: Home Health Workers in the Shadow of the Welfare State*, forthcoming

from Oxford University Press. Press Release, "Governor Edgar & Legislature Slammed for Balancing Budget on Backs of Disabled," November 13 [1992]; "Homecare Workers Demand Legislature Override Governor's Veto," November 17 [1992], both in Service Employees International Union Local 880 Records,, M2001–162, box 4, folder 27, Wisconsin Historical Society, Madison, WI (hereafter 880 Records).

2. "Local 880 Members March on Springfield, Override Governor's Veto," *Local 880 Voice* (February 1993): 1, 3; Service Employees International Union Records, SEIU Publications, Local 880, Archives of Labor and Urban Affairs, Wayne State University.

3. Bob Pool, "Faithful Rally Across U.S. to Keep King Dream Alive," *Los Angeles Times* (April 5, 1988); Victor Merina, "Home-Care Workers Rally, Gain Support in Pay Issue," *Los Angeles Times* (December 23, 1987).

4. Jess Walsh, "Creating Unions, Creating Employers: A Los Angeles Home-Care Campaign," in Mary Daly, ed., *Carework: The Quest for Security* (Geneva: ILO, 2001), 219–33; Linda Delp and Katie Quan, "Homecare Worker Organizing in California: An Analysis of a Successful Strategy," *Labor Studies Journal* 27 (Spring, 2002): 1–23; Cameron Lynne MacDonald and David A. Merrill, "'It Shouldn't Have to Be a Trade': Recognition and Redistribution in Care Work Advocacy," *Hypatia* 17 (Spring, 2002): 67–83; Jennifer A. Parks, *No Place Like Home? Feminist Ethics and Home Health Care* (Bloomington, IN: University of Indiana Press, 2003); and Lynn May Rivas, "Invisible Labors: Caring for the Independent Person," in Barbara Ehrenreich and Arlie Russell Hochschild, eds *Global Woman: Nannies, Maids, and Sex Workers in the New Economy* (New York: Metropolitan Books, 2003), 70–84.

5. Penny H. Feldman, Alice Sapienza, and Nancy M. Kane, *Who Cares for Them? Workers in the Home Care Industry* (Westport, CT: Greenwood Press, 1990).

6. See Kristin Jenkins Gerrick, "Note and Comment: An Inquiry into Unionizing Home Healthcare Workers: Benefits for Workers and Patients," 29 *American Journal of Law & Medicine* 117 (2003); Peggie R. Smith, "Organizing the Unorganizable: Private Paid Household Workers and Approaches to Employee Representation," 79 *North Carolina Law Review* 45 (2000); Molly Biklen, "Note: Healthcare in the Home: Reexamining the Companionship Services Exemption to the Fair Labor Standards Act," 35 *Columbia Human Rights Law Review* 113 (2003).

7. Mary Romero, *Maid in the USA* (New York: Routledge, 1992); Tera Hunter, *To 'Joy My Freedom* (Cambridge, MA: Harvard, 1997); Phyllis Palmer, *Domesticity and Dirt: Housewives and Domestic Servants in the United States, 1920–1945* (Philadelphia, PA: Temple University Press, 1989); Emily Abel, *Hearts of Wisdom: American Women Caring for Kin, 1850–1940* (Cambridge, MA: Harvard, 2000); Evelyn Nakano Glenn, "From Servitude to Service Work: Historical Continuities in the Racial Division of Paid Reproductive Labor," *Signs* 18 (Autumn, 1992): 1–43; Susan Strasser, *Never Done: A History of American Housework* (New York: Pantheon, 1982).

8. Steven Dawson and Rick Surpin, *Direct Care Health Workers: The Unnecessary Crisis in Long-Term Care,* Report Submitted by the Paraprofessional Health Care Institute to Aspen Institute (January 2001), 8, at www.paraprofessional.org/publications/Aspen.pdf (accessed October 14, 2005).

9. Paula England, "Emerging Theories of Care Work," *Annual Review of Sociology* 31 (2005): 381–99; Sonya Michel and Rianne Mahon, *Child Care Policy at the Crossroads: Gender and Welfare State Restructuring* (New York: Routledge, 2002); Nancy Folbre, *The Invisible Heart: Economics and Family Values* (New York: New Press, 2001); Evelyn Nakano Glenn, "Creating A Caring Society," *Contemporary Sociology* 29 (January 2000): 84–86.

10. Jane Aronson and Shelia M. Neysmith, "'You're Not Just in There to Do the Work': Depersonalizing Policies and the Exploitation of Home Care Workers' Labor," *Gender and Society* 10 (1996): 59–77; María de la Luz Ibarra, "The Tender Trap: Mexican Immigrant Women and the Ethics of Elder Care Work," *Aztlán* 28 (Fall, 2003): 87–113; Cinzai Solari, "Professionals and Saints: How Immigrant Careworkers Negotiate Gender Identities at Work," *Gender and Society* 20 (June 2006): 301–33; Claire L. Stacey, "Finding Dignity in Dirty Work: The Constraints and Rewards of Low-Waged Home Care Labor," *Sociology of Health and Illness* 27 (2005): 831–54.

11. Rhacel Salazar Parrenas, *Servants of Globalization* (Stanford: Stanford University Press, 2001).

12. For a sample, Susan Himmelweit, "Caring Labor," *ANNALS, AAPSS,* 561 (January 1999): 30, 31, 36–37; Nell Noddings, *Starting at Home: Caring and Social Policy* (Berkeley, CA,: University of California Press, 2002); Eva Feder Kittay, *Love's Labor* (New York: Routledge, 1999); Deborah Stone, "Caring by the Book," in Madonna Harrington Meyer, ed. *Care Work: Gender, Labor, and the Welfare State* (New York: Routledge, 2000); Viviana A. Zelizer, *The Purchase of Intimacy* (Princeton: Princeton University Press, 2005).

13. Susan M. Reverby, *Ordered to Care: The Dilemma of American Nursing, 1850–1945* (New York: Cambridge University Press, 1987); Susan Gelfand Malka, *Daring to Care: American Nursing and Second-Wave Feminism* (Urbana, IL: University of Illinois Press, 2007); Karen Buhler-Wilkerson, *No Place Like Home: A History of Nursing and Home Care in the United States* (Baltimore, MD: Johns Hopkins, 2001).

14. Leon Fink and Brian Greenberg, *Upheaval in the Quiet Zone: A History of Hospital Workers' Union Local 1199* (Urbana, IL: University of Illinois Press, 1989); Dorothy Sue Cobble, "The Prospects for Unionism in a Service Society," in Cameron Lynne MacDonald and Carmen Sirianni, eds *Working in the Service Society* (Philadelphia, PA: Temple University Press, 1996).

15. Marta Fraenkel, *Housekeeping Service for Chronic Patients* (New York: 1942), 68; Maud Morlock, *Homemaker Services: History and Bibliography* (Washington: GPO, 1964), 4.

16. Fraenkel, *Housekeeping Service for Chronic Patients*, 71–2; The Hospital Council of Greater New York, *Organized Home Medical Care in New York City: A Study of Nineteen Programs* (Cambridge, MA: Harvard University Press, 1956), 35–37.

17. Fraenkel, *Housekeeping Service for Chronic Patients*, 93–4; WPA regulations, which limited individuals to 18 months of work relief, accounted for most of the turnover. See also Jarrett, *Housekeeping Service for Home Care of Chronic Patients*, 11, 95–97; http://www.dol.gov/esa/minwage/chart.htm (accessed July 8, 2004).

18. Morlock, *Homemaker Services*, 4.

19. Mary Poole, *The Segregated Origins of Social Security: African Americans and the Welfare State* (Chapel Hill, NC: University of North Carolina Press, 2006).

20. "Extension of Old-Age and Survivors Insurance to Additional Groups of Current Workers," Report of the Consultant Group, in U.S. Congress, House of Representatives, Committee on Ways and Means, *Hearings Before the Committee on Ways and Means on H.R. 7199, Social Security Amendments of 1954*, 83rd Congress, 2nd Sess. (Washington DC: GPO, 1954), 875.

21. U.S. Department of Health, Education, and Welfare, *Homemaker Services in the United States: Report of the 1959 Conference*, Public Health Service Publication 746 (Washington: GPO, 1960), 18.

22. Morlock, *Homemaker Services*, 11.

23. Jean Kallenberg to Maude Morlock, December 29, 1948, box 119, file 4–11-6, RG102, CV 1945–48.

24. Clara Mae Ellis, "Selective Areas of Service to Older People," *Public Welfare News* (North Carolina) (December 1958): 7–8; Myra Mitchiner, "Homemaker Service Keeps Families Together," *Public Welfare News* (North Carolina) (December 1958): 4, in North Carolina State Library; *Homemaker Services for the Aged in North Carolina*, Information Bulletin No. 30 (Raleigh, NC: North Carolina State Board Of Public Welfare, 1960), 3, North Carolina State Library; "Manual Homemaker Service," North Carolina State Board of Public Welfare, June 1963, North Carolina State Library; Maud Morlock, "Report of Field Visit: North Carolina," February 2, 1954, pp. 13–15, U.S. Children's Bureau, CF 1953–54, box 620, RG102, National Archives and Records Administration, College Park, Maryland (hereafter NARA).

25. Transcript of Interview with Virginia Cloer, Dorothy Hicks, and Eleanor Anderson Charlotte, NC, June 11, 1997 by Johanna Schoen, 7; Transcript of Interview with Murlene Wall, Charlotte, NC, June 19, 1997 by Johanna Schoen, 15–16, both in authors' possession; Annie May Pemberton, "Homemaker Services for the Aged," *Public Welfare News* (September 1962): 6, North Carolina State Library.

26. Lurry to Morlock, April 28, 1945, U.S. Children's Bureau, , CF 1953–54, box 620, RG102, NARA.

27. "Our Homemakers," *The Welfarer* (November 1949): 10, McMillan Library, Human Resources Administration, New York (hereafter HRA); U.S. Department

of Health, Education and Welfare, Public Health Service, Division of Public Health Methods, *Homemaker Services in the United States: Report of the 1959 Conference* (Washington: GPO, 1960), 75.

28. U.S. Department of Health, Education, and Welfare, Public Health Service, Division of Public Health Methods, *Homemaker Services in the United States, 1958: Twelve Statements,* Public Health Service Publication No. 645 (Washington: GPO, 1958), 11.

29. "Welfare's Homemakers Honored with Ten-Year Service Awards," *The Welfarer* (August 1959): 3; "A Decade of Service," *The Welfarer* (July 1961): 11; Robert Alan Shick, "The Contracting Out of Local Government Services: New York City Home Health Care," Ph.D. dissertation, New York University, 1989, 48.

30. *Homemaker Services in the United States, 1958: Twelve Statements,* 11.

31. "Homemaker Service in a Public Welfare Agency," 1–2, 6.

32. Maud Morlock to Wado C. Wright, July 5, 1947, RG102, CF 1949–52, box 414, 4–11–6; Dora Goldfarb, "Homemaker Service for the Aged," esp. 3, 6, file "September 1949," both in U.S. Children's Bureau, CF 1949–52, box 413, RG102, NARA; Jewish Family Service, NY, "A Different and Economical Service to the Aged: Report on the Community Homemaker Service for the Aged Administered by the Jewish Family Service 1945–1950," 2–3, U.S. Children's Bureau, CF 1949–52, box 413, folder: July 1950, RG102, NARA.

33. For more on this see, Boris and Klein, *Caring for America,* chapter 2.

34. E. M. Bluestone, "Home Care and the Practitioner," *Postgraduate Medicine* 24 (2) (August 1958): 139.

35. New York City Department of Hospitals, *Annual Report 1949* (New York: Department of Hospitals), 32.

36. Ibid., 109. Of those receiving housekeeping service, over half had daily visits; another quarter had a visit every two or three days, and the rest had a visit every week. Still, the Hospital Council insisted that the "primary services rendered by home care . . . [were] . . . visits by a physician, a social worker, and a nurse"; important supplementary services included lab tests, x-rays, and furnishing of sick-room supplies and equipment, 109, 111–12.

37. *Social Welfare in New York State in 1962,* 96th Annual Report (Albany, NY: State Department of Social Welfare, 1963), 2–3; "The New Public Welfare System: A Progress Report on the 1962 Amendments to the Social Security Act," in *Social Welfare in New York State in 1964,* 99th Annual Report (Albany, NY: State Department of Social Welfare, 1965), 10.

38. Wilbur Cohen to Mr. John Nolan, June 5, 1963, General Records of the Department of Health, Education, and Welfare, Office of the Secretary, Secretary's Subject Correspondence, box 219, File: 1963, Jan–June, RG 235, NARA .

39. Office of Economic Opportunity, *A Nation Aroused,* 1st Annual Report, 1965, 41, "The War on Poverty, 1964–1968," Part I: The White House Central Files, microfilm edition, reel 9, box 125, microfilm edition.

40. *Homemaker Services in Public Welfare,* 4–5.

41. Fred Powledge, *New Careers: Real Jobs and Opportunity for the Disadvantaged*, Public Affairs Pamphlet No. 427 (New York: Public Affairs Committee, 1968), 8, 11, 4; Frank Riessman, *New Careers: A Basic Strategy Against Poverty*, with introduction by Michael Harrington (New York: A. Philip Randolph Educational Fund, 1966), 7, 9; Arthur Pearl and Frank Riessman, *New Careers for the Poor: The Nonprofessional in Human Service* (New York: The Free Press, 1965), 249–51.

42. Edith F. Lynton, *The Subprofessional: From Concepts to Careers* (New York: National Committee on Employment of Youth, September 30, 1967), 78–79, 85.

43. "Housekeeping Aide Project Trains Mothers in Management and Child Care," *The Welfarer* (September 1964): 1, 6; *1964 Annual Report of the City of New York Department of Welfare*, April 1965; "Training and Employment for Mothers in Part-Time Occupations," *The Welfarer* (March 1967): 1, 8–10; "Two Anti-Poverty Projects Approved," *The Welfarer* (December 1965): 10, all from McMillan Library, HRA. Annie Creola Fenton, "The Housekeeping Aide and Training Project in the New York City Department of Welfare Bureau of Special Services," M.S.W. thesis, New York: Fordham University, 1966.

44. Francis Caro and Arthur Blank, *Home Care in New York City: The System, The Providers, The Beneficiaries* (New York: Community Service Society of New York, July 1985), 123–33; Shick, "The Contracting Out of Local Government Services," 57–58.

45. U.S. Senate, *The Older Americans Act of 1965: A Compilation of Materials Relevant to H.R. 3708, As Amended by the Special Subcommittee on Aging, of the Committee on Labor and Public Welfare* (Washington D.C.: GPO, 1965); Laura Katz Olson, *The Political Economy of Aging: The State, Private Power, and Social Welfare* (New York: Columbia University Press, 1982), 189; David K. Brown, "Administering Aging Programs in a Federal System," in William P. Browne and Laura Katz Olson, eds. *Aging and Public Policy: The Politics of Growing Old in America* (Westport, CT: Greenwood Press, 1983), 204.

46. Community Council of Greater New York, "Report of the Home Health and Housing Program, Citizens' Committee on Aging, January 1967 to December 1969," Revised Edition (July 1970), 1–2, McMillan Library, HRA.

47. "Report of the Home Health and Housing Program," 1–17.

48. *Report of the Special Committee on Aging*, 58th Assembly—Oregon State Legislature (Salem, Oregon, January 1975), 11, 13; Elizabeth Kutza, "Long-Term Care in Oregon," Institute on Aging, Portland State University, 1994, in J. Klein's possession.

49. Buhler-Wilkerson, *No Place Like Home*, 200–01.

50. Katherine Ricker-Smith, "An Historical and Critical Overview of the Development and Operation of California's In-Home Supportive Services Program," San Francisco Home Health Service, Grant HEW-100–78-0027, December 31, 1978, 31–36.

51. Citizens' Committee on Aging, Community Council of Great New York, "Systems Analysis of the Home Attendant Program," January–December 1977,

McMillan Library, HRA; Office of the Comptroller of New York, Bureau of Audit and Control, "Report on the Quality of Care and Operating Practices of the Home Attendant Program: Summary of Significant Observations," October 25, 1978, New York State Library, II.

52. U.S. House of Representatives, Select Committee on Aging, *New York Home Care Abuse*. Hearing, 6 February, 1978. 95th Congress, 2nd Sess. (Washington: GPO, 1978), 27.

53. "Systems Analysis of the Home Attendant Program," 11; Bureau of Audit and Control, "Report on the Quality of Care and Operating Practices of the Home Attendant Program," 7; Peter Kihss, "Home Care Plan for Oldsters Scored," *New York Times* (July 16, 1976); Memo, to David A. Grossman, from Karen M. Eisenstadt, Subject: "A Program for Improving City Services to the Aging," October 6, 1972, 19–20, box 34, folder 606, reel 17, Subject Files, Papers of Mayor Lindsay, Municipal Archives, New York, NY.

54. "Report on the Quality of Care;" "Aide Stays by Elderly Women's Side While Pay Remains in Computer," *New York Times* (May 6, 1977); Peter Kihss, "Program to Aid Elderly, Sick Poor Marked by Fraud, State Audit Says," *New York Times* (December 15, 1977); New York State Department of Social Services, Metropolitan Regional Audit Office, "Audit of Home Attendant Services, New York City Department of Social Services, #76–835-S-029–58," August 1977, McMillan Library, HRA, 8, 14–18.

55. "Report on Quality of Care," VI–VII.

56. Andrew Szasz, "The Labor Impacts of Policy Change in Health Care: How Federal Policy Transformed Home Health Organizations and Their Labor Practices," *Journal of Health Politics, Policy, and Law* 15 (1) (Spring, 1990): 194–97; Feldman, Sapienza, and Hunt, *Who Care for Them?*, 7–8, 55–57; Administration on Aging, *Human Resources in the Field of Aging: Homemaker-Home Health Aide Services*, AoA Occasional Papers in Gerontology, no. 2 (Washington, D.C.: U.S. Department of Health, Education, and Welfare, 1977), 2–3, 7, 18–19; Caro and Blank, *Home Care in New York City: The System, The Providers, The Beneficiaries*, 13; Jane Gross, "New Options (and Risks) in Home Care for Elderly," *New York Times*, March 1, 2007.

57. Keith Kelleher, "ACORN Organizing and Chicago Homecare Workers," *Labor Research Review* no. 80 (1985): 41.

58. SEIU International v. State of Illinois, *Hearing Officer's Recommended Opinion and Dismissal*, State Labor Relations Board, Case No. S-RC-115, Oct. 24, 1985, box 11, folder 3, 2–4, 9–10; Keith Kelleher to All Staff and Leadership, July 9, 1985, box 4, folder 35, 880 Records.

59. "Kelleher, "ACORN Organizing and Chicago Homecare Workers," 37–40; Vanessa Tait, *Poor Workers' Unions: Rebuilding Labor from Below* (Boston, MA: South End Press, 2005); Fred P. Brooks, "New Turf for Organizing: Family Child Care Providers," *Labor Studies Journal* 29 (4) (2005): 51–52.

60. "Discount Foundation Application Summary," n.d., c. 1986, 1; Kelleher, "ACORN Organizing," 37–40.

61. Keith Keller, "A History of SEIU Local 880, 1983–2005," unpublished manuscript (2005), 27, 51, in authors' possession.

62. "N.H.S. Contract Victory. Strike is Off," *The Homemakers' Voice*, "Special Contract Issue," n.d., pg. 1, box 8, folder 12; Mark Heaney to Keith Kelleher, June 10, 1985, box 11, folder 41; Kelleher to Mr. Olson/Heaney, June 17, 1985, box 11, folder 41, 880 Records.

63. Keith Kelleher to John Sweeney, December 5, 1986, in box 4, folder 36; "Year End/Year Begin Report-1986," January 2, 1987, 3; "Year End/Year Begin Report," December 30, 1989, 2; "Year End/Year Begin Report," July 1, 1993, 4, all in box 8, folder 41, 880 Papers; Msgr. John J. Egan to Dr Jean Otwell, January 2, 1985, box 3, folder 39, Records; "Homecare: Where the Heart Is," *Healthcare Worker Update* (Winter/Spring 1991), 9.

64. Les Lester, "SEIU Urges Probe," *Chicago Defender* (May 9, 1991); "SEIU Local 880 Action on Lynn Martin—Agenda," "Songs and Chants," box 7, folder 2, 880 Records,.

65. Kelleher, "A History of SEIU Local 880," 39–42, 49–51.

66. Carol Moseley Braun to Suter, December 1, 1986, box 1, folder 2, 880 Records.

67. To: Harry Kurshenbaum from Keith Kelleher, Re: DORS Background, February 1, 1993, box 11, folder 15, 880 Records.

68. "Local 880 Service Employees International Union, AFL-CIO, CLC Year End/Year Begin Report," December 29, 1990, box 8, folder 41, 880 Records.

69. Memo to Kurshenbaum, Larry Kngelstein to Eugene Moats, November 14, 1989, box 11, folder 5; Memo to Gene Moats From Keith Kelleher Re: Meeting with Janice Salini, et al., March 24, 1992, box 1, folder 32, 880 Records.

70. Audrey McCrimon to Joan Walers, March 10, 1992; Access Living, "Major Victory for the Disability Community in Illinois," August 20, 1992, both in box 11, folder 13, 880 Papers; Bessie Cannon, "Home Care Programs Are Good Investment," *Chicago Sun Times* (November 14, 1992); Ray Sons, "Elderly Poor Pinned by Budget's Brutality," *Chicago Sun Times* (August 23, 1992); Neil Steinberg, "Disabled Stage New Battle Here," *Chicago Sun Times* (May 17, 1992); "Disabled to Get Home Aid," *Chicago Sun Times* (August 20, 1992).

71. Rose Gallagher to Dear Legislator, April 8, 1991; Keith Kelleher to Gene Moats, April 8, 1991, "Minimum Wage Impact": NHS Offer to SEIU Local 880, 3/29/91; "What Local 880 Wants for the IDOA and DORS Budgets;" all in box 7, folder 1, 880 Records. Included in this folder are copies of proposed legislation and letters to legislators.

72. On DORS, see Keith Kelleher, "A History of SEIU Local 880, 1983–2005," unpublished manuscript (2005), in authors' possession.

73. *See* Brooks, "New Turf for Organizing," 53.

74. Memo from Pat Ford to Bob Muscat, May 1, 1996, box 9, folder, "SEIU, Local 616—Homecare Worker's Center Project," Tim Sampson Papers, Labor Archives, San Francisco State University.

75. Marta Russell, "California Scheming," *The Disability Rag* (November/December, 1993): 7.

76. For example, William Endicott, "Emergency Aid Okd for Aged, Blind, Disabled," *Los Angeles Times* (January 23, 1975); "Governor Changes Mind: Bill to Pay In-Home Attendants Signed," *Los Angeles Times* (July 20, 1983).

77. Julie Murray Brenman to Debra Newman, Memorandum on Wages for IHSS Providers, October 24, 1996; "Confidential: Labor Negotiations Information" to San Francisco IHSS Public Authority Governing Body Members from Staff on Collective Bargaining Team, December 10, 1996, Karen Sherr Papers, in authors' possession.

78. "Californian Dreams," *Shadow Economy and Trades Unions* (Duisburg: WAZ-Druck, March 2000), 26.

79. "The Campaign to Improve the In-Home Supportive Services Program," Sherr Papers; Peter Fimrite, "Home Health-Care Workers Get Raise," *San Francisco Chronicle* (December 28, 1995); "San Francisco Homecare Contract," *News from the Home Front* (Fall, 1997); Karen Sherr interview with E. Boris, July 3, 2009; Candace Howes quoted in Eileen Boris, Gwon Chang, Linda Delph, Ruth Matthias, and Carol Zabin., "Workforce Needs in California's Homecare System," *CPRC Briefing Paper,* May 2004, 2. See also Howes' chart, "California IHSS Homecare Workers Wages and Benefits Negotiated with SEIU and United Domestic Workers union," May 31, 2004, in authors' possession.

80. Interview with Danny Villasenor and interview with Rosie Byers, both by Boris and Klein, United Healthcare Workers-West San Francisco Office, September 8, 2008.

81. Breakfast Meeting with Home Care Workers, interview with Lola Young by Boris and Klein, September 6, 2008, United Healthcare Workers-West Leadership Convention, San Jose, CA.

CHAPTER EIGHT

Solvents of Solidarity: Political Economy, Collective Action, and the Crisis of Organized Labor, 1968–2005

Joseph A. McCartin

As the twenty-first century began, there was no denying that the American labor movement was in crisis. Private sector unionization rates had dropped below ten percent, lower than at any point since the early twentieth century. The once powerful industrial unions that had emerged during the labor upheavals of the 1930s were in decline, or, in the case of United Automobile Workers, even struggling for survival amid the economic crisis and restructuring of the auto industry. The hopes that had animated the labor movement following the 1995 election of AFL-CIO president John Sweeney and his New Voices slate, which had promised to reverse labor's slide, had begun to dim.

The sense of crisis in the labor movement became clear in the aftermath of the disappointing 2004 presidential election, which saw President George W. Bush win a second term in office. Those election returns brought long-simmering conflicts within the labor movement to the surface and led to calls for a change in leadership and direction for the AFL-CIO. Within months of the election several of the federation's largest unions, including the Service Employees International Union (SEIU), the Teamsters, UNITE-HERE, and the United Food and Commercial Workers, came together behind a set of demands for the reorganization of the AFL-CIO. Calling themselves the Change to Win coalition, these unions alleged that labor had failed to keep pace with changes in the economy and to do enough to promote new organizing. They demanded that the AFL-CIO push smaller unions to merge with larger ones in overlapping jurisdictions, compel unions to step up their organizing operations, and consolidate the governance of the AFL-CIO in a smaller executive committee in which the largest unions would hold sway. According to SEIU president Andy Stern, it was time for labor to "confront its own underlying structural impediments and those of its affiliates." No longer could labor tolerate having 13 unions in the airline industry, which did not coordinate their actions, 12 unions competing to organize hotel workers, and 30 unions that fought to organize the nation's health care workers, Stern argued. Such overlap "created confusion, unnecessary competition, and conflicting approaches to the same employer." It was time to restructure the labor movement for the era of globalization, Stern and his allies proclaimed.[1] When the majority of the AFL-CIO's affiliates rejected Stern's plan, arguing among other things that it threatened to override the autonomy and democratic governance of the smaller unions, the dissidents broke away to form their own federation called Change to Win.

The founding of Change to Win (CtW) excited many labor observers. Some hailed the new federation as a sign of labor's revival and compared it to the Congress of Industrial Organization of the 1930s.[2] But the CtW did not enjoy the quick take-off that had marked the CIO's birth. While SEIU, CtW's leading force, continued to thrive in the first years after the creation of the new federation, CtW itself sputtered. Only a year into the life of CtW even Stern was forced to admit, "We were overly ambitious at the start about what we could do."[3]

The fact that CtW soon found itself confronting the same difficulty organizing reinforced a growing consensus within the labor movement regarding labor's crisis, a consensus that transcended the factional divisions that had surfaced with the CtW/AFL-CIO conflict. Despite the public dissension that existed between these two rival factions, there was actually much agreement among union leaders about the need for unions to devote more resources to organizing and to win changes in America's ineffectual labor law that would enable workers to organize unions more easily. As overall union density declined to 12 percent, leaders of AFL-CIO and CtW unions alike spoke in quite similar terms. Even as Andy Stern bemoaned the fact that "every single day that I worked with the AFL-CIO it represented a smaller and smaller portion of the workforce," AFL-CIO president John Sweeney agreed with Stern about the need to make new organizing labor's "number one priority."[4] And both Stern and Sweeney strongly supported passage of the Employee Free Choice Act (EFCA), a bill which promised to reinvigorate labor laws that employers had long since learned to evade, ignore, and exploit to their own advantage.

Unions began mobilizing strong support behind the effort to enact EFCA prior to the 2005 split, and they remained united on the need to pass the bill even after the CtW broke from the AFL-CIO. The bill promised to remedy the obvious weaknesses of U.S. labor law through three key legal provisions that union leaders of both federations believed were critical. One provision would guarantee workers in each workplace covered by federal labor law the right to have a union certified as their representative if a majority of them signed authorization cards asking for representation. The "card-check" provision would free workers from the necessity of going through a certification election supervised by the National Labor Relations Board (NLRB)—something workers would otherwise have to do unless an employer voluntarily agreed to accept the showing of cards as sufficient for the certification of the bargaining agent. A second provision would substantially increase the penalties that could be levied by the NLRB against employers who commit unfair labor practices in an effort to deny workers their right to organize. A third provision of the act provided for the intervention of an arbitrator when both sides are unable to reach an agreement on their first contract.[5] That the leaders of the AFL-CIO and CtW, for all of their differences on other issues, continued to work together for the passage of EFCA after 2005, emphasizes the degree to which all labor leaders, no matter their federation allegiances, had come to see the need to jump-start organizing and reform labor law as the keys to labor's revival.

But whether reforming labor law and marshaling more union resources in the service of new organizing would be enough to reverse labor's decline became less clear as the first decade of the new century drew to a close. The history of organized labor's decline between 1968 and 2005 suggests that the influence of labor law or the structure of unions or labor federations may have been much less important than a structural shift in the American political economy which made the construction of workers' solidarity more difficult to achieve than at any time since the rise of mass production industries at the turn of the last century. The chapter that follows attempts to move beyond an examination of labor's decline as a question of dropping union density caused by flawed labor laws or union structures and reframes it as a problem of eroding solidarity, a problem acutely revealed by the near disappearance of the strike as weapon of organized labor. The chapter analyzes how that problem developed in the years since the 1960s, and suggests what besides the enactment of labor law reform or new union structures will be required if unions are to return as a powerful force in the U.S. workplace. While recognizing that there is a rich scholarly discourse on culture and its influences on workers' expressions of solidarity, this chapter focuses on the emergence of structural impediments to collective action and argues that ultimately these have been the determinative factors in shaping labor's recent history.[6]

A Crisis of Union Density and the Right to Organize

Of course the most widely cited measure of union decline is union density, or the percentage of eligible workers who are organized. Density figures do indeed provide unambiguous evidence of labor's decline since the 1960s: between 1968 and 2004, union density dropped by more than half (see Table 9.1). What is ominous about these figures is their relentless downward spiral. Only once in that 36-year span, in 1979, did union density rise from one year to the next. Pointing in an unbroken downward slope, union decline transcended recessions and recoveries, Republican and Democratic administrations alike.

Perhaps in part because the decline of union density occurred with such apparent inexorability during the 1970s and after, scholars who sought to explain this phenomenon tended to focus their attention on two variables whose significance seemed difficult to dispute: employer resistance to unionization and the inadequacies of labor law in protecting workers against that resistance. As early as 1984, leading scholars began to point to effective employer resistance as an explanation for labor's decline.[7] Over time, a growing number of analysts argued for the significance of a

Table 9.1 Non-Agricultural Employment and Union Membership Density, 1968–2004

Year	Non-Agricultural Wage and Salary Workforce* (In thousands)	Percentage of Non-Agricultural Workforce Claiming Membership in Unions**
1968	64,512	28.2
1969	66,719	28.0
1970	68,771	27.8
1971	68,807	27.2
1972	70,695	26.6
1973	72,903	26.6
1974	75,810	26.2
1975	74,994	24.6
1976	76,674	24.5
1977	79,314	24.1
1978	83,073	23.4
1979	86,440	24.4
1980	88,148	23.3
1981	87,983	21.7
1982	87,775	21.0
1983	86,764	20.3
1984	90,416	19.1
1985	93,555	18.2
1986	96,327	17.7
1987	98,100	17.3
1988	101,065	17.0
1989	103,158	16.6
1990	105,410	16.3
1991	104,280	16.3
1992	104,706	16.0
1993	105,441	16.0
1994	108,098	15.7
1995	110,646	15.1
1996	111,267	14.7
1997	113,981	14.2
1998	117,028	14.1
1999	119,627	14.0
2000	123,291	13.6
2001	124,889	13.4
2002	123,395	13.2
2003	124,501	12.9
2004	125,433	12.5

* Source: Bureau of Labor Statistics, http://data.bls.gov (accessed February 25, 2006).
** Sources: Barry T. Hirsch, David A. Macpherson, and Wayne G. Vroman, "Estimates of Union Density by State," *Monthly Labor Review* (July 2001): 54; and Bureau of Labor Statistics, "Union Members in 2005" USDL 06–99, January 20, 2006. At: http://www.bls.gov/news.release/pdf/union2.pdf.

robust union avoidance industry that arose in the 1970s and after. This industry included management consulting firms such the Burke Group, law firms such as Jackson Lewis that specialize in defeating organizing drives, and industrial psychologists such as Charles L. Hughes, the founder of the Dallas-based Center for Values Research, who advise companies on ways to discourage union thinking among their employees. As the leading student of this industry, John Logan, argues, "the principal actors in the union avoidance industry are not, strictly speaking, 'new.' " Yet over the past three decades participants in this industry have not only multiplied in number, they have perfected union resistance techniques with devastating results for labor.[8]

Successful union resistance was aided by the weaknesses of U.S. labor law. When Congress amended the Wagner Act in 1947 by passing the Taft-Hartley Act over the veto of President Harry S. Truman, a number of provisions were written into law that proved disastrous for labor over decades. Among other things, the Taft-Hartley Act recognized employers' right to speak out against the unionization of their workers, gave states the power to ban union shop agreements, and gave workers the right to decertify unions already established in their workplaces. Although such provisions led labor to characterize Taft-Hartley from the outset as a "slave labor act," in fact it took decades before the full importance of these changes became visible.[9]

By the end of the century employers were taking advantage of the law to engage in union resistance campaigns so fierce as to earn the condemnation of Human Rights Watch and other international organizations.[10] One 2009 study of U.S. employers' tactics cataloged a litany of abuses. It found that in 57 percent of union elections employers illegally threaten to close facilities if workers choose union representation. In 34 percent of unionization campaigns, employers illegally discharge workers for actively taking part in union organizing. And in 63 percent of cases, supervisors use one-on-one meetings to discourage workers from choosing union representation. Survey data also indicates that employer opposition to unions intensified and became harder edged in the new millennium. The incidence of cases where employers use ten or more union resistance tactics in a single campaign more than doubled between 1999 and 2003. At the same time employers proved less likely to use rewards such as unscheduled raises, favors, or the introduction of employee involvement programs in an effort to win worker loyalty.[11] In many ways, the nation's largest private sector employer, Wal-Mart, led the way in union resistance.[12]

The increasing aggression by employers led to a sharp decline of organizing through the National Labor Relations Board (NLRB). In 1970, 276,353 workers won union representation as a result of 7,733 union representation elections conducted by the board. By 2005, only 64,502 workers won representation through NLRB elections. Even more significant, the number of union elections held dropped by 72 percent from the 1970 figure to a mere 2,137: unions were increasingly giving up on the system as employers and the union avoidance industry perfected ways of frustrating unionization campaigns that relied on the NLRB.[13]

Survey evidence indicated that millions of workers would unionize if they felt the law would protect their efforts.[14] Thus, labor and its allies focused on passing EFCA in an effort to repair the broken NLRB system. Previous efforts to amend the Taft-Hartley Act in 1965–66, and 1977–78 died due to filibusters in the U.S. Senate. Because the filibuster has proven to be such an effective tactic to block labor law reform, the chances of passing EFCA seemed tenuous even after the 2008 election of President Barack Obama, who supported the bill. Yet it is by no means certain that if labor's supporters enacted a version of labor law that included such features as card-check union recognition, it would be enough to reverse labor's decline. This point becomes clearer if one considers the history of another measure of worker solidarity, the strike. Examined through the lens of the strike, the problem of finding solutions to labor's crisis appears even more daunting.

A Crisis of Collective Action: The Disappearing Strike

Looking at the history of the strike reframes the narrative of labor's decline in some surprising ways. While the decline of union density between the 1955 and 2005 appeared relentlessly predictable from year to year, such was not the case for the strike. Strike activity in the United States did not wane consistently over time like union density. Rather, the frequency of strikes plummeted rapidly and unexpectedly.[15] The timing and circumstances surrounding that development reveal a great deal about the crucial role that shifts in political economy played in undermining the conditions conducive to workers' construction of solidarity.

From the end of World War II through the late 1970s, the strike served as an effective weapon for U.S. workers. Between 1947 and 1979, there was only one year (1963) in which the U.S. Bureau of Labor Statistics registered fewer than 200 major work stoppages (defined as events involving at least 1,000 workers for at least 24 hours). Moreover, the number of work stoppages held remarkably steady over this period. Overall the 1950s were the most strike-prone decade in post-World War II American history. During that decade, the United States averaged 351 major work stoppages annually (i.e. strikes or lockouts involving at least 1,000 workers and lasting for at least 24 hours) and strike militancy hit a peak in 1952 at 470 work stoppages involving 2,746,000 workers. Though not quite as high, strike rates remained healthy for the 1960s and 1970s, averaging 286 per year over this period. Moreover, during the middle ten years of those decades, the years from 1965 to 1974, U.S. workers were every bit as militant as they had been in the 1950s, averaging 344.4 major stoppages annually.[16]

Not only did the measure of strike activity hold fairly steady during the 1960s and 1970s overall, in the public sector strike activity actually grew rapidly in this period. There were only 36 total strikes of any size staged by public sector workers in the United States in 1960. That number rocketed up to 412 by 1970 and to 536 by 1980.[17]

Remarkably, during the years before 1980, the propensity of workers to strike appeared to be unconnected to union density. In the public sector, strike rates rose along with rising union density, as might be expected. But in the private sector strike rates held steady or witnessed slight increases even as union density figures continued to sink.

Because strike militancy had appeared so healthy though the 1960s and 1970s, it was impossible to predict how rapidly strikes would decline in the following two decades. After 1981, the BLS never registered more than 100 major work stoppages in any year.[18] During the 1980s, the annual average of major work stoppages plummeted to 83; during the 1990s the annual average slipped to 34. Between 1980 and 2004, work stoppages dropped rapidly to the point that strike activity in the early twenty-first century was but a fraction of the level that prevailed during the 1950s. While the United States averaged more than 350 major work stoppages annually in the 1950s, that annual average fell to under 25 in the first five years of the new century (see Table 9.2).

From time to time, occasional union victories—such as the 15-day nationwide strike by the Teamsters against United Parcel Service (UPS) in 1997, in which the union won full time employment for 10,000 part-time workers—led some observers to predict the return of labor militancy. But there was no turnaround. The decline of the strike, which had come on far more rapidly and with much less predictability than the decline of union membership, continued to gather momentum after the turn of the millennium.[19]

Table 9.2 Work Stoppages Involving 1,000 workers or More, 1948–2004

YEAR	Number of Work Stoppages	Number of Workers* (Thousands)	Worker/Days Idle** (Thousands)	Percent of Estimated Total Working Time Lost
1948	245	1,435	26,127	0.22
1949	262	2,537	43,420	0.38
1950	424	1,698	30,390	0.26
1951	415	1,462	15,070	0.12
1952	470	2,746	48,820	0.38
1953	437	1,623	18,130	0.14
1954	265	1,075	16,630	0.13
1955	363	2,055	21,180	0.16
1956	287	1,370	26,840	0.20
1957	279	887	10,340	0.07
1958	332	1,587	17,900	0.13
1959	245	1,381	60,850	0.43
1960	222	896	13,260	0.09
1961	195	1,031	10,140	0.07
1962	211	793	11,760	0.08
1963	181	512	10,020	0.07
1964	246	1,183	16,220	0.11
1965	268	999	15,140	0.10
1966	321	1,300	16,000	0.10
1967	381	2,192	31,320	0.18
1968	392	1,855	35,367	0.20

(Continued)

Table 9.2 Cont'd

YEAR	Number of Work Stoppages	Number of Workers* (Thousands)	Worker/Days Idle** (Thousands)	Percent of Estimated Total Working Time Lost
1969	412	1,576	29,397	0.16
1970	381	2,468	52,761	0.29
1971	298	2,516	35,538	0.19
1972	250	975	16,764	0.09
1973	317	1,400	16,260	0.08
1974	424	1,796	31,809	0.16
1975	235	965	17,563	0.09
1976	231	1,519	23,962	0.12
1977	298	1,212	21,258	0.10
1978	219	1,006	23,774	0.11
1979	235	1,021	20,409	0.09
1980	187	795	20,844	0.09
1981	145	729	16,908	0.07
1982	96	656	9,061	0.04
1983	81	909	17,461	0.08
1984	62	376	8,499	0.04
1985	54	324	7,079	0.03
1986	69	533	11,891	0.05
1987	46	174	4,481	0.02
1988	40	118	4,381	0.02
1989	51	452	16,996	0.07
1990	44	185	5,926	0.02
1991	40	392	4,584	0.02
1992	35	364	3,989	0.01
1993	35	182	3,981	0.01
1994	45	322	5,020	0.02
1995	31	192	5,771	0.02
1996	37	273	4,889	0.02
1997	29	339	4,497	0.01
1998	34	387	5,116	0.02
1999	17	73	1,996	0.01
2000	39	394	20,419	0.06
2001	29	99	1,151	#
2002	19	46	660	#
2003	14	129	4,091	0.01
2004	17	171	3,344	0.01

* Number of workers involved includes only those workers who participated in work stoppages that began in the calendar year. Workers are counted more than once if they are involved in more than one stoppage during the reference period. Numbers are rounded to the nearest thousand.
** Days idle include all stoppages in effect during the reference period. For work stoppages that are still ongoing at the end of the calendar year, only those days of idleness in the calendar year are counted.
# Less than .005.
SOURCE: Source: U.S. Bureau of Labor Statistics http://www.bls.gov/news.release/wkstp.t01.htm (accessed July 1, 2005).

Why Strikes Declined: The Restructuring of the American Political Economy

Unlike the graph that traced declining union membership, which remained constant in its downward arc over more than three decades, it was possible to pinpoint the period when the incidence of strikes sharply diminished in the United States. The turning point came in the years between 1979 and 1983. During that brief span, the number of recorded major work stoppages declined by an astonishing 73 percent, never again recovering to pre-1979 levels. Indeed, after 1984 the strike activity of U.S. workers never again reached even 30 percent of what it had been in 1979, and by 2000 the number of major work stoppages was only 17 percent of what it had been when the slippage began 21 years earlier.

This turning point is significant. Looking more closely at the larger forces that came together in this period has the potential for revealing important clues not only regarding the reasons for the disappearance of the strike, but for labor's decline in general. In retrospect it seems clear that between 1979 and 1983 a remarkable confluence of events and forces occurred, suddenly altering the terrain upon which workers and unions operated in ways that made striking successfully far more difficult than ever before. During these years structural economic and political changes came together in a way that devastated worker militancy. Specifically, the intersection of six developments proved crucial: the economic turmoil of the late 1970s; the growing phenomenon of deregulation which undermined the stability of workers in many highly unionized industries; the first effects of a new stage in the process of globalization made possible by the shipping container, the satellite, and the computer; a wave of plant closings that foretold the accelerating phenomenon of de-industrialization and signaled the rise of a service economy where work stoppages were more difficult to stage; the resurgence of conservatism in the face of economic crisis; and the spreading use of striker replacements from the public to the private sector. Each of these developments demands brief examination.

Economically, the years 1979–83, were the most difficult the United States faced between the Great Depression and the end of the century. The combined impact of inflation and unemployment—a dual phenomenon that economists called "stagflation"—reached its peak in the middle of this period, as inflation rose to a post-World War II high of 13.5 percent and unemployment rose to 7.2 percent. This produced a combined inflation-unemployment "misery index" of 20.5 (a 6.8 point increase over 1979). This sudden dose of inflation was in part intentional, coming about due to the policies of the Federal Reserve Bank of the United States, under the leadership of its chairman, Paul Volcker. Appointed to his post by Democratic President Jimmy Carter in 1979, Volcker was determined to control inflation, which had hovered between 5.8 and 7.6 percent in the three years prior to his appointment, and to protect the U.S. dollar, which was coming under increasing international economic pressure. In order to reach his objectives, Volcker intended to induce an economic slowdown, which he did by raising the interest rates charged by the Federal Reserve to a postwar high, driving up the inflation rate nationally, and triggering a recession. Volcker's economic shock therapy was followed quickly by the recession he believed was necessary to throttle inflation.[20] Unemployment hit a post-World War II high of 10.8 percent in 1982. The economic slowdown soon subdued inflation. By 1984 it was down to 1.9 percent. Yet it was not until 1987 that unemployment finally receded below the 7 percent mark.[21]

Yet aggregate unemployment figures do not adequately reveal the extent of insecurity experienced by workers in this period. During 1981–83, 12.3 percent of the U.S. workforce experienced at least one involuntary job loss. And the job loss rate for blue-collar workers was 21.2 percent, almost three times the rate of the next most affected group, sales and administration workers.[22]

The insecurity experienced by workers during this recession was further exacerbated by structural changes in the U.S. economy that were introduced by policies of deregulation in the late 1970s and early 1980s. The Airline Deregulation Act of 1978 was the first of several efforts to remove regulations from employment sectors where unions had become strong (in part due to such regulatory structures). Encouraged by economist Alfred Kahn, who argued that deregulation would promote competition, lower airfares, and lead to economic growth, a Democratic Congress passed the legislation which in turn was signed by Democratic president Jimmy Carter. Kahn proved right about airfares. They were driven down by 30 percent between 1976 and 1990. But the act also destabilized employment in the industry as the deregulated environment created opportunities for unprincipled corporate raiders like Frank Lorenzo, who took over Continental Airlines and Eastern Airlines in the 1980s. Lorenzo filed for bankruptcy in order to abrogate his companies' contracts with unions. His tactics soon pressured other airlines to demand concessions from their unions.[23]

Airline deregulation was quickly followed by the deregulation of interstate trucking. The Motor Carrier Act of 1980 brought a new level of competition to an industry where profit margins could be razor thin. Under the provisions of the act, the number of licensed motor carriers soared over the next decade. Competition reduced costs, as predicted. But in order to remain competitive trucking companies pressured workers to absorb more of the costs of the industry and the Teamster Master Freight Agreement, which had once provided stability in the industry, collapsed under the strain of the new competitive forces.[24]

A third development whose effects became visible during the critical years of 1979–83 was the onset of a new stage of globalization made possible in part by the containerization of shipping. Malcolm McLean, a trucking magnate from North Carolina is credited with shipping the first container—it was transported from New Jersey to Texas in 1956. But the first international shipping via container vessel between the United States and Europe did not come until 1966; shipping between the United States and Asia via container was not under way until 1968. Yet once in place, containerization transformed world shipping and the global distribution of manufacturing facilities within the space of a decade. By 1980, 73 percent of goods between the United States and Europe and 80 percent of goods shipped between the

United States and Asia moved via container. Containerization lowered prices for shipping and increased the speed by which goods could be loaded, offloaded, and trucked to their final destinations. By doing so it began to shrink the globe, especially when supplemented with satellite communication and computerization, making it easier for U.S. companies to send production offshore and import manufactured goods into the United States. The United States did not experience its first postwar trade deficit until 1971. But trade deficits soon rocketed upward from 6 billion in 1976 to 109 billion by 1984. By the early 1980s it was clear that a new era of globalization had begun.[25]

The containerization of shipping and the growth of imports into the U.S. economy hit one longtime union stronghold, the nation's manufacturing industries, especially hard. By 1982, economists Barry Bluestone and Bennett Harrison were documenting what they called the "deindustrialization of America."[26] Although basic industries such as steel and auto had begun shedding jobs as early as the 1950s, this process seemed to accelerate at the end of the 1970s.[27] The U.S. economy lost 2.4 million manufacturing jobs between 1979 and 1983. To some extent these job losses resulted from a monetary policy pursued by the Reagan administration, which had the effect of favoring imports over exports. President Ronald Reagan's Secretary of the Treasury Donald Regan, like Chairman of the Federal Reserve Volcker, sought to strengthen the U.S. dollar in the early 1980s. They pursued this policy with tremendous success in the early 1980s. The value of the U.S. dollar against a broad mix of international currencies jumped by 35 percent between January 1981 and November 1982. The strong dollar gave U.S. foreign policy greater leverage, which the Reagan administration sought. But the strong dollar made imports cheaper to American consumer and U.S. exports more expensive to foreign buyers. The steel and auto industries suffered especially heavy losses as a result. Steel witnessed a wave of plant closings beginning with the shuttering of Youngstown Sheet & Tube in September 1977. Meanwhile, the auto industry shed 100,000 jobs between 1979 and 1982.[28] As manufacturing jobs disappeared, employers not surprisingly found that they could pay less to secure the labor of workers who feared that their jobs might be next to go. The real average hourly wage in manufacturing dipped by five percent between 1979 and 1982. The effects of this decline rippled across the economy. As the historically higher wages in manufacturing declined, hourly wages in the service sector dropped even more during this period.[29]

As manufacturing jobs declined, the importance of the service sector as a trend-setter in labor relations rose accordingly. In contrast to industrial workers, service sector workers were more likely to be part-time, less likely to be organized in unions, and less prone to strikes. The food service and retail sectors accounted for few strikes, and the corporate behemoths such as McDonald's or Wal-Mart that emerged in these sectors remained union free and immune to work stoppages.[30]

As the political economy shifted, increasing insecurity gripped nearly all American workers in the late 1970s and early 1980s, even those who had been fortunate enough to enjoy union representation. The instability helped energize the conservative movement even as it pushed Democrats in the direction of neo-liberalism and a harder-line stance against former allies in the labor movement. In retrospect the rise of conservatism seems to have been over-determined. But it was not experienced that way. The Congressional elections of 1974 saw the labor movement achieve its greatest success ever in a mid-term election, as the candidates it endorsed helped put the Democratic Party in solid control of both the U.S. House and Senate. With high hopes, unions helped elect Democratic President Jimmy Carter in 1976. But the Carter administration turned out to be a bitter disappointment, in part because the nation's economic tribulations pushed politics further in a conservative direction in the late 1970s.

Jimmy Carter won the presidency amid economic turmoil, when the verities of liberal political economy seemed to be turned on their heads by the phenomenon of stagflation. To fight the inflationary component of this economic malaise, Carter was determined to control inflation and the growth of the federal budget. Helping reinforce this tendency was a growing "tax revolt" that was brewing across the country in the mid-1970s. Because real wages began to stagnate after 1973 even as prices (including the costs of state, local, and national governments) rose, tax bills began to feel higher to most working families. This bred resentment against taxes among a growing number of working-class voters. Politicians soon learned to manipulate this resentment effectively. Voters in California enacted a radical tax cut in June 1978 called Proposition 13, spawning similar initiatives in many states. The popularity of the antitax movement led many elected Democratic leaders at all levels of government, to join President Carter in embracing tax reduction and balanced budgets.[31]

The resulting political climate in the late 1970s introduced deep tensions between the labor movement and its former allies in the Democratic Party. Nowhere was this clearer than in relations between the public sector union movement and its erstwhile allies. Organized labor's greatest source of optimism in the 1970s stemmed from the swift rise of public sector unions. Between 1955 and 1975, the number of government workers organized in unions had grown ten-fold. Democratic allies had facilitated this growth: Democratic big city mayors, such as Robert Wagner Jr of New York and Joseph Clark of Philadelphia, had begun collectively bargaining with municipal employees in the 1950s; Democratic governor Gaylord Nelson of Wisconsin signed the first statewide collective bargaining law for public workers in 1959, and Democratic president John F. Kennedy issued Executive Order 10988, introducing collective bargaining into the federal government in 1962. During the economic boom of the 1950s and 1960s, the public supported the demands of often-underpaid government workers in struggles such as the 1968 Memphis sanitation strike. However, the shifting economy of the 1970s altered the terrain on which public sector unions operated.[32]

In the mid-to-late 1970s public sector unions confronted less sympathetic Democrats at every level of government. Mayor Maynard Jackson of Atlanta provided one example. Jackson had won election as the first black mayor of a big southern city in 1973, in part due to the goodwill he had won as an advocate for underpaid black municipal employees while serving as Atlanta's deputy mayor in the early 1970s. But as chief executive of a city that was hard pressed by the fiscal climate of the mid-1970s, Jackson distanced himself from his former allies among municipal workers. When Atlanta sanitation workers struck for higher wages in 1977, Jackson took a hard line. Refusing to negotiate on the wage issue, Jackson threatened to replace sanitation strikers if they did not return to work within 48 hours. When the workers balked at Jackson's threat, he issued dismissal notices and the strike quickly collapsed. Nor was Jackson alone in taking a tough stance against public employees in the late 1970s. Fellow Democratic mayors Ed Koch in New York, Dianne Feinstein in San Francisco, and Wes Uhlman of Seattle all confronted municipal unions in this period and reaped political rewards for "standing up to" public workers' demands. On the federal level, meanwhile, Jimmy Carter disappointed public sector workers by withdrawing his support for a liberalization of the Hatch Act (which constrained the political activities of federal workers), consistently endorsing lower pay increases for federal employees than were recommended by the government's pay agent, and signing the Civil Service Reform Act of 1978, which many federal employees saw as a weak alternative to legislation which they had hoped would grant them greater power and autonomy in collective bargaining.[33]

Squeezed by wage-sapping inflation on the one hand and increasingly stringent budgetary realities on the other, public workers responded with greater militancy in the late 1970s even when their union leaders counseled patience. "I urge you to think twice before calling any strike," Lester Asher, general counsel for the Service Employees International Union, told a public workers' conference in November 1978. But government workers facing inflation and stagnating pay were not inclined to accept such advice. In 1979 an all-time record 593 government strikes involved a quarter of a million government workers and resulted in nearly three million idle workdays. In the first six months of 1980, the strike rate broke another record. A vicious cycle had emerged in which fiscally pressed governments resisted union demands, leading government workers to launch unpopular strikes, which in turn led politicians into more confrontations with unions.[34]

It is in this context that we must understand the most significant strike of late twentieth century, the 1981 walkout of the Professional Air Traffic Controllers Organization (PATCO) against the administration of President Ronald Reagan. PATCO had emerged in 1968 in response to the introduction of collective bargaining in the federal service. By the early 1970s, it won recognition as the official bargaining agent of the controllers. In the mid-1970s PATCO was able to enhance its stature among federal workers' unions by getting the Civil Service Commission to accede to a pay-boosting job classification upgrade for many of its members. But by the late 1970s relations between PATCO and the Carter administration broke down as controllers' demands for further improvements in pay and working conditions ran up against the fiscal restraint of the Carter administration. In frustration, PATCO endorsed the election of Ronald Reagan in 1980 in hopes that a Reagan administration would meet the controllers' demands. Reagan won election, but PATCO's hopes were quickly disappointed in the 1981 contract negotiations. The union responded by calling for a strike on August 3, 1981, an action forbidden by federal law.

Ronald Reagan's handling of the PATCO strike proved devastating for labor. Reagan refused to negotiate with strikers and threatened to dismiss them if they did not return to work within 48 hours. More than 11,000 controllers—some three-quarters of the workforce handling the nation's air traffic—lost their jobs when they refused to heed Reagan's warning. The AFL-CIO protested the firings, and some called for a national mobilization on behalf of the PATCO strikers. But a majority of the public supported Reagan's move, and no mass mobilization materialized. Within weeks it became clear that the strike had been broken.[35]

The PATCO strike had an immediate effect on public sector labor relations. Union leaders worried that Reagan's action would encourage other chief executives to confront unions. "[N]ow we will have thousands of little Ronald Reagans across the country in every town saying, 'Fire them,' whenever public employees confront them in a labor dispute," one union leader predicted.[36] Fearing that their strikes would backfire as badly as the PATCO strike, public sector workers scaled back their militancy markedly in the early 1980s. According to one careful study, the number of government workers' strikes dropped by 40 percent between 1980 and 1982; the number of workdays lost due to those strikes fell by 50 percent.[37] In New York State, the apparent impact of the PATCO strike was clear. During the years 1974–81, New York averaged 20 public sector strikes per year; in a similar span of years after the PATCO strike the average plummeted to a mere two strikes per year.[38]

The impact of the PATCO strike on the private sector may have been even more profound, for that conflict, more than any other event, helped popularize the tactic of striker replacement, the sixth crucial development of the years 1979–84. Since the U.S. Supreme Court's 1938 decision in the case of *NLRB v. Mackay Radio & Telegraph Company* it was understood that private sector employers had the right to replace striking workers in disputes involving economic issues.[39] However, in the years after World War II it had not been common for private sector employers to attempt to break strikes by hiring permanent replacement workers. Between 1950 and 1980, there was only one documented case of employers attempting to permanently replace strikers per 76 major work stoppages. Authors Charles R. Perry, Andrew M. Kramer, and Thomas J. Schneider of the University of Pennsylvania's Wharton School, observed that replacing strikers was not "institutionally popular" in the corporate community; most employers did not have the political will to break strikes before PATCO. But in the years after 1981 that changed. Perry and his collaborators pro-duced a popular pamphlet in 1982 called *Operating During Strikes* that took its cue from Reagan's action and encouraged private employers to follow the president's example.[40] Many employers did just that; employers were ten times more likely to use permanent replacement workers in the decade after PATCO. Between 1982 and 1989, prominent employers including Phelps-Dodge, Greyhound, International Paper, and Hormel hired permanent replacements to break strikes. So too did many smaller employers.[41] When President Bill Clinton endorsed legislation that would block employers from permanently replacing striking workers, the legislation failed to clear a 1994 Senate filibuster.

Why U.S. Workers Did Not Recover the Capacity to Strike

It is not hard to see why the years 1979–84 provided the turning point for the use of the strike in the United States. The confluence of several developments in those crucial years dramatically weakened the strike weapon. But the incidence of major strikes continued to plummet through the 1990s and into the new century. What prevented workers from regaining the capacity to wage successful strikes after this tumultuous transitional period? The answer to this question involves more than the failure to secure legislation banning permanent replacement of strikers. Nor can it be explained solely by reference to a sudden upsurge in anti-union culture, for anti-unionism's cultural influence has hardly been confined to the recent period in American history.[42] Rather, at least three trends in the U.S. political economy during the years since 1981 fostered a climate that made waging and winning strikes increasingly difficult. These were the expansion of globalization and free trade, the first negative effects of which had become visible for many workers in the 1970s; the stagnation in income growth which made workers less able than ever to take on the costs and sacrifices involved in waging successful strikes; and the spread of neoliberal policies of de-regulation and privatization, which further increased workers' insecurity.

The first of those factors, the growing impact of free trade in the global economy, was increasingly evident in the last two decades of the twentieth century. During these years, the U.S. government relentlessly pursued a free trade agenda. That push enjoyed bipartisan support: the Republican administrations of Ronald Reagan and George H. W. Bush, and the Democratic administration of Bill Clinton differed little in their approach to trade questions. Indeed, it was the Clinton administration that ushered in the two most important developments in U.S. trade policy in the late twentieth century: the North American Free Trade Agreement (NAFTA) which Clinton signed over the objections of his union supporters in 1994 and the free-trade promoting World Trade Organization (WTO), which the United States joined in 1995, much to the chagrin of labor and environmental activists.

The impact of globalization and trade liberalization was not unique to the United States during these years. [43] But arguably no workers were more vulnerable to the pressures of globalization than those in the United States. No industrialized nation was as accessible to import-laden container ships, nor did any other advanced nation directly abut a low-waged labor market along a thousand mile border, as the United States did with Mexico. Between 1994 and 2004 alone, AFL-CIO economists estimate, the U.S. lost 900,000 jobs as a direct result of NAFTA.[44] While trade liberalization promoted growth in some sectors of the U.S. economy, in general unionized jobs were lost and lower waged, non-union jobs added since the United States began dismantling its trade barriers. Evidence indicates that workers became increasingly fearful of their jobs in the new economic climate. After 1979, measures of both job stability (the incidence of workers' long-term employment) and job security (workers' ability to retain jobs when their performance has been satisfactory) declined markedly. No doubt this growing insecurity helped erode the level of strike militancy among U.S. workers: workers' feared that walkouts might cost them their jobs.[45]

As jobs grew less secure in the era of globalization, they also became less remunerative. Real wage growth stagnated for most U.S. workers between the early 1970s and the mid-1990s, providing a second powerful force that undermined workers' capacity to strike. Average hourly wages rose by only 6 cents between 1973 and 1995.[46] As income ceased growing, the personal savings dropped from 7.9 percent of aggregate income in 1980 to 4.2 percent in 1990.[47] Meanwhile personal indebtedness as a share of annual income rose from 71 percent in 1979 to 103 percent in 1999. Finally, and not surprisingly, the rate of consumer bankruptcies per 1,000 adults more than tripled between 1980 and 1997.[48] It is not difficult to apprehend the impact of these changes on workers' ability to strike. Since most state laws limit or prohibit the extension of public unemployment benefits to striking workers, and since unions generally pay but a small fraction of their normal incomes to strikers in the form of strike benefits, strikes involve a considerable financial risk for workers who may be increasingly less able to shoulder that risk. And while workers might have been tempted to strike to improve their lot, their sense of the futility of striking seems to have overridden that temptation.

The spread of neoliberal economic policies was a third factor that tended to undermine workers' capacity to act collectively. Deregulation was extended to more unionized sectors of the economy in the 1990s, including print and telecommunications industries where unions had held a strong foothold. Signing the Telecommunications Reform Act of 1996, President Clinton promised that the bill would "help to create an open marketplace where competition and innovation can move as quick as light."[49] The legislation certainly introduced rapid changes in the industry, but often at the expense of job stability for its unionized workers. In 2000 24 percent of telecommunications workers were unionized; by 2008 the figure had dropped to 19 percent.[50] Across the board it seemed that the costs of deregulation were increasingly shifted from government and employers to workers in the late twentieth century, in what Jacob Hacker aptly calls "the Great Risk Shift."[51]

Neoliberal policy-making had an especially significant impact on government, which saw increasing privatization and contracting out, a trend that magnified the sense of insecurity experienced by workers who had been among the most militant in the United States in the 1970s.[52] Sanitation workers, who had helped lead the public sector upsurge since the 1968 Memphis sanitation strike, were among those most affected by privatization. In 1973, only 14 percent of cities contracted out trash collection, but by 1979 30 percent did so. In the 1980s that proportion continued to rise. According to one study, sanitation services became "the prime example of how cities can benefit from cooperation with private enterprise." "Blue-collar workers are generally the first to be fired when a state or local government decides to contract out a service," complained one union official.[53] It was easy to understand the motivations of municipal officials: privately employed sanitation workers earned nine percent less on average than their publicly employed counterparts.[54] But it was not only blue-collar government workers who saw their leverage diminish. Teachers were not immune to the threat of privatization or the chilling effect it helped exert on public sector strikes. As charter schools spread in the 1990s, public school teachers felt increasing pressure from school boards. In Pennsylvania, whose teachers were more strike prone than those in any other state, the incidence of teacher strikes trended sharply downward after the state placed new restrictions on strikes in 1992 and implemented charter schools in 1997. Between 1970 and 1992, Pennsylvania averaged nearly 28 teachers' strikes per year. After 2000, the average dropped to 8.6.[55] By 2004, *Education Week* pointed to Pennsylvania as the clearest illustration of a nationwide "long-term trend away from teachers' strikes."[56]

Union Density, the Right to Organize, and the Capacity to Act Collectively

Considering the trends that unfolded in the late twentieth century, it is little wonder that the U.S. strike rate reached a historic low point in 2002. That year the BLS recorded only 19 major work stoppages involved merely 46,000 workers—only one-sixtieth of the number of workers involved in major work stoppages in 1952. Clearly, transformations in the American political economy had sharply curtailed the effectiveness of strikes for American workers.

This is not to say that the decline of strikes was simply a by-product of structural forces. To do so would be to ignore the agency of workers. In the final analysis strikes declined because fewer workers chose to advance their interests collectively through strikes. Whether such choices were motivated by fear, a resurgent culture of individualism, a pragmatic reading of the balance of forces in the national and global markets, or other factors is less important than the fact that workers increasingly made choices in dealing with their work life that did not involve relying on the solidarity of the strike.

Despite the near disappearance of the strike as a significant weapon for workers, this phenomenon has received far less attention from unions and their allies than declining union density. Workers' apparent inability or unwillingness to engage in strikes receives much less analysis than the violations of their rights to organize. Yet these problems are scarcely separable. To be sure, the relationship between union density and workers' capacity to strike has not always been straightforward. Between the mid-1950s and the late 1970s, for example, declines in union density did not translate directly into declining rates of major work stoppages. As union density dropped from 30 percent in 1960 to 23 percent by 1980, the annual average of major work stoppages actually increased slightly. During the 1960s, the United States averaged 283 major work stoppages per year; in the 1970s the annual average increased to 288. But it is difficult to conclude that the decline in strikes and the decline in union density did not become mutually reinforcing trends by the end of the century, as union density fell below 14 percent by 2000 and the annual average of major work stoppages dropped below 35 per year.[57] After all, workers join unions in order to win greater leverage in their dealings with their employers. As workers found it increasingly difficult to pressure their employers through the use of labor's traditional strike weapon, it is not surprising that fewer of them were willing to brave the systematic intimidation to which employers tended to subject them in order to organize unions and win contracts.

An examination of the decline of the strike in recent decades thus holds an important lesson for labor advocates. It suggests that while reforming labor law in ways that would protect workers right to form unions or improving the effectiveness of national labor federations might be necessary responses to labor's crisis, they are also likely to be insufficient responses. For the crisis of organized labor that emerged in the last third of the twentieth century was not only measured by the erosion of workers' rights to organize or the failure of unions to devote greater resources to organizing, but also by the erosion of workers' capacity to act collectively even when organized. That latter problem is not likely to be remedied by changes in labor law or the structure of union federations alone. It will require sustained efforts to counteract the solvents of solidarity produced by decades of deregulation, privatization, globalization, and increasing inequality, making it again possible for workers to achieve the effective level of collective action that once—not so long ago—was symbolized by the power of their picket lines.

Notes

1. Andy Stern, *A Country that Works: Getting America Back on Track* (New York: Free Press, 2006), 78, 80. For a survey of union organizing strategies, see Kate Bronfenbrenner and Robert Hickey, "Changing to Organize: A National Assessment of Union Organizing Strategies," in Ruth Milkman and Kim Voss, eds *Rebuilding Labor: Organizing and Organizers in the New Union Movement* (Ithaca, NY: Cornell University/ILR Press, 2004), 17–61.
2. Ruth Milkman, "A More Perfect Union," *New York Times* (June 30, 2005); Harold Meyerson, "Labor's Big Split: Pain Before Gain," *Washington Post* (July 26, 2005).
3. Stern quoted in Harold Meyerson, "Hard Labor," *The American Prospect* (July/August 2006): 48.
4. Stern, *A Country that Works*, 79; Sweeney quoted in *Washington Post* (August 25, 2004).
5. Employee Free Choice Act, H.R. 1409, S. 560.
6. One of the most thought-provoking recent statements of the importance of culture can be found in Nick Salvatore and Jefferson Cowie, "The Long Exception: Rethinking the Place of the New Deal in American History," *International Labor and Working-Class History* 74 (September 2008): 3–32. Their essay makes a forceful case for the persistence of individualism in American political culture.

7. See for example, Richard B. Freeman and James Medoff, *What Do Unions Do* (New York: Basic Books, 1984), and Thomas Kochan and Robert McKersie, *The Transformation of American Industrial Relations* (New York: Basic Books, 1986).

8. Robert Michael Smith, *From Blackjacks to Briefcases: A History of Commercialized Strikebreaking and Unionbusting in the United States* (Athens, OH: Ohio University Press, 2003); John Logan, "The Union Avoidance Industry in the United States," *British Journal of Industrial Relations* 44 (4) (December 2006): 651–75.

9. "Slave labor act," quotation from Joseph G. Rayback, *A History of American Labor* (New York: Free Press, 1966), 400. On the Taft-Hartley Act, see Melvyn Dubofsky, *The State and Labor in Modern America* (Chapel Hill, NC: University of North Carolina Press, 1994), 202–22; R. Alton Lee, *Truman and Taft-Hartley: A Question of Mandate* (Lexington, KY: University of Kentucky Press, 1966).

10. Lance Compa, *Unfair Advantage: Workers' Freedom of Association in the United States under International Human Rights Standards* (Ithaca, NY: Cornell University Press, 2004).

11. Kate Bronfenbrenner, "No Holds Barred: The Intensification of Employer Opposition to Organizing," *Economic Policy Institute Briefing Paper #235* (Washington, DC, 2009), 2–3.

12. Nelson Lichtenstein, "How Wal-Mart Fights Unions," *Minnesota Law Review* 5 (2) (2008): 1462–1501.

13. Bronfenbrenner, "No Holds Barred," 8.

14. Richard B. Freeman, "Do Workers Want Unions? More than Ever," *Economic Policy Institute Issue Brief, #182* (Washington, D.C.: Economic Policy Institute, 2007).

15. For alternative interpretations of the recent history of the strike in the United States, see Josiah Bartlett Lambert, *"If the Workers Took a Notion": The Right to Strike and American Political Development* (Ithaca, NY: Cornell University Press, 2005), and Joseph A. McCartin, "Approaching Extinction? The Declining Use of the Strike Weapon in the United States, 1945–2000," in Sjaak van der Velden, Heiner Dribbusch, Dave Lyddon, and Kurt Vandaele, eds *Strikes Around the World, 1968–2005: Case Studies of Fifteen Countries* (Amsterdam: Aksant Academic Publishers, 2007), 133–54.

16. Here I am using the data on major work stoppages registered by the U.S. Bureau of Labor Statistics. The data are not without inherent analytical problems. From 1947 to 1981, the BLS cataloged strikes of all sizes. After 1981, it recorded only "major work stoppages" involving at least 1,000 workers for at least 24 hours. Thus, any effort to address patterns over decades before and after 1981 requires that one focus only on major work stoppages. Questions can be raised about the reliability of conclusions based on data that does not measure smaller work stoppages. But the most careful students of this question, L. J. Perry and Patrick J. Wilson, who studied the relationship between small work stoppages and larger work stoppages during the 1947–81 period, concluded that "the small

disputes do not, by and large, determine the overall shape of the data over time." Rather, trends in small strikes tended to correspond to those in the larger strikes during most of this period. Thus it is reasonable to assume that the pattern of large strikes reflects the overall patterns of strikes and as larger strikes have diminished, all strikes have diminished. See L. J. Perry and P. J. Wilson, "Trends in Work Stoppages: A Global Perspective," Working Paper No. 47, 2004, Policy Integration Department, Statistical Analysis Unit. Geneva: International Labor Organization. Available at: http://papers.ssrn.com/sol3/papers.cfm?abstract_id=908483 (accessed May 28, 2009).

17. U.S. Bureau of Labor Statistics, *Work Stoppages in Government, 1980* (Washington: Government Printing Office, 1981), 4.

18. See BLS data, http://www.bls.gov/news.release/wkstp.t01.html (accessed May 28, 2009).

19. For a fuller discussion of the decline of the strike, see McCartin, "Approaching Extinction?" 133–54.

20. William Greider, *Secrets of the Temple: How the Federal Reserve Runs the Country* (New York: Simon & Schuster, 1987), 1–123.

21. BLS statistics, http://data.bls.gov/PDQ/servlet/SurveyOutputServlet (accessed May 28, 2009).

22. Lawrence Mishel, Jared Bernstein, and John Schmitt, *The State of Working America* (Ithaca, NY: Cornell University Press, 2001), 237.

23. For a survey of labor relations in the airline industry during this period, see Jean T. McKelvey, ed. *Cleared for Takeoff: Airline Labor Relations Since Deregulation* (Ithaca, NY: ILR Press, 1988).

24. On trucking deregulation, see Michael H. Belzer, *Sweatshops on Wheels: Winners and Losers in Trucking Deregulation* (New York: Oxford University Press, 2000).

25. Mark Levinson, *The Box: How the Shipping Container Made the World Smaller and the World Economy Bigger* (Princeton: Princeton University Press, 2006); "U.S. Trade in Goods and Services - Balance of Payments (BOP) Basis," U.S. Census Bureau, Historical Series, March 13, 2009, http://www.census.gov/foreign-trade/statistics/historical/index.html (accessed May 25, 2009).

26. Barry Bluestone and Bennett Harrison, *The Deindustrialization of America: Plant Closings, Community Abandonment, and the Dismantling of Basic Industry* (New York: Basic Books, 1982); Jefferson Cowie and Joseph Heathcott, "The Meanings of Deindustrialization," in Jefferson Cowie and Joseph Heathcott, eds *Beyond the Ruins: The Meanings of Deindustrialization* (Ithaca: Cornell University Press, 2003), 1–17.

27. For more on the decline of steel and auto jobs in the period before the 1970s, see Judith Stein, *Running Steel, Running America: Race, Economic Policy, and the Decline of Liberalism* (Chapel Hill, NC: University of North Carolina Press, 1998), and Thomas Sugrue, *The Origins of the Urban Crisis: Race and Inequality in Postwar Detroit* (Princeton: Princeton University Press, 1996).

28. "Shifts in Auto Industry Employment, 1979–98," *Monthly Labor Review* (September 28, 1999).

29. "Employees on Nonfarm Payrolls by Major Industry Sector: Historical," Table B-1, BLS; "Average Hours and Earnings of Production or Nonsupervisory Workers on Private Nonfarm Payrolls by Major Industry Sector, 1964 to Date," Bureau of Labor Statistics tables available at http://data.bls.gov (accessed January 27, 2006).

30. For more on the labor practices of these trendsetting companies, see Nelson Lichtenstein, *The Retail Revolution: How Wal-Mart Created a Brave New World of American Business* (New York: Metropolitan Books, 2009); Eric Schlosser, *Fast Food Nation: The Dark Side of the All American Meal* (Boston, MA: Houghton Mifflin, 2001).

31. On labor and Carter, see: Taylor Dark, "Organized Labor and the Carter Administration: The Origins of Conflict," 761–82, and Gary M. Fink, "Fragile Alliance: Jimmy Carter and the American Labor Movement," 783–803, both in Herbert D. Rosenbaum and Alexej Ugrinsky, eds *The Presidency and Domestic Policies of Jimmy Carter* (Westport, CT: Greenwood Press, 1994).

32. Mark H. Maier, *City Unions: Managing Discontent in New York City* (New Brunswick, NJ: Rutgers University Press, 1987), chapter 4; Francis Ryan, *Everyone Royalty: AFSCME, Municipal Workers, and Urban Power in 20th Century Philadelphia* (Philadelphia, PA: Temple University Press, forthcoming), chapters 4–5; Joseph C. Slater, *Public Workers: Government Employee Unions, the Law, and the State, 1900–1962* (Ithaca, NY: ILR Press, 2004); *The Crisis in Public Employee Relations in the Decade of the 1970s* ed. Richard J. Murphy, and Morris Sackman (Washington, D.C.: Bureau of National Affairs, 1970).

33. Joseph A. McCartin, " 'Fire the Hell Out of Them': Sanitation Workers' Struggles and the Normalization of the Striker Replacement Strategy in the 1970s," *Labor: Studies in the Working-Class History of the Americas* 2 (3) (Fall, 2005): 67–92; "AFL-CIO, Independents Split over Carter Personnel Plan," *Government Employee Relations Report* (March 6, 1978), 9.

34. Lester Asher, "Remarks at the SEIU Public Workers Conference, November 13–16, 1978 Service Employees International Union," *Problems Confronting Public Workers* (Washington, D.C.: Service Employees International Union, 1978), 11; Bureau of Labor Statistics, U.S. Department of Labor, Bulletin No. 2110, *Work Stoppages in Government* (Washington, DC: Government Printing Office, 1980), 4; "Public Sector Strikes on the Increase," *Government Union Critique* (September 26, 1980), 4.

35. Arthur B. Shostak and David Skocik, *The Air Controllers' Controversy: Lessons from the PATCO Strike* (New York: Human Sciences Press, 1986); Willis J. Nordlund, *Silent Skies: The Air Traffic Controllers' Strike* (Westport, CT: Praeger, 1998); Michael Round, *Grounded: Reagan and the PATCO Crash* (New York: Garland Publishers, 1999).

36. Anonymous union leader quoted in, "Air Controllers' Strike," *Facts on File Yearbook 1981* (New York: Facts on File News Services, 1982), 772.

37. David Lewin, "Public Employee Unionism in the 1980s: An Analysis of Transformation," in Seymour Martin Lipset, ed. *Unions in Transition: Entering the Second Century* (San Francisco, CA: Institute for Contemporary Studies, 1986), 247.

38. Ronald Donovan, *Administering the Taylor Law: Public Employee Relations in New York* (Ithaca, NY: ILR Press, 1990), 205–06.

39. *NLRB v. Mackay Radio & Telegraph Company*, 304 U.S. 333 (1938); James B. Atleson, *Values and Assumptions in American Labor Law* (Amherst, MA: University of Massachusetts Press, 1983), chapter 1.

40. Charles R. Perry, Andrew M. Kramer and Thomas J. Schneider, *Operating During Strikes: Company Experience, NLRB Policies, and Government Regulations*, Labor Relations and Public Policy Series, No. 23 (Philadelphia, PA: Wharton School Industrial Research Unit, 1982).

41. Peter Rachleff, "Is the Strike Dead? An Historical Look at the Future," *New Labor Forum* (Summer, 2003): 87–96; Jonathan D. Rosenblum, *Copper Crucible: How the Arizona Miners' Strike of 1983 Recast Labor-Management Relations in America* (Ithaca, NY: ILR Press, 1994). Four articles by Timothy J. Minchin document the use of replacement workers by smaller employers in the 1980s. See: "Broken Spirits: Permanent Replacements and the Rumsford Strike of 1986," *New England Quarterly* 74 (1) (March 2001): 5–31; "'Labor's Empty Gun': Permanent Replacements and the International Paper Company Strike of 1987–88," *Labor History* 47 (1) (February 2006): 21–42; "Permanent Replacements and the 'Social Accord' in Calera, Alabama, 1974–1999," *Labor History* 41 (4) (2001): 371–96; and "Torn Apart: Permanent Replacements and the Crossett Strike of 1985" *Arkansas Historical Quarterly* 59 (1) (2000): 30–58.

42. See for example, Lawrence Richards, *Union-Free America: Workers and Anti-Union Culture* (Urbana, IL: University of Illinois Press, 2008).

43. See the essays in *Strikes Around the World, 1968–2005: Case Studies of Fifteen Countries*, ed. Sjaak van der Velden, Heiner Dribbusch, Dave Lyddon, and Kurt Vandaele (Amsterdam: Aksant Academic Publishers, 2007).

44. R. E. Scott, "The High Price of 'Free' Trade: NAFTA's Failure Has Cost the United States Jobs Across the Nation," Economic Policy Institute, Briefing Paper #147, November 17, 2003.

45. Mishel, et al., *State of Working America*, 234, 242.

46. These figures are measured in 1999 dollars. See data in Mishel et al., *State of Working America*, 115.

47. Paul Krugman, *Peddling Prosperity: Economic Sense and Nonsense in the Age of Diminished Expectations* (New York: W. W. Norton, 1994), 262.

48. Mishel et al., *State of Working America*, 276, 283.

49. Clinton quoted in Andrew Rich, *Think Tanks, Public Policy, and the Politics of Expertise* (New York: Cambridge University Press, 2004), 121.

50. "Union Affiliation of Employed Wage and Salary Workers by Occupation and Industry," Bureau of Labor Statistics, http://www.bls.gov/cps/cpslutabs.htm (accessed May 28, 2009).

51. Jacob Hacker, *The Great Risk Shift: The New Economic Insecurity and the Decline of the American Dream* (New York: Oxford University Press, 2006).

52. Thomas Frank, *The Wrecking Crew: How Conservatives Rule* (New York: Metropolitan Books, 2008), 42–43, 93–94, 138–39, 254–55, 261, 263–64.

53. John D. Hanrahan, *Government for Sale: Contracting Out—The New Patronage* (Washington, D.C.: AFSCME, 1977), 191.

54. Oliver D. Cooke, *Rethinking Municipal Privatization* (New York: Routledge, 2007), 47–48; Gary Hoover and James Peoples, "The Privatization of Refuse Removal and Labor Costs," *Journal of Labor Research* 24 (2003): 293–306.

55. Harris Zwerling, "Pennsylvania Teachers' Strikes and Academic Performance," Pennsylvania State Education Association, 2009, http://www.psea.org/general.aspx?ID=882 (accessed on May 25, 2009); Elizabeth Weaver, "Pennsylvania Teachers: Number One in Strikes," Allegheny Institute Report #07–06, August 2007 (Pittsburgh, PA: Allegheny Institute, 2007).

56. Bess Keller, "Few Teachers' Strikes Mark U.S. Landscape: Contracts Remain Unsettled in Many Big-City Districts," *Education Week* (October 6, 2004).

57. U.S. Bureau of Labor Statistics, "Union Members in 2005," USDL 06–99, January 20, 2006, at http://www.bls.gov/news.release/pdf/union2.pdf (accessed January 27, 2006).

PART II

NEW DIRECTIONS IN U.S. LABOR HISTORY

CHAPTER NINE

Sensing Labor: The Stinking Working-Class after the Cultural Turn

Daniel E. Bender

"The real secret of class distinctions . . . can be summed up in four frightful words," noted George Orwell, "*the lower classes smell.*" The evidence he produced in his land-mark *Road to Wigan Pier*, a participant observation study of industrial, Depression-era Britain, was physically overwhelming and designed to disgust middle-class readers. From the stench of exhausted, sweaty workers sharing the same filthy bed to the sight of black cockroaches scurrying on pasty white sheets of tripe, Orwell related the repulsive parts of working-class life. Labor historians would be appalled. We have been trained to treat our working-class subjects with dignity. We document—and, at times, celebrate—their "agency," their ability to shape their own destinies and histories.

Yet the working class does stink—at least according to many of the same sources we have long utilized as labor historians. Their food reeks: smelly fish, greasy fried chicken, or, perhaps, oily fast food. Their clothes bear the odors of the traces of their labor: slaughterhouse blood, sweat, coal dust, cheap perfume, or cleaning products. For many observers, even workers' bodies themselves smelled, a sure sign of their inferior class and racial status. They emitted strange odors that repulsed social reformers, factory investigators, welfare officials, and slummers. These observers regularly cited these odors as evidence of class divisions that were rooted in culture, bodies, and biology, as much as economics. Moreover, they claimed odors as justification for policies and politics that sought to transform radically the most intimate details of working-class lives. For Orwell, "physical repulsion" was the most insur-mountable of social boundaries: "for no feeling of like or dislike is quite so funda-mental as a *physical* feeling."[1]

Workers interacted with other workers and across the class divide. They did so in ways that provoked sensual responses—smell as well as taste, sound, touch, and sight. This recognition is critical as labor historians continue to struggle to adapt their craft to transformations in the larger American historiography. In particular, labor historians have been especially reluctant to consider the methods and questions of cultural history. This resistance can be traced to several factors: first, the basis of labor history in understandings of culture that contrast sharply with those of cultural historians; second, the difficulty of adapting cultural historiography to the activist and public historical goals of labor history; and third, the focus of cultural historians on economic elites and consumption to the exclusion of working people and labor. The historicizing of sensual responses—the history of the senses—is important not simply for its potential to deepen our understanding of cross- and intra-class interaction, but also for the way its insights can bridge divides between labor history and cultural history in ways that strengthen both fields. In particular, the history of the senses can integrate into labor history some key cultural historical questions while retaining the longstanding strengths of labor history in social history. A multisensory analysis can broaden our conception of working-class subjectivity, representations of the working class, and the construction of class as a category of analysis. Such an approach can help link definitions of culture, long dominant in labor history, to those that have influenced the "new cultural history."

This chapter, then, argues for greater attention to the history of the senses as an example of how to broaden the engagement of labor historians with different definitions of culture that have, in large measure, determined the kinds of questions we ask. It begins with a survey of labor historians' dependence on anthropological definitions of culture, which has put the field at odds with cultural historians. It offers the conclusion that the history of the senses can bridge the gap between a labor history doggedly entrenched in social history and a cultural history that pays little attention to issues of class. Initially, labor historians were deeply influenced by notions of culture as a resource. That is, culture represented an important common and shared tool around which to construct strategies and movements of resistance. Because of the centrality of this idea of culture, borrowed heavily from anthropology, labor historians have been comparatively slow to consider the understandings of culture that emerged from the "New Cultural History" of the 1980s and 1990s. Notions of culture as a resource have remained critical in labor history, even as some historians have examined the engagement of working people with mass culture. However, we still know less about the working class, not simply as consumers of mass culture, but as objects of cultural analysis. The history of the senses, as Orwell's quote suggests, illuminates not only the literary or artistic responses to working people, but also the far more wide-ranging physical responses.

The history of senses is an emerging field. Rooted in cultural history, historical anthropology, and cultural studies, the history of the senses also offers profound possibilities to expand the scope of social history. For labor history, the history of the senses can provide new ways of understanding class that include but also transcend definitions of class as a set of shared experiences. Class can be conceived of as a set of cultural representations, cultural differences, and physical perceptions that are experienced in multisensory ways. The study of the senses also can broaden the public presentation of labor history, a key commitment of historians who seek to connect the insights of scholarship with the needs of communities and social movements for historical perspective and memory.

Labor History and the Spirit of Reconstruction

From its emergence in the 1970s, the now not-as "New Labor History" has focused on reconstruction, that is, the rediscovery of the lives of normal Americans. The focus was more on shared experiences than on physical responses or perceptions. As one of the field's earliest practitioners and leading scholars David Brody wrote in 1983: "The spirit of discovery is strongly felt by scholars seeking to reconstruct the historical experience of ordinary people."[2] The continuing centrality of reconstruction has tied working-class history closely to social history and rendered many of its practitioners suspicious of cultural history because of its direct critique of social history. As Brody wrote: "labor history is at one with the entire field of social history." Or, as Leon Fink has argued, "labor history has thus become one of the mainsprings within the larger field of social history."[3] It was through social history that the new labor historians moved labor history back into history departments (from economics departments) and vastly expanded the possible topics of analysis.

In the 1980s, this dedication to reconstruction made the New Labor History one of American history's most politically contentious, publicly engaged, and rapidly growing fields. The drive to reconstruct remains the political lifeblood of working-class history; it has produced meticulous depictions of workers' lives in nearly all parts of the nation at all periods of time; sustained and preserved invaluable archives in universities, labor unions, and state and local historical societies; and forced the revamping of the American history survey and synthesis. The New Labor History emerged in the waning moments of the New Left academic revolt when history departments were still resistant to historical narratives that foregrounded social conflict and that were accessible to a broader public.[4]

More than 30 years later, though, with the subjectivity of historical writing almost universally acknowledged and the working class an accepted and important subject of analysis, there is a sense both within and outside of the field that working-class history is self-contained and increasingly isolated. At a moment when labor historians are seeking greater coherence through a thriving Labor and Working-Class History Association (LAWCHA) and are feeling a renewed urge to develop a synthesis of American working-class history, questions of crisis linger over the field.[5]

In particular, labor history seems increasingly isolated as scholars in other fields, such as foreign relations or history of women and gender, have enthusiastically engaged with the possibilities of cultural history. Labor history has been slow to accept the concepts and methods of "the cultural turn."[6] In other fields, historians have come to focus on how social categories are constructed and draw liberally on literary and cultural theorists to rethink the role of the historian in the interpretation of evidence and the creation of narrative analyses. Labor historians have misgivings about cultural historians. Many labor historians accurately note a marked absence of class analysis in the new cultural history. While cultural historians describe gender, race, ethnicity, sexuality, and other categories of difference, like disability, as socially and culturally constructed, they tend to see class as static, a material base upon which other notions of difference are defined and re-defined.

The reluctance of cultural history to engage with issues of class and labor history's focus on reconstruction together have made it difficult to analyze the complex interactions of class with gender, race, ethnicity, and sexuality. In particular, within existing definitions of class within labor history, there is little potential to analyze the visceral, physical, and sensual responses to difference—even if these responses are amply visible in the key sources that labor historians have long utilized.[7]

If understandings of categories of difference have separated cultural and labor history, so, too, have commitments to public scholarship. Cultural history has retreated from politics and the public. The combination of academic and public history much cherished by labor historians is increasingly rare, leaving what David Thelen calls "this feeling of isolation from public audiences."[8] Labor historians, profoundly committed to accessible scholarship, have bemoaned what they regard as retreat to the esoteric and theoretical.[9] In the context of labor history's established methodology, the study of ideas as much as of people, of language as much as of action, might seem reactionary. The reconstruction of working-class life, from the outset, had a specific, political goal. It provided the evidence of working-class unity and popular resistance to capitalism at a moment when many labor leaders doggedly clung to the expiring accords of the Cold War and welfare state. At the same time, labor history as the history of working people could become a tool of empowerment by giving local communities a sense of place in a history of their own that emphasized unity and struggle. Allying themselves with union democracy movements and labor education programs, labor historians sought to provide rank-and-file and working-class community activists a voice through a connection to a usable past.[10] They sought to move beyond texts aimed solely at an academic audience by creating a new kind of history that stressed readability and accessibility. In addition to popular texts, they arranged community forums, exhibits, and workshops and produced films and documentaries that helped to advance an alternative history of ordinary people that would otherwise have disappeared. For many labor historians, the theoretically turgid style of cultural history seemed at odds with their public commitments.[11]

Because of labor historians' focus on reconstruction, we have come to know a great deal about how working people lived and labored; yet, to borrow from Orwell, we know little about how they smelled. Over the course of 30 years, labor historians have produced a remarkable patchwork history of working-class communities and workplaces from Troy, New York to Butte, Montana and from textile mills to autoplants to working-class homes. At the same time, labor historians challenged notions of what was acceptable historical evidence and who were legitimate subjects of analysis. Labor historians have sought to preserve long-forgotten and disappearing materials: union and proletarian newspapers, memoirs, as well as ethnic and labor association records. They have also sought to collect oral histories of ordinary Americans and to use their voices in the re-writing of American history.[12] Given this commitment to new kinds of sources, labor historians could prove leaders in advancing the history of senses—if this history can, in turn, support the kinds of questions and methods so critical to labor history.

Labor History and the Question of Culture

The new labor historians defined class as intertwined with the means of production and with culture. Their predecessors like John Commons or Philip Taft, understood class as a purely economic relationship, focused largely on the labor movement, and cast trade unions as an exceptionally American source of political moderation. Pioneering labor historians, among them David Montgomery and Herbert Gutman, viewed class as the product of common experiences and they focused, not on political moderation, but on a vast range of resistant traditions and customs.[13] This focus naturally raised the question of culture. Influenced by E. P. Thompson's monumental *Making of the English Working Class* and his understanding of class as the composite of common experiences, they created a historiography that recognized the centrality of culture in helping workers make sense of their labor and lives.[14] Culture, they argued, was "customs in common" that were central to how working people formulated, advanced, and implemented strategies of resistance.

Significantly, where labor historians readily accepted the idea that working-class politics and identity emerged from common experiences, their understandings of culture provided little opportunity to examine the way perceptions of difference provoked sensory reactions of disgust, fear, or attraction. These reactions are crucial as class, undoubtedly, is not only experienced, it is described and represented. Cultural history, potentially, offers the methodological tools to analyze this notion of class.[15] Where cultural historians have come to understand culture broadly as "threaded through all social practices," as Stuart Hall writes, labor historians have understood culture as something concrete.[16] Cultural history, then, has focused on representation, and ideology and, draws frequently from the literary theorists of the cultural turn, from Michel Foucault to Frederic Jameson. Labor history is indebted to an understanding of culture, but one grounded in cultural anthropological scholarship, particularly that of Sidney Mintz.[17]

A pioneering generation of labor historians cast culture and society as distinct and separate. As Michael H. Frisch and Daniel J. Walkowitz suggested in 1983 in a summary of then recent work in labor history, "society is the arena." Therefore, as Susan Porter Benson wrote, culture "is the set of frameworks, attitudes, and accepted standards of behavior that one draws upon in dealing with society." Culture, in this reading, is how historical actors approached the "real-world circumstances" of daily life.[18] Culture is a "resource," as Herbert Gutman asserted in echoing Mintz, that workers used collectively to confront the adversity dealt them by capital.[19] Labor historians have traced the "making" of community and workplace cultures that different groups of working-class Americans have used to confront the depredations of capital in and around the point of production. While this materialist definition of culture has come under criticism by a few labor historians and cultural critics, it remains a critical methodological tool for many labor historians seeking to write "thick" descriptions of working-class communities and collective resistance.[20]

Such a definition of culture, however, has several major limitations. First, the anthropological definition privileges group behavior, assuming a singular group identity and political consciousness. Such an approach, as the cultural historian of ethnicity Peggy Pascoe has noted, ignores conflict and difference within communities.[21] It leaves little room for multiple and conflicting identities and, therefore, artificially privileges class conflicts. In fact, such conflicts existed within the context of relationships of gender, race, and ethnicity and difference that, as Orwell suggests, may have been expressed through physical disgust. Second, the notion that society is distinct from culture, in other words, that society is something that can be reconstructed by the careful combing of archives by the skilled historian, is misleading. In fact, the experiences of the least powerful are rarely well chronicled in archival sources; their resistance is frequently more individual than collective.[22]

The labor history of the least powerful has benefited from a cultural approach that allows historical subjects to define the terms and methods of their resistance. The first generation of labor historians of women and people of color has generally searched for the evidence of collective resistance to capital. These historians sought to find examples of "organized women workers" and unionized minorities.[23] But the archives that labor historians have so profitably mined tend to concentrate on those powerful enough to leave the documentary evidence of collective resistance, and for the most part this has meant white, male organized workers. At the same time, the very notion of women's, African-American, or Asian-American labor history depends on the idea of labor history as a field with a past. In this context, the labor history of women and people of color is cast—and isolated—as a branch from the main trunk of labor history. Women and people of color were often ignored by previous generations of oral historians and their resistance was frequently so subtle and so hidden that it did not make its way into the mainstream press. Historians have, therefore, examined the culturally specific ways these workers described their situation and their relationships to those in power.[24] They have examined how the words and symbols workers used to represent themselves and their masters, what the anthropologist James Scott calls "hidden transcripts," became the basis for everyday acts of resistance.[25] The study of "hidden transcripts" has questioned the privileging of visible, potentially heroic kinds of resistance.

Labor historians, in their search for an American anticapitalist tradition, have focused on direct actions, like strikes, riots, violence, and boycotts. As a result, labor historians generally have paid little attention to what George Rawick called "working-class self-activity," those everyday resistant actions that rarely find their way into social historical sources. Sabotage, malingering, lying, stealing, drunkenness, absenteeism, shirking, tramping, quitting, singing, gossiping, and dressing are now studied as proletarian hidden transcripts, but are still often described as distinct from heroic radical resistance.[26] The study of hidden transcripts highlights how the questions of working-class history can be revisited with new methodologies. Historians have revised how and by whom social categories are defined, and have explored the language ordinary people used to identify commonality, to describe social injustice, and to advance strategies of resistance. Revisiting the social historical themes of labor and working-class history highlights how the field of labor history can be better diversified to consider the history of workers of color and women workers as more than add-ons to the main thread of labor history that began with the study of male, industrial wage-earners. As Robin D. G. Kelley wrote: "for all of its radical moorings, 'history from below' started out very manly and very white . . .."[27] While the study of hidden transcripts has helped the field critique its manly and white origins, Alice Kessler-Harris, perhaps the leading historian of gender and labor in the United States, accurately acknowledges that "the language of 'work' and 'workers' still conjures up male images."[28]

Despite resistance, some historians (often who do not identify themselves primarily as labor historians) have engaged with the cultural turn in order to examine, in particular, working-class leisure and the engagement with popular culture. Kathy Peiss early on suggested that working-class Americans, female and male, were enthusiastic participants in consumer capitalism. Even if, as Charlie McGovern has noted, advertisers and producers imagined their ideal consumer as female and middle class, workers purchased dime novels, dress patterns, radios, and mass produced foods. Michael Denning has described the working-class "accents" of American popular culture.[29] Notably, such authors have suggested that through popular culture, workers were able to express dissatisfaction with shopfloor drudgery and articulate longings, if not for socialism or utopia, at least for material pleasure. Matt Garcia, for example, highlights the centrality of theatres and dance halls in the interethnic organizing of Southern California's farms.[30] Similarly, scholars are exploring how ordinary people have drawn on popular culture to shape their self-representation as strikers and workers.[31] The engagement with leisure and popular cultural economies allowed marginalized communities, especially immigrants and African Americans, to articulate conceptions of racial justice and ideals of manhood and womanhood. Davarian Baldwin has recently identified a "marketplace intellectual life." Through their participation in leisure economies, African Americans were able to find forums in the cultural industries of film, beauty, and sports to debate strategies of resistance. Historians like Nan Enstad and Frances Couvares have suggested that popular culture must be explored for how it is used and produced by working-class subjects. Workers were producers, as well as consumers, of popular culture. The study of working-class cultural production includes its creation and its reception. The country music song or hip-hop album can be examined for the experience of their writers and performers, as well as for its received meanings, the site of their performance, and the process of sampling and rewriting to match new contexts.

If this admittedly limited engagement with cultural historical methods has expanded a specific set of questions about consumption and leisure, we still know little about class as a constructed category of analysis. We still face the critical question about how the class divide was perceived and represented by working people and others, including elites. The history of the senses can offer answers by recognizing that the perception and representation of class difference involved a set of common experiences. In this way, working people remain actors and agents who have experienced the demands of work, the rigors of family, the joys of leisure, the enchantment of popular culture, and the gaze of elites, social reformers, artists, and politicians.

Labor, Culture, and the Working-Class Subject

The act of reconstruction has sought to resurrect working-class actors as historical agents and to restore to them their power to shape their destinies. The focus of this project, as a result, has tended to obscure differences and conflict within the working class. It has also become unidirectional. That is, labor historians have generally examined how working people have engaged with (and resisted) managers, corporations, social reformers, and political parties. We know a great deal less about how working people have been described, studied, and represented, for example, by elites. Moreover, with a handful of exceptions, cultural historians have offered little to the study of the working-class subject, beyond general suggestions that working-class communities were objects of fear or contempt. While cultural history has elucidated middle-class and elite understandings of faraway peoples and colonized subjects, it has rarely explored the domestic, working-class "other." Yet workers were and remain subjects of intense study and analysis. Matthew Frye Jacobson provocatively suggests that immigrant workers and colonized peoples were, in fact, considered in the same conversations and using the same methods.[32] Jacobson's insight highlights a key aim of a cultural labor history: understanding difference within working-class communities, as well as efforts to define and naturalize hierarchies of class alongside those of gender and race.

Notions of culture as a resource have tended to describe communities as united in resistance. More recently, the work of a few scholars offers insight into ways of examining the social and cultural construction of difference within working-class communities and the representation of work. They have identified the role of ideologies of gender, race, and ethnicity in the consolidation and splintering of working-class communities. They have explored how such ideologies are formed and reformed in local contexts as well as in the broader framework of migration and diaspora.[33] And, they point out the role of conceptions of difference in definitions of a woman's wage, free labor, and blue-collar, white-collar, and professional work.[34] Scholars draw upon literature, music, and art for changing representations of labor.[35] Such cultural analyses also permit the historian to explore working-class self-representation, the ways ordinary people gave historically specific meanings to social categories, like "worker," "wife," "father," "breadwinner," "professional," and "employer." The vast number of social histories of American labor has—unintentionally perhaps—

demonstrated that such categories have no universal meaning. Their connotations have varied dramatically from place to place and from era to era. A cultural approach recognizes that categories exist only through their expression and representation. Analysis shifts from relations between social groups to the very process through which these groups are represented and, therefore, constituted.[36]

Workers are actors and agents—they are also subjects of study and analysis. As Elizabeth Faue demonstrates in her recent biography of the labor journalist Eva McDonald Valesh, the fate of workers, their living conditions, and the state of their bodies have been the focus of intense interest. In fact, Valesh distanced herself from her working-class roots largely through the journalistic gaze.[37] Ava Baron and Eileen Boris, similarly, have argued that laboring bodies become "spectacles" and "objects of law and social policy, weak, disordered, violated, or just out of place." As Baron and Boris have noted: " 'The body' itself is elusive and multivariate: Its appearance as unchanging and material masks complexity and cultural variability. It simultaneously is signified and signifier. It is a work, a product of human labor, and something that does work, masking the social power attached to bodily differences."[38] Their work suggests that the same documents that labor historians have relied on to reconstruct the social history of the working class can be revisited for what they reveal about the representations of class and class difference. Government documents and census data, welfare and reform reports, social surveys, artistic representations, photographs, autobiographies, and images, among many other key sources, highlight working-class lives only through the medium of cross-class and intra-class cultural interaction. The extension of Baron and Boris' analysis of bodies to consider the insights of the history of the senses is worthwhile. Bodies, after all, are more than isolated objects or spectacles. Bodies interact in multi-sensory ways through the act, experience, and perception of smell, taste, sight, sound, and touch. This recognition can, in the final analysis, serve the ends of social history and the labor history project of reconstruction.

Sensing the Working Class

An important development in recent American history has been a critique of historians' overwhelming dependence on the visual, that is, on printed sources, images, and narratives that describe what was or could have been seen. The emerging history of the senses offers a great deal to the study of the American working class beyond this focus on a single sense. It suggests a broader history of the working-class subject and presents an understanding of culture that bridges the anthropological and the literary. Methodologically, the study of the senses can better integrate culture into social history. For historians of the senses, culture remains something that is experienced, even utilized. It is also perceived, threaded through all human interaction. Such a hybrid conception of culture can expand labor historians' longstanding goal of reconstruction. It also offers exciting new potentials for the public engagement of labor history.

Like labor history itself, the study of the senses has long been intertwined with the history of emergent capitalism. One of the originators of the multidisciplinary study of the senses, Marshall McLuhan, argued for a "great divide" in the history of human sensory perception. The printed book and the subsequent mass production of literary material made the industrial West dependent principally on seeing; the non-West, meanwhile, remained predominantly oral. The broad strokes and generalizations of McLuhan's "great divide" theory have—not surprisingly—come under intense scrutiny from historians and historical anthropologists alike.[39] As Constance Classen, David Howes, and Mark Smith have independently demonstrated, society, even after industrialization, has remained multisensory and the distinctions between sight, taste, sound, and smell are often blurred.[40] They have also realized that senses are not pan-historical universals. In other words, even if a sound has been recorded and available to historians generations removed, they do not hear the sound in the same way as their subjects. A recipe remade with complete faithfulness to ingredients from one of numerous historic cookbooks does not taste the same way to its later day cook, as it might have to a nineteenth-century migrant or a middle-class Depression-era family. The smells of the city, the sound of factories, or the feel of human flesh must be historicized. As Classen notes, "sensory perception is a cultural, as well as a physical act."[41]

Scholars, beyond labor history, have examined the ramifications of this realization that the history of the senses demands attention not only to representation, but also to experience. How did the plantation South smell? What is the significance of frequent writing of whites, both Northern and Southern, about the smell of slaves and freedman? Mark Smith's studies of the senses in the antebellum South have provided a nuanced reconstruction of plantation life, beyond the oft-analyzed visual accounts provided by travelers. At the same time, Smith has demonstrated how black and white Southerners and Northern visitors defined race itself through the process of perception and, then, recorded that perception. Historians, he notes, have generally focused on those perceptions, not the act of perceiving, that is, the moments when and the fashion in which historical agents translated sensory responses into categorical beliefs about difference.[42]

Labor history is almost as dependent as the history of slavery on indirect sources, that is, on material written by those in power about the powerless and subaltern. The history of the senses offers new ways of reading the experience of the most disenfranchised in the words, deeds, and perceptions of the elite. While historians influenced by the work of James Scott have uncovered much evidence of hidden resistance by reading such sources "across the grain," a multisensory analysis can connect the histories of working-class identity and resistance to those of elite representations of working people. We can depend on the rich detail of archival sources, but we must still examine why and how sensory responses have been recorded or omitted. Why are the sources labor historians have depended upon so frequently rich in sensory descriptions? Why are political judgments and policy justifications embedded in descriptions that deliberately evoke sensory responses? So often the elite voices that narrate our sources provoked disgust or curiosity (and, frequently, both) in order to elicit intellectual response.

Upton Sinclair's familiar *The Jungle* (1906) provides a vivid example of the possibilities of a multisensory labor history. The socialist novel evoked visceral responses, hitting the public first in the stomach and, only, later in the voting and legislating brain. It provides a portrait of work in Chicago's meatpacking factories and of life in the surrounding immigrant districts.[43] Its descriptions are so vivid that some labor historians have been wary of employing the novel, beyond dramatic color. Sinclair's political and outsider perspective, seemingly compromises the novel's reliability. The novel has become the property of the literary scholar, not the social historian.[44] In fact, in its drama, the novel only amplifies the style of legislative documents, reform tracts, or political broadsides. The novel is truly archetypical of the kind of primary sources that serve labor historians well. If *The Jungle* reveals little about the political consciousness of immigrant meatpackers, it highlights the way elites described immigrant workers in multisensory ways. For instance, the novel begins with a wedding ceremony in a neighborhood saloon. The greasy smells of the foreign food blend with sweaty aromas of the workers. The frenetic music testifies to the workers' primitivism; the industrial city merged with the savage jungle. The primal smells of slaughterhouse are infused into the skins and clothes of the workers. Their low racial status is confirmed by the contrast with elite tourists to the slaughterhouse who are overwhelmed by the stench. As it traces the descent of Jurgis Rudkis from virile proletarian manhood to primitive bestiality, the novel describes a debased working class. For Sinclair, as for so many of his contemporaries, the racial and gendered status of workers is revealed by the coarseness of their senses. Subaltern status was a sensory fact. If Sinclair believed that he (and other elite and outside critics) had neutral aromas, the workers he observed demonstrated their inferior status and outsider position through their stench. Outside observers like Sinclair engaged in the act of smelling whereas their subjects simply smelled—they reeked. Equally, for Sinclair, they were noisy. Their food was overpoweringly strong. Their skin was coarse and their touch animalistic. Visually, they seemed oblivious to the tawdry surroundings of their lives. Sinclair would have agreed with Orwell: the working class smells.

The history of the senses expands our understandings of class as a category of analysis and illuminates its connections to other constructed categories of difference, especially race and gender. Sound, taste, and smell have been equally important in efforts to define class hierarchies as physical superiority or inferiority, akin and related to racial hierarchies. Beyond novels like *The Jungle*, government documents, factory inspection reports, and journalistic accounts provide historians with key statistical information and first-hand descriptions of a range of different workplaces, from sweatshops to bakeries to car plants to nursing homes. The sensory responses of observers are as important as their statistical data. New York's factory inspectors, for example, described the smell of sweatshops, as much as the disorderly and cramped surroundings. Inspectors contrasted their own disgust with the seemingly disregard of immigrant workers. One typical report from 1893 declared that sweatshops "smell as powerfully and poisonously as the wretched toilers themselves."[45] Such sensory responses revealed the intertwined racial and class differences separating inspectors from workers. Similarly, when the sociologist Edward Ross characterized new immigrant workers in his classic *The Old World in the New*, he recorded his sensory responses to workers. One of his sources described Jews as "an invading slime . . . they are loud, noisy . . . pushing and vulgar." Sound and smell merged with tactile metaphors to confirm racial inferiority. Even manners of eating became evidence of difference and character: "They eat enormously. Noisily and repulsively. They devour their food rapidly—bolt it—with little mastication."[46] Ross' repulsion belied his hostility to immigrant workers. When the Rev. C. H. Parkhurst expressed his hostility to immigration in 1885, he also evoked the perceived smells and "infection" of recent arrivals through the metaphor of "a stream of sewage from northwestern Europe discharging among us its reeking and continuous filth." Moreover, he denied the industrial usefulness of immigrants through negative sensory cues. The efforts of immigrants worked towards shit, not invention. He bemoaned the immigrants' "defecating energy at work among us."[47]

Observers most often described the least powerful workers in ways that provoked powerful sensory responses. When the socialist William Noyes defended his—and many other socialists'—hostility to African-American workers and his belief that they could play little role in the Socialist Party, he turned immediately to the logic of physical repulsion. His insistence on permanent racial hierarchy ("we have no hope that the Ethiopian can change his skin") depended on multisensory disgust. "Physically the negroes are as a race repulsive to us," he declared. He was repulsed in particular by their "odor, even of the cleanest of them . . . " He marveled, in fact, that Southern whites' demands for servility and service trumped the abomination of touch. The Northerner (and the socialist) wondered that the Southerner could tolerate black touch: "He hears of gentlewomen being shampooed and otherwise physically touched by negresses, he sees their children fondled and kissed by negro nurses . . . he sees white folks' food cooked and served by negroes." For Noyes, remarkably, miscegenation was subsumed within this broader array of skin-crawling, cross-class touch.[48]

A sensual approach suggests that much of the labor history source base explains class difference as something that is physically experienced. In this way, the study of experience and representation intersect. Still, representations that served varying political ends offered different sensual cues. Sinclair turned especially to smell to depict class as an ethnic and racial divide. In contrast, visual cues have been key to representations of class as a spatial divide. Social welfare activists, from the Pittsburgh Survey at the beginning of the twentieth century to Great Society Community Action Program workers, have produced detailed maps of urban poverty and social geography. Visual markers reinforced their maps. The Pittsburgh Survey displayed dramatic images of workers and their neighborhoods shrouded in chiaroscuro. When such urban reformers described the city in terms of darkness and daylight, ocular metaphors became markers of class difference and moral quality.

Shining lights equally represented middle-class reform.[49] The association of darkness and light, night and day continue to define urban class boundaries. Dark street corners or shadowy alleys remain ocular cues to urban decline or "underclass" ghettos.

The history of the senses also expands the study of working-class politics: the resistance, organizing, and beliefs of working people themselves and efforts at social control. In fact, so many of the efforts to control, regulate, or reform working-class lives can be linked though what we might term "sensory control." Labor historians have described scientific management, notably, as the control of work processes by managers; the managers' brain was back under the managers' cap. Scientific management was also a direct control of workers' bodies and their senses. Eating was determined now by a time-clock, not the pangs of the stomach. Workers' developed new sensual responses to the product they produced. They touched a small, indistinguishable part of the subject, but, likely, never held the finished product. This acute physical and tactile disenfranchisement from production was magnified by the ways scientific management penetrated the sounds and smells of the factory into working-class neighborhoods. Many proletarian novels, such as Thomas Bell's *Out of This Furnace*, for example, describe the mournful cry of the factory whistle. The mine whistle even provided the title for Tillie Lerner's short story, "The Iron Throat." The whistle was "like some guttural voiced metal beast."[50] Ford's five-dollar day (and welfare capitalism, in general) extended scientific management's sensory control into most aspects of workers' lives. The company welfare department claimed dominion over workers' food, hygiene, and personal deportment. Workers were expected to surrender taste, smell, and sound in return for a higher wage. The service industries that expanded at the end of the twentieth century demanded as much sensory control as earlier scientifically managed industry. The domestic worker, like the nurse or home healthcare worker, must cope with unpleasant or unsafe odors without comment or complaint. Changing notions of hygiene have cast the touch of restaurant or food service workers as a source of contamination. They are clad now in plastic or latex gloves, as removed from their product as an assembly line worker.

In addition to technologies of the senses like electrification, the "liberal project" described by Patrick Joyce of rational and incremental reform of proletarian homes and workplaces depended on sensory control.[51] This project reached back into the late nineteenth century as settlement house workers sought to regulate proletarian sensory alterity. That is, they promoted middle-class norms of smell, sound, and taste. They offered classes in hygiene to combat the perceived problem of immigrant filth, encouraged alternative recipes to immigrant foods, and organized classical music concerts. In the post-World War II years, public housing advocates even organized around the putrid conditions of urban life. Rhonda Williams documents the efforts of Baltimore housing advocates who organized against the stench of chicken blood from a nearby slaughterhouse. Meanwhile, urban planning officials, like New York City's Roger Starr, criticized public housing projects as slums by referring to the prevalent stench of urine and strong cooking odors.[52]

By contrast, working-class resistance—including hidden transcripts—can be read as a search for what we might term "sensory autonomy." For Kelley, hip-hop, played especially loud, seizes urban public space. Similarly, Elizabeth Fones-Wolf describes the class conflict that surrounded radio in the 1930s and 1940s. Trade union radio and juke joints are united in the contest over space, sound, and bodies.[53] They have their origins in disparate motivations, but actually are connected in larger contestations over sensory control. Workers often resisted the enforced silence of the workplace, whispering or singing when managers' backs were turned. Did they feel a particular triumph in piercing the auditory regime of the workplace? Elite critics or nativists even described immigrant language—the sound of something incomprehensible—as foreign, even primitive. Language was also potentially alarming, a kind of auditory autonomy outside of the control of managers or employers. Perhaps it was for this reason—in addition to the advantages in preventing shopfloor organizing—that numerous employers throughout the twentieth century have deliberately combined workers who speak different languages in the same workroom. Touch is also profoundly contested. One of the few elements of work that is increasingly regulated by law and the state is physical contact. Even as health regulations or bargaining rights have been eroded, laws about permissible touch have been clarified and expanded in the context of debates over sexual and workplace harassment. By the early 1990s, the *New York Times* noted a slew of new books that guided managers in determining when physical and oral contact—touching and joking, especially— became part of a "hostile" work environment.[54] The contemporary manager has ever more ability to hire and fire at will—but little legal right to touch an employee.

The senses were key to the ways working people physically expressed their multiple identities in spaces often firmly regulated by the state and by management. Workers defined their subjectivity in multisensory ways—and, through sensual responses, traced their differences from others. Through the examination of such responses labor historians can better understand the fracturing of working-class communities, especially along lines of race and gender. When white workers listened to the minstrel show, they heard sounds that reminded them of racial difference. They were not just "seeing race," as David Roediger has put it; they were hearing race. Similarly, when white working-class men tasted chow mein in one of San Francisco's Chinese restaurants that catered primarily to single men, they tasted racial difference. Kathleen Barry insightful analysis of airline work identifies the "wages of femininity." She argues that the glamour associated with working as stewardess was embodied in ever more revealing uniforms. Her work raises the important questions about whether the tactile feel of the working uniform obscures or confirms the sense of a particular job as professional, blue collar, manly, or feminine. It behoves the historian to examine the ways working people defined racial and gendered differences through sound, taste, and smell, in addition to sight.

In sum, the history of senses revisits and expands key questions in labor history about power, resistance, and identity. Moreover, the study of senses bridges the methodological gap between cultural and social history by defining class as something that is both experienced and represented. Class remains defined by experience, that is, the experience of smell, sound, taste, sight, and touch. At the same time, we can understand class in terms of ideology and representation—as Orwell's distasteful quote suggests. This broader understanding of class moves studies, for example of the body and of popular culture, once peripheral to labor history, to its core. The study of bodies is transformed by the study of sense. Janet Zandy's examination of the cultural representation of working people's hands or Edward Slavishak's analysis of the industry that provided prosthetics to injured workers provide new perspectives to the cultural history of working-class bodies. By focusing on hands, Zandy highlights the way hands—aged, rough, or callused—and touch become a focus for cultural conversations surrounding work. Likewise the sight of disabled factory workers transformed representations of industry from civic progress to social degeneration. Insights like those of Zandy and Slavishak, and the history of senses more broadly, restore flesh, bones, and blood to bodies. The body is removed from its solitary, individual existence and placed in its context.

Similarly, the study of popular culture merges with urban social history in, for example, the study of sound. As Clare Carbould has noted, Harlem sounded dramatically different to its proletarian residents than to outside observers. Where African Americans heard "a distinctive and valuable culture," white critics recorded sounds that confirmed primitivism. Oral culture was both a social resource in the years of the Harlem Renaissance and a question of ideology and representation.[55]

When the history of the senses bridges methodological gaps between social and cultural history, it supports the underlying commitment of many labor historians to the creation of a usable past. As it bridges definitions of culture, a sensual approach provides a way of maintaining, even expanding, the public focus of labor history even while integrating new understandings of culture. Most public labor history remains dependent on sight and aurality/orality. From websites to museums, labor historians have collected and exhibited visual documents and oral histories that tell "labor's stories" about resistance, immigration, and the experience of work. Yet sensory history could add much to these stories. We have told visual and oral stories, but, in ignoring the remaining senses, we neglect the historical stakes in controlling sensory perception.

The public labor historian is challenged to recreate either digitally or physically the experience of smell or taste. For example, as I have argued elsewhere, the sweatshop (and the racial and class politics that surrounded it) cannot be faithfully exhibited without attention to the persistent complaints about smell.[56] The uniqueness of on-going debates over the sweatshop lay, less in their complex system of contracting out labor, and more in their racialized association with debased immigrant workers. When labor historians interrogate the way critics of sweatshops have for a century focused on their filth and smells, they can engage the public in arguments about how ideas about race have shaped the experience of working people. The history of the senses presents significant challenges to public history. It also offers possibility to bring viewers and visitors ever closer to usable pasts. Exhibits, digital technologies, and museums must be revisited. The historical dependence of what Tony Bennett calls the "exhibitionary complex" on visuality can be interrogated—and overcome. In the end, the public might become less of a viewing and distanced visitor and more of an engaged participant.

Conclusion: Renovating the Social

In a recent review essay, Daniel J. Walkowitz urged historians to "renovate 'the social' in its relationship to the cultural."[57] The concern of labor historians with the cultural turn has a long genealogy. A few have embraced the methods of the new cultural history especially to elucidate the experiences of working women and people of color. Even so, historians have been wary of departing from the essential social concerns of labor history: the common experiences of workers, their collective and individual resistance, and the applicability of scholarly work in the public realm. Their concern has some basis. After all, cultural history has rightfully been criticized for its exclusive focus on an ill-defined middle class and for its disinterest in class as a constructed category of analysis. However, labor history, once an iconoclastic field of history, must not become a bastion of methodological conservatism, overly devoted to its iconographic past.

Within the expanding field of cultural history, labor history can renovate the social, partly by connecting older understandings of culture as a resource with the definitions that have guided cultural historians in their study of race, popular and mass culture, gender and the body, and representation. This connection, however, is difficult to forge. It demands linking anthropological and literary methods and logics. The history of the senses offers a workable road-map, as it is grounded equally in cultural studies and historical anthropology.

Orwell, it seems, provokes discomfort. Where labor historians have been drawn to proletarian heroism, Orwell highlights disgust. And yet, so, too, do so many other chroniclers of working-class lives. The class line appears in so many circumstances in the language of disgust and repulsion. If we admit that the working class stinks, then we recognize the way that class could be tasted, smelled, touched, heard, and seen. The senses were realms of contest, sources of control, and the means of autonomy. Arguing for the labor history of the senses is, in fact, to help articulate a social history of working-class culture and a cultural history of the working-class experience.

Notes

1. George Orwell, *On the Road to Wigan Pier* (London: Victor Gollancz, 1937). Emphasis in original. For a close reading of Orwell's interpretation of the stinking working class, see Constance Classen, David Howes, and Anthony Synnett, *Aroma: The Cultural History of Smell* (New York: Routledge, 1994), 166–67.

2. David Brody, "Workers and Work in America: The New Labor History," in *Ordinary People and Everyday Life* (Nashville, TN: American Association for State and Local History, 1983), 139–55.
3. Quoted in J. Carroll Moody, "Introduction" in J. Carroll Moody and Alice Kessler-Harris, eds *Perspectives on American Labor History: The Problem of Synthesis* (DeKalb, IL: Northern Illinois University Press, 1989), ix–x.
4. Among the key original works of the "New Labor History" are: Herbert Gutman, *Work, Culture, and Society in Industrializing America: Essays in American Working Class and Social History* (New York: Alfred Knopf, 1976); and David Montgomery, *Worker's Control in America: Studies in the History of Work, Technology, and Labor Struggles* (New York: Cambridge University Press, 1979). Subsequent work, often by the students of Gutman and Montgomery, further developed the themes of the New Labor History and often came to consider new types and groups of workers. See: Thomas Dublin, *Women at Work: The Transformation of Work and Community in Lowell, Massachusetts, 1826–1860* (New York: Columbia University Press, 1979); Susan Porter Benson, *Counter Cultures: Saleswomen, Managers, and Customers in American Department Stores, 1890–1940* (Urbana, IL: University of Illinois Press, 1986); Elizabeth Faue, *Community of Suffering and Struggle: Women, Men and the Labor Movement in Minneapolis, 1915–1945* (Chapel Hill, NC: University of North Carolina Press, 1991); Daniel J. Walkowitz, *Worker City, Company Town: Iron and Cotton Worker Protest in Troy and Cohoes, New York, 1855–84* (Urbana, IL: University of Illinois Press, 1978); Leon Fink, *Workingmen's Democracy: The Knights of Labor and Americans Politics* (Urbana, IL: University of Illinois, 1983).
5. For recent efforts to synthesize American working-class history, see Nelson Lichtenstein, *State of the Union: A Century of American Labor* (Princeton: Princeton University Press, 2002); Bruce Nelson, *Divided We Stand: American Workers and the Struggle for Black Equality* (Princeton: Princeton University Press, 2002); Priscilla Murolo and A. B. Chitty, *From the Folks Who Brought You the Weekend: A Short, Illustrated History of Labor in the United States* (New York: The New Press, 2001); Jacqueline Jones, *A Social History of the Laboring Classes: From Colonial Times to the Present* (Malden, MA: Blackwell Publishers, 1999). For one discussion of the "crisis" in labor history, see the roundtable on the future of labor history in *International Labor and Working-Class History* 46 (Fall, 1994): 7–92.
6. For important texts describing "the cultural turn," see: Fredric Jameson, *The Cultural Turn: Selected Writings on the Postmodern 1983–1998* (London: Verso, 1998); Perry Anderson, *the Origins of Postmodernity* (London: Verso, 1998); Terrence J. McDonald, ed., *The Historic Turn in the Human Sciences* (Ann Arbor, MI: University of Michigan Press, 1996); David Chaney, *The Cultural Turn: Scene-Setting Essays on Contemporary Social History* (London: Routledge, 1994).
7. For essays that explore the social construction of difference, see Eileen Boris and Angélique Janssens, eds *Complicating Categories: Gender, Class, Race and Ethnicity* (Cambridge: Cambridge University Press, 1999).

8. David Thelen, "The Practice of History" *Journal of American History* 81 (Spring, 1989): 942–43. On the cultural turn in history and its relationship to social history, see Lynn Hunt, ed., *The New Cultural History* (Berkeley, CA: University of California Press, 1989); Victoria E. Bonnell and Lynn Hunt, eds *Beyond the Cultural Turn: New Directions in the Study of Society and Culture* (Berkeley, CA: University of California Press, 1999).

9. See Geoff Eley, "Is All the World a Text? From Society History to the History of Society Two Decades Later" in Terence McDonald, ed., *The Historic Turn in the Human Sciences* (Ann Arbor, MI: University of Michigan Press, 1996). Melvyn Dubofsky presents one particularly antagonistic, but not untypical, dismissal of historians of the cultural turn who "use jargon or arcane academic language to establish their credential as intellectuals . . . " Melvyn Dubofsky, *Hard Work: The Making of Labor History* (Urbana, IL: University of Illinois Press, 2000), 4.

10. James Green, *Taking History to Heart: The Power of the Past in Building Social Movements* (Amherst, MA: University of Massachusetts Press, 2000), 1–167; Annelise Orleck, *Storming Caesars Palace: How Black Mothers Fought Their Own War on Poverty* (Boston: Beacon Press, 2005).

11. See, for example, Daniel J. Walkowitz, *The Molders of Troy* (Schenectady; WMHT-TV with Bowling Green Films, Inc. 1979); Studs Terkel, *Working: People Talk About What They Do All Day and How They Feel About What They Do* (New York: Pantheon, 1974); *Jeremy Brecher, Strike!* (Boston, MA: South End Press, 1972); Roy Rosenzweig and David Thelen, *The Presence of the Past: Popular Uses of History in American Life* (New York: Columbia University Press, 1998).

12. Rick Halpern, "Oral History and Labor History: A Historiographic Assessment after Twenty-Five Years," *Journal of American History* 85 (2) (1998): 596–610.

13. John R. Commons et al., *History of Labor in the United States,* vols 1–4 (New York: Macmillan, 1918–35); Philip Taft, *The A.F. of L. from the Death of Gompers to the Merger* (New York: Harper, 1959); David Montgomery, *Citizen Worker: The Experience of Workers in the United States with Democracy and the Free Market during the Nineteenth Century* (New York: Cambridge University Press, 1995); Gutman, *Work, Culture, and Society,* 3–118; Bruce Laurie, *Artisans into Workers: Labor in Nineteenth-Century America* (Urbana, IL: University of Illinois Press, reprint 1997), 6–14; Alice Kessler-Harris, *Gendering Labor History* (Urbana, IL: University of Illinois Press, 2006), 134; Roy Rosenzweig, *Eight Hours for What We Will: Workers and Leisure in an Industrial City, 1870–1920* (New York: Cambridge University Press, 1983); Fink, "American Labor History," 233–34.

14. E. P. Thompson, *Making of the English Working Class* (New York: Vintage Books, 1963). On the influence and historiography of Thompson, see Harvey J. Kaye and Keith McClelland, eds *E.P. Thompson: Critical Perspectives* (Philadelphia, PA: Temple University Press, 1990).

15. In addition, cultural historians have questioned social historians' definition of experience as an objective experience that, therefore, can be shared in common. Joan W. Scott, "The Evidence of Experience," *Critical Inquiry* 17 (Summer, 1991):

773–97 understands experience not as something real, but as located within a discursive context. This insight is key to the linguistic turn that has informed both cultural history and the critique of the New Labor History. See: Gabrielle M. Spiegel, ed., *Practicing History: New Directions in Historical Writing after the Linguistic Turn* (New York: Routledge, 2005).

16. On different understandings of culture, see: Stuart Hall, "Cultural Studies: Two Paradigms" in Nicholas Dirks, Geoff Eley, and Sherry Ortner, eds *Culture/ Power/History* (Princeton: Princeton University Press, 1994), 520–38; William H. Sewell, Jr, "The Concept(s) of Culture" in Bonnell and Hunt, eds *Beyond the Cultural Turn*, 35–61.

17. Sidney Mintz, "Foreword" in Norman Whiten, Jr and John F. Szwed, eds *Afro-American Anthropology: Contemporary Perspectives* (New York: The Free Press, 1970).

18. Michael H. Frisch and Daniel J. Walkowitz, eds *Working-Class America: Essays on Labor, Community, and American Society* (Urbana, IL: University of Illinois Press, 1983), xii; Susan Porter Benson, *Counter Cultures: Saleswomen, Managers, and Customers in American Department Stores, 1890–1940* (Urbana, IL: University of Illinois Press, 1986), 2–3.

19. Gutman, *Work, Culture, and Society in Industrializing America*, esp. 16–19;

20. Clifford Geertz, *The Interpretation of Cultures* (New York: Basic Books, 1973). For examples of the continuing importance (and usefulness) of this definition of culture, see Eric Arnesen, Julie Greene, and Bruce Laurie, eds *Labor Histories: Class, Politics, and the Working-Class Experience* (Urbana, IL: University of Illinois Press, 1998), 8–9; Gunther Peck, *Reinventing Free Labor: Padrones and Immigrant Workers in the North American West, 1880–1930* (New York: Cambridge University Press, 2000). For one labor historical critique of this definition, see Elizabeth Jameson, *All That Glitters: Class, Conflict, and Community in Cripple Creek* (Urbana, IL: University of Illinois Press, 1998), esp. 10–11 and William Powell Jones, *The Tribe of Black Ulysses: African American Lumber Workers in the Jim Crow South* (Urbana, IL: University of Illinois Press, 2005), 60–88.

21. Peggy Pascoe, "Race, Gender, and Intercultural Relations: The Case of Interracial Marriage," *Frontiers* 12 (1991): 5–18.

22. One of the results of the cultural turn is an examination of the role of the historian in the production of narratives and in the reconstruction of the social. See: Karen Halttunen, "Cultural History and the Challenge of Narrativity" in Bonnell and Hunt, eds *Beyond the Cultural Turn*, 165–84.

23. See, for example, Alice Kessler-Harris, "Where Are the Organized Women Workers?" *Feminist Studies* 3 (9) (Fall, 1975): 92–110; Barbara Mayer Wertheimer, *We Were There: The Study of Working Women in America* (New York: Pantheon, 1977); Joe William Trotter, Jr, *Black Milwaukee: The Making of an Industrial Proletariat, 1915–1945* (Urbana, IL: University of Illinois Press, 1985); Herbert Gutman, "The Negro and the United Mine Workers of America: The Career and Letters of Richard L. Davis and Something of Their Meaning, 1890–1900" in

Julius Jacobson, ed. *The Negro and the American Labor Movement* (Garden City, NY: Anchor Books, 1968), 49–127.

24. For examples of how to move women and people of color to the center of labor history methodology, see: David Roediger, "What If Labor Were Not White and Male? Recentering Working-Class history and Reconstructing Debate on the Unions and Race," *International Labor and Working-Class History* 51 (1997): 72–95; Alice Kessler-Harris, "Treating the Male as 'Other': Redefining the Parameters of Labor History," *Labor History* 34 (2–3) (1993): 190–204.

25. James Scott, *Domination and the Arts of Resistance: Hidden Transcripts* (New Haven, CT: Yale University Press, 1990); James Scott, *Weapons of the Weak: Everyday Forms of Peasant Resistance* (New Haven, CT: Yale University Press, 1985). On the application of the ideas of Scott to the study of the working class, see Robin D. G. Kelley, " 'We Are Not What We Seem': Re-thinking Black Working-Class Opposition in the Jim Crow South," *Journal of American History* 80 (June 1993): 75–112; Tricia Rose, *Black Noise: Rap Music and Black Culture in Contemporary America* (Hanover, NH: Wesleyan University Press, 1994).

26. George Rawick, "Working-Class Self-Activity," *Radical America* 3 (March–April 1969): 23–31; Robin D. G. Kelley, *Race Rebels: Culture, Politics, and the Black Working Class* (New York: The Free Press, 1994), esp. 161–228; Nan Enstad, *Ladies of Labor, Girls of Adventure: Working Women, Popular Culture, and Labor Politics at the Turn of the Twentieth Century* (New York: Columbia University Press, 1999); Tera Hunter, *To 'Joy My Freedom: Southern Black Women's Lives and Labors after the Civil War* (Cambridge: Harvard University Press, 1997).

27. Kelley, *Race Rebels*, 6. See, also, Ava Baron, "Gender and Labor History: Learning from the Past, Looking to the Future" in *Work Engendered: Toward a New History of American Labor* (Ithaca, NY: Cornell University Press, 1991), 1–46. This is not in any way to diminish the enormous contribution of scholars like Gutman and Montgomery, only to suggest that the work of other scholars, some not as tied to this particular brand of social history, has been and will be critical in understanding the history of "ordinary Americans."

28. Kessler-Harris, *Gendering Labor History*, 10.

29. Kathy Peiss, *Cheap Amusements: Working Women and Leisure in Turn-of-the-Century New York* (Philadelphia, PA: Temple, 1986); Michael Denning, *Mechanic Accents: Dime Novels and Working-Class Culture in America* (New York: Verso, 2nd edition, 1998); Denning, *Culture in the Age of Three Worlds* (New York: Verso, 2004); Charles F. McGovern, *Sold American: Consumption and Citizenship, 1890–1945* (Chapel Hill, NC: University of North Carolina Press, 2006).

30. Matt Garcia, *A World of Its Own: Race, Labor and Citrus in the Making of Greater Los Angeles, 1900–1970* (Chapel Hill, NC: University of North Carolina Press, 2001).

31. Enstad, *Ladies of Labor, Girls of Adventure*; Paula Rabinowitz, *Labor and Desire: Women's Revolutionary Fiction in Depression America* (Chapel Hill, NC: University of North Carolina Press, 1991); Blake Allmendinger, *The Cowboy: Representations*

of Labor in an American Work Culture (New York: Oxford University Press, 1992); Nicholas K. Bromell, *By the Sweat of the Brow: Literature and Labor in Antebellum America* (Chicago: University of Chicago Press, 1993); Kathryn Oberdeck, "Popular Narrative and Working-Class Identity: Alexander Irvine's Early Twentieth Century Literary Adventures" in Arnesen, Greene, and Laurie, eds *Labor Histories*, 201–29; Michael Denning, *The Cultural Front: The Laboring of American Culture in the Twentieth Century* (London: Verso, 1996); Barbara Melosh, *Engendering Culture: Manhood and Womanhood in New Deal Public Art and Theater* (Washington, D.C.: Smithsonian Institution Press, 1991); Peter La Chapelle, *Proud to Be an Okie: Cultural Politics, Country Music, and Migration to Southern California* (Berkeley, CA: University of California Press, 2007); José M. Alamillo, *Making Lemonade out of Lemons: Mexican American Labor and Leisure in a California Town, 1880–1960* (Urbana, IL: University of Illinois Press, 2006).

32. Matthew Frye Jacobson, *Barbarian Virtues: The United States Encounters Foreign Peoples at Home and Abroad* (New York: Hill and Wang, 2000).

33. Linda Gordon, *The Great Arizona Orphan Abduction* (Cambridge: Harvard University Press, 1999); Paul Gilroy, *The Black Atlantic: Modernity and the Double Consciousness* (Cambridge: Harvard University Press, 1993); Marcel van der Linden, "Transnationalizing American Labor History," *Journal of American History* 86 (3) (1999): 1078–92; Nancy Hewitt, *Southern Discomfort: Women's Activism in Tampa, Florida, 1880s–1920s* (Urbana, IL: University of Illinois Press, 2001).

34. Amy Dru Stanley, *From Bondage to Contract: Wage Labor, Marriage, and the Market in the Age of Slave Emancipation* (Cambridge: Cambridge University Press, 1998); Jonathan A. Glickstein, *Concepts of Free Labor in Antebellum America* (New Haven, CT: Yale University Press, 1991); Alice Kessler-Harris, *A Woman's Wage; Historical Meanings and Social Consequences* (Lexington, KY: University of Kentucky Press, 1990); Daniel J. Walkowitz, *Working With Class: Social Workers and the Politics of Middle-Class Identity* (Chapel Hill, NC: University of North Carolina Press, 1999).

35. Hunt, ed., *The New Cultural History*, 4–6.

36. Kathleen Barry, *Femininity in Flight: A History of Flight Attendants* (Durham, NC: Duke University Press, 2007), 174–210; Ardis Cameron, "Boys Do Cry: The Rhetorical Power of the 'New' Labor History," *Labor* 1 (Fall, 2004): 97–108; Elizabeth Faue, "Reproducing the Class Struggle: Class, Gender and Social Production in U.S. Labor History," *Mitteilungsblatt des Instituts fur Soziale Bewegungen* (Heft 25, 2001), 47–66.

37. Elizabeth Faue, *Writing the Wrongs: Eva Valesh and the Rise of Labor Journalism* (Ithaca, NY: Cornell University Press, 2002). On the working-class subject, see also: Paige Raibmon, "The Practice of Everyday Colonialism: Indigenous Women at Work in the Hop Fields and Tourist Industry of Puget Sound," *Labor* 3 (3) (2006): 23–56; Joshua Brown, *Beyond the Lines: Pictorial Reporting, Everyday Life, and the Crisis of Gilded Age America* (Berkeley, CA: University of

California Press, 2002); Frank Tobias Higbie, *Indispensable Outcasts: Hobo Workers and Community in the American Midwest, 1880–1930* (Urbana, IL: University of Illinois Press, 2003).

38. Ava Baron and Eileen Boris, "The Body as a Useful Category for Working-Class History" *Labor* 4 (Summer, 2007): 23–43; Joel Dinerstein, *Swinging the Machine: Modernity, Technology, and African American Culture between the World Wars* (Amherst, MA: University of Massachusetts Press, 2003).

39. Marshall McLuhan, *The Gutenberg Galaxy* (Toronto: University of Toronto Press, 1962); Walter Ong, *Orality and Literacy: The Technologizing of the World* (New York: Routledge, 1982).

40. Constance Classen, *World of Sense: Exploring the Senses in History and Across Cultures* (New York: Routledge, 1993); David Howes, *Sensual Relations: Engaging the Senses in Culture and Social Theory* (Ann Arbor, MI: University of Michigan Press, 2003); Mark M. Smith, "Producing Sense, Consuming Sense, Making Sense: Perils and Prospects for Sensory History," *Journal of Social History* 40 (June 2007): 841–58.

41. Constance Classen, "Foundations for an Anthropology of the Senses," *International Social Science Journal* 153 (September 1997): 401.

42. Mark M. Smith, *Listening to Nineteenth-Century America* (Chapel Hill, NC: University of North Carolina Press, 2001); Smith, *How Race is Made: Slavery, Segregation, and the Senses* (Chapel Hill, NC: University of North Carolina Press, 2006). See also Shane White and Graham White, *The Sounds of Slavery: Discovering Africa American History through Songs, Sermons, and Speech* (Boston, MA: Beacon, 2005).

43. James R. Barrett, *Work and Community in the Jungle: Chicago's Packinghouse Workers, 1894–1922* (Urbana, IL: University of Illinois Press, 1990); Roger Horowitz, *Negro and White, Unite and Fight!: A Social History of Industrial Unionism in Meatpacking, 1930–90* (Urbana, IL: University of Illinois Press, 1997), 11–12.

44. James R. Barrett, "Remembering *The Jungle* (1906)," *Labor* 3 (Winter, 2006): 7–12.

45. George McKay, "The Sweating System" in *Eighth Annual Report of the Factory Inspector of the State of New York, 1893* (Albany, NY: James B. Lyon, State Printer, 1894), 787–97.

46. Edward A. Ross, "Ethnological Notes," Edward A. Ross Papers, Wisconsin Historical Society, box 26, folder 11; Edward Alsworth Ross, *The Old World in the New: The Significance of the Past and Present Immigration to the American People* (New York: The Century Co., 1914).

47. Rev. C. H. Parkhurst, "Is Christianity Declining?" *North American Review* 41 (July 1885): 25–34.

48. William Noyes, "Some Proposed Solutions to the Negro Problem," *International Socialist Review* 2 (December 1901): 401–03.

49. Maurine Greenwald, "Visualizing Pittsburgh in the 1900s: Art and Photography in the Service of Social Reform" in Maurine Greenwald and Margo Anderson, eds *Pittsburgh Surveyed: Social Science and Social Reform in the Early Twentieth Century* (Pittsburgh: University of Pittsburgh Press, 1996), 124–52; Daniel E. Bender, *American Abyss: Savagery and Civilization in the Age of Industry* (Ithaca, NY: Cornell University Press, 2009).

50. Thomas Bell, *Out of this Furnace* (Pittsburgh: University of Pittsburgh Press, 1976 [1941]); Tillie Lerner, "The Iron Throat" in Granville Hicks, et al., eds *Proletarian Literature in the United States: An Anthology* (New York: International, 1935).

51. Patrick Joyce, *The Rule of Freedom: Liberalism and the Modern City* (London: Verso, 2003).

52. Rhonda Y. Williams, *The Politics of Public Housing: Black Women's Struggles Against Urban Inequality* (New York: Oxford University Press, 2004), 146; Roger Starr, *The Urban Choices: The City and its Critics* (Ann Arbor, MI: University of Michigan Press, 1967), 89.

53. Elizabeth Fones-Wolf, *Waves of Opposition: Labor and the Struggle for Democratic Radio* (Urbana, IL: University of Illinois Press, 2006).

54. Barbara Presley Noble, "When the Subject Is Harassment: Tomes of Advice on How to Avoid the Syndrome—or Minimize its Effects," *New York Times* (July 12, 1992), 94.

55. Clare Corbould, "Streets, Sounds and Identity in Interwar Harlem," *Journal of Social History* 40 (June 2007): 859–94. See also: Roger Horowitz, *Putting Meat on the American Table: Taste, Technology, Transformation* (Baltimore, MD: Johns Hopkins University Press, 2006).

56. Daniel E. Bender, "Sweatshop Subjectivity and the Politics of Definition and Exhibition," *International Labor and Working-Class History* 61 (Spring, 2002): 13–23.

57. Daniel J. Walkowitz, "Critical Junctions: Anthropology and History Beyond the Cultural Turn (review)," *Journal of Social History* 40 (Summer, 2007): 1011–13.

CHAPTER TEN

Re-Imagining Labor: Gender and New Directions in Labor and Working-Class History

Elizabeth Faue

Nearly thirty years have passed since David Montgomery extolled the virtues of workplace culture, the fraternal work ethic, and worker resistance against scientific management in his landmark book, *Workers' Control in Industrial America.*[1] His influential volume spurred a wave of studies of shop floor resistance and the emerging labor relations regime in the Progressive era. Manufacturing firms slowly replaced old systems of labor control, where craft custom and personal relationships set the pace of work, with rational systems, including Taylor's scientific management and time-studies of production. Montgomery detailed how workers resisted in small and large ways the imposition of the new system of workplace control and established grassroots resistance to the new management regime. Working-class men were central to Montgomery's argument, but women factory operatives—outside of Montgomery's purview—were less able and less committed to opposing the new factory order. In all of this, the focus of the argument was on grassroots resistance to the larger movements of Capital and its technology of surveillance and control.

Less direct but still influential was Montgomery's tentative, slender discussion of manliness, masculinity, and brotherhood as central to labor ideology and practice. His focus on the masculine work culture of the skilled trades, however, laid the groundwork for scholarship in the next three decades that embraced gender differences in the construction, practice, and language of labor solidarity. Drawing on his work, but also the work of historical sociologists such as Cynthia Cockburn and historian Joan Scott, feminist labor historians explored how men and women had different work cultures and experiences.[2] Ironically, attention to the use of working-class ideals of manhood and the use of gendered (masculine) political language in the labor movement had two consequences. First, it made gender central to labor history and incorporated gender analysis, and thus women's experience, into the field as a whole; second, it made masculinity, a hitherto unexplored aspect of working-class life, central to women's history.

How women's labor history became gendered labor history and in turn reshaped the larger field is the subject of this essay. I begin by outlining the development of labor history and women's labor history in the twentieth century. Exploring key texts, I show how socialist feminist theory, discursive gender analysis, and the exploration of working-class masculinities and womanhood reinvigorated historical understandings of work, the labor movement, and labor history. The resurgence of feminist activism, the employment of gender analysis in the social sciences and the humanities, and the continued growth in and impact of women's labor force participation have given energy and political meaning to studies of class formation and class protest. They focus not only on women, women's work, or women's labor activism in a narrow or even a national sense. They explore, instead, diverse "masculinities," representations of womanhood, and the "performance" of gender, persistent forms of gender discrimination and sexual harassment, and the gendered character of craft work and unskilled and sweated labor. Explorations of gender in labor and working-class history have led not only to studies of working-class subjectivity but also to gendering our understanding of capitalism and class politics.

Labor History in the Twentieth Century

The earliest academic work in labor history was under labor economist John Commons and his students at the University of Wisconsin. The Wisconsin School was primarily concerned with the development of American labor unions as economic institutions and on the legal and political framework of trade unionism. Their studies focused on skilled white workingmen; and they paid little attention, except as exceptional cases, with women as workers or, for that matter, with immigrant and African American workers. When they did discuss women workers, it was to record and describe their difference from men in labor protest and union activism, not to ask analytical questions about its origin and impact. For labor historians of the Progressive era, women's wage work and their lack of enthusiasm for union organization, in the face of labor union hostility, became a problem to be solved tactically, not a structural or cultural obstacle that demanded change. Echoing the public voice of the labor movement, labor and working-class historians envisioned labor as a mostly masculine enterprise, in which women played a marginal and subordinate role.[3]

For Helen Marot, a Progressive labor reformer associated with the Commons School, labor activism was a gendered activity—"masculinity" and "femininity" determined its form, its character, and its language of representation. While women, Marot observed, made good strikers, their role in the labor force and the family made them poor unionists; men, in contrast, were the foundation upon which the labor movement was built. Workingmen in the trades in particular were more institutionally conservative and thus stable; they were invested in their skill as property and in their role as family provider. Such men, embracing the values of craft unionism, made the best unionists, while women workers, mainly unskilled workers, had less investment in or support for permanent organization. Burdened with family responsibilities and social expectations, women occasionally displayed the tenacity of revolutionists but not the steadfastness required of unionists and labor leaders.[4]

Writing only a few years before the tumultuous labor revival of World War I, Marot had evidence to support her formulation. The Uprising of the 20,000 had given renewed energy to the International Ladies' Garment Workers Union, but it was men who had made the Protocols of Peace in which the union became the bargaining agent for the garment trade.[5] Women frequently led the demonstrations in the epic "Bread and Roses" strike in Lawrence, Massachusetts; the fiery Elizabeth Gurley Flynn inspired them to hang on in the desperate days of January, but it was men who negotiated the agreement ending the strikes.[6] In strikes in mining, packinghouse, and steel industries, where women stood out in the crowd, gave rousing speeches like Mother Jones, and even suffered and died at the hands of police and private armies, as women and children did during the Ludlow massacre, they came to represent the victims of Capitalism at its most destructive.[7] Still, the figures of Samuel Gompers, Big Bill Haywood, and Eugene Debs dominated the mass-market, labor, and radical presses.[8]

Despite the writings of labor reformers like Marot, the voice of labor in the Progressive Era remained primarily masculine and muscular, both in the tones of conservative trade unionism and in the radical accents of the Industrial Workers of the World. As a representation of working-class struggle, the Worker towered over smaller images of Capital and the State in cartoon, poster art, and in proletarian fiction.[9] For labor historians, the naturalness of gender ideology, and how gendered assumptions permeate the languages of work, protest, and politics, made it possible to write about workingmen and manhood both uncritically and unselfconsciously.

Over the years, labor's public face remained the same during the triumph of industrial unionism in the 1930s, the workplace conflicts of World War II and the postwar strike wave, and while the labor rebellions of the 1970s raged. Despite women's increased presence in the workplace, labor organizing, leadership, and even membership continued to be gendered male. The rank-and-file rebellions of the decade occurred against the backdrop of men in industrial unions, even as corporations outsourced production, closed factories, and abandoned mines and even as the women's struggles for pay equity and gender equality offered new stories, diverse voices, and new forms of organization.[10] It took the emergence of the women's movement of the 1960s and 1970s to make possible re-envisioning the labor movement, and labor history, in a new gender-conscious and feminist way.

Women's Labor History

When the new women's history came of age in the 1980s, it was guided by concerns derived from the women's movement, especially socialist feminist theories about women workers and their participation in social movements and working-class politics. Historians further asked what women's condition had been historically and how public work and social class shaped their lives in a broad spectrum of nations and cultures. Studies exploring women's status and work inside the home and in the paid labor force, and relationships between men and women, saw capitalism and its social relations, at least since the fifteenth century, as determining women's place in society and their role in history. This perspective made women's labor history one of the more popular areas of study and argued for connections between women's status and their labor force participation, even during the long nineteenth century, when women wage workers represented only a small fraction of the female population generally.[11]

Following the revival of women's history as an academic field, feminist historians began to explore women's relationship with the labor movement and especially sex discrimination and exclusion. Scholars in the United States such as Alice Kessler-Harris and Nancy Gabin and sociologist Ruth Milkman probed what role women played in a working-class movement defined and led by men and governed by ideas of men's authority. Implicating labor unions in creating—or, at the very least, perpetuating—the sexual division of labor, feminist labor historians documented the historical origins of contemporary sex segregation of the labor market and the labor movement.[12] An underlying assumption was that men and women, historically and culturally, had different attitudes toward and models of work and family relations. For most of the nineteenth and early twentieth centuries, differences in men's and women's labor force participation over the life course reinforced this assumption.[13]

As these early writers acknowledged, the paradigm of divided lives and segmented worlds did not fully describe working-class lives. Women's labor historians tentatively began to rethink labor history as a whole from the perspective of gender (men and women), family, household, and community. They argued that, while working-class families harbored both competing and collective interests, family ideology shaped men's and women's public identities—women as part of domestic ideology and men in terms of the family wage.[14] The different family roles, life cycles, and life chances of working-class men and women altered how they saw themselves in relationship to ethnic communities, labor unions, and political organizations; so too did ideas about manhood and womanhood and the proper role of men and women. While they shared forms of collective protest with men, historians argued, working-class women developed gender-specific repertoires for their own collective actions that drew their power, in part, from traditional understandings of masculinity and femininity.[15] Finally, family and community provided context and meaning not only to working-class women's protest but also to organized workingmen, as they became invested in the roles of citizen worker and family provider.[16]

Early works in the new women's history focused on what we might now consider the iconic image of women wage-earners—most specifically, as factory operatives, an occupation that employed only a minority of working women. Most income-producing work for women came, instead, through domestic labor and outwork. Manufacturing work for women, while visible and controversial, was the arena of only the "lucky" few.[17] Studying factory labor was, however, familiar ground. Progressive labor historians already had relayed the story of the mill girls of Lowell, Massachusetts, the shirtwaist strikers of 1910 New York, the collar workers of Troy, New York, and their industrial counterparts. For the most part, women's labor historians argued, the experience of being a workingwoman was widely shared and accepted, even as few working women thought of themselves as regular wage-earners or even potential members of working-class movements. Thomas Dublin, Daniel Walkowitz, Christine Stansell, Mary Blewett, Susan Levine, and Carole Turbin, among others, traced the growth of a women's trade union consciousness, even as they confirmed that workingmen primarily saw labor protest and labor reform as masculine and work as a masculine realm.[18]

While studies of working women centered on nineteenth-century female operatives in the textile, garment, and shoe industries, historians of the twentieth century launched their research on women in working-class communities but also covered a broad range of women's occupations in service and clerical sector as well as manufacturing. Elizabeth Jameson, Mary Murphy, Ardis Cameron, Laurie Mercier, myself, and others studied labor struggles in working-class communities as expressive of gendered class politics. Patricia Cooper, Sharon Hartman Strom, Sue Cobble, and Venus Green explored how working women in cigar-making, clerical work, domestic service, waitressing, and in communications shaped work culture and labor activism along gender and race lines.[19] The collective portrait that women's labor historians painted was of female labor force participation that increased gradually over the course of the twentieth century even as it changed in composition, character, and duration. A greater proportion of women engaged in waged and salaried work, with longer work careers, as married women and as mothers. They have constituted a growing proportion of the paid labor force and the labor movement, changes that have made women workers' participation increasingly significant over time. Historians further have shown working women's encounter with a workplace of male design and authority and permeated with a masculine culture of class confrontation and cross-class fraternal bonds. Working women learned to make their jobs their own, forming same-sex bonds in workplace and community and forging a work culture and language of protest that reflected women's values.[20]

Beyond the workplace, working-class women have had a role to play in the labor movement not only as workers but as wives and family members. Historians asked how non-wage-earning women experienced and identified class and how they imagined and explained labor activism in a culture that undervalued and even opposed women's public activism. Several studies of working-class women's activism in union auxiliaries, consumer politics, and political parties suggested that gendered class politics did not end at the factory door.[21] Rather, working-class men and women had gendered understandings of what constituted community and solidarity. Those understandings were not always or often political. In his autobiography, *Seventy Years of Life and Labor*, American Federation of Labor president Samuel Gompers wrote of "class feeling," which was an understanding that one's experience and position was determined by class and social injustice but not primarily by a political understanding. Women's labor activism, like men's, was the translation and mobilization of that feeling as class consciousness.

Labor Feminism and Working-Class Womanhood

The connection between women's labor force participation and their labor activism raised questions about the history and evolution of labor feminism across the nineteenth and twentieth centuries. The new women's history, while it tipped its hat to women's workplace activism, generally focused on the largely middle-class women's movement. It oriented its narrative to one of increased feminist activism over the twentieth century, culminating in the emergence of the women's liberation movement and contemporary feminism in the mid-1960s. For women's labor historians, early efforts to organize women workers through the Women's Trade Union League seemed to provide a model of cross-class women's activism and suggest the origins of contemporary labor feminism. More than that, the militant labor activism Helen Marot celebrated among women in the Progressive era has been seen as an expression of working-class feminism.[22] Working women's activism throughout the twentieth century gave rise to questions of women's status and role in the labor movement and in society. Beginning in the 1930s, women in the automobile and electrical industries, in hotel and restaurant work, in service employment, and in public sector jobs sought equal pay and equal opportunity on the shop floor and in the union. The passage of equal pay and civil rights legislation in the 1960s, especially Title VII, offered working women the tools to challenge sex discrimination in both workplace and union.[23] Focusing attention on gender conflict and competition in the workplace, feminist labor historians opened up debates on the relationship between the labor movement and working women but also on the relative weight and significance of gender in class politics generally.[24]

While these debates in many ways replicated feminist arguments over gender difference and equality in the pursuit of women's political agenda, women's labor history—and gendered labor history—moved beyond the divide. As Kathleen Barry's recent book, *Femininity in Flight*, argues, working women found common cause with labor organizations and sought to find their own justice outside labor's confines. Barry's book builds upon the findings of women's labor historians over the past two decades. Concerned with both the cultural meanings of gender and the legal and political practices that structured women's inequality in the labor force, she shows how working women both arrived at and later challenged their subordinate position in the labor movement. Contrasting the construction of femininity in the airline industry with the masculine culture of unionism, Barry explains the emergence of labor feminism among a group of women workers publicly characterized as accommodating and submissive. She thus bridges the divide between organized feminism and women in the labor movement.

A complex and compelling study of flight attendants' effort to unionize and struggle against discrimination, Barry's *Femininity in Flight* examines the origins of the occupation, its feminization in the early years of the airline industry, and the path toward unionization from the 1940s to the 1980s. Primarily organized under the institutional umbrella of the Airline Pilots Association (ALPA), the flight attendants' union repeatedly sought an independent charter and autonomous governance, but it came up against the strictures of the Railway Labor Act, which governed airline transit, and against the paternalism and often open sexism of the pilots' union.

Because their occupation was feminized and paid what Barry calls, "the wages of glamour," flight attendants faced not only male competition within workplace and union, but informal and direct sexual harassment from employers, co-workers, and customers. The gender dynamics of flight crews, with the male-dominated (until relatively recently) cockpit and predominantly (although not entirely) female flight attendants, created additional tensions and underlined male authority structure of workplace and union. Still, changes in the attendants' attire and in their public image contributed to the sometimes hostile work environment for women. While the image of the flight attendant in the early years of commercial flying was that of a nurse or hostess, it rapidly changed after World War II. Revealing work uniforms and suggestive slogans ("Fly Me!" as one exuberant ad campaign had it) objectified women flight attendants who saw their role as one of customer service and plane safety.[25]

Femininity in Flight focuses on the struggles of unionized flight attendants in two arenas—one in the labor movement, where flight attendants sought early on to separate from the pilots' union, and the other with employers on the issues of salaries, working conditions, and selective and restrictive employment policies. Early on, major airlines adopted hiring practices that banned married women, women above the age of 35, and women who became pregnant. In addition, the relatively high wages and travel benefits available to women flight attendants gave employers the ability to hire selectively in terms of height, weight, and appearance. Moreover, they could and did mandate workplace appearance, including hair style, uniform dress and shoes, and make-up. Employer practices created uniformity among women flight attendants but also forced many women unwillingly into early retirement and limited as well their personal lives.[26]

These issues gave flight attendants added incentive not only to push for autonomous unions, which would give priority to their needs and demands, but also to pursue other forms of work organization and litigation. With the advent of Title VII of the Civil Rights Act and organized feminism, flight attendants, along with other women workers, took on the airlines, highly sexualized advertising and uniform policies, challenged strictures on appearance, race, age, marital status, and maternity; and fought for wages and salaries commensurate with their skills, both in superior service and in guaranteeing passenger safety. Related to these struggles were concerns about occupational health and safety for airline attendants in the jet age of pressurized cabins and also with airlines serving on an irregular basis as transport for toxic substances. In seeking ways to address these problems, flight attendants sometimes sought allies within different factions of unions in the airline industry. They came to understand how the governing structures of unions and their politics could either limit or advance working women's ability to make wage gains or improve conditions.[27]

In *Femininity in Flight*, Kathleen Barry constructed a study of the flight atten-dants that employs methods from cultural and gender history as well as the social sciences. Her hybrid approach capitalizes on the best scholarship in gender and labor history over the past two decades. More than that, however, she is able to take seriously the gender differences within the flight attendants' world and struggles while also granting their pursuit of gender equality within the workplace, the labor movement, and society. There was no contradiction in the efforts of flight atten-dants' embrace of the class politics of unionization and their complementary efforts to seek autonomy from male unions and the gender politics required to make their airborne workplace safer and more hospitable for working women. Understanding the gender conflict underlying the relationship of women to male-dominated union organizations, and in the wider economic and cultural context, allows Barry and her readers to consider that class consciousness and trade union consciousness and identity were at times both problematic as well as positive for women in flight. Barry's embrace of labor feminism sees it not as a contradictory but a complemen-tary struggle for gender and class goals.

Labor Masculinities

The late 1980s set the stage for the parallel development of a labor history sensitive to and driven by gender analysis of working-class men's history. Historian Joan Scott published a series of essays in the mid-1980s, later collected in *Gender and the Politics of History*, that led the way in probing how gender shaped politics historically and how politics in turn relied on gendered discourse. Applied to the study of working-class politics and the labor movement in the United States, Scott's approach opened up questions about working-class masculinity and its expression in a muscular and masculinist labor ideology.[28] The construction and meanings of working-class man-hood remained among the unasked questions in labor and working-class history until the 1990s. What limited discussion there had been of working-class manhood did not view the language of manhood and masculinity as problematic for either working-class organization or for women in the industrial workplace. Following on questions about gender relations in the workplace, several feminist scholars began to explore how masculinity and the language of manhood shaped labor ideology and politics. *Work Engendered: Towards a New History of American Labor*, edited by sociologist Ava Baron, was the first collection of essays on labor history to take seri-ously the challenge of integrating gender analysis into the narrative of working-class American history.[29] Apart from its goal of centrally addressing women's relationship to and relations within the labor movement, the book's authors analyzed how the language and methods of masculine labor limited and at times curtailed women's labor activism and union membership.[30] Arguments about labor organizations and work subcultures expanded to incorporate language and practice along a broader continuum of class politics and experience.

Since the publication of *Work Engendered*, male historians have taken up the challenge of understanding how masculine language and manhood as an ideal have characterized class politics in the United States. Steve Meyer linked men's horseplay on the shop floor to the sexual politics of unionism, Gregory Kaster formulated the ideology of "labor's true man," Daniel Bender argued that sexual harassment reinforced the masculine hierarchy of workplace and union, and Joshua Greenberg explored how workers "advocated the man." Prolific studies have explored the importance of manliness and manhood in workplace and union and also suggest new ways to understand working-class masculinities.[31]

Even as women labor historians probed the constructions of masculinity and femininity with regard to working women's activism, new studies looked toward how working-class men defined masculinity in their own terms. The evolving history of working-class masculinities posits distinctions between rough and respectable manhood along lines of age, life course, skill, occupation, but also ethnicity and race.[32] In the nineteenth century, these divisions were clearest among those who worked in the skilled trades and those who were engaged in unskilled manual labor, whether in canal digging, dock work and hauling, or railroad construction. Easier access to the trades and the decline of apprenticeship as an institution led both to greater transience among young working-class men and to the growth of an urban youth subculture.[33]

The craft worker bore a significantly different relationship to the labor market and civil society than the unskilled roustabout. Each of the skilled trades unions, from cigar makers and carpenters to printers, iron workers, hatters, and machinists, developed a code of manly behavior on and off the job. Craft unions, including the federated trades of the AFL and the railway brotherhoods, embraced voluntarism with regard to state action, a labor ideology that was at once nativist and racially exclusive; at the same time, honorable manhood in the crafts envisioned the skilled worker as the head of household, a home-owner, and a patriotic, if contentious, citizen. Possessing skill as a property, craft unions sought to control access to the labor market through union contracts and closed shops and maintained complex systems of apprenticeship and journeymen status to limit entry to the trade. Craft union practices were defined by and defended through the language of manliness and autonomy, even as they relied upon collective action and control. For these reasons, women workers, and semiskilled immigrant and African American workingmen, were excluded by union custom and rule from membership.[34]

By the twentieth century, the dilution of skill in the workplace, greater managerial control over work processes, diminished power of working-class men in family life, and the decline of working-class men's institutions like the barbershop, volunteer fire companies, boxing clubs, street gangs, and taverns led to a revitalization of masculine aggression and the rough culture of the shop floor.[35] It was not only in industries where men dominated the workforce: in garment work, where the labor force was overwhelmingly female, and where women occupied the least well-paid and least skilled positions, male co-workers and supervisors could and did intimidate them and engaged in workplace-based sexual harassment. As historian Daniel Bender argues, such acts of aggression and interpersonal violence helped to reinforce men's authority and maintain the sexual division of labor, even as workingmen perceived themselves as vulnerable to unemployment and risk from injury or from chronic and even fatal occupational disease.[36]

Interpersonal violence in working-class households and communities has had little attention, but studies of working-class men and urban crime, based on police and court records, suggest a conflation between physicality (whether in work or leisure) and working-class masculinities. Heightened gender conflict, particularly in times of economic distress, led to escalating rates of male violence against women in private households and families; in times of relative prosperity, however, working-class men were more likely to seek validation in contests against other men and even in involuntary manslaughter against other assertive workingmen. In an essay, Pamela Haag noted how working-class men expressed uncertainty in violence against women and how masculinity was constructed in the physical assertion of authority against subordinates. While Haag does not compare these patterns to middle- and upper-class violence, her research resonates with other studies of working-class masculinity and physical contestation, in and out of the workplace.[37]

Stephen Norwood's *Strike-Breaking and Intimidation: Mercenaries and Masculinity in Twentieth Century America* implicitly critiques the construction of working-class masculinity and the valorization of violence on both sides of the class line.[38] Like Kathleen Barry's *Femininity in Flight*, Norwood's book is the culmination of two decades of scholarship on gender and labor activism. It has the distinction, moreover, of covering a topic long neglected in labor history—that of strikebreaking and union-busting—and of interpreting it through the gendered lens of twentieth-century labor relations. Norwood draws upon the rich literature of gendered labor history to reveal the often problematic association between working-class manhood and the propensity for violence. He further explores the racial and ethnic dimension of working-class masculinity in labor conflict as he explores how working-class men encountered a sometimes-armed and confrontational labor movement on the one hand and armed and legally sanctioned opposition to labor unions and strikes on the other. This violent world of labor conflict informs his portrait of Harry Bennett, the mastermind behind Henry Ford's offensive against labor.

What is refreshing in Norwood's analysis is his take on masculine violence as a problematic of turn-of-the-century labor relations. While many labor historians uncritically celebrate the ability of workers (male or female) to physically challenge employers and police in collective action, there has been little discussion of the repercussions of such violence or how it reflects larger patterns of class and industrial violence in the United States. To a great extent, Norwood fills the bill, taking on difficult subjects such as the gang-like violence of strikebreakers and paid armed guards and their shared vision of a physically intimidating and even brutal masculinity.

He also addresses the complex position of African American strikebreakers, both as workers and as armed military police, in labor conflicts of the early twentieth century. Community leaders extolled the opportunities that strikebreaking offered, especially when black men were excluded from labor unions and most industrial employment. The often visceral racial conflict between white and black workers, and pervasive working-class racism, made it possible to rationalize replacing workers; strikebreaking also legitimated African American violence both in self-defense and as part of the job. Despite being widely used in strikes, African American men were rarely given permanent employment in industry. Over time, growing reluctance to employ African American strikebreakers and the rise of a more racially egalitarian industrial union movement put an end to the practice.[39]

Norwood's study suggests that the social difference among working-class strikers and strikebreakers was small indeed. Strikers and strikebreakers came from the same backgrounds, had similar work histories—at least prior to taking on strikebreaking as an occupation, and of necessity participated in the same masculine working-class culture that placed a premium on physical prowess and confrontational style. The infamous Harry Bennett, head of Henry Ford's Service Department, lacked education, but he dominated hiring and firing and kept Ford non-union for nearly two decades. Yet he and his strikebreaking team had to be able to blend into the working-class community in order to report on and analyze workingmen's attitudes toward work and unionization. Strikebreakers valorized violence—in the workplace and on the picket line, and they relied on their ability to confront and control, if not eliminate, worker discontent using the weapons at their disposal—from blackjacks to police batons, local ordinances, and personal fisticuffs.[40]

Adrift in a Sea of Masculinity: A Conclusion of Sorts

Struggles between male strikers and strikebreakers obscure other forms of labor solidarity and subversion in labor history. Because labor unionism, from its origins, was defined as masculine in character, and the appropriate place for women as being outside the labor movement, albeit in a supporting role, union authority and governance has seen women members either as problematic (they lower men's wages and compete for jobs) or as nonexistent (women's labor struggles are not well covered or understood). The functioning of organizations, and especially of bureaucratic ones, has been gendered, and the fundamental terms in which workers function within unions are guided by such informal and unacknowledged gender beliefs and practices. In several studies, going back to the first wave of feminist scholarship in the 1970s, historians and sociologists have tried to come to grips with how corporations, workplaces, and unions encode gender in their organizational culture. In each case study, the critical factor appears to be the proportion of men and women and the relative timing of their entry into the organization. Much as has been suggested earlier, the central terms of organization, both in the workplace and in labor organizations, have interpreted authority and legitimacy as masculine, despite women's participation in and support for an organization's goals. This understanding, along with the reality of private gender conflict and public cooperation, suggests that women have remained subordinate in the labor movement for historical reasons as well as contemporary needs.[41]

The new literature on gender in labor history has made masculinity problematic in class terms and thus renewed feminist understandings that the social and intimate relations between men and women were and are political—not simply a matter of private individual behavior and private lives best kept silent. Recent studies of working-class violence, especially the suggestive studies of workplace conflict between men and women and the pervasiveness of sexual harassment, underwrite an older truth as well, that men's weapons were not only psychological intimidation and economic control but also physical and emotional violence. The cultural understandings of manhood and womanhood were different for the working classes, and for the racial and ethnic groups within them, even as men's and women's class experience and identity were centrally shaped by their gender. The role of violence in validating and pursuing class agendas, however, can and should be debated, even as class politics was and is constituted by and inseparable from gendered language and behavior.

In simple terms, work, solidarity, and protest were and to a great extent still are defined as primarily male and connected to physical outcomes, while family life, division, and passivity are defined as essentially female and ephemeral. Still, we must ask what makes it possible for women to walk a picket line, petition for rights, and sue for restitution, given these cultural expectations; how those who do not participate in the white male culture of unionism imagine themselves in solidarity, and how gender both empowers as well as limits class activism? Finally, how have such gender ideals, which have underwritten much of labor history, changed in a deindustrializing economy, where male jobs, and the solidarity that they created, disappear, even as women's jobs—and their labor union membership—are newly important for working-class families and the economy writ large? How have racial and ethnic differences among men and women workers altered how they think about their own gendered and class roles as working-class Americans?

The recent literature on gender in labor history suggests that these questions must be explored beyond the shop floor, if we are at all to make sense of how class identity is gendered and also ethnically and racially defined. A prolific field of scholarship for over a half century, labor history has documented, described, and analyzed class experience in the United States but primarily as collective and public phenomena and as expressions of work relations. What historians have not done is to follow through with our more fundamental and even philosophical questions about how working-class individuals come to be—their life chances and life courses, their emotional histories and their subjective understandings, all of which require not just gender analysis but feminist understandings of what gender difference and equality have meant and might mean.

Despite the proliferating studies of masculinities, and an even longer literature on women, we still do not know as much about family lives and affiliations and what they mean in the context of work and class politics. How working-class subjects come to be remains one of the most compelling directions for research, especially in the arenas of adolescence, sexuality, and the formation and transformation of political consciousness.

Some promising beginnings can be found in working-class and labor biography. The careful reconstruction of the lives of labor activists has shed light not only on individual paths to political activism and social mobility but also on the origins of class feeling and class consciousness.[42] The work of Canadian historian Craig Heron on working-class masculinity has engaged some of the important life course issues that shape working-class lives in a capitalist society. Studies of working-class childhood and adolescence, from child labor through education and marriage, have tended to be narrow in scope, but they also provide some insight on the gendered subjectivities of working-class men and women. George Chauncey's work on gay men in New York, while it crosses class boundaries, suggests a way into thinking about sexuality and consciousness for working-class men.[43]

Recent scholarship has focused primarily on a different divide—one between the deindustrializing developed world and the fast-industrializing but impoverished underdeveloped areas of the world. Education and even communications technology have spread faster and farther in the latter areas than in the United States. What is more, the developed world has outsourced much of its vital labor to these regions, which they neither understand nor seek to control. Globalization has changed workers' lives and altered the rate at which countries integrate and find new resources; labor conflict, among working-class men and women, has risen outside the Western postindustrial world, and gender shapes these relations as well. Labor historians concerned with gender in the postindustrial economy, and the persistence of gender inequalities in rapidly industrializing countries, are focusing on how the language and practices of masculinity and femininity structure interactions in this new world of labor. As the world of work is increasingly centered in the information sector, and moves away from the old paradigms of the labor theory of value rooted in a manufacturing economy, historians have only begun to explore how class experience, consciousness, and politics take shape within the global economy and the ways that class and class politics continue to be profoundly gendered in origin, meaning, and consequence.

Notes

1. David Montgomery, *Workers' Control in Industrial America* (Cambridge: Cambridge University Press, 1979).
2. Cynthia Cockburn, *In the Way of Women: Men's Resistance to Women in Organizations* (Ithaca, NY: ILR Press, 1991), employs socialist feminist thought on patriarchy and at the same time provides a model for the sociological study of gender and organizations. See also Joan Wallach Scott, *Gender and the Politics of History* (New York: Columbia University Press, 1988).

3. Elizabeth Faue, "Reproducing the Class Struggle: Class, Gender and Social Reproduction in U.S. Labor History," *Amerikanische Arbeitergeschichte Heute*, ed. Irmgard Steinisch, *Mitteilungsblatt des Instituts fur soziale Bewegungen* (Bochum: Ruhr Universitaet, 2001), 47–66, takes on the changing meanings of gender difference in labor and working-class history.

4. Helen Marot, *American Labor Unions* (New York: Henry Holt, 1914), 68–74. Elizabeth Faue, *Writing the Wrongs: Eva Valesh and the Rise of Labor Journalism* (Ithaca, NY: Cornell University Press, 2002), 148–59, summarizes the gendered ideology of craft unionism.

5. Daniel E. Bender, *Sweated Work, Weak Bodies: Anti-Sweatshop Campaigns and Languages of Labor* (New Brunswick, NJ: Rutgers University Press, 2004), esp. 155–80; Richard Greenwald, *The Triangle Fire, the Protocols of Peace, and Industrial Democracy in Progressive Era New York* (Philadelphia, PA: Temple University Press, 2005), 25–93.

6. Ardis Cameron, *Radicals of the Worst Sort: Laboring Women in Lawrence, Massachusetts, 1860–1912* (Urbana, IL: University of Illinois Press, 1993).

7. On the gendered representation of women workers, see, among others, Elizabeth Faue, " 'The Dynamo of Change': Gender and Solidarity in the American Labour Movement of the 1930s," *Gender and History* 1 (2) (Summer, 1989): 138–58; Ruth Siefert, "The Portrayal of Women in the German-American Labor Movement," in Hartmut Keil, ed. *German Workers' Culture in the United States, 1850–1920* (Washington, D.C., Smithsonian Institute Press, 1988), 109–36; Mary E. Frederickson, "Heroines and Girl Strikes: Gender Issues and Organized Labor in the Twentieth-Century American South," in Robert H. Zieger, ed. *Organized Labor in the Twentieth-Century South* (Knoxville, TN: University of Tennessee Press, 1991), 84–112; David Demarest, "Representations of Women in Narratives of the Great Steel Strike of 1919," in John H. Hinshaw and Paul Le Blanc, eds *US Labor in the Twentieth Century* (Amherst, NY: Humanity Books, 2000), 82–91.

8. The ideal of working-class heroism, gendered masculine, in opposition to victimhood, gendered feminine and in age both children and the elderly, is now commonly understood in labor history. See Scott, *Gender and the Politics of History*, 93–112; Faue, " 'Dynamo of Change'", and the thoughtful discussion of heroism and martyrdom in Bryan K. Garman, *A Race of Singers: Whitman's Working Class Hero from Guthrie to Springsteen* (Chapel Hill, NC: University of North Carolina Press, 2000); Rebecca N. Hill, *Men, Mobs, and Law: Anti-Lynching and Labor Defense in U.S. Radical History* (Durham, NC: Duke University Press, 2008).

9. There is a growing literature on gender and labor representations in the nineteenth and twentieth centuries. See, for example, Faue, 'Dynamo of Change'; Paula Rabinowitz, *Labor and Desire: Women's Revolutionary Fiction in Depression America* (Chapel Hill, NC: University of North Carolina Press, 1991); Melissa Dabakis, *Visualizing Labor in American Sculpture: Monuments, Manliness and the Work Ethic, 1880–1935* (Cambridge: Cambridge University Press, 1999); Laura Hapke, *Labor's Text: The Worker in American Fiction* (New Brunswick, NJ: Rutgers

University Press, 2001); Bender, *Sweated Work, Weak Bodies*; Edward Slavishak, *Bodies of Work: Civic Display and Labor in Industrial Pittsburgh* (Durham, NC: Duke University Press, 2008).

10. Studies of rank-and-file rebellions in the 1970s largely focus on men, with little reference to developments in women's labor force participation or union organization. See Sheila Cohen, "The 1968–1974 Labor Upsurge in Britain and America: A Critical History and a Look at What Might Have Been," *Labor History* 49 (2008): 395–418; Stanley Aronowitz, *False Promises: The Shaping of American Working Class Consciousness* (New York: McGraw Hill, 1973); Dan Georgakas and Marvin Surkin, *Detroit, I Do Mind Dying: A Study in Urban Revolution* (New York: St. Martin's, 1975); Dan La Botz, *Rank-and-File Rebellion: Teamsters for a Democratic Union* (London and New York: Verso, 1990); Philip W. Nyden, *Steelworkers Rank and File: The Political Economy of a Union Reform Movement* (New York: Bergin and Garvey, 1984); Glenn Perusek and Kent Worcester, *Trade Union Politics: American Unions and Economic Change, 1960s– 1990s* (Atlantic Highlands, NJ: Humanities Press, 1995). For exceptions, see recent studies by Dennis Deslippe, Kathleen Barry, and Dorothy Sue Cobble, cited and discussed below.

11. See the landmark volume *Liberating Women's History: Theoretical and Critical Essays*, edited by Berenice A. Carroll (New York: Harper and Row, 1974); note also Sheila Rowbotham, *Hidden From History: Rediscovering Women in History from the 17th Century to the Present* (New York: Pantheon, 1974).

12. James Kenneally, "Women in Trade Unions, 1870–1920," *Labor History* 14 (1) (Winter, 1973): 45–55; Alice Kessler-Harris, "Where are the Organized Women Workers?" *Feminist Studies* 3 (Fall, 1975): 92–110; Milton Cantor and Bruce Laurie, eds *Class, Sex and the Woman Worker* (Westport, CT: Greenwood Press, 1977); Ruth Milkman, "Organizing the Sexual Division of Labor: Historical Perspectives on Women's Work and the American Labor Movement," *Socialist Review* 49 (January–February 1980): 95–150; Nancy Gabin, "'They Have Placed a Penalty on Womanhood': The Protest Actions of Women Auto Workers in Detroit Area Locals, 1945–1947," *Feminist Studies* 8 (Summer, 1982): 373–98; Ann Schofield, "Rebel Girls and Union Maids: The Woman Question in the Journals of the AFL and the IWW, 1905–1920," *Feminist Studies* 9 (Summer, 1993): 335–58; Sharon Hartman Strom, "Challenging 'Woman's Place': Feminism, the Left, and Industrial Unionism in the 1930s," *Feminist Studies* 9 (Summer, 1983): 359–86; Ruth Milkman, ed. *Women, Work and Protest: A Century of US Women's Labor History* (Boston, MA: Routledge and Kegan Paul, 1985), especially Alice Kessler-Harris, "Problems of Coalition-Building: Women and Trade Unions in the 1920s," 110–38.

13. See Rosalyn Feldberg and Evelyn Nakano Glenn, "Male and Female: Job Versus Gender Models in the Sociology of Work," *Social Problems* 26 (June 1979): 524–38. This perspective informed much subsequent labor history. See, for example, Leslie Woodcock Tentler, *Wage-Earning Women: Industrial Work and*

Family Life in the United States, 1900–1930 (New York: Oxford University Press, 1979); Alice Kessler-Harris, *Out to Work: A History of Wage-Earning Women in the United States* (New York: Oxford University Press, 1982), and occupational studies such as Patricia Cooper, *Once a Cigar Maker: Men, Women and Work Culture in American Cigar Factories, 1900–1919* (Urbana, IL: University of Illinois Press, 1987).

14. See Martha May, "Bread Before Roses: American Workingmen, Unions, and the Family Wage," in Ruth Milkman, ed. *Women, Work, and Protest* (Boston, MA: Routledge and Kegan Paul, 1985), 1–21; Alice Kessler-Harris, *A Woman's Wage: Historical Meanings and Social Consequences* (Lexington, KY: University of Kentucky Press, 1990); Lawrence Glickman, "Inventing 'the American Standard of Living': Gender, Race, and Working Class Identity, 1880–1925," *Labor History* 34 (2/3) (Spring–Summer, 1993): 221–35; For the English case, Wally Seccombe, "Patriarchy Stabilized: The Construction of the Male Bread-Winner Wage Norms in 19th Century Britain," *Social History* 11 (1986): 53–76. A more recent study pushes this perspective into the late twentieth century. See Rebecca R. Scott, "Dependent Masculinity and Political Culture in Pro-Mountaintop Removal Discourse, Or, How I Learned to Stop Worrying and Love the Dragline," *Feminist Studies* 33 (Fall, 2007): 484–509.

15. For examples of how collective action is shaped by gendered meanings and repertoires, see Jacquelyn Dowd Hall, "Disorderly Women: Gender and Labor Militancy in the Appalachian South," *Journal of American History* 73 (1986): 354–82; Mary E. Triece, *On the Picket Line: Strategies of Working-Class Women during the Depression* (Urbana, IL: University of Illinois Press, 2007). See also the creative use of gender in a social movement perspectives in Karen Beckwith, "Collective Identities of Class and Gender: Working-Class Women in the Pittston Coal Strike,: *Political Psychology* 19 (March 1998): 147–67; Karen Beckwith, "Gender Frames and Collective Action: Configurations of Masculinity in the Pittston Coal Strike," *Politics and Society* 29 (2001): 297–330.

16. For early formulations, see Louise Tilly, "Paths of Proletarianization: Organiza-tion of Production, Sexual Division of Labor, and Women's Collective Action," *Signs: A Journal of Woman and Culture* 7 (Winter, 1981): 400–17; Carole Turbin, "Reconceptualizing Family, Work and Labor Organizing: Working Women in Troy, 1860–1890," *Review of Radical Political Economics* 16 (1) (1984): 1–16; Harold Benenson, "The Community and Family Bases of U.S. Working Class Protest, 1880–1920," *Research in Social Movements, Conflicts and Change* 8 (1985): 109–32. See also Alice Kessler-Harris, "Treating the Male as 'Other': Re-defining the Parameters of Labor History," *Labor History* 34 (Spring–Summer, 1993): 190–204; Johanna Brenner, "On Gender and Class in U.S. Labor History," *Monthly Review* 50 (6) (November 1998).

17. For an analysis of women's labor force participation and occupational shifts, see Elyce Rotella, *From Home to Office: U.S. Women at Work, 1870–1930* (Ann Arbor, MI: University of Michigan Research Press, 1981); Alice Kessler-Harris, *Out to*

Work: A History of Women Wage-Earners in the United States (New York: Oxford University Press, 1982); Lynn Y. Weiner, *From Working Girl to Working Mother: Female Labor Force Participation in the United States, 1820–1980* (Chapel Hill, NC: University of North Carolina Press, 1985); Claudia Goldin, *Understanding the Gender Gap: An Economic History of Women* (New York: Oxford University Press, 1990).

18. Daniel J. Walkowitz, *Worker City, Company Town: Iron and Cotton Workers' Protest in Cohoes, New York, 1855–1885* (Urbana, IL: University of Illinois Press, 1978); Thomas Dublin, *Women at Work: The Transformation of Work and Community in Lowell, Massachusetts, 1826–1860* (New York: Columbia University Press, 1979); Susan Levine, *Labor's True Woman: Carpet Weavers and Labor Reform in the Gilded Age* (Philadelphia, PA: Temple University Press, 1984); Mary Blewett, *Men, Women and Work: Class, Gender and Protest in the New England Shoe Industry, 1780–1910* (Urbana, IL: University of Illinois Press, 1988); Carole Turbin, *Working Women of Collar City: Gender, Class and Community in Troy, New York, 1864–1886* (Urbana, IL: University of Illinois Press, 1992).

19. For community studies of women's activism, see Cooper, *Once a Cigar Maker;* Ardis Cameron, *Radicals of the Worst Sort: Laboring Women in Lawrence, Massachusetts, 1860–1912* (Urbana, IL: University of Illinois Press, 1993); Mary Murphy, *Mining Cultures: Men, Women and Leisure in Butte, 1914–1941* (Urbana, IL: University of Illinois Press, 1997); Elizabeth Jameson, *All That Glitters: Class, Conflict and Community in Cripple Creek* (Urbana, IL: University of Illinois Press, 1998); Laurie Mercier, *Anaconda: Labor, Community and Culture in a Montana Smelter City* (Urbana, IL: University of Illinois Press, 2001). Women's occupational studies include David M. Katzman, *Seven Days a Week: Women and Domestic Service in Industrial America* (New York: Oxford University Press, 1978); Margery W. Davies, *Woman's Place is at the Typewriter: Office Work and Office Workers, 1870–1930* (Philadelphia, PA: Temple University Press, 1982); Susan Porter Benson, *Counter Cultures: Saleswomen, Managers and Customers in American Department Stores, 1890–1940* (Urbana, IL: University of Illinois Press, 1986); Darlene Clark Hine, *Black Women in White: Racial Conflict and Cooperation in the Nursing Profession, 1890–1950* (Bloomington, IN: Indiana University Press, 1989); Phyllis M. Palmer, *Domesticity and Dirt: Housewives and Domestic Servants in the United States, 1920–1945* (Philadelphia, PA: Temple University Press, 1989); Mary Romero, *Maid in the U.S.A.* (New York: Routledge, 1992); Sharon H. Strom, *Beyond the Typewriter: Gender, Class, and the Origins of Modern American Office Work, 1900–1939* (Urbana, IL: University of Illinois Press, 1992); Dorothy Sue Cobble, *Dishing It Out: Waitresses and Their Unions in the Twentieth Century* (Urbana, IL: University of Illinois Press, 1991); Venus Green, *Race on the Line: Gender, Labor, and Technology in the Bell System, 1880–1980* (Durham, NC: Duke University Press, 2001).

20. For examples of how industrial work fed both confrontation and fraternal bonds, see Wayne Lewchuk, "Men and Monotony: Fraternalism as a Managerial

Strategy at Ford Motor Company," *Journal of Economic History* 53 (4) (1993): 824–56; Lisa M. Fine, "Rights of Men, Rites of Passage: Hunting and Masculinity at Reo Motors of Lansing, Michigan, 1945–1975," *Journal of Social History* 33 (Summer, 2000): 805–23; Lisa M. Fine, *The Story of Reo Joe: Work, Kin and Community in Autotown, U.S.A.* (Philadelphia, PA: Temple University Press, 2004). Another arena where women confronted an evolving work culture permeated and structured by gender ideology and roles, see Angel Kwolek-Folland, *Engendering Business: Men and Women in the Corporate Office, 1870–1930* (Baltimore, MD: Johns Hopkins University Press, 1994). As heirs to a nineteenth-century vision of the self-made man, business workplaces embraced a bi-polar ideal of masculinity—individually competitive and yet imbued with a cooperative and paternalistic work ethic. See Clark Davis, *Company Men: White Collar Life and Corporate Culture in Los Angeles, 1892–1941* (Baltimore, MD: Johns Hopkins University Press, 2000).

21. For examples of women's labor activism as consumers and auxiliary members, see Marjorie Penn Lasky, " 'Where I Was a Person': The Ladies' Auxiliary in the 1934 Minneapolis Teamsters' Strike," in Milkman, ed. *Women, Work and Protest*, 181–205; Ann Schofield, "An 'Army of Amazons': The Language of Protest in a Kansas Mining Community, 1921–22," *American Quarterly* 37 (5) (Winter, 1985): 686–701; Margaret Rose, " 'From the Fields to the Picket Line': Huelga Women and the Boycott, 1965–1975," *Labor History* 32 (Summer, 1990): 271–93; Susan Levine, "Workers' Wives: Gender, Class and Consumerism in the 1920s United States," *Gender and History* 3 (Spring, 1991): 45–64; Dana Frank, "Gender, Consumer Organizing, and the Seattle Labor Movement, 1919–1929," in Baron, ed. *Work Engendered*, 273–92; Darlene Clark Hine, "The Housewives' League of Detroit," in Nancy Hewitt and Suzanne Lebsock, eds *Visible Women: New Essays on American Activism* (Urbana, IL: University of Illinois Press, 1993), 223–42; Annelise Orleck, " 'We Are That Mythical Thing Called the Public,' " *Feminist Studies* 19 (Spring, 1993): 147–72; Melinda Chateauvert, *Marching Together: Women of the Brotherhood of Sleeping Car Porters* (Urbana, IL: University of Illinois Press, 1994); Karen Beckwith, "Lancashire Women against Pit Closures: Women's Standing in a Men's Movement," *Signs* 21 (4) (Summer, 1996): 1034–68; Caroline Waldron Merithew, " 'We Were Not Ladies': Gender, Class and a Women's Auxiliary's Battle for Mining Unionism," *Journal of Women's History* 18 (2) (2006): 63–94.

22. There is a vast literature on the Women's Trade Union League. Most relevant for our discussion here is Nancy Schrom Dye, *As Equals and As Sisters: Feminism and Unionism in the Women's Trade Union League of New York* (Columbia, MO: University of Missouri Press, 1979); Nancy Maclean, '*The Culture of Resistance*': *Female Institution-Building in the International Ladies' Garment Workers' Union* Michigan Occasional Papers in Women's Studies, 21 (Ann Arbor, MI: University of Michigan, 1982); Annelise Orleck, *Common Sense and a Little Fire: Women and Working Class Politics in the United States, 1900–1965* (Chapel Hill, NC: University

of North Carolina Press, 1995); Jennifer Guglielmo, "Italian Women's Proletarian Feminism in New York City Garment Trades, 1890s-1940s," in Donna R. Gabaccia and Franca Iacovetta, eds *Women, Gender and Transnational Lives: Italian Workers of the World* (Toronto: University of Toronto Press, 2002), 247–98; Diane Kirkby, *The Power of Pen and Voice: Alice Henry's Life as an Australian-American Labour Reformer* (Cambridge: Cambridge University Press, 2002). Nan Enstad, *Ladies of Labor, Girls of Adventure: Working Women, Popular Culture, and Labor Politics at the Turn of the Twentieth Century* (New York: Columbia University Press, 1999) has provided a different take on militant women's labor activism and re-reads the history of the Uprising of the 20,000 as part of a working-class women's feminism that embraced popular culture and consumerism..

23. Nancy Gabin, *Feminism in the Labor Movement: Women and the United Auto Workers, 1935–1975* (Ithaca, NY: Cornell University Press, 1990), did pioneering work on the postwar period. See also Dorothy Sue Cobble, "Recapturing Working-Class Feminism: Union Women in the Postwar Era," in Joanne Meyerowitz, ed. *Not June Cleaver: Women and Gender in Postwar America* (Philadelphia, PA: Temple University Press, 1994); Dennis A. Deslippe, "Organized Labor, National Politics, and Second Wave Feminism in the U.S., 1965–1975," *International Labor and Working Class History* 49 (1996): 143–65; Dennis A. Deslippe, *'Rights, Not Roses': Unions and the Rise of Working-Class Feminism, 1945–1960* (Urbana, IL: University of Illinois Press, 2000); Dorothy Sue Cobble, "'A Spontaneous Loss of Enthusiasm': Workplace Feminism and the Transformation of Women's Service Jobs in the 1970s," *International Labor and Working Class History* 56 (Fall, 1999): 23–44; Nancy Maclean, "The Hidden History of Affirmative Action: Working Women's Organizations in Workplace Struggles in the 1970s and the Gender of Class," *Feminist Studies* 25 (1999): 43–78.

24. See the "Roundtable on Dorothy Sue Cobble, The Other Women's Movement: Workplace Justice and Social Rights in Modern America," *Labor: Studies in Working-Class History in the Americas*, 2 (4) (Winter, 2005): 43–62, especially responses by Alice Kessler-Harris and Elizabeth Faue.

25. Kathleen M. Barry, *Femininity in Flight: A History of Flight Attendants* (Durham, NC: Duke University Press, 2007).

26. Barry, *Femininity in Flight*; Eileen Boris, "Desirable Dress: Rosies, Sky Girls, and the Politics of Appearance," *International Labor and Working Class History* 69 (Spring, 2006): 123–42.

27. For similar struggles, see Gabin, *Feminism in the Labor Movement*; Deslippe, *Rights, Not Roses*; Susan M. Hartmann, *The Other Feminists: Activists in the Liberal Establishment* (New Haven, CT: Yale University Press, 1998); Mary Margaret Fonow, "Protest Engendered: The Participation of Women Steelworkers in the Wheeling-Pittsburgh Steel Strike of 1985," *Gender and Society* 12 (6) (1998): 710–28; Dorothy Sue Cobble, *The Other Women's Movement: Workplace Justice and Social Rights in Modern America* (Princeton: Princeton University Press, 2005).

28. Scott, *Gender and the Politics of History.*
29. See Ava Baron, ed., *Work Engendered: Towards a New History of American Labor* (Ithaca, NY: Cornell University Press, 1991). For overviews of recent literature, see Ava Baron, "Masculinity, the Embodied Male Worker, and the Historian's Gaze," *International Labor and Working-Class History* 69 (Spring, 2006): 143–60; Ava Baron and Eileen Boris, "'The Body' at Work: How Useful a Historical Concept?" and responses by John F. Kasson, Susan Glenn, and Valerie Burton in *Labor: Studies in Working Class History in the Americas* 4 (2) (Summer, 2007): 23–63.
30. For feminist scholarship on masculinity and the trades, see Anne Phillips and Barbara Taylor, "Sex and Skill: Notes toward a Feminist Economics," *Feminist Review* 6 (October 1980): 79–88; Cooper, *Once a Cigar Maker*; Mary Blewett, "Manhood and the Market: The Politics of Gender and Class among the Textile Workers of Fall River, Massachusetts, 1870–1880," in Baron, ed., *Work Engendered*, 92–113; Nancy A. Hewitt, "'The Voice of Virile Labor': Labor Militancy, Community Solidarity, and Gender Identity among Tampa's Latin Workers, 1880–1921," in Baron, ed. *Work Engendered*, 142–67; Ileen DeVault, "'To Sit Among Men': Skill, Gender, and Craft Unionism in the Early American Federation of Labor," in Eric Arnesen, Julie Greene, and Bruce Laurie, eds *Labor Histories: Class, Politics and the Working-Class Experience* (Urbana, IL: University of Illinois Press, 1998), 259–83; Daniel Bender, "'A Hero . . . for the Weak': Work, Consumption, and the Enfeebled Jewish Worker, 1881–1924," *International Labor and Working Class History* 56 (Fall, 1999): 1–22.
31. Baron, ed., *Work Engendered*, was the opening foray. See also Montgomery, *Workers' Control in America*; Steve Meyer, "Work, Play and Power: Masculine Culture on the Automotive Shop Floor, 1930–1960," *Men and Masculinities* 2 (1999): 115–34; Gregory L. Kaster, "Labour's True Man: Organised Working-men and the Language of Manliness in the USA, 1827–1877," *Gender and History* 13 (April 2001): 24–64; Daniel E. Bender, "'Too Much Distasteful Masculinity': Historicizing Sexual Harassment in the Garment Sweatshop and Factory," *Journal of Women's History* 15 (2004): 91–116; Joshua Greenberg, *Advocating the Man: Masculinity, Organized Labor, and the Household in New York, 1800–1840* (New York: Columbia University Press, 2008).
32. Steven Maynard, "Rough Work and Rugged Men: The Social Construction of Masculinity in Working Class History," *Labour/La Travail* 23 (Spring, 1989): 159–69; Joshua B. Freeman, "Hardhats: Construction Workers, Manliness, and the 1970s Pro-War Demonstrations," *Journal of Social History* 26 (Summer, 1993): 725–44; Steve Meyer, "Rough Manhood: The Aggressive and Confrontational Shopfloor Culture of Auto Workers during World War II," *Journal of Social History* 36 (2002): 125–47.
33. William J. Rorabaugh, *The Craft Apprentice: From Franklin to the Machine Age in America* (New York: Oxford University Press, 1986); Ava Baron, "'Acquiring a Manly Competence': The Demise of Apprenticeship and the Remasculinization

of Printers' Work," in Mark C. Carnes and Clyde Griffen, eds *Meanings for Manhood: Constructions of Masculinity in Victorian America* (Chicago: University of Chicago Press, 1990), 152–63; Christine Stansell, *City of Women: Sex and Class in New York, 1789–1860* (New York: Knopf, 1986); Richard Stott, *Workers in the Metropolis* (Ithaca, NY: Cornell University Press, 1990); Peter Way, "Evil Humors and Ardent Spirits: The Rough Culture of Canal Construction Laborers," *Journal of American History* 79 (4) (March 1993): 1397–1428; Peter Way, *Common Labour: Workers and the Digging of North American Canals, 1780–1860* (Cambridge: Cambridge University Press, 1993); Gunther Peck, *Reinventing Free Labor: Padrones and Immigrant Workers in the North American West, 1890–1930* (Cambridge: Cambridge University Press, 2000), 117–57; Frank Tobias Higbie, *Indispensable Outcasts: Hobo Workers and Community in the American Midwest, 1880–1930* (Urbana, IL: University of Illinois Press, 2003). For black workers, see Michael McCoyer, " 'Rough Mens' in 'the Toughest Places I Ever Seen': The Construction and Ramifications of Black Masculine Identity in the Mississippi Delta's Levee Camps," *International Labor and Working Class History* 69 (Spring, 2006), 57–80.

34. See Montgomery, *Workers' Control in America*; David Bensman, *The Practice of Solidarity: American Hat Finishers in the Nineteenth Century* (Urbana, IL: University of Illinois Press, 1985); Cooper, *Once a Cigar Maker*; Andrew Edward Neather, "Popular Republicanism, Americanism, and the Roots of Anti-Communism, 1890–1925," Ph.D. dissertation, Duke University, 1994; Eric Arnesen, " 'Like Banquo's Ghost, It Will Not Down': The Race Question and the American Railroad Brotherhoods, 1880–1920," *American Historical Review* 99 (December 1994): 1601–33; Faue, *Writing the Wrongs*, esp. 148–59; Paul Michael Taillon. " 'What We Want is Good, Sober Men': Masculinity, Respectability and Temperance in the Railroad Brotherhoods," *Journal of Social History* 36 (2002): 319–38; Bender, *Sweated Labor and Weak Bodies*.

35. This is best seen in the work of Steve Meyer on working men in the automobile industry. See Meyer, "Rough Manhood"; Meyer, "Work, Play and Power: Masculine Culture on the Automotive Shop Floor, 1930–1960," *Men and Masculinities* 2 (1999): 115–34; Meyer, "Workplace Predators: Sexuality and Harassment on the US Automotive Shop Floor, 1930–1960," *Labor* 1 (2004): 77–93. See also Stan Gray, "Sharing the Shop Floor: Women and Men on the Assembly Line," *Radical America* 18 (1984): 69–88; Nancy Quam-Wickham, "Rereading Man's Conquest of Nature: Skill, Myths, and the Historical Reconstruction of Masculinity in Western Extractive Industries," in Roger Horowitz, ed. *Boys and Their Toys? Masculinity, Technology and Class in America* (New York: Routledge, 2001), 91–110.

36. Mary Bularzik, "Sexual Harassment at the Workplace: Historical Notes," in James Green, ed. *Workers' Struggles, Past and Present: A Radical America Reader* (Philadelphia, PA: Temple University Press, 1983), 117–35, was an early work. See in addition to Meyer, "Workplace Predators," cited above, and Bender, " 'Too Much Distasteful Masculinity.'" See also Karen Mason, "Feeling the Pinch: The

Kalamazoo Corsetmakers' Strike of 1913," in Carol Groneman and Mary Beth Norton, eds *To Toil the Livelong Day: America's Women at Work, 1787–1980* (Ithaca, NY: Cornell University Press, 1987), 141–60, esp. 157–59; Enstad, *Ladies of Labor, Girls of Adventure*, 141–45.

37. Pamela Haag, "The 'Ill-Use' of a Wife: Patterns of Working-Class Violence in Domestic and Public New York City, 1860–1880," *Journal of Social History* 25 (1992): 447–77. See also Stansell, *City of Women*; Michael Kaplan, "New York City Tavern Violence and the Creation of a Working-Class Male Identity," *Journal of the Early Republic* 15 (1995): 591–617; McCoyer, "Rough Mens," speaks to workingmen's hostility toward women. Older studies of domestic violence are relevant here. See Linda Gordon, *Heroes of Their Own Lives: The Politics and History of Family Violence* (New York: Viking, 1988), and Elizabeth H. Pleck, *Domestic Tyranny: The Making of Social Policy against Family Violence from Colonial Times to the Present* (New York: Oxford University Press, 1987).

38. Stephen H. Norwood, *Strike-Breaking and Intimidation: Mercenaries and Masculinity in Twentieth Century America* (Chapel Hill, NC: University of North Carolina Press, 2002).

39. Norwood, *Strikebreaking and Intimidation*, 78–113.

40. See also Robert Michael Smith, *From Blackjacks to Briefcases: A History of Commercialized Strikebreaking and Unionbusting in the United States* (Athens: Ohio University Press, 2003), which provides additional insights into strike-breaking but expends little effort in teasing out the gender implications.

41. Rosabeth Moss Kanter, *Men and Women of the Corporation* (New York: Basic Books, 1977); Cynthia Cockburn, *Brothers: Male Dominance and Technological Change* (London: Pluto Press, 1983); Jeff Hearn and Wendy Parkin, "Gender and Organizations," *Organization Studies* 4 (1983): 219–42; Jeff Hearn, *The Gender of Oppression: Men, Masculinity and the Critique of Marxism* (New York: St. Martin's Press, 1988); Elizabeth Faue, "Paths of Unionization: Community, Bureaucracy and Gender in the Minneapolis Labor Movement of the 1930s," in Baron, ed. *Work Engendered*, 296–319; Cockburn, *In the Way of Women*; Fonow, "Protest Engendered"; Gregory Wood, "The Paralysis of the Labor Movement: Men, Masculinity and Unions in the 1920s," *Michigan Historical Review* 30 (Spring, 2004). See also the contemporary evaluations in Dorothy Sue Cobble, ed., *The Sex of Class: Women Transforming American Labor* (Ithaca, NY: Cornell University Press, 2007). For gay and lesbian issues in labor, see Kitty Krupat and Patrick McCreery, eds *Out at Work: Building a Gay-Labor Alliance* (Minneapolis, MN: University of Minnesota Press, 2001).

42. Recent labor biographies include Paula F. Pfeffer, *A. Philip Randolph, Pioneer of the Civil Rights Movement* (Baton Rouge, LA: Louisiana State University Press, 1990); Elaine J. Leeder, *The Gentle General: Rose Pesotta, Anarchist and Labor Organizer* (Albany, NY: SUNY Press, 1993); Craig Phelan, *Divided Loyalties: The Public and Private Life of John Mitchell* (Albany. NY: SUNY Press, 1994); Richard Griswold del Castillo and Richard A. Garcia, *Cesar Chavez: A Triumph of Spirit* (Norman, OK: University of Oklahoma Press, 1995); James R. Barrett,

William Z. Foster and the Tragedy of American Communism (Urbana, IL: University of Illinois Press, 1999); Craig Phelan, *Grand Master Workman: Terence Powderly and the Knights of Labor* (Westport, CT: Greenwood Press, 2000); Yvette Richards, *Maida Springer, Pan-Africanist and International Labor Leader* (Pittsburgh: University of Pittsburgh Press, 2000); Elliott Gorn, *Mother Jones, the Most Dangerous Woman in America* (New York: Hill and Wang, 2001). For a wonderful study of working-class autobiography, see Mary Jo Maynes, *Taking the Hard Road: Life Course in French and German Workers' Autobiographies in the Era of Industrialization* (Chapel Hill, NC: University of North Carolina, 1995). See also Mary Jo Maynes, Jennifer L. Pierce, and Barbara Laslett, *Telling Stories: The Use of Personal Narratives in the Social Sciences and History* (Ithaca, NY: Cornell University Press, 2008).

43. Craig Heron, "'Boys Will Be Boys': Working-Class Masculinities in the Age of Mass Production," *International Labor and Working-Class History* 69 (2006): 6–34. But see also his "The Boys and Their Booze: Masculinities and Public Drinking in Working-Class Hamilton, 1890–1946," *Canadian Historical Review* 86 (September 2005): 411–52. The literature on working-class youth and older workers in the United States is scant, in part because family history has focused on the middle class. For some recent studies, see David Nasaw, *Children of the City: At Work and At Play* (New York: Oxford University Press, 1986); Jacquelyn Dowd Hall, James Leloudis, Robert Korstad, Mary Murphy, Lu Ann Jones, and Christopher P. Daly, *Like a Family: The Cotton Mill Workers' World* (Chapel Hill, NC: University of North Carolina Press, 1987); Jeffrey Ryan Suzik, "'Building Better Men': The CCC Boy and the Changing Social Ideal of Manliness," *Men and Masculinities* 2 (1999): 152–79; Todd Alexander Postol, "Masculine Guidance: Boys, Men and Newspapers, 1930–1939," in Horowitz, ed. *Boys and Their Toys?,* 169–96; Ronald D. Cohen, *Children of the Mill: Schooling and Society in Gary, Indiana, 1906–1960* (New York: Routledge Falmer, 2002); Julia Grant, "A 'Real' Boy and Not a Sissy: Gender, Childhood and Masculinity, 1890–1940," *Journal of Social History* 37 (2004): 829–51; Stephen Lassonde, *Learning to Forget: Schooling and Family Life in New Haven's Working Class, 1870–1940* (New Haven, CT: Yale University Press, 2005); Gregory Wood, "'Beyond the Age of Earning': Masculinity, Work and Age Discrimination in the Automobile Industry, 1916–1939," *Labor* 3 (2006): 91–120; George Chauncey, *Gay New York: Gender, Urban Culture, and the Making of the Gay Male World, 1890–1940* (New York: Basic Books, 1994).

CHAPTER ELEVEN

The Limits of Work and the Subject of Labor History

Zachary Schwartz-Weinstein

In recent decades, social and academic understandings of what "labor" is have been called into question on multiple fronts. Thus, the subject of labor history and the broader theoretical and social understandings of what constitutes "work" have also been thoroughly challenged and profoundly troubled. This is not a completely new development. Feminist scholars and the new social movements that emerged amidst the germination of what sociologist and world-systems theorist Immanuel Wallerstein has called "the world revolution of 1968" leveled important and powerful critiques against the limits of labor history's gaze, as, indeed, did the New Social Historians of the 1960s and 1970s who rebuked the Commons school for its institutionalist focus and blindness to everyday lived experiences and struggles. In this moment of neoliberalism's apogee and crisis, how scholars should understand what forms of activity and social life are involved in capitalism's relentless pursuit of surplus value is worthy of consideration. What does and what does not constitute "labor" has once again become important ground on which to think about the future of labor history research. If earlier critiques of labor history hinged largely upon the invisibility of particular groups of waged workers within the discipline, recent work has expanded the subject of critique. Moving away from new labor history's original project of problematizing Fordist consensus and historicizing its crisis, new questions point the way towards a labor history which might speak more directly to more recent crises in the constitution and management of work and workers. Drawing on sources which have included 1970s Marxist feminist critiques of productive labor as well as intersectional scholarship and activism at the articulation points of race, gender, class, and (sometimes) sexuality, labor studies' cultural turn has been an important, but not exclusive vehicle for such considerations. These recent interventions suggest the potential benefits of a sustained critical interrogation of productive labor's categoric occlusions, of the worlds of labor formally outside of or marginal to the wage relation. This marginality and invisibility is a central characteristic of a post-Fordist, flexible labor force which looks noticeably different in many ways from that at which the scholarly critiques of the 1970s and 1980s were directed. In this essay, I am interested not only in the criteria by which we assess the practices and acts which belong under labor history's rubric, but also in how historians can map and respond to the reconstituted landscapes of contemporary labor, to its increasingly socialized and precarious character.

As I signal above, I am proposing two directions in which historians' attempts to wrestle with these concerns might range. First, I suggest that labor history look to the processes of marginalization and accumulation which constrict and expand the definitions of work and the classes of workers. Such a project entails a continuing critical engagement with the history of the discipline and the limits and possibilities of the Marxist categorization and theorization of labor to which so much of labor history has been so productively affixed.

Second, I urge a focus on how newly "labored" (and de-labored) forms of work are situated in relation to contemporary and historical capitalisms and articulations of race, gender, and nation. Labor historians could and should continue to document the "laboring" of particular activities and groups, the way particular activities have become recognizable as work and labor, and how the subjects who perform it have become knowable as "workers," both within and outside of wage labor. But in suggesting that labor history continue to reorient its gaze, to shift the forms of work and workers with whom it is most concerned, I pay special attention to questions of racialized and gendered service work and the growing literature on affective labor.

How and when work is or is not recognizable as "work" is not a merely academic question. One need only point to two recent high-profile National Labor Relations Board (NLRB) decisions involving nurses' job classifications and graduate employee teaching assistants to recognize the ways in which questions rooted in the political economy and cultural politics of work quickly assume juridical import and tangible effects. In both *Brown University vs. the United Auto Workers* (2004) and *Oakwood Healthcare Inc.* (2006), the NLRB excised entire categories of workers from the ranks of "labor"—the nurses because they helped train new hires, the graduate teachers and researchers because they were "primarily students." The *Brown* decision[2] and *Oakwood Healthcare Inc.*[3] serve as high-profile examples of the socially constructed limits of "work," particularly in its relationship to wage labor and Fordist employment structures. These NLRB decisions made clear the political ambiguities and legal contests over what sociologist Maurizio Lazzarato has called "immaterial labor," the labor which produces the cultural and informational content of the commodity.[4] They evinced the similarly contradictory position (and gendered subordination) of what Arlie Russell Hochschild, in a formulation which has become a classic one for feminist sociology of work, called "emotional labor," the work of modulating others' emotional states by instrumentally managing ones' own feelings.[5] Hochschild's pioneering study strongly echoes in the later formulation of literary theorist Michael Hardt and autonomist Marxist political philosopher Antonio Negri. Hardt and Negri employed the post-structuralist frameworks of Foucault and Deleuze (especially the Deleuzian engagement with Spinoza) to adapt Hochschild's "emotional labor" into "affective labor." This is labor "in the bodily mode," labor which produces social relationships, social life, collective feelings, and thus the entire biopolitical edifice of the Deleuzian "society of control"—a modular, diffuse and decentralized networked inheritor of the old "disciplinary" power of the Fordist state/industry compact.[6]

These cases made clear the broad politico-economic implications of this labor, its complex cultural politics and social location. It was the communicative aspect of the gendered and affective dimensions of nurses' caring labor which the NLRB confused with a supervisory function. The board majority hinged its ruling on the legal definitions of the verbs "assign" and "direct" and the phrase "independent judgement." On the other hand, the cognitive labor of Brown University's lumpen professoriate proved, for the board, (strategically) indistinguishable from the traditional duties of the student, duties which have generally not been understood as labor. To be a student, the NLRB declared, is not to be a worker. The labor board ruling collapsed teaching work into an apprenticeship putatively outside of the realm of productive labor. Teaching's status as work was entirely contingent on how and where it is situated by employers in relation to formal and informal structures of employment, training, professional development, voluntarism, and apprenticeship.

African American studies scholar Fred Moten and social theorist Stefano Harney have posed their counterargument to this logic in terms which directly engage the questions this essay considers.[7] Moten and Harney evince a radical concern for the diffusion of social labor beyond the formal and explicit divisions of classroom labor. The commodity produced by academic labor, they argued, is inherently collaborative, and requires student labor as a condition of its completion. This dispute thus dramatized several of the features of the world of emotional and affective work which demonstrate the stakes of the socially constructed availability of "labor" as a social and legal descriptor. In particular, Brown exhibited the notion that one should love the job enough to see it as vocation rather than work. It also evinced the blurry edges produced by the collaborative and cooperative nature of labor premised on interpersonal interaction and communication, and the uneasy and contested dynamics of commodification as it operates within forms of labor which rely upon being in common.

These two labor board decisions, then, serve as examples both of the ways in which "labor's" often gendered and racialized ideological availability to multiple and disparate forms of human activity characterizes post-Fordist models of labor precaritization, and of the increasingly affective character of many types of contemporary work. They are case studies in how a mostly implicit hierarchy of labor, productive, unproductive, reproductive, waged, and wageless, has contributed to the historical and social construction of value.

Any "hierarchy" here is, of course, what orthodox Marxists would dismiss as merely superstructural. The reproductive labor, for instance, performed by immigrant women domestic workers in New York City is not, once it has been abstracted into labor power and then into exchange value, really of a lesser character than that of a textile worker in Guangzhou, or of a construction worker in New Jersey.

It appears as such, though, within capitalism's own logic, as abject and as subordinate to the hegemony of waged productive labor and managerial and professional "immaterial" production and symbolic analysis. One of the most valuable lessons of the cultural turn, however, has been the very tangible and material effects that ideas, knowledges, and ideology can bring to bear on social life. There's a very real political importance to historicizing what Gramsci would call the "relations of force" that structure the social meaning of work. Conversely, the implicit subordination of affective labor to more analytic and symbolic forms of "informatized production" in even some of the autonomist Marxist literature on immaterial labor and "cognitive capitalism" stands as a particularly ironic example of how particular kinds of work are accorded differential value within particular optics of social and cultural analysis.[8]

Labor historians might begin to rethink labor history's subject, then, might initiate a shift in the subdiscipline's implied and explicit subjects, by first grappling with "productive labor" as a category of analysis and praxis. Doing so would benefit from a brief review of how the topic has been addressed in the work of the feminist and antiracist scholars and activists who have explored and challenged orthodox Marxism's normative hegemony of the urban male manufacturing worker as the subject of history and revolutionary politics. This work has exposed the ideological and economic limits of "productive labor" through attention to the often precarious, low-wage and/or wageless forms of work excluded from its purview, a project for whose extension I argue in this essay. Orthodox Marxists and liberal consensus historians alike saw the precariat, the wageless, and the service sector as social parasites, the dangerous and untrustworthy lumpen proletariat. Antonio Gramsci, for instance, looked upon the formally unwaged labor of housewives as "artisanal" and those who performed it as a fundamentally backwards and potentially conservative social force.[9] Scholars rooted in the social struggles of the 1960s and 1970s, in women of color feminism, and in the red feminist offshoots of Italian autonomia, on the other hand, revealed what were heretofore largely unexamined worlds of labor upon which the accumulation of capital and the production of surplus value were structured.[10]

What had been understood by scholars as productive labor's antonym, as the opposite of (real) work, or as its little-discussed stepchild, in the case of informal, off-the-books, and precarious, low profile "odd jobs," became comprehensible as its indispensable conspirator. What Marx famously called the "fetish of the commodity and its secret" concealed not only the "productive labor" directly and immediately involved in the manufacture of the commodity, but also the multiple forms of labor necessary for the social relations of production to obtain, to facilitate the sale and consumption of commodities, the reproduction and care of workers, bodies, and relationships, and the collective creation of social life. The questions raised by the architects of this historiographic tradition within labor studies demanded a radical expansion of the term "worker" to those who labor in the domains of reproduction and affect, immateriality, cognition, and emotion, for irregular, informal and/or invisible compensation.[11] Although this is a project which began decades ago, its full implications for labor history have been both hotly debated and insufficiently embraced.

Troubling the limits of productive labor allows a reconsideration of conventional understandings of the historical development of capitalism and the Marxian account of the working day. It may allow historians radically different understandings of what the lives of historical subjects mean in expanded context. Still, interrogating the limits of the category of "productive labor" in classical and Marxian political economy does not completely resolve how labor historians might understand the contingent and socially constructed means by which particular acts can become known, politically, legally, and in broader social and cultural frames, as labor. Alone, such a project may not open up labor history's still-too claustrophobic historical protagonist to expanded possibilities. This is why it is necessary to historicize the term's absence, its lack, its exclusion and denial. Such denials are not constant, inevitable, or automatic, but instead occupy historically specific relationships to shifting modes of production and technologies of work, management, and consumption. The instability of labor as a category is, all too frequently, also articulated to racial formations and ideologies of gender. The erasure and denial of labor (and/or "labor") has been and is often a racial project in Michael Omi and Howard Winant's sense of the term, "simultaneously an interpretation, representation, or explanation of racial dynamics, and an effort to reorganize and redistribute resources along particular racial lines."[12] Attempts to demarcate or shift the boundary between work and non-work become a set of claims about race and races and their relationship to the workplace or the place of nonwork and, more broadly, the "economic," with which "race," intersects. The history of work and workers must also continue to grapple with questions of gender, often inseparable from the historical construction of race and races. Classical political economy's definition of labor as actions taken by man to transform the natural world naturalizes particular labors, yokes them to certain bodies and spaces. If history as a discipline has been somewhat less susceptible to such a framework, many labor historians into the 1990s too often collapsed "women" and "gender," failing to develop a gender analysis which would illuminate the kinds of problems this essay explores. Mapping the history of labor's invisibility thus necessitates an account of "labor's" relationship to intersecting histories of capital accumulation, racial formations, and gender. Karl Marx's explication of productive labor as an organizing category of labor within capitalism is foundational to such an account.

"Productive labor," in Marx, is both a limited and expansive category. It is assigned based not on the character of the work itself but rather on its relationship to the production of surplus value. The "determinate material form of the labor, and therefore of its product, in itself has nothing to do with this distinction between productive and unproductive labor."[13] The production of surplus value involves the expropriation, by the capitalist, of more labor from the workers than what their wages pay for. Surplus value is unpaid labor, labor beyond the wage. Capital is "the command over unpaid labor," surplus value is "in substance the materialization of unpaid labor time."[14] Labor is *productive* if and because the worker's unpaid labor time is, or becomes, the capitalist's profit.

In a famous passage from *Capital*'s first volume, Marx wrote,

> A schoolmaster is a productive worker where, in addition to belaboring the heads of his pupils, he works himself into the ground to enrich the owner of the school. That the latter has laid out his capital in a teaching factory, instead of a sausage factory, makes no difference to the relation.[15]

So, for Marx, teaching is productive labor *if* the teacher is paid a wage by a capitalist who profits from the teacher's labor. Other service industry work straddled the productive/unproductive divide in similar terms; a waiter or cook in a restaurant or hotel is a productive laborer because she is paid a wage to labor that her employer might profit, a wage which does not pay her the full value of her work. The labor of a cook in a private home, or a butler, however, would be "unproductive," because his or her labor consumes, rather than generates, surplus value.[16] It is important to note here that for Marx, production was increasingly socialized; workers who never put a "hand to the object" may nevertheless have been "an organ of the collective labourer," performing "subordinate functions" no less productive to the generation and extraction of the commodity's value.[17] Still, as the British socialist and political scientist Ralph Miliband noted, some forms of work Marx foreclosed from "productive labor" no matter their relationship to the production of surplus. Clerical work, in Marx's time still something of an elite and decidedly male profession, was not productive labor because clerks were not, Marx held, involved in anything resembling a direct manner, in the production of surplus value. But if the unpaid labor of "commercial workers" did not create surplus value, it did "create [the capitalist's] ability to appropriate surplus value, which, as far as this capital is concerned, gives the same result."[18] For Miliband this was evidence that the productive/unproductive distinction was not useful. His judgment was made in hindsight, many decades after the reorganization of production had long since reconfigured the demographics and social relations of clerical and office work and since social movements had begun to mount a concerted challenge to the limits of productive labor as a diagnostic category and a privileged revolutionary subject position. Yet productive labor retains its purchase, informally, at least, within the U.S. division of labor, evident in the racial differentiations in how labor is valued and assigned.[19]

Productive labor may not have been inextricably yoked to manufacturing and extractive industries, which, textiles excepted, were often the purview of male proletarians in the United States. But it was, for Marx, linked to the wage. Absent the wage-relation and the transformation of wages into profits through labor, labor was not productive—at least not in relation to capital or for capitalists.

Scholars have found this privileging of the wage problematic for several major reasons. First, it ascribed to slavery a nebulous and often debated position in the history of capitalism. Was slavery a primitive, antiquated mode of organizing labor superseded by capitalism's constant progress, or was it instead an integral part of the history of capitalist development and industrial modernity? Did the transcontinental slave trade not play an integral role in establishing a transatlantic mode of production based on the colonization of the Americas and the exploitation of indigenous and migrant unfree labor, coexistent with and indispensable to the rise of the European bourgeoisie, the discipline of political economy, and the hegemony of the wage-form? The unfree labor of enslaved people of African descent, as well as that of indentured Europeans, though their indenture was more often explicitly a form of debt to be paid off by the wages (in labor time) of the work they had contracted or been sentenced to perform, generated enormous profits for northern capitalists and southern planters alike and fueled capital accumulation and capitalist expansion.

A second major critique of the link between labor and the wage originated in the socialist feminist debates surrounding the economic significance of the household. For working-class (white) women in the United States, the shift "from household manufacture to wage labor" had begun, as Alice Kessler-Harris notes in her classic *Out to Work*, in the late eighteenth and early nineteenth centuries. As capitalism subsumed previously autonomous, "unproductive" household labor "wifely duties" into New England's textile mills, wage labor opened up to "mill girls" (as well as women who never set foot in one of the factories) a "vision of economic independence[20]" from domestic confinement and drudgery. In the liberal feminist imaginary for which the move Kessler-Harris describes has played such a central role, entrance into the formal sphere of waged work is crucial to women's equality, here understood as the ability to sell one's labor on equal terms and for an equal wage. Some socialist feminists, however, refused to cede the notion that formally wageless household work had ever been truly "unproductive" to capitalism, theorizing it instead as invisible, rigidly gendered labor necessary for capital's constant renewal.

Reproductive labor as a category of analysis which disrupts orthodox's Marxism's masculinist proletarian subject was perhaps most prominently put forward by autonomous Marxist feminists like Selma James and Mariarosa Dalla Costa. The debate over their work marked an important moment for the intelligibility of domestic work as labor within feminist circles in the early 1970s, but the limits of this intelligibility were immediate and noteworthy. Domestic labors performed for others, waged or unwaged, were outside the scope of this conversation, an exclusion which is important precisely because it was foundational to establishing the scope, scale, and politics of academic discourse on reproductive labor—so much so that many subsequent articles mistook the term to refer only to the reproduction of bodies (and maybe households) rather than, as Wally Seccombe noted in his critique of James and Dalla Costa, the reproduction of social relations *and* labor power. Focusing on formally wageless feminized domestic work performed in one's own home allowed for an easy critical articulation of gender, domestic spaces, and invisible labors, but obscured important aspects of the history of reproductive labor which complicated the privileged position of the housewife as object of analysis. Attention to such histories of domestic and other forms of service and caring work both inside and outside the home as a unit of economic reproduction might grant scholars significant insights into the important role these forms of work have played in the development of U.S. capitalism.

Indeed, affective, caring, and other forms of service work are a field which labor history ought to embrace more deliberately and completely. The meteoric rise and statistical hegemony of the tertiary sector over the last quarter-century would itself constitute reason enough for, at the very least, a critical reassessment of the ways in which the discipline of history has addressed service work. The role of service work and service workers in historical and contemporary processes of racialization, the historically contingent gendered context in which such work is performed and represented, and the importance of service work in contemporary conversations about neoliberal biopolitics[21] and transnational migration make such a project all the more urgent.

Feminist historians first took up questions of service, domestic, and caring work en masse amidst the ferment of the women's liberation movement during the 1970s and early 1980s. In some of the most groundbreaking work of the era, historians shifted labor history's gaze to state regulation of sex workers and the class politics of public health policy, traced the commodification of household labor, and explored the emergence of a feminized proletariat in the nineteenth-century American city.[22] By the late 1980s, Susan Porter Benson, Dorothy Sue Cobble, and Phyllis Palmer, among others, were mapping the history of U.S. women's service labor in workplaces which were certainly sites of emotional, even affective labor—the department store sales floor, the restaurant, and the home.[23] Ava Baron's 1991 edited volume *Work Engendered,* one of the major inroads into the field of gender studies and post-structuralist perspectives, included articles on clerical work and food service by Ileen DeVault and Cobble, respectively.[24] Julie Greene, writing in *Frontiers* in 1994, saw in the new amalgamations of gender theory and labor history the potential "for reshaping the historical discipline."[25] But male labor historians, and labor history as a discipline, were nevertheless slow, as Baron notes in her introduction to *Work Engendered,* to embrace not only service work, but also women workers as subjects. Domestic labor, wageless work, and precarious employment have similarly been particularly underdeveloped topics with which labor history has yet to satisfactorily grapple. Here sociology and ethnographic research have been somewhat more successful, but a historical perspective is sorely missed. In the absence of such a perspective we lose key insights into the political economy of transnational labor migrations. Without an account of wagelessness, precarity, and forms of labor excluded from the orthodox Marxist category of productive labor, meanwhile, or of forms of labor rendered invisible or peripheral to orthodox Marxist optics because of such labor's affective and communicative characteristics, labor history risks a dangerous and parochial inability to understand living labor's broader dimensions. The remainder of this essay looks specifically at histories of affective labor, service work, and domestic work, their imbrications with historically constructed racialized and gendered subjectivities, and the centrality of ambiguities over their status as labor to their socialization and representation.

Domestic work serves as a particularly good example for talking about both the porous boundaries of labor and the subjects of historical inquiry because of its foundational relationship to the proliferation of service sector jobs in the late twentieth century and the discursive practices which frame it and articulate it to social struggles. Labor historian Jacqueline Jones, for instance, has chronicled the long history of African American women's domestic labor (waged and wageless) in the homes of others. Jones argues that for recently emancipated black women after the civil war, unwaged domestic work performed in their own families became a far less oppressive and alienating space than in the white households where they worked for wages.[26] An account of domestic work and its legibility or illegibility as labor, therefore, necessitates consideration of the ways in which this work's relationship to industrial capitalism has been sutured by the histories of slavery, struggles over post-emancipation wage labor arrangements, and the racialization of low wage service work in the nineteenth and twentieth centuries. If domestic work was not productive labor inside the home, how was it understood when it was outsourced as waged labor to others? The history of racialized domestic service employment over the last two centuries has been marked by constant struggle and negotiation between employers and workers, refracted through and constructed within the history of pre-and post-emancipation ideologies of class, sexuality, domesticity, femininity, and race. Tera Hunter, a historian of labor, race, and gender in the nineteenth century, describes the struggles which black women domestic workers and washerwomen organized and in which they took part from emancipation through World War I and the first Great Migration of African-American proletarians from the rural and urban south to the cities of the Northeast and Midwest. Hunter describes a constant struggle on the part of Atlanta's black service workers to assert control and limits over the terms of their newly free labor, forming unions both clandestine and open, as well as engaging in a wide array of infrapolitical negotiations and tactics.[27]

In the twentieth century the geography and cultural politics of domestic work were radically transformed by new labor migrations and the new international division of labor, suburbanization and white flight from cities at and after midcentury, and the entry of upper and middle-class women into professional workplaces. The experiences of an increasingly globalized class of domestic service workers hold important lessons about the definitions and limits of labor. Describing an experience of staying with a Latino professor in El Paso, Texas, the sociologist Mary Romero was struck by her host's relationship to his undocumented teenage maid, whom he treats badly. When Romero, responding to her host's children's abusive behavior toward the worker, helped her to clean dishes, she was met with nervous disdain and bourgeois guilt from the employer. This professor viewed his maid neither as an employee nor as a "member of the family," but instead, Romero observed, as a "charity case," a recipient of good works. Domestic labor here is framed, at least by the professor intimidated, Romero suggests, by what he presumed to be her radical Chicana politics, as benevolent instruction in the ways of industrial modernity and as economic patronage.[28] The invisibility of housework, Romero found, extends into waged domestic work. "Domestic workers and their employers," she wrote, "are caught up in a complex dialectic as they construct and reconstruct the organization of housework." Waged domestic labor raised, for Romero, important contradictions within middle-class feminism, and staged an encounter between housewives and domestics over "labors of love" (and thus not labor proper) for which both were responsible in their own homes.[29] Middle-class women's increased mobility involved the exploitation of racialized low-wage workers who were often employed or had been employed in a wide spectrum of service sector jobs. Reproductive labor was thus outsourced from the home to the market, or from formally private spaces into overtly "public" workplaces (even if as low profile janitorial or food service staff).

"Wifely" housework's separation from "real work" rendered paid housework marginal by association. Indeed, this marginality, this estrangement from "real work," extended out of the home and into the expanding service sector at large. The ambiguities attached to the various components of waged domestic service work, to the affective and emotional labor of caring for and interacting with children and other charges, as well as with the principal employer, and the menial labor of cleaning floors, cooking, and doing laundry, have had material effects for domestic workers. That menial tasks also have immaterial *affects* is part of the problem. Part of the value of domestic labor is the way it makes the employer feel about the work, about her or his home, kitchen, clothes, and/or status. The intersections of informality, expectation, and ambiguity have often become a site of struggle and negotiation between workers and their employers.

Pierette Hondagneu-Sotelo has chronicled the implications of and struggles over the ambiguities which obtain in domestic labor arrangements extensively. Nannying, housekeeping, and home cleaning were and are precarious work not only because they are informal and without job security but also because deducing what must be done is itself often labor(ious), and must be accomplished through trial and error. One of Pierette Honagneu-Sotelo's informants, an employer of domestic labor who was herself a pediatric nurse described an "ideal nanny/housekeeper" as "somebody who can know what you need before you have to ask-like just know you that well." This worker must "become adept at reading subtle cues" from her "harried, hard-working single parent" employer.[30] The many employers whom Hondagneu-Sotelo interviewed described a varied set of desired relationships with their domestic workers, and multiple strategies for producing or compelling the desired affects and carriage from employees. Workers whom Sondagneu spoke to also expressed a variety of reactions to how their employers communicated with them and how employers wished to be involved in or removed from the labor process. One nanny/housekeeper complained to Hondagneu-Sotelo of her employer's expectation that she "constantly seek out her employer to ask how she might be of service," finding it illogical that she was expected to "regularly enter [the employer's] home office or sitting room to ask if she had any requests." Why, asked the domestic worker, "can't she come tell me."[31] Ambiguity over domestic labor contracts and job descriptions have often entailed a need for domestic workers to be flexible in accommodating the changing wishes and requirements of employers. As Hondagneu-Sotelo notes, this often meant "raises in work duties without raises in pay," expectations raised without similar adjustments in compensation. Particular ideas about what kinds of work particular domestics can reasonably be expected to perform have often been clearly racialized. White Anglo nannies, Hondagneu-Sotelo noted, "are generally not expected to do housecleaning work," but "Latinas regularly are."[32] The emotional aspects of domestic work, such as child care, and the friendships that sometimes formed between domestic workers and their employers, could compel even more labor from employees, but the affective nature of the labor could also be a tool for workers to make claims based upon their relationships with their charges, their greater parenting skill and expertise than parents themselves, and their integration into family units.[33] The frequent absence of the employer during work hours contributed to ambiguity surrounding what work domestics are supposed to perform and the schedule by which they are supposed to perform it. A potentially positive aspect of this ambiguity, Hondagneu-Sotelo found, is the space it allows workers to ignore directives and work on their own terms, however surreptitiously. Such autonomy, however, was both a source of managerial anxiety and an inspiration for the production of new technologies, such as nannycams and baby monitors, to help nervous employers keep tabs on their hired help.[34]

Romero claimed that domestic labor is devalued because of the formal estrangement of reproductive labor from measurements of capitalist productivity, that domestic work is not automatically low-wage or racialized, but is socially constituted as such. The intimacy between employer and employee common to domestic service work both produced and reproduced domestic labor's exceptional relationship to "real work." Yet this intimacy is itself a commodity, produced through the affective labor of domestic workers, and, as in Arlie Russell Hochschild's account of Delta Airlines flight attendants in the early 1980s, a terrain of routinization and alienation from the workers' own emotions.[35] Flight attendants, like domestic workers and other service workers, often labored to conceal that they labor. Part of the job was to pretend that it was not a job, which may have meant performing contentment or simply invisibility. In her recent book *Femininity in Flight*, Kathleen M. Barry historicizes this labor and links it to the historical struggles over the autonomy, racial composition, and sexualization of the U.S. flight attendant labor force between the 1950s and the 1980s. Barry also names the affect which flight attendants labored to produce as "glamour," a mixture of gendered distinction and luxurious consumption which became increasingly and overtly sexual throughout the 1970s. This overt commoditization of flight attendants' presumed sexual availability inspired a feminist ferment, culminating in the formation of the autonomous flight attendants' organization "Stewardesses for Womens' Rights."[36] These developments mirrored similar ones in other industries, such as the proliferation of clerical worker unions and feminist groups throughout the 1970s and early 1980s and the later emergence of domestic worker organizations and workers centers, such as the Domestic Workers Association in Los Angeles (founded 1990), with which Hondagneu-Sotelo is involved as both an activist and an ethnographer, and Domestic Workers United in New York City (founded 2000).[37]

These workers' labor produced affects. Affective labor obtains differently for different forms of service work but, like the history of the rise of service work more broadly, the affects their labor produced are generative sites for understanding contemporary articulations and disarticulations of labor. For labor historians, affect is relevant not only because of its complicity in labor's invisibility, but because the presence of affects likely signifies the presence of labor which may or may not be understood as such. Affect and emotion work may thus constitute a vast archive for labor historians to engage in much the same way that historians of gender and cultural studies scholars have begun to do.

The ethnographic accounts provided by Romero and Hondagneu-Sotelo, and the recovered historical narrative offered by Tera Hunter represent intimately supervised and surveilled caring work as careful and constant sites of contestation and negotiation. This contestation is, however, conversant with and productive of historical shifts and cycles in caring work's supervision and surveillance. "Affect," as the militant Madrid research collective Precarias a la Deriva argue, "flows precariously." Caring work's sexualized flows and commodified displacements exist in an instrumental relationship to the affective products and cultural logics of neoliberal globalization and the war on terror. But care workers' affective labor might also, however, oppose "the securitary logic reigning in the precaritized world" through forms of cooperation and collective independence.[38] This is what Michael Hardt calls "the potential of necessary affective labor." The gendered labor of service workers and care work, what Hardt calls "biopower from below," is "firmly embedded as a necessary foundation for capitalist accumulation and patriarchal order." But what makes caring work necessary for contemporary capitalism also makes it powerful. Thus, Hardt suggests that the production of affects may hold enormous subversive or liberatory potential.[39]

Historians might further explore the scope and character of the commodities which service work produces. We might take up the implications and trace the development of the social, interactive character of so much of this precarious and ideologically devalued labor. We might undertake an archival practice which understands "labor" as a socially constructed and unevenly available term and looks for labor in places where the archive obscures it, places where we are not accustomed to seeing work or workers. Labor historians may, in historicizing "real work" and the labor marginal to and/or excluded from it, be able to mark opportunities for labor movements to forge complex solidarities and alliances. We may be able to write a far more complex and compelling histories with radically different protagonists. Such an archival practice, crucially, can offer new insight into the historical articulation of race, gender, and work, can locate the workplace, defined broadly, as a site where racial and gender formations are produced and reproduced in the most quotidian interactions with employers and coworkers, family and customers. Historians may find that such a practice also helpfully illuminates the political economy of reproductive labor and the cultural dimensions of its emotional and affective components.

Historicizing work's limits may speak to the possibilities for a broader critical inquiry into the scope and scale of the institutions and ideological apparatuses of contemporary and historical social and cultural life-worlds. There is too much at stake in struggles over what constitutes work, and what "labor" occludes, marginalizes, and excludes, to shy from such political and critical engagements.

And in thinking about what it might mean to reorient labor history's subject, we might take inspiration from the cultural historian Michael Denning's recent exhortation that scholars refuse to see "bread-winning factory worker as the productive base on which a reproductive superstructure is erected." Instead Denning urges us to "imagine the dispossessed proletarian household as a wageless 'base' of subsistence labor,—the 'women's work of cooking, cleaning, and caring'—which supports a 'superstructure' of migrant wage seekers," proletarian globe-hoppers and daily commuters alike, "who are ambassadors to, or perhaps hostages to, the wage economy." If, as Denning argues, "Unemployment precedes employment . . . both historically and conceptually," then living labor precedes so-called productive labor." This is Denning's response to Achille Mbembe's demand that "a 'biopolitics of our age' must attend to 'the biopolitics of joblessness.'" Capitalism, Denning explains, begins "not with the offer of a job, but with the imperative to 'earn' a living." "Proletarian" becomes a synonym not for wage labor but for its preconditions—"dispossession, expropriation, and a radical dependence on the market." It isn't wage labor that creates a proletariat, rather, but what David Harvey calls "accumulation by dispossession," a far more generalized phenomenon. Thus, for Denning "wageless life, not wage labor, is the starting point in understanding the 'creative destruction' of the free market," in theorizing social life beginning from the accumulation not of capital, but instead of living labor, waged and wageless, "working" and "not working."[40] Where shall labor historians, then, take the remarkable insight that "you don't need a job to be a proletarian?"

Notes

1. Immanuel Wallerstein, "New Revolts Against the System," *New Left Review*, 18 (2002): 33.
2. National Labor Relations Board, *Brown University and International Union, United Automobile, Aerospace, and Agricultural Implement Workers of America, UAW AFL-CIO, Petitioner*, Case 1-RC-21368, July 13, 2004.
3. National Labor Relations Board, *Oakwood Healthcare Inc.* Case 7-RC-22141, September 29, 2006.

4. Maurizio Lazzarato. "Immaterial Labor," in Paolo Virno and Michael Hardt, eds *Radical Thought in Italy: A Potential Politics* (Minneapolis, MN: University of Minnesota Press, 1997).
5. Arlie Russell Hochschild. *The Managed Heart: The Commercialization of Human Feeling* (20th Anniversary Edition) (Berkeley, CA: University of California Press, 2003).
6. Michael Hardt and Antonio Negri. *Empire* (Cambridge, MA; Harvard University Press, 2001); Gilles Deleuze, "Postscript on the Society of Control," *October* 59 (Winter, 1992): Cambridge: MIT Press, 3–7; Michael Hardt, "Affective Labor," *Boundary 2* 26 (2) (1999): especially p. 96.
7. Fred Moten and Stefano Harney, "Doing Academic Work," in Randy Martin, ed. *Chalk Lines: The Politics of Work in the Managed University* (Durham, NC: Duke University Press, 1998), 154–80.
8. See Emma Dowling's critique in her "Producing the Dining Experience: Measure, Subjectivity, and the Affective Worker." *Ephemera: Theory and Politics in Organization* 7 (1): 2. See also Nick Dyer-Witheford, "Cyber-Negri: General Intellect and Immaterial Labour," in S. Murphy and A. Mustapha, eds *The Philosophy of Antonio Negri: Resistance in Practice* (London: Pluto Press. 2005).
9. See Mariarosa Dalla Costa and Selma James, *The Power of Women and The Subversion of Community* (Bristol, England: Falling Wall Press, 1972), 55 n. 20.
10. Dalla Costa and James, *The Power of Women.* See also Leopoldina Fortunati, *The Arcane of Reproduction: Prostitution, Labor, and Capital* (New York: Autonomedia, 1989); Patricia Hill Collins, *Black Feminist Thought: Knowledge, Consciousness, and The Politics of Empowerment* (New York: Routledge, 2000); Teresa Arnott and Julie Matthaei. *Race, Gender, and Work: A Multicultural Economic History of Women in the United State* (Boston, MA: South End Press, 1996).
11. For some recent work in this tradition, see Mignon Duffy, "Doing the Dirty Work: Race, Labor, and Gender in Historical Perspective," *Gender & Society* 22 (3) (2007). Jennifer Morgan's *Laboring Women: Reproduction and Gender in New World Slavery* (Philadelphia, PA: University of Pennsylvania Press. 2004) offers a particularly valuable history of racialized reproductive labors in seventeenth and eighteenth century new world slavery as well as a strong rebuke of accounts of reproduction and reproductive labor which do not take into account the ways such categories have been profoundly racialized. The connections, Morgan writes, "between commodification, production, and reproduction are nowhere as clear, nor as unexplored, as in African American History."
12. Michael Omi and Howard Winant, *Racial Formation in the United States: From the 1960s to the 1990s* (Second Edition) (New York: Routledge, 1994), 56.
13. Karl Marx, *Theories of Surplus Value* (Amherst, NY: Prometheus Books, 2000), 159.
14. Karl Marx, *Capital Vol 1* (New York: Penguin Classics, 1992), 672.
15. Ibid., 644.
16. Marx, *Theories of Surplus Value*, 159.

17. Marx, *Capital Vol. 1*, 644. See also Ralph Miliband, *Divided Societies: Class Struggle in Contemporary Capitalism* (Oxford: Oxford University Press, 1989), 38–41.
18. Marx, *Capital Vol III*, (New York: Penguin Books, 1991), 406–08. See also Miliband, *Divided Societies*.
19. See, for instance, Hondagneu-Sotelo's discussion of racial inequalities in the expectations of the particular forms of service work particular domestic workers are expected to perform, which I discuss below. For struggles over access to particular forms of work for people of color in the United States, see David E. Bernstein, *Only One Place of Redress: African Americans, Labor Regulations, and the Courts from Reconstruction to the New Deal* (Durham, NC: Duke University Press, 2001) and Nancy MacLean, *Freedom Is Not Enough: The Opening of the American Workplace* (Cambridge, MA: Harvard University Press and the Russell Sage Foundation, 2006). See also Robert H. Zeiger, *For Jobs and Freedom: Race and Labor in America since 1865* (Lexington, KY: University Press of Kentucky, 2007).
20. Alice Kessler-Harris, *Out to Work: A History of Wage Earning Women in The United States* (20th anniversary edition) (Oxford: Oxford University Press, 2003), 20–45.
21. See Pheng Cheah, "Biopower and the New International Division of Reproductive Labor," *Boundary 2* 34 (1) (2007): 79–113.
22. Judith Walkowitz, *Prostitution and Victorian Society: Women, Class, and the State* (Cambridge: Cambridge University Press, 1980); Susan Strasser, *Never Done: A History of American Housework* (New York: Owl Books, 2000 [1982]); Christine Stansell, *City of Women: Sex and Class in New York, 1789–1860* (Urbana, IL: University of Illinois Press, 1987); Alice Kessler-Harris, *Out to Work: A History of Wage-Earning Women in the United States* (Oxford: Oxford University Press, 2003 [1982]).
23. Susan Porter Benson, *Counter Culture: Saleswomen, Managers, and Customers in American Department Stores 1890–1940* (Urbana, IL: University of Illinois Press, 1988); Dorothy Sue Cobble, *Dishing It Out: Waitresses and Their Unions in the Twentieth Century* (Urbana, IL: University of Illinois Press, 1991); Phyllis Palmer. *Domesticity and Dirt. Housewives and Domestic Servants in the United States, 1920–1945* (Philadelphia, PA: Temple University Press, 1989). See also Julie Greene's review essay "Working Gender" in *Frontiers: A Journal of Women's Studies* 14 (3) (1994).
24. Ava Baron, ed., *Work Engendered: Toward a New History of American Labor* (Ithaca, NY: Cornell University Press, 1991).
25. Greene, "Working Gender."
26. Jacqueline Jones, *Labor of Love, Labor of Sorrow* (Vintage Books Edition) (New York: Vintage, 1995).
27. Tera Hunter, *To 'Joy My Freedom: Southern Black Women's Lives and Labors after the Civil War* (Cambridge, MA: Harvard University Press, 1998). See 24–27, for instance.

28. Mary Romero, *Maid in the USA* (10th Anniversary Edition) (New York: Routledge, 2002), 30–34.
29. Ibid., 73.
30. Pierrette Hondagneu-Sotelo, *Doméstica: Immigrant Workers Cleaning and Caring in the Shadows of Affluence* (Berkeley, CA: University of California Press, 2001), 141.
31. Ibid., 145.
32. Ibid., 148.
33. Ibid., 154–58.
34. Hondagneu-Sotelo, *Doméstica*, 140 and Romero, *Maid in the USA*, 61.
35. Hochschild, *The Managed Heart*.
36. Kathleen M. Barry. *Femininity In Flight: A History of Flight Attendants* (Durham, NC: Duke University Press, 2007).
37. See Dorothy Sue Cobble, *The Other Women's Movement: Workplace Justice and Social Rights in Modern America* (Princeton: Princeton University Press, 2004). See also John Hoerr, *We Can't Eat Prestige: The Women Who Organized Harvard* (Philadelphia, PA: Temple University Press, 1997). Also Toni Gilpin, Dan Letwin, Gary Isaac, and Jack McKivigan, *On Strike For Respect: The Clerical and Technical Workers' Strike at Yale University 1984–85* (Urbana, IL: University of Illinois Press, 1995); Hondagneu-Sotelo, *Doméstica*, 220–29, and http://www.domesticworkersunited.org/ (accessed September 13, 2009).
38. Precarias a la Deriva, "A Very Careful Strike," translated by Franco Ingrassia and Nate Holdren, in *The Commoner*, no. 11 (Spring/Summer, 2006). See especially 38–41.
39. Hardt, "Affective Labor," 98–100.
40. Michael Denning, "The Spectre of Wageless Life," conference working paper presented at "Practicing Transnational Cultural Studies: Dialogues between Working Groups at Yale and New York Universities, Voluntown, CT, May 11–13, 2008, 5.

PART III

RESOURCES

Labor and Working-Class History Chronology

1619	African slaves first brought to Virginia
Early 1660s	Slave labor laws codified in Virginia
1763	Members of James Miller's 15th regiment, stationed in Quebec, mutiny over cutbacks in pay and provisions at the close of the Seven Years' War
1765	Stamp Act protests of artisans and laborers
1785	General Society of Mechanics and Tradesmen founded in New York City
1788	Artisans participate in Federal processions in support of the Constitution
1790	Moses Brown and William Almy establish the Rhode Island textile mill system in Pawtucket, Rhode Island
1806–15	Journeymen Cordwainers in Philadelphia (1806), New York (1810), and Pittsburgh (1815) are indicted under criminal conspiracy charges for striking
1813	Francis Cabot Lowell founds the Boston Manufacturing Company, which capitalizes textile mills in Waltham, Massachusetts
1824	Frances Wright speaks in New York City advocating political and social equality for workers' and women's rights
1829	Workingmen's Party established in New York City. Thomas Skidmore publishes *The Rights of Man to Property*
1830s	White workers, defining a free labor ideology that included a sense of popular whiteness, chase African Americans off the Boston Common on the 4th of July. In this same decade, white middle-class reformers express concern over racial mingling at Pinkster and Negro Election Day celebrations and successfully ban them
1833	General Trades Union formed in New York City

1833–38	Journeymen's societies in the conflict trades (printers, cordwainers, tailors, carpenters, and others) coordinate 168 strikes in demand of the ten-hour day. Strikes fail in Baltimore and Boston but are successful in Philadelphia.
1834	National Trades Union formed
1835	New York Supreme Court finds in *People v. Fisher* that journeymen cordwainers from Geneva conspired to restrain trade when they organized themselves and struck for higher wages in 1829
1840	Washingtonian Temperance Society founded by six Baltimore artisans; by 1843 the organization has 3 million members
	Ten-hour workday is established for federal employees
1840–45	*Lowell Offering*, a monthly magazine, is written and published by working women. At the same time, a distinct ideology is articulated in contemporary diaries, sermons, periodicals, and advice books that defines women's proper role to be focused on and limited to the home. This "cult of true womanhood"—which dominates middle-class understandings of women's roles throughout rest of the nineteenth century—calls upon women to uphold the values of "purity, piety, domesticity, and submission"
1844	Representatives from various craft unions and labor reform movements form the New England Workingmen's Association
1845	George Henry Evans founds the National Reform Association in New York with the rallying cry of "Vote Yourself a Farm!"
1847–1850s	New Hampshire, Pennsylvania, Maine, Rhode Island, Ohio, and California pass ten-hour labor laws
1852	Longshoreman's United Benevolent Society plans to secure waterfront jobs for its mostly white and Irish membership, limiting job opportunities for African Americans and increasing tensions between blacks and Irish in New York City
1853	The Know Nothing (American) Party becomes the voice for political nativism, which is embraced by some native-born workers who resent recent immigrants. These labor nativists blame the immigrants for lowering wages and engaging in "slop work" in the nation's growing factories
1855	William Poole, a native-born American butcher, is killed in a New York bar fight and becomes a martyr to the labor nativist cause
	By 1855 Irish men and women largely displace African American workers in New York City on the docks and in service work

1863	New York City draft riots, expressing both class-based grievances and racial conflict, last for three days and result in the deaths of 74 people
	International Workingmen's Association (IWA) established
1864	The first female labor union, the Collar Laundry Union, is formed in Troy, New York
1865–1915	25 million immigrants arrive in the United States (mostly the "new immigrants" from Southern and Eastern Europe), many of whom form the backbone of the growing industrial working class
1866	National Labor Union is formed, welcoming skilled and unskilled laborers and farmers and supporting the eight-hour day, cooperatives, and currency reform; lasts until 1872 when it is transformed into the National Labor Reform Party and is defeated at the polls
1869	Knights of Labor founded among a group of garment cutters in Philadelphia welcoming all producers in mixed assemblies; reaches over 100,000 members by 1884
1874	Tompkins Square Riot expresses frustrations of the unemployed, who are attacked by the police
1876	Workingmen's Party of the United States formed
1877	Great railroad strikes in protest of wage cuts and speed-ups along the Pennsylvania and Baltimore and Ohio Railroads in Martinsburg, West Virginia, Pittsburgg, Pennsylvania, and Chicago, Illinois
1877	Socialist Labor Party established
1877	Farmers Alliances formed first in Texas and then throughout the South and West to confront the problems of debt and credit
1881	Federation of Organized Trades and Labor Unions established welcoming craft unions only
1882	First September Labor Day parade held in New York City. This becomes a national holiday in the United States in 1894
1883	The anarchist International Working People's Association (IWPA) is formed in Pittsburgh
1884	Bureau of Labor established
1886	March and April: Great Southwest Railroad Strike ends in defeat as strikebreakers disagree with their militant comrades' tactics. May 1: the first labor May Day demonstrations are held across America largely in support of the eight-hour day. May 4: peaceful protest meeting in Haymarket Square, Chicago ends in tragic bombing blamed on anarchists triggering what becomes the

nation's first red scare. December: the American Federation of Labor is founded in Columbus, Ohio representing 25 national trade unions with Samuel Gompers as its president

1887	Four of the "Haymarket Eight"—anarchists convicted of the May 4th bombing—are executed in Chicago after one of the most controversial trials of the century
1888	United Hebrew Trades formed among garment workers in New York
1890	United Mine Workers established
1892	The Populist Party is formed out of the old Farmers Alliances
1892	Homestead Strike ends in failure for the Amalgamated Association of Iron, Steel and Tin Workers and marks the end of unions in steel for more than four decades
1893	Western Federation of Miners (WFM) established
1894	Jacob Coxey, a Populist, leads a march on Washington calling for a government response to high unemployment
	Pullman Strike and Boycott
1895	National Association of Manufacturers established. It would become a foe of labor unions, organizing open shop drives and lobbying against them into the twentieth century.
1898	U.S. Supreme Court in *Holden v. Hardy* upholds an eight-hour law for Utah miners because mining, as a "dangerous industry," deserves such state protection
1901	International Ladies' Garment Workers Union (ILGWU) formed in New York
	Socialist Party of America founded and led by Eugene Debs
1904	The Social Democratic Party in Milwaukee elects nine aldermen to the Common Council who challenge the agenda and procedures of the Council to be more responsive to the people. By 1910 socialists in Milwaukee see their candidate elected as mayor and send Victor Berger to Congress.
1905	Industrial Workers of the World (IWW) founded in Chicago by Eugene Debs, William, "Big Bill" Haywood, and others
1908	U.S. Supreme Court in *Muller v. Oregon* upholds a ten-hour Oregon law as applied to women, arguing that women deserve such special protection as "bearers of the race"
1909	"Uprising of the 20,000" garment workers in New York over pay, workplace safety, and workplace control

1911	Triangle Shirtwaist Factory fire in New York kills 146 women
1912	IWW helps organize 30,000 mill hands in Lawrence, Massachusetts and wins a wage increase after a lengthy strike
1913	IWW supports striking silk workers in Paterson, New Jersey but the strike is lost despite the successful Paterson Pageant held at Madison Square Garden (supported by John Reed and Mabel Dodge) that won support for the strikers among radicals and progressives
	United States Commission on Industrial Relations, chaired by Frank Walsh, leads 154 days of public hearings on the state of the nation's industrial relations. Walsh's report calls for the democratization of industrial life
	U.S. Department of Labor established
1914	Amalgamated Clothing Workers of America (ACWA) formed in Chicago
	Clayton Act declares that antitrust acts should not forbid the existence of unions
	Ludlow Massacre leaves 2 children and 11 women dead after the Colorado National Guard attacks a tent village of striking coal miners and their families
1917	Espionage Act passed. IWW headquarters around the country are raided by federal agents and mass trials of "Wobblies"—including the trial of William Haywood and 100 fellow Wobblies in Chicago—effectively cripple the organization
1918	Sedition Act amends Espionage Act—over 2,000 people would be prosecuted and 900 convicted for dissent under these acts during the war, including Eugene Debs and other Socialist Party and union leaders
	National War Labor Board established to enforce the eight-hour day, equal pay for women, the right of workers to organize and bans on delays of production
1919	Great Strike Wave of over 3,600 walkouts (22% of the total workforce) including Seattle shipyard workers, steelworkers, and the Boston police
1919–20	The Red Scare takes place, which consisted of vigilante violence and government prosecution of anarchists, socialists, and communists, including the nationwide "Palmer raid" arrest of over 6,000 people and the deportation of 249 aliens to Russia. Many left-led unions, like New York City's Teacher's Union, became targets of government imposed loyalty oaths.

1919	U.S. Supreme Court sustains restrictions on free speech ("clear and present danger" test) in *Schenck v. United States*
1920s	Many large employers pursue the open shop using company unions, employee representation plans, and corporate welfare. Most workers in industrial cities remain divided along the lines of race and ethnicity within their respective urban enclaves. Yet some create a vibrant working-class culture sustained by institutions that include cooperative housing agreements (like the Amalgamated houses), resorts, and summer camps (like Camp Unity)
1923	U.S. Supreme Court strikes down a minimum wage law for women in *Adkins v. Children's Hospital,* arguing the women have "a right to make their own bargains"
1925	A. Philip Randolph helps found the Brotherhood of Sleeping Car Porters
1929	Great Depression begins that lasts through the 1930s resulting in a 25 percent unemployment rate by 1932
1930s	Throughout the South there is an explosive growth in Holiness, Pentecostal, and fundamentalist churches, as well as in Bible institutes, evangelical radio programs, and itinerant revivalists. These institutions help many Southern workers cope with the tough times of the Depression
1933	Communist Party members in cities like New York, Chicago, and Minneapolis help organize Unemployment Leagues and tenant strikes in protest of the joblessness and evictions resulting from the Great Depression
	National Industrial Recovery Act (NIRA) section 7a provides protection for workers to organize. It is stricken down by the Supreme Court in 1935
1934	Successful general strikes are held in Minneapolis (Teamsters), San Francisco (longshoremen), and Toldeo (Auto-lite workers) contributing to a growth in industrial organization. Strikes in the textile industry fail
1935	National Labor Relations Act (Wagner Act) provides federal recognition of workers' rights to engage in collective bargaining and freely elect representative unions
1935	Nurse companions, homemakers, and other in-home care workers are left out of New Deal labor law reforms along with domestic servants. When the New Deal ushered in old age insurance, unemployment benefits, collective bargaining, minimum wages, and maximum hour limits, these mostly female and minority workers were rendered ineligible

	Committee for Industrial Organization formed within the AFL
1936	December 1936–March 1937 United Auto Workers sit-down strike at General Motors wins union recognition
1937	Memorial Day massacre at Republic Steel when 10 workers are killed and 90 wounded as striking SWOC members and families gather outside the plant and are met by police
1938	After disputes within the AFL, John L. Lewis helps found an independent Congress of Industrial Organizations (CIO)
	Fair Labor Standards Act bans child labor and established maximum hour and minimum wage requirements
1940	Smith Act passed making it illegal to advocate the overthrow of the government. Twenty-nine Teamsters and SWP leaders from Minneapolis and New York are indicted and 18 are convicted under this law in 1941. Such prosecutions—which were later aimed at the CP—not only weaken these radical political parties but also disrupt local union organizing
1941	January: Strike at Allis Chalmers plant in Milwaukee. March: National Defense Mediation Board created by FDR to enforce no strike pledge. May: Strike at North American Aviation ends with army seizure of the plant. June: Executive Order 8802 establishes the Fair Employment Practices Commission. October: UMW strike among the "captive mines"
1942	During World War II, 6 million women enter the paid labor force (75% of whom were married)
1942–43	During World War II, 800,000 industrial jobs are brought to the South and there are some union successes due to the support of the FEPC and National War Labor Board
	Battle between Catholic anticommunist workers in the Connecticut Brass Valley and communist organizers of Mine-Mill ends with the expulsion of union leaders and organizers with communist ties
1943	Wildcat strikes throughout all major industries involve over 3,000 work stoppages and 2 million workers.
	Smith-Connally War Labor Disputes Act mandates that unions issue written strike notices followed by a 30-day cooling-off period
1946	CIO launches its organizing campaign in the South known as Operation Dixie
1945–46	Postwar strike wave involves 5,000 work stoppages and 4.6 million workers

1947	Taft-Hartley Act passed—includes a mandate for union leaders to sign affidavits that they are not members of the Communist Party or risk losing access to the NLRB
	New York State passes the Condon-Wadlin Act that made strikes by state and local government workers illegal
1948	Labor-management accord reached between UAW and GM includes cost of living adjustment but no union say over production
1949	CIO expels unions it believes are influenced by communists
1955	AFL and CIO officially merge, with George Meany as president and Walter Reuther as head of the Industrial Union Department
1957	The McClellan Committee (Senate Select Committee on Improper Activities in the Labor and Management Field) exposes corruption in many unions, including the Teamsters, fostering negative public opinion of unions
1958	Mayor Robert Wagner, Jr of New York issues Executive Order 49, which allows municipal unions to bargain collectively with government agencies
1959	United Steel Workers lead a successful national strike
	Landrum-Griffin Act passed to protect individual workers from corrupt union officials
1962	President Kennedy issues Executive Order 10988, which allows federal government employees to bargain collectively
1963	Blue-collar workers comprise only 36.4 percent of the workforce; wholesale, retail, service, and government jobs rise to 57 percent
	March for Jobs and Freedom held in Washington D.C. by the Negro American Labor Council, civil rights organizations, and some unions
1964	Title VII of the Civil Rights Act prohibits discrimination in employment on the basis of race, color, religion, national origin, or sex
1965	César Chávez leads the Farm Workers Association in support of a strike called by the Agricultural Workers Organizing Committee against the grape growers of Delano county, California; the two groups merge in 1966 to form the United Farm Workers Organizing Committee (UFWOC)
1967	UAW leaves the AFL-CIO in protest of the federation's support for the Vietnam war

	AFSCME membership grows to 350,000
	Taylor Law passed in New York State outlawing strikes by public employees
1968	Urban sanitation workers from Local 1733 AFSCME sustain a two-month strike in Memphis for labor and civil rights
1970	Grape growers sign contracts with UFWOC
1978	Airline Deregulation Act destabilizes employment in the industry
1979	U.S. Steel closes 15 mills in eight states; from 1979 until 1995 the steel industry loses over 400,000 jobs (going from 600,000 to 169,000)
1980	"Containerization" transforms U.S. shipping and dock work as 73 percent of goods between the United States and Europe and 80 percent between the United States and Asia move via container
1981	PATCO (Professional Air Traffic Controllers' Organization) goes on strike over unsafe working conditions; President Reagan dismisses 11,000 strikers and authorizes the hiring of replacement workers, crushing PATCO
	UAW reunites with AFL-CIO
1983	Between 1979 and 1983 the United States loses 2.4 million manufacturing jobs, partly due to Reagan's monetary policies that favor imports
mid-late 1980s	SEIU launches "justice for janitors" campaigns around the nation
1984	Hotel Employees and Restaurant Employees Union (HERE) organizes Yale University's support staff
1993	Family and Medical Leave Act passed
1994	Clinton signs the North American Free Trade Agreement, which AFL-CIO economists estimate cost the United States 900,000 jobs by 2004
1995	ILGWU, ACWA, and TWU merge as UNITE (Union of Needle Trades, Industrial and Textile Workers) with a combined membership of only 220,000
	The United States joins the World Trade Organization (WTO)
1995	John Sweeney, former head of SEIU, becomes AFL-CIO president and calls for militant organizing
1996	Telecommunications Reform Act deregulates the industry at the expense of unionized workers' security
1997	Workers at United Parcel Service (organized by the Teamsters) strike and win concessions for full- and part-time workers

1999	74,000 California home attendants vote to join the Service Employees International Union (SEIU)
2001	NLRB ruling in favor of the Graduate Student Organizing Committee-United Auto Workers (GSOC-UAW) at New York University considers graduate students as workers of the university and recognizes their right to organize
2003	HERE & UNITE work together on the Immigrant Workers Freedom Ride, the Yale strike, and H&M organizing campaign
2004	UNITE and HERE merge to create UNITE-HERE
	NLRB rules 3–2 in favor of Brown University and against the UAW, reversing the 2001 NYU decision and declaring that graduate student teaching and research assistants are "primarily students" and not workers protected by the NLRA
2005	Seven unions (the International Brotherhood of Teamsters, the Laborers' International Union of North America, the Service Employees International Union, the United Brotherhood of Carpenters and Joiners of America, the United Farm Workers, the United Food and Commercial Workers International Union, and UNITE-HERE) leave the AFL-CIO to form a new affiliation, the Change to Win coalition
	AFL-CIO and Change to Win support the Employee Free Choice Act (EFCA); they continue to fight for this reform today
2006	National Labor Relations Board, with new anti-union members appointed by George W. Bush, issues a 3–2 split ruling in *Oakwood Health Care Inc*, holding that Registered Nurses who mentor or help to train new employees are supervisors under the law and, therefore, not workers who could be covered by the National Labor Relations Act or eligible to vote in an NLRB-supervised election for union representation

Resources

Archives

- **Georgia State University Southern Labor Archives**, Special Collections & Archives, Georgia State University Library, 100 Decatur Street SE, Georgia State University, Atlanta, Georgia 30303–3202
  Phone: 404–413-2880, Fax: 404–413-2881, Email: archives@gsu.edu
  http://www.library.gsu.edu/spcoll/pages/area.asp?ldID=105&guideID=510 (accessed March 21, 2010).

- **The Kheel Center for Labor-Management Documentation & Archives,** Catherwood Library Kheel Center, 227 Ives Hall, Cornell University, Ithaca, NY 14853
  Tel: 607–255-3183, Fax: 607–255-9641
  http://www.ilr.cornell.edu/library/kheel/ (accessed March 21, 2010).

- **Labor Archives & Research Center,** J. Paul Leonard Library, San Francisco State University, 1600 Holloway Avenue, San Francisco, CA 94132
  Phone: 415–338-1854 Email: libweb@sfsu.edu
  http://www.library.sfsu.edu/about/depts/larc.php (accessed March 21, 2010).

- **Library of Congress, Labor History Sources in the Manuscript Division**, Manuscript Division, Library of Congress, 101 Independence Ave. SE, Washington, D.C. 20540–4680
  Phone: (202) 707–5387
  Fax: (202) 707–7791
  http://www.loc.gov/rr/mss/laborlc.html (accessed March 21, 2010).

- **Tamiment Library and Robert F. Wagner Labor Archives,** New York University, 70 Washington Square South, 10th Floor, New York, NY 10012
  Tel: 212–998-2630, Fax: 212–995-4225
  http://www.nyu.edu/library/bobst/research/tam/ (accessed March 21, 2010).

- **U.S. Labor and Industrial History Audio Archive**, Prof. Gerald Zahavi Department of History, University at Albany 1400 Washington Ave., Albany, NY 12222
Tel. (518) 442–4780
http://www.albany.edu/history/LaborAudio/ (accessed March 21, 2010).

- **The Walter P. Reuther Library of Labor and Urban Affairs**, Walter P. Reuther Library, Wayne State University, 5401 Cass Ave., Detroit MI 48202
Tel: 313–577-4024
http://www.reuther.wayne.edu/ (accessed March 21, 2010).

- **Wisconsin Historical Society,** 816 State Street, Madison, WI 53706–1417
http://www.wisconsinhistory.org/libraryarchives/readroom/labor.asp (accessed March 21, 2010).

Journals

International Labor and Working Class History Cambridge University Press.

Labor History Routledge.

LABOR: Studies in Working-Class History of the Americas Duke University Press.

Radical History Review Duke University Press.

On-line Exhibits and Resources

- **Center for Labor Research and Education:**
http://www.labor.ucla.edu/ (accessed March 21, 2010).

- **Chicago Anarchists on Trial:**
http://memory.loc.gov/ammem/award98/ichihtml/ (accessed March 21, 2010).

- **The Dramas of Haymarket:**
http://www.chicagohistory.org/dramas/ (accessed March 21, 2010).

- **H-Labor:**
http://www.h-net.org/~labor/ (accessed March 21, 2010).

- **Kheel Center—Triangle Factory Fire Exhibit:**
http://www.ilr.cornell.edu/trianglefire/ (accessed March 21, 2010).

- **The Labor Project:**
http://libweb.uoregon.edu/dc/labor/ (accessed March 21, 2010).

- **The Labor Trail:**
http://www.labortrail.org/ (accessed March 21, 2010).

- Seattle General Strike Project:
  http://depts.washington.edu/labhist/strike/ (accessed March 21, 2010).

- University of Washington, University Libraries, List of Labor History Websites.
  Links to sites dealing with General Labor History Sites, Strikes, Unrest & Tragedies, Working Conditions & Working Life, Photographs and Posters.
  http://www.lib.washington.edu/subject/History/tm/labor.html (accessed March 21, 2010).

- U.S. Bureau of Labor Statistics:
  http://www.bls.gov/ (accessed March 21, 2010).

Professional Organizations

- The Illinois Labor History Society, 28 E. Jackson, Chicago, IL 60604
  Phone: (312) 663–4107
  http://www.kentlaw.edu/ilhs/ (accessed March 21, 2010).

- Labor and Working-Class History Association, Sanford Institute, Duke University, Box 90239 Durham, NC 27708–0239
  Email lawcha@duke.edu
  http://www.lawcha.org/ (accessed March 21, 2010),

- The New York Labor History Association, c/o Robert F. Wagner Labor Archives, 70 Washington Square South, 10th floor, New York, NY 10012
  Phone: 212-998-2636
  http://www.ilr.cornell.edu/nylha/ (accessed March 21, 2010).

Further Reading

Chapter One: Memoirs of an Invalid: James Miller and the Making of the British-American Empire in the Seven Years' War

Anderson, Fred. *Crucible of War: The Seven Years' War and the Fate of Empire in British North America, 1754–1766*. New York: Random House, 2000.

—. *A People's Army: Massachusetts Soldiers and Society in the Seven Years' War*. Chapel Hill, NC: University of North Carolina Press, 1984.

Brewer, John. *The Sinews of Power: War, Money and the English State, 1688–1783*. London: Routledge, 1989.

Brumwell, Stephen. *Redcoats: The British Soldier and War in the Americas, 1755–1763*. New York: Cambridge University Press, 2002.

Frey, Sylvia R. *The British Soldier in America: A Social History of Military Life in the Revolutionary Period*. Austin, TX: University of Texas Press, 1981.

Gipson, Lawrence Henry. *The British Empire before the American Revolution*, vol. VII, *The Great War for the Empire: The Victorious Years 1758–1760*. New York: Alfred A. Knopf, 1949 and vol. VIII, *The Great War for Empire: The Culmination, 1760–1763*. New York: Knopf, 1953.

Lemisch, Jesse. *Jack Tar vs. John Bull: The Role of New York's Seamen in Precipitating the Revolution*. New York: Garland, 1997.

Linebaugh, Peter and Marcus Rediker. *The Many-Headed Hydra: Sailors, Slaves, Commoners, and the Hidden History of the Revolutionary Atlantic*. London: Verso, 2000.

Mackillop, Andrew. *"More Fruitful than the Soil":: Army, Empire and the Scottish Highlands, 1715–1815*. East Linton, Lothian, Scotland: Tuckwell Press, 2000.

Marshall, P. J. ed. *The Oxford History of the British Empire, Vol. II, The Eighteenth Century*. Oxford: Oxford University Press, 1998.

Parker, Geoffrey. *The Military Revolution: Military Innovation and the Rise of the West, 1500–1800*. Cambridge: Cambridge University Press, 1988.

Stone, Lawrence ed. *An Imperial State at War: Britain from 1689 to 1815*. London: Routledge, 1994.

Chapter Two: Losing the Middle Ground: Strikebreakers and Labor Protest on the Southwestern Railroads

Arnesen, Eric. " 'The Quicksands of Economic Insecurity': African Americans, Strikebreaking, and Labor Activism in the Industrial Era." Eric Arnesen, ed., *The Black Worker: Race, Labor, and Civil Rights Since Emancipation*. Urbana, IL: University of Illinois Press, 2007, 41–71.

Baron, Ava. "Gender and Labor History: Learning from the Past, Looking to the Future" in Ava Baron, ed. *Work Engendered: Toward a New History of American Labor.* Ithaca, NY: Cornell University Press, 1991.

Brody, David. "Free Labor, Law, and American Trade Unionism" in Stanley L. Engerman, ed. *Terms of Labor: Slavery, Serfdom, and Free Labor.* Stanford, CA: Stanford University Press, 1999.

Case, Theresa A. "The Radical Potential of the Knights' Biracialism: The 1885–1886 Gould System Strikes and Their Aftermath." *Labor: Studies in Working-Class History of the Americas,* vol. 4: 4 (Winter 2007).

Case, Theresa A. *The Great Southwest Railroad Strike and Free Labor.* College Station, TX: Texas A&M Press, 2010.

Dubofsky, Melvyn. "The Federal Judiciary, Free Labor, and Equal Rights" in Richard Schneirov, Shelton Stromquist, Nick Salvatore, eds. *The Pullman Strike and the Crisis of the 1890s: Essays on Labor and Politics.* Urbana, IL: University of Illinois Press, 1999, 159–78.

Fink, Leon. "From Autonomy to Abundance: Changing Beliefs About the Free Labor System in Nineteenth-Century America," in Stanley L. Engerman, ed. *Terms of Labor: Slavery, Serfdom, and Free Labor.* Stanford, CA: Stanford University Press, 1999.

Keyssar, Alexander. *Out of Work: The First Century of Unemployment in Massachusetts.* Cambridge: Cambridge University Press, 1986.

Minchin, Timothy J. " 'Labor's Empty Gun': Permanent Replacements and the International Paper Company Strike of 1987–88." *Labor History,* vol. 47: 1 (2006), 21–42.

Rosenbloom, Joshua L. *Looking for Work, Searching for Workers: American Labor Markets during Industrialization.* New York: Cambridge University Press, 2002.

Sidbury, James. *Ploughshares into Swords: Race, Rebellion, and Identity in Gabriel's Virginia, 1730–1810.* Cambridge: Cambridge University Press, 1997.

Stromquist, Shelton. *A Generation of Boomers: The Pattern of Railroad Labor Conflict in Nineteenth-Century America.* Chicago, IL: University of Illinois Press, 1987.

Taillon, Paul Michel. *Good, Reliable, White Men: Railroad Brotherhoods, 1877–1917.* Urbana, IL: University of Illinois Press, 2009.

Chapter Three: Rethinking Working-Class Politics in Comparative-Transnational Contexts

Berger, Stefan. *British Labour Party and German Social Democrats, 1900–1931.* Oxford: Oxford University Press, 1994.

Cowie, Jefferson. *Capital Moves: RCA's Seventy Year Quest for Cheap Labor.* Ithaca, NY: Cornell University Press, 1999.

Davies, Sam ed., *Dockworkers: International Explorations in Comparative Labour History, 1790–1970.* Aldershot: Ashgate, 2000.

Eley, Geoff. *Forging Democracy: The History of the Left in Europe, 1850–2000.* New York: Oxford University Press, 2002.

Gabaccia, Donna. *Italy's Many Diasporas.* Seattle, WA: University of Washington Press, 2000.

Katznelson, Ira and Aristide Zolberg. *Working-Class Formation: Nineteenth-Century Patterns in Western Europe and the United States.* Princeton, NJ: Princeton University Press, 1986.

Kirk, Neville. *Comrades and Cousins: Globalization, Workers and Labour Movements in Britain, the USA, and Australia from the 1880s to 1914.* London: Merlin Press, 2003.

Linebaugh, Peter and Marcus Rediker. *The Many-headed Hydra: Sailors, Slaves, Commoners and the Hidden History of the Revolutionary Atlantic.* Boston, MA: Beacon, 2000.

Lucassen, Jan, ed. *Global Labour History: A State of the Art.* New York: Peter Lang, 2006.

Magnusson, Warren. *The Search for Political Space Globalization, Social Movements, and the Urban Political Experience.* Toronto: University of Toronto Press, 1996.

Rodgers, Daniel T. *Atlantic Crossings: Social Politics in a Progressive Age.* Cambridge: Harvard University Press, 1998.

van der Linden, Marcel. *Workers of the World: Essays Toward a Global Labour History.* Leiden: Brill, 2008.

van der Linden, Marcel and Jürgen Rojahn. *The Formation of Labour Movements, 1870–1910: An International Perspective.* Amsterdam: Brill, 1990.

Chapter Four: No Common Creed: White Working-Class Protestants and the CIO's Operation Dixie

Carpenter, Joel A. *Revive Us Again: The Reawakening of American Fundamentalism.* New York: Oxford University Press, 1997.

Chappell, David L. *A Stone of Hope: Prophetic Religion and the Death of Jim Crow.* Chapel Hill, NC: University of North Carolina Press, 2004.

Fannin, Mark. *Labor's Promised Land: Radical Visions of Gender, Race, and Religion in the South.* Knoxville, TN: University of Tennessee Press, 2003.

Flynt, Wayne. *Poor But Proud: Alabama's Poor Whites.* Tuscaloosa, AL: University of Alabama Press, 2001.

Goldfield, Michael. *The Color of Politics: Race and the Mainsprings of American Politics.* New York: The New Press, 1997.

Griffith, Barbara S. *The Crisis of American Labor: Operation Dixie and the Defeat of the CIO.* Philadelphia, PA: Temple University Press, 1988.

Honey, Michael K. *Southern Labor and Black Civil Rights: Organizing Memphis Workers.* Urbana, IL: University of Illinois Press, 1993.

Korstad, Robert Rogers. *Civil Rights Unionism: Tobacco Workers and the Struggle for Democracy in the Mid-Twentieth Century South.* Chapel Hill. NC: University of North Carolina Press, 2003.

Minchin, Timothy J. *What Do We Need a Union For? The TWUA in the South, 1945–1955.* Chapel Hill, NC: University of North Carolina Press, 1997.

Pope, Liston. *Millhands and Preachers: A Study of Gastonia.* New Haven, CT: Yale University Press, 1942.

Simon, Bryant. *A Fabric of Defeat: The Politics of South Carolina Millhands, 1910–1948.* Chapel Hill, NC: University of North Carolina Press, 1998.

Waldrep, G. C. *Southern Workers and the Search for Community: Spartanburg, South Carolina.* Urbana, IL: University of Illinois Press, 2000.

Chapter Five: A. Philip Randolph, Black Anticommunism, and the Race Question

Anderson, Jervis. *A. Philip Randolph: A Biographical Portrait.* New York: University of California Press, 1972.

Bates, Beth Tompkins. *Pullman Porters and the Rise of Protest Politics in Black America 1925–1945*. Chapel Hill, NC: University of North Carolina Press, 2001.

Berg, Manfred. *"The Ticket to Freedom": The NAACP and the Struggle for Black Political Integration*. Gainesville, FL: University Press of Florida, 2005.

Feldman, Glenn. *Before Brown: Civil Rights and White Backlash in the Modern South*. Tuscaloosa, AL: University of Alabama Press, 2004.

Haynes, John Earl, Harvey Klehr, and Alexander Vassiliev. *Spies: The Rise and Fall of the KGB in America*. New Haven, CT: Yale University Press, 2009.

Isserman, Maurice. *Which Side Were You On?: The American Communist Party during the Second World War*. Middletown, CT: Wesleyan University Press, 1982.

Korstad, Robert Rodgers. *Civil Rights Unionism: Tobacco Workers and the Struggle for Democracy in the Mid-Twentieth-Century South*. Chapel Hill, NC: University of North Carolina Press, 2003.

Naison, Mark. *Communists in Harlem during the Depression*. Urbana, IL: University of Illinois Press, 1983.

Pfeffer, Paula F. *A. Philip Randolph, Pioneer of the Civil Rights Movement*. Baton Rouge, LA: Louisiana State University Press, 1990.

Power, Richard Gid. *Not Without Honor: The History of American Anticommunism*. New York: The Free Press, 1995.

Rosswurm, Steve, ed. *The CIO's Left-Led Unions*. New Brunswick, NJ: Rutgers University Press, 1992.

Schrecker, Ellen. *Many are the Crimes: McCarthyism in America*. Princeton, NJ: Princeton University Press, 1998. (Original hardback Boston, MA: Little, Brown and Company, 1998).

Chapter Six: The Contextualization of a Moment in CIO History: The Mine-Mill Battle in the Connecticut Brass Valley During World War II

Cochran, Bert. *Labor and Communism: The Conflict That Shaped Unions*. Princeton, NJ: Princeton University Press, 1977.

Feurer, Rosemary. *Radical Unionism in the Midwest, 1900–1950*. Urbana, IL: University of Illinois Press, 2006.

Filippeli, Ronald L. and Mark D. McColloch. *Cold War in the Working Class: The Rise and Decline of the United Electric Workers*. Albany, NY: State University of New York Press, 1995.

Freeman, Joshua. *In Transit: The Transport Workers Union in New York*. New York: Oxford University Press, 1989.

Gilpin, Toni, "Left By Themselves: A History of the United Farm Equipment and Metal Workers Unions." PhD dissertation, Yale University, 1993.

Korstad, Robert Rogers. *Civil Rights Unionism: Tobacco Workers and the Struggle for Democracy in the Mid-Twentieth-Century South*. Chapel Hill, NC: University of North Carolina Press, 2003.

Levenstein, Harvey A. *Communism, Anticommunism, and the CIO*. Westport, CT: Greenwood Press, 1981.

Mercier, Laurie. *Anaconda: Labor, Community, and Culture in Montana's Smelter City*. Urbana, IL: University of Illinois Press, 2001.

Rosswurm, Steve, ed. *The CIO's Left-Led Unions*. New Brunswick, NJ: Rutgers University Press, 1992.

Schatz, Ronald W. *The Electrical Workers: A History of Labor at General Electric and Westinghouse, 1923–1960*. Urbana, IL: University of Illinois Press, 1983.

Stepan-Norris, Judith and Maurice Zeitlin eds. *Left Out: Reds and America's Industrial Unions*. New York: State University of New York Press, 2003.

Zieger, Robert H., *The CIO, 1935–1955*. Chapel Hill, NC: University of North Carolina Press, 1995.

Chapter Seven: Organizing the Carework Economy: When the Private Becomes Public

Biklen, Molly. "Note: Healthcare in the Home: Reexamining the Companionship Services Exemption to the Fair Labor Standards Act." 35 *Columbia Human Rights Law Review* 113 (2003).

Boris, Eileen and Jennifer Klein. *Caring for America: Home Health Workers in the Shadow of the Welfare State*. New York: Oxford University Press, forthcoming 2011,

—. "'We Were the Invisible Workforce': Unionizing Home Care," in Dorothy S. Cobble, *The Sex of Class: Women Transforming American Labor*. Ithaca, NY: Cornell University Press, 2007, 177–93.

—. "Organizing Home Care: Low Waged Workers in the Welfare State." *Politics and Society*, vol. 34: 1 (March 2006), 81–106.

Delp, Linda and Katie Quan. "Homecare Worker Organizing in California: An Analysis of a Successful Strategy." *Labor Studies Journal* 27 (Spring, 2002), 1–23.

Feldman, Penny H., Alice Sapienza, and Nancy M. Kane.. *Who Cares for Them? Workers in the Home Care Industry*. Westport, CT: Greenwood Press, 1990.

Ness, Immanuel. "Organizing Home Health Workers: A New York City Case Study," *Working USA* (November–December 1999), 59–95.

Parks, Jennifer A. *No Place Like Home? Feminist Ethics and Home Health Care*. Bloomington, IN: University of Indiana Press, 2003.

Rivas, Lynn May. "Invisible Labors: Caring for the Independent Person," in Barbara Ehrenreich and Arlie Russell Hochschild, eds. *Global Woman: Nannies, Maids, and Sex Workers in the New Economy*. New York: Metropolitan Books, 2003, 70–84.

Smith, Peggie. "Aging and Caring in the Home: Regulating Paid Domesticity in the 21st Century." 92 *Iowa Law Review* 1837 (2007).

Tait, Vanessa. *Poor Workers' Unions: Rebuilding Labor from Below*. Boston, MA: South End Press, 2005.

Walsh, Jess. "Creating Unions, Creating Employers: A Los Angeles Home-Care Campaign," in Mary Daly, ed., *Carework: The Quest for Security*. Geneva: ILO, 2001, 219–33.

Chapter Eight: Solvents of Solidarity: Political Economy, Collective Action, and the Crisis of Organized Labor, 1968–2005

Compa, Lance. *Unfair Advantage: Workers' Freedom of Association in the United States under International Human Rights Standards*. Ithaca, NY: Cornell University Press, 2004.

Dubofsky, Melvyn. *The State and Labor in Modern America.* Chapel Hill, NC: University of North Carolina Press, 1994.

Friedman, Gerald. *Reigniting the Labor Movement: Restoring Means to ends in a Democratic Labor Movement.* New York: Routledge, 2007.

Lambert, Josiah Bartlett. *"If the Workers Took a Notion": The Right to Strike and American Political Development.* Ithaca, NY: Cornell University Press, 2005.

Lichtenstein, Nelson. *The Retail Revolution: How Wal-Mart Created a Brave New World of American Business.* New York: Metropolitan Books, 2009.

—. *State of the Union: A Century of American Labor.* Princeton, NJ: Princeton University Press, 2002.

McCartin, Joseph A. "Re-Framing U.S. Labour's Crisis: Reconsidering Structure, Strategy, and Vision." *Labour/Le Travail* 59 (Spring 2007), 133–48.

Moody, Kim. *Workers in a Lean World: Unions in the International Economy.* New York: Verso, 1997.

Rosenblum, Jonathan D. *Copper Crucible: How the Arizona Miners' Strike of 1983 Recast Labor-Management Relations in America.* Ithaca, NY: ILR Press, 1994.

Silver, Beverly J. *Forces of Labor: Workers' Movements and Globalization since 1870.* New York: Cambridge University Press, 2003.

Smith, Robert Michael. *From Blackjacks to Briefcases: A History of Commercialized Strikebreaking and Unionbusting in the United States.* Athens, OH: Ohio University Press, 2003.

van der Velden, Sjaak, Heiner Dribbusch, Dave Lyddon, and Kurt Vandaele, eds. *Strikes Around the World, 1968–2005: Case Studies of Fifteen Countries.* Amsterdam: Aksant Academic Publishers, 2007.

Chapter Nine: Sensing Labor: The Stinking Working-Class after the Cultural Turn

Baron, Ava and Eileen Boris. "The Body as a Useful Category for Working-Class History." *Labor* 4 (Summer, 2007), 23–43.

Bender, Daniel E. *American Abyss: Savagery and Civilization in the Age of Industry.* Ithaca, NY: Cornell University Press, 2009.

Boris, Eileen and Angélique Janssens, eds. *Complicating Categories: Gender, Class, Race and Ethnicity.* Cambridge: Cambridge University Press, 1999.

Cameron, Ardis. "Boys Do Cry: The Rhetorical Power of the "New" Labor History." *Labor* 1(Fall, 2004), 97–108.

Classen, Constance and David Howes, and Anthony Synnett. *Aroma: The Cultural History of Smell.* New York: Routledge, 1994.

Denning, Michael. *Culture in the Age of Three Worlds.* New York: Verso, 2004.

Dinerstein, Joel. *Swinging the Machine: Modernity, Technology, and African American Culture between the World Wars.* Amherst, MA: University of Massachusetts Press, 2003.

Enstad, Nan. *Ladies of Labor, Girls of Adventure: Working Women, Popular Culture, and Labor Politics at the Turn of the Twentieth Century.* New York: Columbia University Press, 1999.

Garcia, Matt. *A World of Its Own: Race, Labor and Citrus in the Making of Greater Los Angeles, 1900–1970.* Chapel Hill, NC: University of North Carolina Press, 2001.

Howes, David. *Sensual Relations: Engaging the Senses in Culture and Social Theory.* Ann Arbor, MI: University of Michigan Press, 2003.

Scott, Joan W. "The Evidence of Experience" *Critical Inquiry* 17 (Summer, 1991), 773–97.
Smith, Mark M. "Producing Sense, Consuming Sense, Making Sense: Perils and Prospects for Sensory History," *Journal of Social History* 40 (June, 2007), 841–58.

Chapter Ten: Re-imagining Labor: Gender and New Directions in Labor and Working-Class History

Baron, Ava, ed. *Work Engendered: Towards a New History of American Labor.* Ithaca, NY: Cornell University Press, 1991.
Barry, Kathleen. *Femininity in Flight: A History of Flight Attendants.* Durham, NC: Duke University Press, 2007.
Bender, Daniel E. *Sweated Work, Weak Bodies: Anti-Sweatshop Campaigns and the Languages of Labor.* New Brunswick, NJ: Rutgers University Press, 2003.
Cameron, Ardis. *Radicals of the Worst Sort: Laboring Women in Lawrence, Massachusetts, 1860–1912.* Urbana, IL: University of Illinois Press, 1993.
Cobble, Dorothy Sue. *The Other Women's Movement: Workplace Justice and Social Rights in Modern America.* Princeton, NJ: Princeton University Press, 2005.
Enstad, Nan. *Ladies of Labor, Girls of Adventure: Working Women, Popular Culture, and Labor Politics at the Turn of the Twentieth Century.* New York: Columbia University Press, 1999.
Faue, Elizabeth. *Community of Suffering and Struggle: Women, Men and the Labor Movement in Minneapolis, 1915–1945.* Chapel Hill, NC: University of North Carolina Press, 1991.
Green, Venus. *Race on the Line: Gender, Labor, and Technology in the Bell System, 1880–1980.* Durham, NC: Duke University Press, 2001.
Horowitz, Roger, ed. *Boys and Their Toys? Masculinity, Technology, and Class in America.* New York: Routledge, 2001.
Kessler-Harris, Alice. *Gendering Labor History.* Urbana, IL: University of Illinois Press, 2006.
Norwood, Stephen. *Strikebreaking and Intimidation: Mercenaries and Masculinity in Twentieth Century America.* Urbana, IL: University of Illinois Press, 2002.
Scott, Joan Wallach. *Gender and the Politics of History.* New York: Columbia University Press, 1988.

Chapter Eleven: The Limits of Work and the Subject of Labor History

Barry, Kathleen M. *Femininity In Flight: A History of Flight Attendants.* Durham, NC: Duke University Press, 2007.
Dalla Costa, Mariarosa and Selma James. *The Power of Women and the Subversion of Community.* Bristol, England: Falling Wall Press, 1972.
Hardt, Michael. "Affective Labor." *Boundary 2*, vol. 26: 2 (1999).
Hardt, Michael and Antonio Negri. *Commonwealth.* Cambridge: Harvard University Press, 2009.
Hochschild, Arlie Russell. *The Managed Heart: The Commercialization of Human Feeling.* 20th Anniversary Edition. Berkeley, CA: University of California Press, 2003.
Hondagneu-Sotelo, Pierrette. *Doméstica: Immigrant Workers Cleaning and Caring in the Shadows of Affluence.* Berkeley, CA: University of California Press, 2001.

McDonald, Cameron and Carmen Sirianni, eds. *Working in the Service Society.* Philadelphia, PA: Temple University Press, 1996.

Mies, Maria. *Patriarchy and Accumulation on a World Scale: Women in the International Division of Labour.* London: Zed Books, 1986.

Parrenas, Rhacel Salazar. *Servants of Globalization: Women, Migration, and Domestic Work.* Stanford, CA: Stanford University Press, 2001.

Precarias a la Deriva. "Precarias: First Stutterings of Precarias a la Deriva." http://www.sindominio.net/karakola/antigua_casa/precarias/balbuceos-english.htm (accessed September 28, 2009).

—. "A Very Careful Strike," translated by Franco Ingrassia and Nate Holdren, in *The Commoner* No. 11, Spring/Summer 2006.

Strasser, Susan. *Never Done: A History of American Housework.* New York: Owl Books, 2000.

Index

Made in the USA
Lexington, KY
22 November 2011